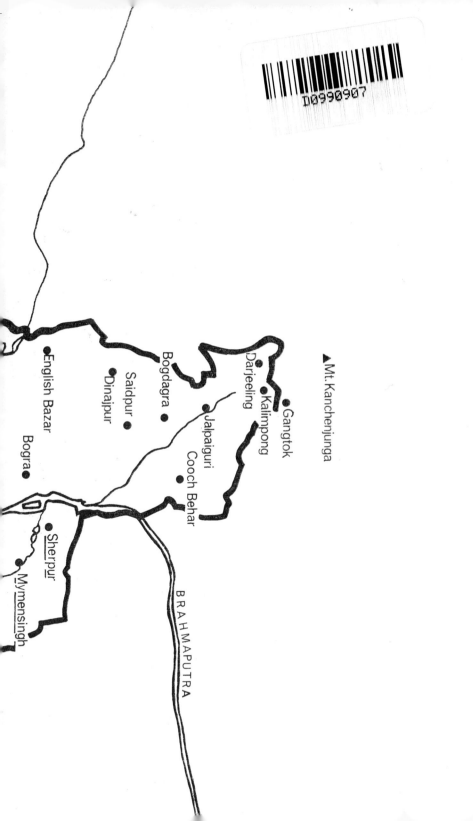

▲Mt. Kanchenjunga

●Gangtok

●Kalimpong

Darjeeling●

Bogdagra●

●Saidpur

●Dinajpur

●English Bazar

Jalpaiguri●

Cooch Behar●

Bogra●

●Sherpur

●Mymensingh

BRAHMAPUTRA

PORTRAIT OF A DIRECTOR
SATYAJIT RAY

By the same author
EISENSTEIN
PAUL ROBESON
PANDITJI: A PORTRAIT OF JAWAHARLAL NEHRU

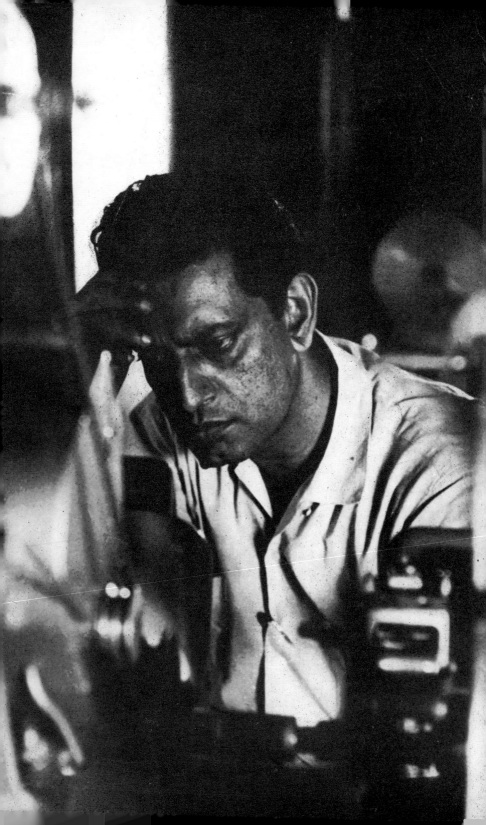

PORTRAIT OF
A DIRECTOR
Satyajit Ray

By

MARIE SETON

INDIANA UNIVERSITY PRESS
BLOOMINGTON & LONDON

Library of Congress catalog card number: 75-108946

ISBN: 0 253-16815-5

Printed in Great Britain

To
SANDIP
Fourth Generation Ray, Artist

"Each race contributes something essential to the world's civilization in the course of its own self-expression . . . The essential contribution of India, is simply her Indianess; her great humiliation would be to substitute or to have substituted for this own character (*svabhava*) a cosmopolitan veneer, for then indeed she must come before the world empty-handed."

Ananda Coomaraswamy in *The Dance of Shiva;* from an essay published in *The Athenaeum,* 1915

ACKNOWLEDGEMENTS

As is evident from the text of this book, a great many people generously contributed their thoughts on Ray's work, loaned letters and donated illustrations. In this connection I especially wish to thank Bansi Chandragupta, James Lester Peries and A. Huq.

Throughout the writing of it, Satyajit Ray was constantly giving me illustrations, actually many more than are here used. His generosity was boundless; but never at any point did he influence the style of the book nor any opinion expressed in it. For this I am most grateful. But it could not have been written so far as the family history is concerned without the unstinting help of Uncle Subimal Ray.

At a later stage, I am indebted for assistance in illustrations to the British Film Institute and to Contemporary Films, and I wish to thank John Gillett for having read the original first draft of the manuscript and for his useful suggestions; no less I am grateful to Josephine Marquand for further suggestions as to how to cut what was at first a very long manuscript. This book could not have been written without a great deal of help from the many people who flit in and out of the text.

I am indebted to Anandam Film Society, Bombay, for illustrations reproduced from the special issue of *Montage* devoted to Ray; to *Sight and Sound*; to *Now*, Calcutta; and to *Punch* for the ffolkes cartoon; also to the National Library, Calcutta for aiding me with material on the Brahmo Samaj and the Tantric aspects of Hinduism.

I must also thank the Indian High Commission in London for checking the maps which form the endpapers.

MARIE SETON

CONTENTS

Contents

APPENDICES *(by Satyajit Ray)*

LIST OF ILLUSTRATIONS

(Between pp. 94 and 95)

I.
Kalinarayan Gupta, Satyajit Ray's maternal great-grandfather.
Dwarkanath Ganguli, noted Brahmo Samaj crusader.
Kadambini Basu, India's first woman doctor. *(Satyajit and Subimal Ray)*

II.
Upendrakishore Ray (1863–1915), Printer, Writer, Painter, Illustrator, Musician.
Sukumar Ray (1887–1923), Writer and Illustrator. *(Satyajit and Subimal Ray)*

III.
Satyajit (Manik) Ray at the age of three.
Satyajit with Sandip, aged 3. *(A. Huq)*
1935—Manik at fourteen with his mother, Suprabha. *(Satyajit Ray)*
The Family. *(A. Huq)*

IV.
1941—Brush drawing by Satyajit Ray of Bijoya Das. *(Satyajit Ray)*

V. Ray's Sun Temple of Konarak Studies, 1943.
A small figure carved as a medallion. Pencil study.
Crayon Study of one of the many loving couples. *(Satyajit Ray)*

VI.
Two Pencil Studies of the dancer-musician figures on the Sun Temple of Konarak, Orissa. *(Satyajit Ray)*

VII. *Pather Panchali (Song of the Little Road)*, 1950–55.
Discarded scene between Durga and Apu.
Shanti Chatterjee cutting Chunibala Devi's hair.
Chunibala Devi as Old Indir. *(Satyajit Ray)*

VIII. *The Apu Trilogy.*
Subir Bannerjee, the first Apu. *(Satyajit Ray)*
Pinaki Sen Gupta, the second Apu. *(The National Film Archive)*
Apu's son, Kajal (Alok Chakravarty). *(Contemporary Films)*

IX.
The Family in *Pather Panchali*, 1950–55. *(Satyajit Ray)*
Karuna Banerji as the Mother; Kanu Bannerjee, as the Father. *(Satyajit Ray)*
The young girl, Durga, Uma Das Gupta, steals for love of Old Indir, Chunibala Devi. *(Satyajit Ray)*

X.
The Death of Durga. (*Satyajit Ray*)
The Return of Harihar, the Father. (*Satyajit Ray*)
The Villagers come to bid the family farewell. (*Satyajit Ray*)

XI–XIV.
Sketches for proposed musical short, 1951. (*Satyajit Ray*)

XV. *Aparajito* (*The Unvanquished*), 1956.
Harihar reading the Scriptures on the Ghats. (*The National Film Archive*)
The Death of Harihar, the Father. (*Satyajit Ray*)
Shot No. 224. The Mother, Sarbojaya, watching a scene where her son
is acting. (*Satyajit Ray*)

XVI.
Apu makes efforts to follow in his father's footsteps as a priest. (*Satyajit
Ray*)
The Adolescent Apu. Sumiran Kumar Ghosal. Shot No. 323. (*The
National Film Archive*)
Shot No. 398—Apu has returned from Calcutta. (*Satyajit Ray*)

(*Between pp. 158 and 159*)

XVII. *Apur Sansar* (*The World of Apu*), 1959.
Apu, the young man, Soumitra Chatterjee, in the opening scene.
(*Satyajit Ray*)
The Bridal Chamber. (*Satyajit Ray*)
Sequence No. 6. Apu returning home finds his brother-in-law, Murari,
waiting to tell him of Aparna's death in childbirth. (*Satyajit Ray*)

XVIII. Set for the Calcutta Attic Stairs. Sequence No. 4.
Apu brings Aparna to his attic room across the railway tracks.
They come to the first floor.
They continue going up to the attic. (*Satyajit Ray*)

XIX. *Jalsaghar* (*The Music Room*), 1957–8.
Chhabi Biswas as Biswambhar Roy, the improvident landlord.
The second *jalsa*—musical soirée—just before the storm rises to its
crescendo.
The final *jalsa*. (*Satyajit Ray*)

XX. *Devi* (*The Goddess*), 1959–60.
Sharmila Tagore as Daya and Soumitra Chatterjee as her husband,
Umaprasad. Sequence No. 1.
Chhabi Biswas as Daya's father-in-law, Kalikanker Roy. Sequence No. 2.

XXI.
A page from the script of *Devi*.
Daya enshrined by her father-in-law as an incarnation of the Goddess.
(*Satyajit Ray*)

XXII.
A page from the script of *Devi*. (*Satyajit Ray*)
Umaprasad finds Daya out of her mind. (*The National Film Archive*)

B

LIII.
Sound Stage for recording. New Theatre Studio, Calcutta.
He directs his musicians as he does his actors and edits sound as he edits picture. (*A. Huq*)
Ray recording music with James Ivory. (*National Film Archive*)

LIV.
Bijoya with Satyajit during pause in *Kanchenjunga* music recording session.
"The expressiveness of his hands in explaining . . ." (*A. Huq*)

LV. Ray Abroad.
1963, recording a discussion with the author for the BBC in the author's London flat. (*David Muir*)
1966, with Akira Kurosawa in Tokyo. (*Satyajit Ray*)

LVI.
January 1965, the International Film Festival, New Delhi. (*Satyajit Ray*)
1962 as juror with James Quinn of the British Film Institute at the Berlin Film Festival. (*Harry Croner*)

LVII.
Satyajit and his own shadow, like the shadow of his father and grand-father. (*A. Huq*)

LVIII. *Paras Pathar* (*The Philosopher's Stone*), 1957–8.
Tulsi Chakravarty as Parash Dutta with the magic stone.
The Duttas have grown rich.
      Kapurush-o-Mahapurush (*The Coward and the Holy Man*), 1965.
The "Saint" discourses to his disciples. (*Satyajit Ray*)

LIX. *Goupi Gyne and Bagha Byne*, 1968.
Sketch of Halla Army arrayed for the battle that never takes place.
Ray directing the above scene in Jaisalmer with the camels.
Goupi, Topen Chatterji, the singer, and Bagha, Rabi Ghosh, the drummer, arrive at Halla bent on preventing the war. (*Satyajit Ray*)

LX.
Ray's *Goupi Gyne* sketches.
Satyajit decorating a clay pot for film, Rajasthan.
The boys have the first of their magic meals. (*Satyajit Ray*)

LXI.
Musicians wait for the singing contest to start.
Ray directing Santosh Dutt as the Bad King of Halla and Jahar Roy as his Prime Minister.
Goupi and Bagha in the Palace of Shundi. (*Satyajit Ray*)

LXII.
The Bad King of Halla, Santosh Dutt, with his Prime Minister, Jahar Roy.
The Good King of Shundi, Santosh Dutt, with Goupi and Bagha.
Goupi and Bagha sing and drum to the soldiers of Halla. (*Satyajit Ray*)

LXIII. *Aranyer Din-Ratri* (*Days and Nights in the Forest*), 1969–70. (*Satyajit Ray*)

LXIV. *Pratidwandi* (*Siddhartha and the City*), 1970.

WHO'S WHO

"ADIB", pen name of Shamlal, noted critic and now Editor-in-Chief of *The Times of India*.

AUDY, one of the two producers of Ray's *Kanchenjunga*.

BANERJI, CHANDANA, Calcutta schoolgirl who interprets Ratan in *The Postmaster*.

BANERJI, KARUNA, the non-professional actress who created the role of the Mother in *Pather Panchali*; also appears in the same role in *Aparajito*, and in *Devi* and *Kanchenjunga*. Is a talented writer of perceptive essays and comments.

BANERJI, RANKI, played Durga as a little child in *Pather Panchali*.

BANNERJEE, BIBHUTI BHUSAN, author of the noted novel *Pather Panchali* and the sequel, *Aparajito*; also *Panage*, famine story.

BANNERJEE, Mrs., the author's wife who favoured Satyajit Ray directing the film of *Pather Panchali*.

BANNERJEE, KALI, professional actor in *Monihara*.

BANNERJEE, KANU, the professional actor who was cast for the father, Harihar, in *Pather Panchali*.

BANNERJEE, SUBIR, the first and youngest Apu in *Pather Panchali*.

BANNERJEE, TARASHANKAR, originally a political worker among Bengali villagers, he became the author of the stories on which Ray's film *Jalsaghar* is based and also the novel, *Abhijan*, the film of which Ray scripted and finally directed.

BANSAL, R. D., well-known Bengali film producer and distributor associated with Ray's films from 1963 to 1967.

BASU, KADAMBINI, first woman B.A., married her mentor, Dwarkanath Ganguli, whose daughter by a previous marriage married Ray's grandfather, Upendrakishore Ray. She became a highly successful doctor.

BHAGAT, USHA, secretary to Mrs. Indira Gandhi; Joint Secretary of Federation of Film Societies of India.

BHAT, M. D., Chairman of the Central Board of Film Censors in 1955 and played a major role in *Pather Panchali* receiving the President's Gold Medal; subsequently Chairman of Film Finance Corporation.

BHATIA, VANRAJ, professional musician; critic of Ray's music.

BISWAS, CHHABI, noted Bengali film star and Ray's leading actor in *Jalsaghar, Devi* and *Kanchenjunga*. Killed in a motor accident during the run of the last-mentioned film.

BOSE, AJIT, of Aurora Films, Calcutta; financier of *Aparajito*. One of Bengal's major producers.

BOSE, DEBIKI, noted Bengali film director of the older generation.

BOSE, DILIP, cousin of Satyajit Ray; correspondent in Darjeeling for the *Statesman*; appears for a moment in *Kanchenjunga*.

BOSE, NANDALAL, important Bengali painter and instructor of Satyajit Ray at Tagore's Santineketan.

BOSE, NITIN, the son of Ray's paternal great-aunt, became a well-known film director in the early 1930s.

BOSE, Lady J. C., wife of famed scientist and founder of Widows' Home, Vidyasagar Bani Bhavan, where Ray's mother taught embroidery.

BOSE, RAJSHEKAR, scientist and author writing under the name 'Parasuram'. One of his stories serves as base of Rays film *Paras Pathar*.

CHAKRAVARTY, one of the two producers of *Kanchenjunga*.

CHAKRAVARTY, AJOY, painter and maker of puppet film, who knew Ray at Santineketan.

CHAKRAVARTY, ALOK, appears as Apu's son, Kajal, in *Apur Sansar*.

CHAKRAVARTY, TULSI, professional actor appearing as pundit-grocer in *Pather Panchali*; appears as leading character in *Paras Pathar*. Died soon after.

CHANDRAGUPTA, BANSI, Ray's Art Director, first worked for Jean Renoir and was formerly a painter. Kashmiri by origin.

CHATTERJEE, ANIL, appears as the Postmaster in Tagore's story; also as Anil, the playboy son in *Kanchenjunga* and as the young husband in *Mahanagar*.

CHATTERJEE, BIJOY, producer of *Abhijan*.

CHATTERJEE, HEREN, professional singer chosen by Ray for his first acting role as the Father in *Mahanagar*.

CHATTERJEE, K. N., journalist friend of Ray's father Sukumar. They were both in England together in 1911.

CHATTERJEE, SOUMITRA, having had some experience as an amateur actor with his own group, Ray selected him to play the adult Apu in *Apur Sansar*. Subsequently, Chatterjee has appeared as the younger son in *Devi*, as Amulya in the Tagore story, *Samapti*; Narsingh in *Abhijan*; Amul in *Charulata*; and the Coward in *Mahapurush*. Has starred in numerous films directed by other directors in Bengal. Cast by Ray for leading role in the famine film, Ashari Shanket, 1969.

CHATTERJI, SHANTI, one of the original members of Ray's unit.

CHATTERJI, TOPEN, cast for the young singer in *Goupi Gyne and Bagha Byne.*

CHAUDHURY, NILIMA ROY, one of the two Darjeeling college girls to appear as the "girl friends" in *Kanchenjunga.*

CHOUDHURY, ANIL, Ray's Production Manager from *Pather Panchali* onwards. One of the first to join Ray's unit.

CHOUDHURY, ASIT, Calcutta producer and distributor of some of Ray's films, notably *Teen Kanya.*

CHUNIBALA DEVI, the ancient actress who created the role of old Indir in *Pather Panchali.*

DAS, CHARUCHANDRA, half-brother of Ray's mother, Suprabha Das, and father of Ray's wife Bijoya.

DAS, P. K., younger brother of Ray's mother and with whom he went to live after the death of his father, Sukumar.

DAS GUPTA, APARNA, known as Rina; daughter of critic and film maker, Chidananda. She appears as tomboy heroine of *Samapti* Subsequently, she has adopted the screen as a career. Has lately appeared in Hindi films made in Bombay.

DAS GUPTA, CHIDANANDA, fellow founder with Ray of the Calcutta Film Society. Retired after many years as publicity man of Imperial Tobacco to devote himself to film making; has always been well-known critic. His first film, financed by the Calcutta Film Society, was *Portrait of a City.*

DAS GUPTA, HARI, documentary film director trained in Hollywood; assistant to Jean Renoir on *The River.* Maker of numerous films.

DAS GUPTA, UMA, the girl, Durga, in *Pather Panchali.* Has not acted since. She has put on record that when invited to meet Satyajit Ray, she put on a pearl necklace to impress him, which he promptly told her she must take off. She learned all the dialogue of Durga from the original script, then found it had been revised during the eight months' halt in shooting. This, too, was to impress him. "He never treated me like a child. I used to babble away to him as with my companions. He used to speak to me as if he was my own age."

DEY, ALOKENATH, Ray's Assistant Music Director from *Pather Panchali* onwards. Is a skilful flautist.

DEY, PRITHWISH, one of the men convicted in the Jessop Case. Ray had thought of him as a potential actor to appear in Ray's script of *Home and the World.* Sentenced to life imprisonment, Dey, on release became an observer during the making of *Mahanagar*. When finally tested for acting ability he proved to have little.

DUTT, DULAL, Ray's editor who had had some slight experience of editing when he joined Ray's unit for *Pather Panchali*. Has worked with Ray ever since and is a much valued member of the unit.

DUTT, SANTOSH, interpreter of both the Good King and the Bad King in *Goupi Gyne*.

DUTTA, NEPAL, Calcutta cinema owner and joint producer of Ray's *Goupi Gyne*.

DUTTA, PURNIMA, daughter-in-law of Nepal, Producer of *Chhuti*, 1966.

DUTTA, SAILEN, one of Ray's assistants and a basic member of his unit.

GANDHI, Mrs. INDIRA, daughter of Prime Minister Jawaharlal Nehru; President of the Congress Party 1959–60; Vice-President of Federation of Film Societies of India 1961–66; Prime Minister of India since January 1966.

GANDHI, MAHATMA, "Father of the Nation" of independent India. Propounder of passive resistance. Born 1869; assassinated February, 1948.

GANGULI, BIDHUMUKHI, daughter of Dwarkanath Ganguli, married Ray's grandfather, Upendrakishore.

GANGULI, DWARKANATH, famous member of the Brahmo Samaj and father of Ray's paternal grandmother, Bidhumukhi.

GHATAK, RITWIK, Bengali film director with unusual and experimental approach; best known for his first film, *Ajantrick*.

GHOSAL, S., played the adolescent Apu in *Aparajito*.

GHOSH, ATULYA, notorious Congress politician of West Bengal.

GHOSH, BHANU, one of Ray's basic unit; also acts in *Abhijan*.

GHOSH, RABI (in English, Ravi), stage actor appearing as Rama in *Abhijan*; subsequently joint leading role of Bagha in *Goupi Gyne and Bagha Byne*.

GUPTA, ANNADA DEVI, Ray's maternal great-grandmother; possessed of good singing voice.

GUPTA, ANUBA, well-known Bengali screen star appears as Anima in *Kanchenjunga*.

GUPTA, KALINARAYAN, noted in Brahmo Samaj history for his goodness and beauty of his singing and hymns composed by himself; Ray's maternal great-grandfather.

GUPTA, R. P., of J. Walter Thompson, introduced John Huston to Ray during *Pather Panchali* difficulties.

HOME, GAGANCHANDRA, classmate of Ray's grandfather, Upendrakishore and a noted member of the Brahmo Samaj to which
he introduced Upendra during their schooldays.

HUQ, A., an East Pakistani (East Bengal) photographer of great
talent and a devoted friend of Ray's mother and of himself.
Contributes some of the most interesting photographs in this
book.

KAPOOR, SHEMMI, the second of the trio of brothers all of whom
are popular Hindi film stars.

KARLEKAR, Mrs. KALYANI, Ray's cousin.

KHAN, ALI AKBAR, famous sitar player; composer of music for
Ray's *Devi* and other Indian films.

KHAN, USTAD VILAYAT, one of India's three most famous musicians,
Ravi Shankar and Ali Akbar Khan making up the trio. Music
for *Jalsaghar*.

KOUSHIK, student friend of Ray's who is now well-known painter
in Delhi. At present back in Santineketan as Principal of the
Art School (Kala Bhawan).

KRIPALANI, KRISHNA, author of biography of Rabindranath Tagore,
and Mahatma Gandhi; husband of Nandita, Tagore's grand-
daughter; friend of Ray's.

KRIPALANI, NANDITA, Rabindranath Tagore's grand-daughter who
knew Ray at Santineketan; has appeared on the screen and
worked for Delhi's Cottage Industries Emporium. Died 1967.

KUMAR, UTTAM, Bengali star appearing in *Nayak* and *Chiriakhana*.

McCUTCHION, DAVID, an English friend of Ray's, teaching Compara-
tive Literature at Jadhavpur University, Calcutta.

MAHALANOBIS, Professor, famous Indian economist; friend of
Sukumar Ray; adviser on Satyajit's subjects as youth.

MATHUR, Director of Publicity, West Bengal Goverment.

MAZUMDAR, LILA, cousin of Ray's, well-known as a writer of
children's stories. Works for All-India Radio.

MAZUMDAR, KANIKA, well-known screen actress appearing in
Monihara.

MITRA, DURGA DAS, sound recordist for all of Ray's films.

MITRA, NARENDRA, author of stories on which *Mahanagar* is based.

MITRA, SHEMBU, well-known Bengali theatre director.

MITRA, SUBRATA, Ray's cameraman, was observer on Renoir's film,
The River. Cameramen for Ivory-Merchant films, *The Householder* and *Shakespeare Wallah*.

MOOKERJEE, ARUN, young theatre actor appearing as Ashoke in *Kanchenjunga.*

MUKHERJEE, MADHABI, actress playing wife Arati, in *Mahanagar* and Charu in *Charulata;* wife in *Kapurush.*

MUKHERJEE, PRABHAT KUMAR, Hindu author of story on which *Devi* is based.

MUKHERJI, JNANESH, theatre actor playing Josef in *Abhijan.*

NEOGY, PRITHWISH, student at Santineketan with Ray and one of his closest friends. Painter, critic, collaborator with Hari Das Gupta on two films on Konarak and during 1955–56 was Director of Municipal Museum in Ahmedabad designed and built by Le Corbusier.

PERIES, JAMES LESTER, Ceylon film director of *Rekava,* which appeared soon after *Pather Panchali.* Since then has made two further films. *Gamperelya* won top award Third Indian International Festival, 1965.

RAY, BIJOYA, wife of Satyajit Ray. Great grand-daughter of Kalinarayan Gupta, inheriting musical talent.

RAY, SANDIP, only child of Satyajit and Bijoya Ray.

RAY, SUBIMAL, Satyajit's youngest uncle, who lives with him.

RAY, SUPRABHA, (*née,* Das), mother of Satyajit; grand-daughter of Kalinarayan Gupta.

REBI DEVI, professional actress playing unpleasant Mrs. Mukherji in *Pather Panchali,* also appears as mother, Mrs. Mazumdar, in *Mahanagar.*

REDDI, DR. GOPALA, Minister of Information and Broadcasting 1962; former student at Santineketan and Chief Minister of Andhra.

REDWOOD, VICKY, Anglo-Indian girl with some nightclub singing experience, cast as Edith in *Mahanagar.*

REHMAN, WAHEEDA, Muslim star of Hindi films; appears as Gulabi, heroine of *Abhijan.*

ROY, ALOKNANDA, Presidency College student playing heroine in *Kanchenjunga.*

ROY, Mr., Aloknanda's father, an engineer.

ROY, Mrs., Aloknanda's mother, translator of novels into Bengali.

ROY, BIMAL, famous Bengali film director who makes Hindi films in Bombay; most important of his films in Hindi is *Do Bigha Zamin* which introduced neo-realism to Indian cinema.

ROY, DR. B. C., Chief Minister of West Bengal until 1962 when he died; friend of Ray family, and finally arranged State funds for the completion of *Pather Panchali.*

Roy, Kumar, actor in *Monihara* and *Charulata*.

Roy, Raja Rammohan, most famous of 19th-century Bengali reformers and founder of the Brahmo Samaj in 1830. Visited England. Influenced by Unitarianism.

Roy, Soumendu, formerly an assistant cameraman to Subrata Mitra, replaced Mitra for *Teen Kanya* and photographed *Abhijan*.

Royals, Derek, a Darjeeling tea-planter who appears as a tourist in *Kanchenjunga*.

Sanyal, Pahari, noted actor, plays Uncle Jagadish in *Kanchenjunga*; small part in *Paras Pathar*.

Sarkar, Prasenjit, plays the little boy, Pintu, in *Mahanagar*.

Sen, Keshubchandra, leader of the Brahmo Samaj. The movement split after the controversy over his daughter's marriage to the Maharajah of Cooch Behar, the family being idol-worshippers, his views on women and his Messianic aspects.

Sen, K. C. (Bhaya), great-grandson of Keshubchandra Sen; founder of Bandwagon, agency for placing bands and entertainers in Indian night clubs and restaurants.

Sen, Mrinal, one of Bengal's younger film directors; best film is *Baishey Sravana*.

Sen, Nandita, daughter of K. N. Chatterjee and wife of Potla Sen, Ray's Presidency College friend.

Sen, Potla, Satyajit's classmate. Executive of Imperial Tobacco, now in Government service.

Sen, P. C., successor to Dr. B. C. Roy as Chief Minister of West Bengal, 1962.

Sen, Subrata, Left-wing union official, former member of Calcutta Corporation, amateur actor who plays Shankar in *Kanchenjunga*, and role in *Nayak*.

Sen Gupta, Pinaki, plays the young Apu in *Aparajito*.

Shankar, Ravi, world famous sitar player and composer of music for the Apu Trilogy. Music for numerous films, including Norman McLaren's *Chairy Tale*.

Shankar, Uday, famous dancer and elder brother of Ravi.

Singh, Vidya, aristocratic Darjeeling college girl who appears as first girl friend in *Kanchenjunga*.

Sinha, Topen, Bengali film director. One of his best-known films is *Hungry Stones*, from the Tagore story.

Tagore, Abanindranath, painter and poet; one of the famous Tagore family. As painter revived an indigenous style.

TAGORE, DEBENDRANATH, father of Rabindranath and second leader following Raja Rammohun Roy of Brahmo Samaj.

TAGORE, DWARKANATH, grandfather of Rabindranath. Died on a visit to London and is buried in England.

TAGORE, JYOTINDRANATH, one of Rabindranath's older brothers and with whom Rabindranath went to stay in England. Jyotindranath's wife exerted a great influence on the poet.

TAGORE, RABINDRANATH, most famous Indian other than Mahatma Gandhi in first half of 20th century. Poet, dramatist, painter, educational reformer, he won the Nobel Prize in 1914 and was granted a Knighthood, which he returned in protest in 1919. His short stories have now been filmed by numerous directors as well as Satyajit Ray. Like Ray, Rabindranath experimented with music, both Indian and Western. Seeking to bring together the East and the West he was frequently thought of as the universal man.

TAGORE, SHARMILA, grandniece of Rabindranath, was 14 years old when Ray asked her to act Aparna the young bride in *Apur Sansar*. Is now a noted film star. Appears also in *Devi* and *Nayak*. Cast for *Ashari Shanket*, 1969.

THAKURTA, RUMA GUHA, Bijoya Ray's niece who has inherited a Das singing voice, plays Neeli, the Christian schoolteacher in *Abhijan* and the leading role in her husband's film, *Baranasi*, Thakurta having been a member of Ray's unit.

VISWANATHAN, N., a college lecturer who is also well known as an actor in Tamil and Bengali films. He himself is a Tamil. Plays Bannerji, the engineer in *Kanchenjunga*.

PART I

THE RAYS

Chapter 1

SATYAJIT RAY—FIRST IMPRESSIONS

"SOMEDAY I'll make a great film!" remarked Satyajit Ray in 1948 to his friend Chidananda Das Gupta. Das Gupta laughed. He thought Ray was joking. But, in fact, Ray was in deadly earnest though he had not begun his first film, *Pather Panchali*. It would take five years work and only be completed in the summer of 1955. Created against a background of tremendous difficulties, *Pather Panchali* was to bring the unknown Satyajit Ray international acclaim and fame.

When he made his unexpected remark, Ray, Chidananda, and another Das Gupta—Hari—who had returned to Calcutta from Hollywood—had just formed the Calcutta Film Society as a means of seeing and promoting the screening of important international films, past and present. Almost their first act was to purchase a print of Sergei Eisenstein's *Potemkin*.

Ray, his friends and their supporters were in opposition to the outmoded theatrical vulgarity of the Indian film industry's pictures, particularly those with Hindi dialogue produced in Bombay. These Hindi films alone were assured of an extensive national release. Those produced in any of the other one dozen official languages of India were rarely distributed outside their own limited linguistic area.

For over three decades Indian commercial entertainment films had been ground out in ever increasing numbers. The Indian and Japanese industries had competed with each other as to which would produce the largest number of films each year. The output of both exceeded that of Hollywood. But the annual production of Indian films repetitiously and rigidly conformed to a standard formula. Indian production existed on the base of an unshakable conviction that audiences desired an escape from reality; that people would only pay to see excessively long films, from fourteen to twenty-four thousand feet. Distributors and exhibitors demanded that the films should be crammed with the entire gamut of romance, melodrama, cheese-cake, crude comedy, plus a substantial quota

27

of songs and dances. The classic Hindu epics were rehashed a dozen times. The other major category, the so-called "socials", flagrantly imitated Hollywood in a concocted "Indian" setting. Essentially theatrical in setting and acting, the greatest defect of these numberless pictures lay in the absence of any structure in their scenarios.

Location shooting had become almost totally unknown in India. Action in films, including village scenes, was confined to sets mainly designed like stage box sets. Actors came into view and placed themselves within the frame. The camera seldom moved about within the action. Bimal Roy's *Do Bigha Zamin* (*Two Acres of Land*) became one of the few exceptions. An immense amount of unrelieved dialogue marred the cinematic element in the majority of films. Make-up usually resembled that of the stage. Directors seemed oblivious of the visual incongruity of a village girl beautified with lipstick and saris far more expensive than those ever worn by village women, except, perhaps, for their wedding. Ever increasingly, a few male and female stars dominated the entire industry.

Despite their greater literary interest, the Western theatre had laid a heavy hand on Bengali films. Sets employing burlap backcloths and reassembling much-used materials over and over again, offered the camera, no matter how excellent the cameraman, no vistas. Bengali scenarios had almost identical appearance with play scripts. Novels were translated very literally to the screen. The convention of music, singing and dancing belonged to both the tradition of folk and classical Indian drama; but its injection into films had barely attempted to render it either in cinematic terms, or as a logical development of any story. People were given to singing on their death beds, and it was always associated with a love scene. Lovers never kissed, but a range of eroticism had been substituted for the prohibited kiss. There had not arisen a director determined to break these conventions and create an integrated film which could stand honest comparison with the world's outstanding film productions.

In 1948, Satyajit Ray, the outstanding commercial artist of Bengal, together with his friends, recognized this situation. The Calcutta Film Society served to cultivate a greater awareness of film as an art. Following its formation, Ray, who had been making notes on film construction and had also attempted scenario writing, began to write film reviews chiefly for *The Statesman*, the most notable local newspaper. For several years he had been seeing films with his painter friend, Bansi Chandragupta, a Kashmiri, who aimed at becoming an Art Director in a film industry which did not comprehend the meaning of Art Direction. However, in 1950, when Jean Renoir arrived in Calcutta to direct *The River*, Chandragupta gained the opportunity for experience as the assistant Art Director. Ray met Renoir. This resulted in Ray being invited to write an article for the British magazine, *Sequence* (see Appendix I).

By this time, Ray had become the Art Director of a British-owned publicity firm which sent him to London. During four months he saw ninety-nine films of importance. On his journey back to India, he began writing the scenario of *Pather Panchali*. He had been thinking about this story for five years, indeed since 1945 when he had been commissioned to illustrate an abridgement of the novel on which the film is based.

In 1955, after a decade of hopes and tribulations, *Pather Panchali* burst upon Calcutta to be received with immense enthusiasm. Rumours of its uniqueness spread like wildfire across India. Within half an hour of my first arrival in Bombay I was told that a great film had recently been released in Calcutta. That was October 1955. Five weeks later, the film was being screened on Sunday mornings at the Delite Cinema in Delhi, a theatre which presented Bengali pictures to attract the Bengali-speaking community at an early off-hour.

Because the sparse dialogue was subordinated to the imagery, *Pather Panchali* was attracting a largely non-Bengali audience in Delhi. This is where I first saw it screened to an enthralled audience.

In spite of the film's indisputable success, the Secretary of the Ministry of Information and Broadcasting in Delhi was extremely tepid about seeing the film as the most suitable entry for the next Cannes Film Festival. A vulgar colour extravaganza, which was a great commercial success, was being favoured. *Pather Panchali* was, however, so remarkable a film that temporary obstacles of indifference, ignorance or prejudice could not eliminate the certainty that such a contribution to film-making would ultimately find unequivocal appreciation.

Two friends of Satyajit Ray—Krishna Kripalani and his wife, Nandita, a grand-daughter of the poet Rabindranath Tagore—who had both known Ray as a student at the Tagore centre of Santineketan, showed me a letter from him. Despite the acclaim of his film in Bengal, he was now facing further difficulties. The gist of the trouble was that two Americans, who had seen the film's first screening at the Museum of Modern Art in New York, had written to West Bengal's Chief Minister, Dr. B. C. Roy, who had authorized State finance to complete the film. The writers had declared that *Pather Panchali* depicted poverty; therefore it was not a desirable film to be screened abroad lest it serve as unfavourable propaganda.

The British Film Institute had asked me to search for an Indian film meriting screening at the National Film Theatre. Quite obviously *Pather Panchali* merited international release. It appeared that if the Institute would request a copy of the film from the West Bengal Government, there was a reasonable expectation that one might be sent. This might aid in it being sent to Cannes. I wrote to Satyajit Ray to tell him of the Institute's interest.

On arrival in Calcutta, I went to Ray's home on the south side because at that time he had no telephone.

The Rays lived in an upstairs flat off one of the main arteries of Calcutta. Today he lives in a similar but rather larger flat on the next street, Lake Temple Road, It is a moderately prosperous middle-class district in the social stratification between the extreme luxury of expensive Alipore and the descending degrees of poverty that reach incredible depths in other parts of Calcutta—Calcutta, the birthplace of new ideas and paradoxically, of museum traditions.

Every afternoon around teatime the milkmen come with their cows and tether them to the railings of Ray's house, and the other houses. On the landings of those houses with flats, outside the front doors, there are frequent changes of traditional *rangoli* patterns chalked out by housewives as decoration for every Hindu festival. Such patterns are to be found on the threshold of homes of Hindus all over India during Dewali, the Festival of Lights; but much more frequently in the building where Ray lives.

He was out at work but not at film-making. For economic reasons he was still employed as a commercial artist in the firm of D. J. Keymer. His wife, Bijoya, and her two-and-a-half-year-old son, Sandip, were in the living-room. She was welcoming but not talkative. (Pl. III)

There were two things in the Lake Avenue room—square with no unusual features—which made an impression: a number of terracotta Bengali folk toys and several beautifully modelled Buddhistic looking heads. These were modern copies but different in their inner feeling from the commonplace deity figures to be found in many people's homes. They possessed a concentrated serenity and were not in the sentimental vein of popular religious figures.

A second woman, arrayed from head to foot in a borderless white sari—the Bengali widow's *than*—came into the room. She gave the illusion of being unusually tall. Her presence was commanding without being formidable. Her manner had warmth. This was Satyajit Ray's mother, Suprabha.

I asked Mrs. Ray about the heads.

"They are mine," she answered.

Unlike many Hindu women—I did not know that she came of a Brahmo Samaj family and was, therefore, unorthodox—who maintain traditional behaviour, including much reticence, Suprabha Ray talked with free animation.

She said her husband had died when Satyajit was three. Later she had gone to work in a home for widows, teaching sewing. "One day I felt a desire to model heads. I had this feeling for three years and I did these heads. Suddenly, I ceased to feel inspired. I never modelled another head."

Mrs. Ray gave the impression of determination, openness and enthusiasm.

"Satyajit's father was a writer and artist." By the tone of her voice she implied that this was important in relation to her son. "Come, I'll show you his picture."

She took me into a bedroom where her husband's photograph hung on the wall. The face was not handsome in a conventional way. It appeared a rather Victorian face. She explained that he wrote for children and pointed to a watercolour for a book illustration. It was evident that she cherished his memory, as she no less cherished her son and sought to communicate with anyone who appreciated his film.

Unannounced, Satyajit Ray came to see me at the flat where I was staying. It was a bald kind of encounter without polite exchanges and confined to our framing an emphatic letter imperatively requesting the British Film Institute to ask for a copy of *Pather Panchali* from the West Bengal Government to be considered for presentation at the National Film Theatre. Ray said he knew Gavin Lambert, then editor of *Sight and Sound*, and that Lindsay Anderson and he were friendly. Both, he thought, would help.

Ray's enormous height was accentuated by the flowing lines of his traditional Bengali clothes. Yet his hands were slim and sensitive, the wrists unexpectedly slim-boned. His wavy hair was exceedingly well cut giving a decided orderliness to his features, large-scale and massively carved. Ray looked distinct from any easily identified Bengali type where there is often visible evidence of the fusion of Aryan, Mongolian and Dravidian ethnic origins.

C

Indeed, he appeared untypical of any Indian group. As his friend, David McCutchion, later commented: "Satyajit's a bit like Alexander the Great to look at!" His cast of feature suggests the antique, expressive at one moment of sober, even sombre austerity, but the next of spontaneous delight and humour. In any mood Ray must serve as a magnet to photographers. He speaks English with no Indian inflexion. It would be hard to find a more pleasing voice than his, or a more natural way of speaking.

A few days after this meeting I commenced to give six consecutive nights of film discussion at the Indrapuri Studio. Ray came each evening and sat in the third or fourth row of chairs. Even sitting down he was taller than anyone else. While a number of other people gave their opinions and asked questions, Satyajit Ray remained completely silent. He watched the films with concentration and he listened, but gave nothing away. On the third evening I talked about *Pather Panchali*, saying that if shown abroad it would gain world recognition. Though completely Indian, its characters were universal.

Following that session, Ray came along beside me outside the studio and, with no preliminary remark, said: "If you keep on saying the things you are saying about *Pather Panchali*, you'll make yourself a lot of enemies!"

He said he would come and see me the next morning at breakfast time at the Alipore Government hostel where I was staying. Sitting across the breakfast table, Ray's reserve and aloofness in a crowd disappeared. It was not that he talked a great deal, but that he talked with frankness. Being neither critical nor disillusioned, he did not attempt to mitigate Indian faults by citing "our spiritual heritage". He discussed the Indian scene and film censorship objectively. This conversation confirmed the impression made by *Pather Panchali* that Satyajit Ray had profoundly deep Indian roots, a stable pride and devotion to India's humanism. His was not a nationalist pride, but pride in that which was enduring in spirit. Indianess was fused in him with an acute awareness of where traditionalism imposed limitations and attitudes.

While the immediate outward impression made by Ray—because of the traditional garb he wore and the way he wrapped his embroidered stone-coloured shawl around his shoulders—lent the illusion that he might never have stepped beyond the boundaries of his own State of Bengal, there was a subtle intimation that this was not at all the case. He might appear the essence of Bengal yet there was nothing provincial about him. He did not have to put it into words that he had intimate knowledge of what went on, and had gone on for a long time, in the world. There was an indefinable universality in his outlook.

Though I had only been in India two months or so, the most disquieting thing that had struck me in many contemporary artists was their conscious, or unconscious, ambivalence towards the Indian scene. Too many were either led to escape its powerful challenge through a decorative interpretation of the cultural pattern; or else evade grappling with its realities by espousing essentially Western forms and attitudes. Contemporary painting was attractive but usually failed to portray depth.

There seemed to be a lack of equilibrium among artists in seizing upon the potent actualities of their environment, an environment where at one and the same moment there appears the most intense beauty, poignant liveliness and dignity side by side with horror. It was Satyajit Ray's equilibrium which left the most forceful impression.

Pather Panchali did finally arrive at the 1956 Cannes Film Festival. In absentia its creator received the award "for the best human document". As the first film of the now famous Apu Trilogy, it dispelled the long-held feeling that India was unlikely to produce a great film. *Pather Panchali* and *Aparajito*, the second film of the Trilogy, collected between them one dozen major awards, possibly the greatest number of prizes won by any director for two films.

Unheralded at Cannes, *Pather Panchali* was announced for screening on a sultry afternoon towards the end of the Festival. A small, somewhat *distrait* audience, bored by too many cocktail parties and an endless parade of films, gathered to see it. The critics who were there expected nothing more than "the usual Indian film with dances, songs and sacred cows. There were only a few people and the first moments seemed to confirm their worst suspicions. The film's opening seemed slow and solemn."

Among the critics present was Arturo Lanocito of Italy's *Corriere della Sera*. He found "the images were mixing the self-indulgent refinement of aestheticism with some crudity so realistic as to be repulsive". Some people drifted out. Only a very small audience remained when the unexpected began to happen. Lanocito suddenly realized that "the magic horse of poetry" was invading the screen; "the breadth of the story became large, the purity of the images corresponded to the purity of the subject. On very few occasions we had seen on the screen the novel of a childhood spent in the fields told with such felicity of expression . . . we had witnessed a kind of self-revelation of Indian film art."

The next year, 1957, *Pather Panchali* was shown at the first San Francisco Film Festival on the recommendation of the film critic, Albert Johnson. It won the prize for the Best Film and Best Director. By this time, the second film, *Aparajito*, in which Apu, the boy of the first film, passes from child to adolescent to student youth, was completed and entered in the Venice Film Festival. Under René Clair's chairmanship, the Jury awarded the sought-after Golden Lion of St. Mark's to Ray. There followed the David O. Selznick award for the Best Foreign Film of the year. The two films were coupled in the Golden Laurel Awards and Trophy for the years 1959 and 1960.

Following the Venice award, one Italian newspaper had splashed a headline that Ray was the Indian Robert Flaherty. This led to Flaherty's widow, Frances, instigating an invitation to Ray to come to the United States as the first foreign guest at the Robert Flaherty Seminar held in the late summer of 1959. After this brief visit, Frances Flaherty wrote me a letter comparing her husband to Ray: "Ray quiet, self-contained, aloof; Bob restless, ebullient and so warm. Ray, as you know has an impressive presence; when he spoke that presence became articulate in the most beautiful use of the English language I have ever heard. The sensitive exactness of the words he used was again for me the most perfect revelation of why he could make a film like *Pather Panchali*."

During this visit, Edward Harrison, the distributor who had discovered *Rashomon*, released *Pather Panchali* in New York. Until his death in 1967, Harrison would for ever remain utterly devoted to Satyajit as a man as well as an artist. Ray was a great success at the Seminar and in New York, affording something of a surprise to his interviewers. One New York writer commented: Ray "is no dreaming dilettante. A strapping, swarthy chap, with strong features, he talks like a realistic poet, without the slightest foreign accent, looking fresh from the American gridiron."

That autumn, he demonstrated his quiet confidence in Brussels. He had been invited to serve as the seventh Juror for the film festival of the Ten Best Films of All Times. This was his maiden Jury service.

Yet when Ray arrived in Brussels the impression he gave was that he must have sat on several international juries. It seemed he belonged as much to Europe as everyone else present; that he was naturally a part of the world film scene and not the special representative of an Asian country. He was wearing a casual shirt and a pair of trousers which might have been tailored in London.

Ray's amused comment was: "I've made it a condition of my being on the Jury that if I don't wish to vote, I won't vote."

During that week delegations arrived from the Soviet Union, Poland, Britain, France, and most of the countries of Europe, as well as the United States. Frances Flaherty was there. Mixing with all delegates and with his international colleagues on the Jury, Ray accomplished a remarkable feat of diplomacy: he convinced everyone, including the Festival officials, that it was impossible for a single film to be selected from the ten and voted as the best film of all time.

Satyajit Ray reasoned that how could such a choice be made when the films chosen by cinema historians included silent films and sound films? Could *Potemkin* be ranked a greater film than *The Gold Rush?* With utmost tact Ray contrived to have the Best Film of All Time set aside to the satisfaction of every delegate. Instead, the delegates were asked to submit their own additional list of ten great films. The Jurors, all of them younger film directors, decided to select from the ten films, those films of the greatest interest to them. Thus a judgement which would have been unrealistic and arbitrary was waived. No one resented the man from India asserting so much common sense.

In *The Dance of Shiva,* a book by Ananda Coomeraswamy, the author wrote: "We must demand of a coming race that man should act with European energy and think with Asiatic calm— the old ideal taught by Krishna upon the field of battle." He quoted from the *Gita*: "Indifferent to pleasure and pain, to gain and loss, to conquest and defeat, thus make ready for the fight. . . ." These words seem applicable to the character of Satyajit Ray.

With his first two films Satyajit Ray conquered the discriminating appreciation of two continents beyond his own Asia. As early as 1957, he was invited to Japan, the indefatigable Mrs. Kawakita, who had put the Japanese film on the world map, having seen *Pather Panchali* at the National Film Theatre in London. Ray never reached Tokyo until 1966. But then he evoked great admiration with Mrs. Kawakita writing that Ray "is now the greatest of the world cinema".

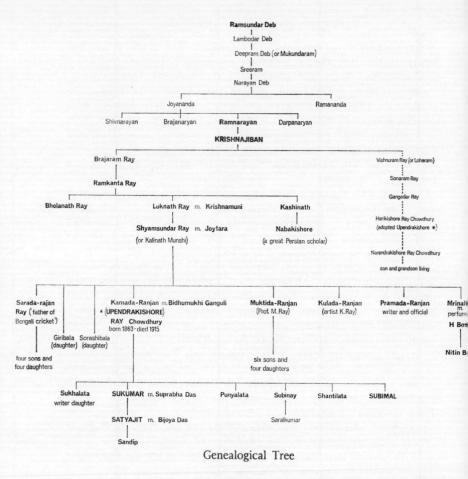

Genealogical Tree

Chapter 2

ANCESTRAL TAPESTRY

As a man, Ray centres his life among his relations as if he were a traditional Indian. His creative preoccupations revolve persistently around family relationships. Only four of his films have, so far, deviated from this pattern, *Abhijan* (1962) and *Nayak* (1965-66), and the short film, *Postmaster*, also *Goupi Gyne* (1968-69).

Not only is Ray's talent inherited, but the independent cast of his mind and the character of his moral outlook are a reflection of a family type. Satyajit's youngest paternal uncle, Subimal, a meticulous-minded former teacher helped—and is frequently quoted below—to reassemble this history of the Ray family. A whole book could be written on the Rays before the birth of Satyajit. Like a film fourteen reels long, each reel depicting a generation, the history of the family reflects the changes in Bengal. The background is changeless, a landscape of coconut forests, bamboo groves and spreading raintrees—a lush greenness reflected in eternal temple tanks round which the family habitations have clustered. For centuries the natural opulence of Bengal tempted outsiders: fair Aryans, dark Dravidians from the Deccan, Turks and Afghans from afar. The Pathan rulers invited in Semitic-Negro men from Egypt and Abyssinia. The last but one of the invaders were Mughuls, or Mongols, whom Genghis Khan had led out of Central Asia. Each came in the time of their power to oust another and reap the benefits of the land. Each added their own ethnic stream as the many rivers and rivulets wend their way to the Ganges Delta. The last to push their way into Bengal were the Europeans, bringing with them Jehovah. Among all the traders and adventurers and missionaries, the British manoeuvred the most successfully. They were the last supreme rulers.

During the unending struggles for supremacy by aliens, Hindu Bengalis learned an outward adaptability to violent circumstances. Concealed within them there congealed an inward conservatism built up to preserve a cultural and religious distinction based on the worship of female deities. A secret core developed in the Bengali soul. It can still be detected today, for when two Bengalis meet they draw together like members of a secret society. Consciously or unconsciously aware that their land has always been invaded, they turn for consolation to their cherished and beautiful mother tongue.

With the onset of Muslim domination in the eleventh and twelfth centuries, Hindu intelligence, more complex than that of the conquering invaders, led to Hindu indispensability to a succession of rulers. The conquered became as bamboos bending in the wind stirred by the battles of outsiders. One such bamboo was the earliest recorded ancestor of the Ray family, Ramsundar Deb, a non-Brahmin of *Kayastha* caste, a caste mainly composed of intellectuals.

Ramsundar first appears as a resident of a village in Nadia district of West Bengal. He must have been born about the middle of the sixteenth century. His descendants for the next three centuries appear to have been devotees of Vishnu, the Preserver. No portrait exists of Ramsundar, but there is a legend that he was very handsome. He decided, "presumably for some mundane purpose", to depart on the hazardous journey from Nadia district to Mymensingh district in East Bengal where Pathan nawabs still ruled. He reached the estate of the Zamindar, the landowner, of Sherpur, who held estates lying south of the Assam foothills. The Zamindar became Ramsundar's patron, and brought him into contact with the ruling Raja of Yasodal. Ramsundar became the Raja's son-in-law. As well as a daughter, a *jaghir* of land was granted to him by the Raja. The extent is unknown but from it Ramsundar and his descendants collected a fair revenue.

Four generations from Ramsundar remained in Yasodal, administering the estates of powerful zamindars and nawabs. During the first half of the eighteenth century, a descendant, Ramnarayan, was appointed a Naib, a rent collector, for a district some considerable distance from Yasodal. On his journeys, haunted by attacks from wild animals and robbers, Ramnaryan took with him his only son, Krishnajiban. The dangers of the journey did not match up with the attractiveness of the rewards. Father and son uprooted themselves and founded a new residential house in the village of Masooa on the banks of the Brahmaputra river within the district where the rents had to be collected.

At this time, when the family title was now changed to Ray, society was in a constant state of flux. Hinduism, with its inner elasticity, managed to attain equilibrium between the contradictory polarizations within the Hindu soul—an innate sagacity in regard to material things and a yearning for spiritual values and philosophic speculation. Hinduism flourishes in a land subjected to yearly devastation by floods, yet dependent for the earth's regeneration upon the torrential storms of the monsoon. In these surroundings, the minds of men are inevitably drawn towards opposing poles, building up material substance for earthly survival, yet unable to forget the presence of vast, inexplicable forces, which they can attempt to tame only by strict ceremonial observances.

The two sons of Krishnajiban, Brajaram and Vishnuram, lived in esteem at Masooa, the younger notably more ambitious in worldly things than the elder. They fell under the influence of a group of Brahmins from the Himalayas. Brajaram developed a love of learning, while Vishnuram fused the traditional attitudes of piety with interest in the accumulation of wealth. They were to hand on these traits to the male heirs of the two branches of the family they founded, thus marking out a continuity of outlook from father to son. For some considerable time the learned Brahmins acted as community advisers to the two brothers and their families living jointly within one compound. Masooa seemed cradled in security.

Suddenly, the village was destroyed by flood. As in the film *Pather Panchali*, the Ray home was devastated. The family, as that of Harihar, was forced to move away. The joint family split up, each brother setting out to follow the dictates of his inherent nature.

Brajaram Ray and his descendants did not seek to acquire any substantial amount of land. They invested their efforts in becoming more learned officials. Vishnuram, on the other hand, acquired land. Brajaram's son, Ramkanta, tall and good-looking, did not have much money. At first, this defeated him in acquiring the bride he desired. A rich landowner rejected him, not having seen him as a prospective son-in-law. His name is lost. But, subsequently, seeing the young Ray at some gathering, he enquired about him. Discovering this was the would-be bridegroom he had rejected, he was so impressed that he reversed his decision and instantly married Ramkanta to his daughter. In due course, Ramkanta became a respected Majumdar.

Though Ramkanta was an official with an interest in things of this world, he had a love of music. After satisfying his gigantic morning appetite—he would consume a basketful of fried rice and a whole jackfruit the weight of which was around four pounds—he would sing devotional songs accompanying himself energetically on the Vishnava *Khole*. When his religiosity reached its climax of excitement, Ramkanta would beat his melon-shaped drum so violently that the instrument would splinter.

He had three sons—Bholanath, Loknath, and Kashinath (whose son became a famous Persian scholar). The eldest of the boys begot no male child, but had the unusual habit of replying to every question in verse. Versifying was to become one of the several artistic talents in succeeding generations.

It cannot have been very long before the handsome and exuberant Ramkanta realized the unusual capacities of his second son, Loknath. Schooled in Sanskrit and Persian, the boy was trained as a surveyor. But he could not fit into the world of zamindars. Orthodox Hinduism failed to satisfy either his mind or his emotions. From an early age Loknath felt compelled to follow a path which the practical-minded orthodox Hindus considered to be dangerous, if not abhorrent. This was the doctrine of Tantra with its worship of feminine deities—Kali and Durga—breaking of caste taboos and, in some groups, the practice of magic rites that were commonly held to be excessively erotic.

Alarmed at his son's increasing preoccupation with Tantric mysteries, Ramkanta stiffened his demands that Loknath marry. After a time the son gave in, seemingly willing to renounce his desire to become a mystic sadhu. A marriage was arranged with the very fair Krishnamuni. But the instant a child was conceived Loknath retreated to contemplation in a hut he had built near the cremation *ghat*. Here, at the *ghat*, the Tantrics practised austerities in pursuit of deep mystic experiences. Loknath's son was born and named Shyamsundar. But his birth failed to draw his father into the normal householder's role, and Ramkanta Ray is said to have ordered his son's Tantric books to be seized and thrown into the river. Loknath's reaction was extreme. His will to live ceased. In three days he was dead. He was thirty-one years old.

The story handed down to Satyajit Ray was that Loknath retreated to his hut, lay down on the ground and while waiting for death, made the accurate prediction that his only son would be like the spreading raintree, producing many progeny, and his descendants would flourish. There is evidence that a tendency to premonition reappeared in at least two of Loknath's descendants, a grandson and a great-grand-daughter.

Left a widow in such extraordinary circumstances, Krishnamuni Ray remained with her only child, Shyamsundar, in the house of her father-in-law. She, who had been compelled to stand aside and see her husband, Loknath, desert his father's house for death, outlived her son. She became the immutable widow of Hindu tradition. Her hair was cut short even if her head was not shaved. She could never again put a streak of vermilion in the parting, the significant line which told, and tells the world, a Bengali woman is a wife.

Custom dictated that the young Krishnamuni remove her earrings and her gold bangles, and to refrain from placing the much-loved *tilak* mark, large or small—the vermilion beauty spot like an all-seeing third eye—above and between her eyebrows. This is a beautification only for the unwed and the wed, prohibited to the widow. Until her death, Krishnamuni was condemned by tradition to wear the borderless white *than*, the widow's sari of dull and unbeautiful weave, worn again by Satyajit's mother nearly a century later.

Perhaps under the mellowed guidance of his grandfather, Ramkanta and his mother, who had nothing but her son to live for, Shyamsundar, like his strange father, grew up studying Sanskrit and Persian. At some unrecorded date he learned English, for now there were new methods of trade and constant changes in administrative methods introduced first by the East India Company—"John Company"—and later by the British Indian Government with its Imperial capital in fast-growing Calcutta.

The extremism of Loknath did not reappear. At a suitable time, Shyamsundar, destined to become a noted Sanskrit scholar, married Joytara, whom her descendants recall as being sufficiently generous of heart to forget her orthodoxy occasionally. Towards the end of his life, Shyamsundar also moved so far from strict orthodoxy as publicly to support the remarriage of a virgin widow in a family he knew.

Shyamsundar's eldest son, Sarada-rajan, was born before the terrible echoes of the Mutiny of 1857 had died down. He grew up to maintain his Hindu orthodoxy and was yet another Ray to become a noted Sanskrit scholar and mathematician. He became Principal of Calcutta's Vidyasagar College.

Sarada-rajan affected properly Victorian cricket clothes on the pitch in duplicate of his English physical double, the famous cricketer, W. G. Grace, and he died with the designation, "Father of Bengali cricket". He was one of Loknath's descendants to be gifted with premonition. Twice this was said to have operated during his lifetime.

The youngest daughter, Mrinalini, became the mother of fourteen children, one of her sons being Nitin Bose, who became a leading Bengal film director before the advent of Satyajit Ray. She was still alive at the age of eighty-five when this book was commenced. Hers was a family which pioneered in many fields, including being the owners of one of the first cars to appear in Calcutta.

In all, Joytara bore Shyamsundar eight children each of whom distinguished him or herself in one way or another, more often than not in education and science for theirs was a period when the scientific and technological ideas of the West were flooding through Bengal. The most remarkable of Shyamsundar's children was Upendrakishore, who would become the grandfather of Satyajit Ray.

The senior branch of the Ray family attained distinction through their intellects with official status masking a tendency to intellectual turbulence and creativity. Meanwhile, acquisition of property had become the preoccupation of Krishnajiban's younger son, Vishnuram, and his descendants. For four generations their estate, acquired after the flooding of Masooa, increased in size. Hariki-shore, only somewhat younger than his relative, Shyamsundar, was now recognized as a zamindar and added the title of nobility, Chowdhury, to his name. He was every inch a zamindar.

The rise in wealth of this side of the Ray family had been encouraged during the eighteenth and nineteenth centuries by the aggressive impact of the rapidly expanding East India Company. Its advent had caused the decline of the old landed aristocracy. Fortunes linked with the Pathan and Mughul rulers were doomed. Thus it was that people with the perspicacity of Vishnuram Ray, his son and his grandson, emerged as the new class of zamindars.

But, behind the façade of charm and affluence, Harikishore Ray Chowdhury maintained a second personality, that of an excessively pious Hindu who fasted with strictest adherence to orthodoxy unassailed by the new ideas about him. He remained untouched by the rational assault on orthodoxy instigated by the famous Bengali reformer, Raja Rammohan Roy (1772–1833), the founder of the Brahmo Samaj. Instead of being influenced, Harikishore, the zamindar, became the President of the Institution for the Spread of the Knowledge of the Hindu Religion, a movement to resist religious liberalism. But by 1863, Harikishore had no son and heir to inherit and carry on the proud traditions of his family. This must have caused him much distress since his orthodoxy demanded a son to light his funeral pyre.

Harikishore Ray's family history was devoid of polygamous marriages. He could not entertain the thought of a second marriage, even though the class to which he belonged by virtue of his wealth often accepted polygamous marriages without question. His family, rich as it was, was a puritan family, so much so that, with the exception of the *Jatra* folk plays with their religious themes, he would permit no dramatic performances within the confines of his property.

Like other Hindu zamindars, rajas and maharajas in need of an heir, even if not sired by themselves, Harikishore, unsuspecting he would later father a son akin in character to himself, searched for a child to adopt from among his relatives. His choice fell on Satyajit Ray's grandfather, born in 1863 and destined to grow up with a temperament and talents utterly divergent from those of Harikishore. It was not a surprising choice since Shyamsundar Ray, much respected, had several sons. There was no bar to a family allowing one of its children to become the adopted heir of a relative. Yet, in this case, the choice was to prove ironic.

The devout zamindar, Harikishore Ray Chowdhury, in that prim Victorian age, was thoroughly ensnared by the traditional idea that fairness and good looks were synonymous. This led him inadvertently to adopt the most unorthodox of his relative's offspring because the boy was the fairest. Thus, Shyamsundar's second son, renamed Upendrakishore Ray Chowdhury, went to live at the zamindari. In time, this boy would become the first Ray to marry out of caste and for love by his own arrangement.

As often happens, a few years after the adoption of Upendra-kishore, his adopted mother gave birth to a son, Narendrakishore. Like his forebears, but less successfully, he would devote himself to the preservation of the inheritance, which he was to share with the adopted Upendra. He, too, would preserve his orthodoxy.

From the first, the adopted son was more absorbed in the charm of his flute than in learning how a zamindari was operated. He even carried his flute to the local Mymensingh Zilla District School. But, in spite of his preoccupation with the flute, he never failed to answer correctly when the master put questions to him. It was here that he first met unorthodox views. They were those of his closest friend and classmate, Gaganchandra Home.

Home was an ardent follower of the Brahmo Samaj, whose members were still militantly crusading for the "worship of the Supreme Being in spirit as opposed to the prevailing idolatry of the land". They crusaded for abolition of blood sacrifice, remarriage of widows, inter-caste marriage and co-education. This movement, of which the Tagores became leaders, served as the spiritual, social and, ultimately, political hub of the period, later known as the Bengal Renaissance.

Raja Rammohan Roy, the Brahmo Samaj founder, had been profoundly influenced by the English Unitarians. Indeed, it was his failure to spread English Unitarianism in Bengal which led him to create a Hindu parallel. He had studied the Vedas and the Upanishads, the Koran and the Bible. He preached that behind their ceremonial trappings, all religions held a central truth. Once this truth was discovered, men of different creeds would feel as brethren. The only fit offering for the Supreme Being should be "days of benevolence towards each other". The Brahmos sang the Psalms of David after chanting the Vedas.

It is possible that Upendrakishore may have heard of the con-version to Brahmoism of a zamindar of moderate means named Kalinarayan Gupta of Kaoraid. He had become a legend in the Dacca district. This man's grand-daughter would become the mother of Satyajit Ray. Kalinarayan, too, had been adopted as a child. From his earliest years he had showed marked kindliness in a generally callous society. In a caste-conscious world where the ancient Laws of Manu had petrified into an obsessive dread of defilement, Kalinarayan had no fear of consorting with people of low caste.

After long and unsatisfactory discussions with the Pundits, Gupta and his wife, Annada Devi, abandoned the presence of any traditional image in their worship and offered only the prayers within their own minds. Soon after this decision Kalinarayan went to the city of Dacca to learn English. Dacca, the opulent capital of Pathan-ruled Bengal and now under British rule, had become a great trading centre. For twenty years, it had served as a fountain for the spread of Brahmo ideas, and for reform. Now, periodically, irate fathers turned to beating their sons and evicting them from their homes for joining the Brahmos.

Kalinarayan Gupta's adopted mother, and old friends, grew anxious that he would lose his faith and virtue if he continued to learn English in Dacca. They begged him to return home. He returned, but he was captivated by what he had heard of the Brahmos. He began to read their literature in his mother tongue By November 1869, when Gupta was thirty-nine years old and, therefore, by orthodox standards, of middle age, he, his wife and their second and third sons, journeyed to Dacca to consecrate themselves to the Brahmo "search for truth".

It amazed and shocked some of the Dacca Brahmos, "who were not yet free and unfettered", to see Babu Kalinarayan's two servants sitting side by side with their master, his wife and his sons, waiting for their collective initiation. Immediately Gupta returned to his zamindari he instituted a Samaj and commenced to teach "uneducated men belonging to the agricultural classes". Through his simple way of exposition many of them grasped the broad truths of pure spiritual religion and gathered round him as his first disciples.

Gupta, who possessed a beautiful and powerful voice, and his wife sang their own devotional songs which became part of the Brahmo hymnal. These were simple and impressive.

Babu Kalinarayan, his hair parted on the left and combed in a sedate and Victorian manner, kept a style of longish beard only growing around his jaw line. With his large visionary eyes, long classical nose and strong but softly moulded lips, he would raise his voice, "sweet in tone" to proclaim, "where love appears, every-thing there turns friendly". (Pl. I)

He abandoned himself to the service of his fellows. From some-where he had learnt the rudiments of medicine and simple opera-tions. He treated people's ills and the villagers regarded the strange zamindar's skill as a gift from God. It was impossible for him to conceive keeping for himself and his family more than they actually required. He instructed the local stationmaster to send anyone who had to wait for a train to his house and he would give them shelter. It was handed down that Gupta went among these unknown guests seeking to find out who was poor and had a long journey ahead. He would give these people money.

The last remembered action of Gupta juxtaposes his selfless, undeviating stability to his ideals with a candid portrait of a community steeped in its own insensitive egocentricity. In his old age, Kalinarayan shocked his village when a man of low caste, a scavenger, became insane. The villagers rejected this deranged man who made a nuisance of himself. But day after day the Zamindar nursed him. When the man died, Kalinarayan lifted the corpse on his shoulders and carried it to the cremation ground. Suddenly, the villagers flocked along the way abjectly entreating the Zamindar to allow them to dispose of the body.

Gupta is said to have told them : "He helped me often in life. It will give me solace to perform his last rites." He walked on singing his hymn composed for the dual purpose of Brahmo festivals and memorials to the dead : "Let us sing that name of God, the very recollection of which is a balm to the heart and removes fear of death. . . ." Kalinarayan Gupta epitomized the idealism and ecstasy latent in the Bengali soul which Brahmoism released after the national tragedy of the Indian Mutiny and the frustrations which followed it.

Brahmoism would not have been born in Bengal, nor flourished there, had there not been deep internal decay. The Brahmos were lighting a torch which others could carry forward for the benefit of India as a whole, even if the later torch-bearers themselves would sink back in time to a self-hypnotized state of eternally intending to do something and then forgetting to carry it through. There were, of course, exceptional men and women, true psychological followers of Rammohan Roy, such as the great Tagores and, in time, Upendrakishore Ray.

When the young Upendra brought home the echoes of his growing Brahmo sentiments, Harikishore was, to put it mildly, disapproving.

From Harikishore's point of view Brahmoism was a dangerous disease, even afflicting those who were not Brahmos. As mentioned, Upendrakishore's respected father, Shyamsundar, was not beyond being influenced. Without the subversion of Brahmoism he would hardly have defended, even in a single case, the remarriage of a virgin widow. The Brahmos were making their opinions felt throughout Hindu Bengal.

They were behind the reformist Act III of 1872 which legalized the remarriage of widows, inter-caste marriages and civil marriages. Even the spate of local criticism had not deterred Shyamsundar Ray. He declared: "I have given my word and I will not take it back. I will attend the wedding!"

Harikishore's wealth and pious pursuit of individual salvation protected him like the glass covers of his Victorian Age from the dust of daily life. He forbade Upendrakishore to mix with the Brahmos or to see his friend, Gaganchandra Home. But Upendrakishore could not end his friendship with Home. He would take his flute and go into the woods and, secretly, meet Home after piping an all-clear. The two boys would then discuss Brahmoism which was percolating through their school. The Headmaster himself became an adherent.

At school, Upendrakishore was displaying "marked mathematical and scientific talents". A passion for art was also emerging. "Alone and unaided he mastered the mysteries of light, shade and perspective." He could not refrain from drawing and sketched on his school books and papers. The teachers noticed Upendrakishore's pronounced artistic inclinations developing hand in hand with a passionate interest in the sciences—the knowledge introduced with such force from the West. Young Ray's multi-sidedness was cemented by his consuming attachment to music, inherited, probably, from his father, Shyamsundar, who was able to compose his own songs for devotion in Sanskrit. On graduation from Mymensingh Zilla School, Upendrakishore was recommended for a Government scholarship.

He departed from Harikishore's zamindari for Calcutta's Presidency College, the oldest centre of the now accepted methods of English education, with its gigantic neo-classical portico, which remains unchanged, supported by Roman-style columns. Shortly after, his own father died.

In the film *Aparajito*, though it depicts a period more than fifty years later than the departure of Satyajit Ray's grandfather for Calcutta, there is a poignant symbol of Apu's transition from rural schoolboy to urban student: Apu puts his feet gingerly into his first pair of European-style shoes and tries to walk in the uncomfortable footwear so grossly unsuited to the tropical Bengal climate. Upendrakishore, though an heir to a zamindari, had never worn such shoes and his feet must have felt as uncomfortably rubbed as Apu's. He could only have been as astonished as Apu at the new and previously undiscovered things he met in the Imperial city of Calcutta.

The most brilliant of Loknath Ray's grandchildren now moved

back to West Bengal from whence the adventurous ancestor, Ramsundar Deb, had travelled to East Bengal four centuries earlier. At Calcutta's Presidency College, Upendrakishore's attention first became fixed on scientific experiment rather than on his artistic leanings. Soon the two became fused in photography. Before long, Upendrakishore "constructed with his own hands a working model of a gyroscope out of a wooden ball and a few bits of wood".

"With his own hands" hints at the upper-class, and even middle-class, Bengali taboos against manual work. Even in Upendrakishore's time this revulsion against all but intellectual work had induced outsiders from other parts of India, particularly Mawaris from Rajasthan, to come into Bengal and exploit the opportunities in business and industrial development. Upendrakishore did not reject the use of his hands for manual work. Perhaps the instinctive dexterity of his grandson, Satyajit, and his son, Sandip, is derived from Upendrakishore.

Upendra, who was remembered as having never lost his temper, again gravitated towards Brahmoism. He was drawn to the most radical group of Brahmos, those of the Sadharan, or Republican Samaj. Founded by the intrepid Dwarkanath Ganguli, and his friends, the Sadharan Samaj opposed the more conservative views on women expressed by the mystic-minded leader, Keshubchandra Sen, who had become surrounded by a torrid mysticism and was claimed as a Messiah.

Brahmin by birth and teacher by profession, as a young man Dwarkanath Ganguli had even shaken up the Brahmos of Dacca by crusading for the education of women in a village of the distant Faridpur district. His assaults on traditionalism and the abuses of society which were flourishing in the 1860s soon led him to sensational forays in saving Kulin Brahmin girl widows from forced immorality. When it was not the plight of women he was concerned about, it was the indentured labourers of the Assam tea plantations. Ganguli took immense risks to investigate their conditions and make them known.

The rise of Garibaldi and the Italian *Resorgimento* movement exerted a profound influence on Ganguli. He evolved the idea of "a United India, derived from the inspiration of Mazzini, or at any rate of bringing all India upon the same political platform". The Constitution of the Sadharan Brahmo Samaj was more advanced in political thought than anything in England at the time. It recognized the principle of universal adult franchise, the clause which would be embodied seventy years later in the Constitution of Free India.

D

Unlike his grandfather, Loknath Ray who willed his own death to maintain his unorthodox convictions, Upendrakishore quietly slid into the Brahmo movement. New factors operating in society were all on his side. If he was summarily disinherited he could survive. He could go to work. After graduating from Presidency College in 1884, Upendrakishore commenced his career as an artist and photogapher. With the death of Harikishore, his adopted father, Upendra took no personal interest in the management of the property.

He said: "I entrust the management to Narendrakishore because I know he can be trusted. Being Harikishore's own son, he has greater right to it. I am satisfied with what he sends me out of the income of the zamindari."

Young Ray was pleased to haunt the Samaj building on Cornwallis Street. He was invited across the road to Dwarkanath Ganguli's home, No. 13. Babu Dwarkanath, long the impassioned partisan of female emancipation, had a whitening moustache decorating a bulldog face that would have suited an English general. His eldest daughter was Bidhumukhi. She was not a very good-looking girl, but young Upendrakishore liked her. Perhaps she was a little overshadowed by her father's newly acquired second wife, Kadambini, formerly Miss Basu, and Babu Dwarkanath's academic Galatea. (Pl. I)

The pretty Kadambini had been one of her ageing husband's earliest pupils at his Bengali Woman's Institute. Daringly, he had prepared her for the 1878 Entrance Examination to Calcutta University when even women in England were barred from universities. Having succeeded in entering the University, Miss Basu created a sensation by holding her own against the gentlemen students. She was deluged with praise and medals. A special reception was held in her honour and attended by the bigwigs when in 1882, Miss Kadambini Basu became the then British Empire's first lady B.A.

The crusading widower was, undoubtedly, very much in love with Kadambini in her distinctly Victorianized silk blouse, and the then fashionable embroidered veil over her hair known by the flirtatious name of "fascinator". Her European-style high-heeled shoes peeped out below her sari. Ganguli persuaded her to hold up her head and assert she was a "person" and, therefore, under the rules, eligible to enter the Calcutta Medical School. The result was that Miss Basu became India's first qualified lady doctor. Presumably, in a gesture of thanks for the confidence inspired, Miss Basu became Dr. (Mrs.) Dwarkanath Ganguli. In Indian usage, her own name, Kadambini, was used in place of her husband's, Dwarkanath.

The Ganguli family atmosphere of a debating society, far from alarming Upendrakishore, induced him to be bold enough to propose that daughter Bidhumukhi, who was not anything like as formidable an example of female emancipation as her new step-mother, become his wife. He was twenty-three when this inter-caste marriage took place in a Brahmo Samaj ceremony in 1885. His admiration for his father-in-law added to his pleasure.

With the paradoxicality of Hindu orthodoxy, his mother, Joytara, was reputed to have remarked : "If my son has accepted as a wife a Brahmin who is also a Brahmo, I am willing to accept her as my daughter-in-law."

Yet, to keep on the undefiled side of her orthodox convictions, Joytara never lived under the same roof with the inter-caste Rays. Instead, she lived with her eldest son, the cricketer, his wife and their four sons and four daughters. Orthodoxy and non-conformity began to dwell in the Ray family in a spirit of equilibrium.

At the outset of their married life, Upendrakishore and Bidhumukhi lived on the first floor at 13 Cornwallis Street, one floor below Babu Dwarkanath and his young Kadambini. It was a sort of reformed and urbanized joint family. Kadambini soon produced a family of seven young children to match her stepdaughter, Bidhumuki's, six. The two youthful families with uncles and aunts and stepnieces and nephews all more or less the same age grew up playing together.

Very early, Upendrakishore's scientific turn of mind had caused him to explore printing methods. By 1885, he had made a study of photo-engraving. Since he possessed a private income from the zamindari, he sent to England to purchase equipment for producing half-tone block printing, then unknown in India. That year, too, he founded his press under the name of U. Ray. He had dropped the title of nobility, Chowdhury, from his name. Later, the press became known as U. Ray and Sons. Upendrakishore installed it in his own home and it was never to be parted from where the family lived, so when Satyajit was finally born he was, from birth, surrounded by technical processes.

Being a perfectionist, Upendrakishore found existing processes too primitive for him. He sorted out rival theories and reached his own conclusions. This subsequently had international repercussions. He commenced experiments on standardization of printing methods. By 1904–5, *Penrose Annual*, for which Ray wrote technical articles, was claiming that "Mr. Ray is evidently possessed of a mathematical quality of mind and he has reasoned out for himself the problems of half-tone work in a remarkably successful manner."

Grandfather Ray had become Calcutta's outstanding printer by working out machines of his own devising—a screen-adjusting machine and a sixty-degree screen and a diaphragm system. Initially this was to aid a perfected reproduction of his own paintings and illustrations for the books he wrote himself. These were to entertain his own children and the flock of related children; for example, his account of prehistoric animal life, *Sekaler Katha*, is still read in Bengal.

Upendrakishore's eldest daughter, Sukhalata, was later to demonstrate a predisposition to premonition. She, too, wrote poetry. In 1956, her poems of family remembrance were published. Scattered through them are intimate observations of people leading their daily lives. Then, suddenly a dramatic but natural incident appears, and the liveliest images of nature, all much akin to the construction and imagery of her nephew, Satyajit's, films. Her poems are in English.

In 1887, when Satyajit's father, Sukumar, was born, Big Sister Sukhalata, only a year older than he was, recalled:

> Dear little brother,
> In the bath-tub splashing water with his hand.

As well as giving an image, there is the revelation of the Anglicized manner of bathing the children. And:

> Then I see him
> Pursuing fleeing girls with a lifted stick,
> The naughty little boy;
> Battering a toy violin to pieces
> To find whence the tunes came.

The inquisitive mind of the father had passed to the son. Similar efforts at investigation would be noted in Satyajit when he was a young child.

Upendrakishore's first family home, as all his later houses, echoed with the strains of Satyajit's grandfather practising and playing to friends on his real violin. The children came into the world, one after another, with silver spoons in their mouths. There was the long line of inherited talents. There was money. There were servants to attend to their wants. Yet their father had protected them before their birth from falling under the self-damaging vices of the zamindar-dominated Bengali society. Even down to Satyajit's time, this society was to cultivate an indolent arrogance saturated with potential creative imagination, but too little sense of reliability.

There was the dual protection of Upendrakishore himself and his rather plain wife. Satyajit's paternal grandmother was much more than a zealous housewife and affectionate mother. She was a "woman", as her youngest son remembers, "of great compassion whose mind could easily discern the secret sorrows and wants of not only friends and relatives but also of those unknown to her". Much has been recalled of Bidhumukhi's sensitive generosity towards strangers.

Her third child, a girl, Punyalata, who grew up to marry a magistrate, arrived on the scene with Sukhalata remembering:

> Father carrying her in his arms,
> Pacing up and down the room,
> To rock her into restful sleep,
> His shadow moving along the sun-lit wall.

This was because Little Sister was ill. The next child born, the boy, Subinay, would always remain close to his elder brother in his trials and tribulations.

Punyalata remembered Elder Brother, Satyajit's father, Sukumar, drawing pictures "rich in imagination and joyful in spirit on his slate, or on paper". At eight years old this embryonic family humorist completed his first creative feat—a poem to "Nadi", the river. Upendrakishore, "with the eye, hand and soul of an artist", was only too eager to watch for what his eldest son would produce next. It took some time, but the next year Sukumar, who showed inventiveness in sport and entertaining all the younger children, produced his second poem, "Tick, Tick, Tong". It was really a translation of "Hickory, Dickory, Dock". Father, who was already writing for children, gave Sukumar's poem to the children's magazine, *Mukul*. At nine, Sukumar emerged an author in print.

Both Punyalata, and the youngest girl, Shantilata, were born in the Cornwallis Street house. Then the family moved to Shivnarayan Das Lane before the last child, Subimal, came into the world. He grew up careful and conscientious, the cherisher of family memories. He was the member of the Ray family to spend the last years of his life in the home of his nephew, Satyajit, and his son, Sandip. Subimal, too, would write children's stories and remain unforgotten by the students he taught.

As the children grew, their father, Upendrakishore, would take them to the latest artistic or industrial exhibitions. He would explain to them everything that was worth knowing about the objects on display. As he stood talking, other children and grown-up people would gather round to listen. Perhaps it was this response to his way of putting things which inspired Upendrakishore to retell the stories from *The Ramayana* and *The Mahabharata* in a series of children's books. These he illustrated himself, as his son, Sukumar, would illustrate his own nonsense verses, and as his grandson, Satyajit, at forty, would have an impulse to illustrate and write stories for children.

In time there appeared the Ray family's most striking fusion of scientific craftsmanship and the creative spirit—the children's magazine, *Sandesh* (*Sweetmeat*). Counting no costs, Upendrakishore's magazine reflected the richness of his own family life.

There must have been great excitement when young stepmother Kadambini Ganguli, with two of her own young children in tow, reappeared in a cloud of glory from far-off Edinburgh where she had captured further medical degrees. And no less of a thrill running through the family and catching up the children when the glamorous modernistic doctor-grandmother was suddenly called to Nepal in 1896 where she cured the Queen Mother, who bestowed a pony on her which ever afterwards drew her carriage. Princely families began to invite Dr. (Mrs.) Ganguli to be their Physician.

Again it was an Indian paradox: that ruling royal families would trust a woman doctor, especially one whose husband was famed for his exploits in exposing the cruelties on English tea plantations towards the frequently kidnapped indentured labourers in Assam; or a husband so disobliging to the supreme British rulers as to identify himself with the recently formed Indian National Congress which for its fifth session held in Bombay, requested the admittance of female delegates. Kadambini was one.

In 1900 Upendrakishore and his family moved to a large house at 22 Sukea Street, now known as Kailash Bose Street.

> Ours was the only house
> In the street at the time,
> To own a telephone line.
> People talked from floor to floor.

writes Sukhalata, also remembering the arrival of Calcutta's first car and gramophone, for father's youngest sister, Auntie Mrinalini, rode in the city's earliest motor car.

The printing press was under the same roof, with the house something between a private technical school and an all-round academy of the arts. The focus in the Ray household was on entertaining and developing the children. The gatherings epitomized what was called the Bengal Renaissance. What educated Bengal thought today was talked about tomorrow in circles all over the country. The symbol of the Renaissance man, Rabindranath Tagore, the multi-sided, often came to visit the Ray family. Rabindranath appreciated the unostentatious spirituality of the Ray home. He enjoyed the gleams of humour mixed with Upendrakishore's aesthetic and scientific discussions. Being himself a master composer in both Indian and Western styles of music, Tagore enjoyed inducing Upendra to play his violin. (Pl. II)

In Calcutta there was a spate of playwriting, with Tagore in the forefront. Earlier, dramatists had arisen influenced by the Western theatre. This had been followed by adaptations of Bengali novels. Subsequently the Tagore brothers, Jyotindranath and Rabindranath, experimented with dramatic forms which incorporated elements from the religious folk theatre of *Jatra*. Though they were written to please himself and not for the professional theatre, Rabindranath's plays later became the symbol of Bengali dramatic talent.

Often when inspired—just as in the case of his creative grandson —Upendrakishore would remove himself from crowded Calcutta. Giving no explanation, he would leave at short notice with one of his servants, or take one of the children with him. He would head for Puri with its expanse of sand and ocean. Or he would make the long journey north to Darjeeling, the Himalayan town on many levels. He would contemplate "the most beautiful snow range in the world", as Satyajit would have one of his own character creations describe the visible peaks in his film, *Kanchenjunga*.

Through the haze of time, Upendra's youngest child, Subimal, recalls his father "gazing intently and meditatively at the scenery before him. Upendrakishore Ray's eyes would draw in the beauty of the thing, his mind would absorb its spirit, his hand would reproduce the whole with appropriate and confident strokes of the brush inspired by the deep and natural reverence he had for his work."

As a description, this could apply to Satyajit Ray for, like his grandfather in painting, he often pauses after shooting a scene, and then shoots it again with the "additions of some delicate touches here and there".

Upendrakishore was a born illustrator and landscape painter.

He had the same feeling for Nature as that revealed in his grandson's films. But as Satyajit is a man of today, there are works of his grandfather which reveal the influence of the British Pre-Raphaelites. One painting is now in a Ray relative's house. It is of Sita, the wife of Lord Rama of the epic. Sita is depicted as a pale Victorian Miss. This painting speaks eloquently of the role of British art education in India at the time.

Upendrakishore Ray

The Indian genius for reconciling the supposedly irreconcilable even operated in the Ray family. When orthodox Narendrakishore Ray Chowdhury appeared from the Mymensingh zamindari and consorted with his adopted brother and his brood of inter-caste children and friends, Narendrakishore still preserved his orthodox ritualism as a leader of the orthodox community by eating separately. He brought his own servants to prepare his orthodox food. Even so, he was prepared to be present at Brahmo ceremonies in Upendrakishore's house.

Over the years, Upendrakishore had been training up a generation of highly skilled craftsmen who would become the finest printers in Bengal. Early in the twentieth century the most skilful of these student apprentices left U. Ray to open a business of his own. After his departure, Upendrakishore discovered that this man had misappropriated funds. Instead of charging him with embezzlement, Upendrakishore only commented : "If he can start a business of his own with the knowledge gained here, let him have his chance."

Upendrakishore was an inherently trusting man. Although he sometimes took his family to the Mymensingh zamindari—as when they all arrived at Bara Masooa "on elephants, and in palanquins"— he never asked embarrassing questions of Narendrakishore Ray Chowdhury about how things were really going financially with the zamindari bequeathed by Harikishore to his own son and the adopted Upendrakishore. Upendrakishore's idealism prevailed in relation to the Mymensingh estate. It seems to have been a family trait in his branch of the family always to look for the best in people's conduct. Even Satyajit, who was to grow up without the benefit of money, lacks natural suspicion. He has never yet sued any publisher or film distributor who owes him money. Grandfather was not a businessman, nor was his son, Sukumar. Perhaps none of the descendants of Brajaram Ray have manifested business acumen.

As time went on, troublesome and unpleasant situations became apparent in distant Mymensingh. Narendrakishore incurred a diversity of difficulties and debts. Suddenly, Upendrakishore was informed that the zamindar had mortgaged part of the estate. He had never insisted upon a definite division as to what was Narendrakishore's and what was his. Upendrakishore was obliged to take a mortgage. The mortgagor was a friend he had known in college. Yet Upendrakishore felt himself secure, especially as Sukumar was manifesting graphic and literary talents, and understood technical processes. Even as a child, Sukumar had shown dramatic talent.

With an open house always full of relatives and enterprising people, the gregarious Sukumar revealed a spontaneous dramatic ability at a very young age. He had roped in his mother's Ganguli half-brothers, and his younger brother, Subinay, to help devise entertainment for the younger children. He used Bengali folk dolls made of paper—dolls often representing ghosts, this being indicated by the backward turn of their feet. Sukumar, and his family assistant directors of his first show, animated these paper dolls by threading the figures with thin string and turning them into dancing puppets.

Now, following in father's footsteps, he was a student at Presidency College. Here he created the home-based Nonsense Club with membership open to those with a flair for the ridiculous, practical joking and, most of all, acting. He was growing tall but not as handsome as his father. Like his great-great-great-uncle Bholanath, who had answered questions in verse, Sukumar instinctively rhymed, putting ideas together in a style somewhat resembling Lewis Carroll and in the spirit of Edward Lear.

At some point before 1911, when Sukumar was sent off to England, Suprabha Das, the rather tall and beautiful teenaged grand-daughter of the visionary Kalinarayan Gupta, was introduced to Sukumar's Nonsense Club. She, like all the Guptas, had a beautiful singing voice. Sukumar, no doubt, had his eye on Suprabha Das before he went to England on a scholarship from Calcutta University to Manchester College of Technology to study photography and half-tone printing.

One evening fifty-one years later, Sukumar's son, Satyajit, started on an enthusiastic hunt through boxes of old papers in search of what he could find of his father's and grandfather's to show me. Almost at the bottom of a tin trunk there lay a bulky pile of Sukumar's letters written to various members of his family. They were either on Northbrook Society stationery or from 12 Thorncliffe Road in Manchester. The letters were long and newsy. In one Sukumar told the story of his arrival in Manchester and visit to the Principal of his College. The small son "ran out to see the Indians and mother said 'Jackie was disappointed and said, "Why, they are only Indian gentlemen. They haven't got their feathers on"!' "

Another described how, in London, he had attended a concert of the violinist, Fritz Kreisler, and had also seen the hand-coloured film of the Delhi Durbar. The London Underground with its electric lifts which he had not experienced before, intrigued him. When Rabindranath Tagore came to London, young Sukumar had a meeting with Sir William Rothenstein of the Tate Gallery. Rothenstein, being one of Tagore's great admirers, made a portrait of the poet. On July 12th, 1912, Sukumar Ray had gone to the Royal Court Theatre—a theatre still devoted to experiment—to see the first presentation of Tagore's play, *Post Office*.

While Sukumar was in England—and frequently visited London —an exhibition of the ultra-modernist painters—Picasso, Braque and Kandinsky—captured his imagination. He wrote an article on their modern painting.

That evening in June 1962, reading the old papers, the work of four generations of Rays—Upendrakishore's, Sukumar's, Satyajit's and the boy, Sandip's—were set side by side. Each reflected the contemporary trends indicative of their own period. Sandip's were decidedly influenced by popular comic strips and his father's films. Nevertheless, there appeared to be a line of continuity in terms of the observation of human character. Here was something of a hereditary creative pattern stretching over four generations.

On Sukumar Ray's return from England in 1914, he married Suprabha Das It was around this time that the family moved into the elegant and interestingly designed house which Upendrakishore had built at 100 Garper Road—the house where Satyajit would be born—in the heart of the intellectual district of North Calcutta. Set in the highly individual stuccoed façade were decorative lotus medallions, which are still there. Two lotus buds form a poetic detail at the corners of the flat roof forming two terraces for games and sleeping out. This gracious, cool house, with an almost rural view of trees and tall palms, must have been an expensive house to build.

The U. Ray and Sons Press and publishing business was housed on the ground floor, with the composing room occupying the front part of the first floor. The family's living accommodation was at the back of this floor and on the second floor. The rooms were quiet, with high ceilings. Behind the house stretched a long garden.

Yet Upendrakishore seldom dwelt in this delightful house of his own design. Though only fifty-three, he had developed the then uncontrollable disease of diabetes. He placed Sukumar and his younger son, Subinay, also a writer of children's stories, in charge of the Press. Sukumar took over the editing of *Sandesh*, where he developed his own mood of nonsense verses, and his frequently surrealist-slanted illustrations. He was being spoken of as perhaps the most original of the coming generation of writers, one of vast promise. (Pl. II)

Upendrakishore knew, even as Sukumar would also learn about himself too early, that his creative talents were doomed to be brought to a premature end. His violin had to be left in silence; his paintbrushes began to gather dust; gradually, even his pen remained unused in the penholder. Still his unorthodox faith had brought to him a quality of mind which enabled Upendra to lie, day after day, and accept the approach of his own dissolution. He brought himself to regard death as a personal friend, perhaps as comforting as Rabindranath Tagore, who often came to see him.

During the last days of his life, Upendrakishore, the instinctive artist, put himself into an essentially mystic, even ecstatic, state of mind. He appeared to have the creative imagination to enjoy, or at least give the impression of enjoying, drawing nearer his exit from life. His final day is like a story designed to leave behind the memory drained of pain and bitterness. In the morning, he noticed a bird chirping for an instant near the window. Then it flew away.

"Did you hear what the bird said?" Upendrakishore is reported to have asked the relatives and friends gathered around. It was as if he was going to tell another story for the children.

"Go your way in peace is what the bird told me . . ." he added.

Before he lapsed into a final coma, Upendrakishore told Bidhumukhi: "Whenever I close my eyes I see a beautiful kind of light, a clear, brilliant light. . . ."

Loknath Ray's grandson glided peacefully out of life like the notes of his boyhood's flute, fading into utter silence on December 20th, 1915.

It is reasonable to consider that the details of his grandfather's and father's death have influenced the attitudes of Satyajit Ray. These memories have been preserved and they may explain why Satyajit consciously turns away from stark and hopeless endings to his films. He has an impulse to leave a question mark.

Like his father, Upendrakishore, and like his son, Satyajit, Sukumar, despite his sense of humour, had intense powers of concentration. He would become entirely oblivious of everything while working out a creative problem from beginning to end. Swift minded, he synthesized words and images. Unfortunately, his literary style is very difficult to translate. Satyajit made an effort to put into English some verses from "The King of Bombaria", from the book, *Abol-Tabol* :

> In the land of Bombaria
> The customs are peculiar.
> The king, for instance, advocates
> Gilded frames for chocolates.
> The queen, who seldom goes to bed
> Straps a pillow round her head.
> The courtiers—or so I'm told—
> Turn cartwheels when they have a cold:
>
> . . . The king's old aunt—an autocrat—
> Hits pumpkins with her cricket bat
> While Uncle loves to dance Mazurkas
> Wearing garlands strung with hookahs.
> All of this, though mighty queer,
> Is natural in Bombaria.

Bubbling with wit and good humour, Sukumar mixed his creative work with a passionate support of the now declining Brahmo Samaj. Difficulties and disappointments were multiplying for him. By 1920, after seven years of marriage, Sukumar and Suprabha remained childless, while the family business was facing accumulating debts.

As Satyajit would say long years after: "My father and grandfather were idealists. They wanted to change so many things"; he concluded, "they were not practical men".

Sukumar (for "Abol-Tabol")

In a moment of ominous foreboding, Sukumar wrote a curious letter to the family friend, Professor Mahalanobis, the noted economist. He said he felt a change coming over him and the change was towards death. He wrote 'death' in English and underlined it. Sukumar was now the third descendant of Loknath to be seized with a sense of premonition which became reality.

The worsening financial situation compelled him to journey to Mymensingh to investigate conditions at the zamindari. He discovered the whole estate was swamped by debt, not only the acreage on which his father, Upendrakishore, had taken a mortgage from his college friend. His visit was disastrous. On his return to Calcutta he carried within him the bacteria of the then fatal disease of blackwater fever. He was thirty-two. Only now did he learn that his wife, Suprabha, was pregnant. Their son, a rather small baby, was born on May 2nd, 1921, and named Satyajit.

Within a month the fever appeared. Sukumar could not shake it off. Though every conceivable treatment was tried, including the traditional, improvement was never more than temporary. Fever penetrated deeper and deeper with the bacteria affecting one organ after another until Sukumar found himself tied to a wheelchair. As his whole system disintegrated, the financial crisis of the business became acute. Some of the best process workers became lazy and careless. Not even Suprabha knew the full extent of the debts. Her husband's illness halted transactions which might have saved them.

Yet Sukumar continued to write. His wit remained unimpaired. Persistently he continued to bring out *Sandesh*. He was able to drown despairing thoughts in what he was doing and find relief in the continued sound of the presses working. He was helped by the companionship of friends who came to see him. Many came, including Rabindranath Tagore. Another was K. N. Chatterjee, who had come to meet him at Victoria Station when he first arrived in London.

Chatterjee recounted to me how conscious he was of the troubles facing Suprabha. He was distressed that there was nothing he could do to help Sukumar whom he regarded as the most talented of the younger generation of Bengal's artists and writers. He would always remember one particular afternoon when he visited the Garper Road house.

Sukumar, in a wheelchair, was in the garden at the back of the house. The two of them were talking together. Suddenly, they noticed Satyajit, who was nicknamed Manik. He was playing with a green toy frog which would leap when its spring was fastened. Then, for the first time, Manik caught sight of a live frog hopping about without a spring. (Pl. III)

"Bang"—frog—"Bang", burbled Manik, toddling over to his father to ask how a frog could hop about without a spring.

But the grown Manik retained no recollection of this mystery of the frogs. His earliest memories are of playing marbles on the tiled floor of the family drawing-room. It appeared to him to be an enormous room. He remembers standing for long periods on the roof of the house looking over to the next compound—the playground of a school for deaf boys, and watching them play football. He would be drawn to stand at the composing-room door watching the men silently working. There was a smell of paraffin. . . .

Sukumar, bedridden and in great pain, used up the last of his dying forces in writing, in verse form, his thoughts on the Brahmo Samaj in the days when it had been a potent force. Now it had shrunk into a narrowed puritanism alien to the rich spirit of the Rays and the poetic and universal vision of Rabindranath Tagore.

On Rabindranath's last visit to Sukumar—August 29th, 1923—when Sukumar felt he was soon to die, Tagore sang nine of his songs to him, some of them songs of joy he had composed. Perhaps Manik, who became Rabindranath Tagore's biographer on film, listened to them.

As death came very close to Sukumar, his streak of premonition turned into a strange dream—that Upendrakishore and some of his dead friends were holding a discussion about Sukumar's future. Visions came to him. Once he said he had seen his youngest sister, Shantilata, who had died, sitting by his bedside. On another occasion, he said he saw his mother's brother, also dead, and one of his intimate friends, who had died, sitting on his bed and looking at him. Evidently, Sukumar Ray had not the slightest doubt as to his survival beyond the moment of death. For him, death was only a withdrawal from the living, a reunion with those he had loved and who had passed out of life before him.

The most vivid image of his father that Satyajit Ray has—it is not clear if it is his own memory or a picture created for him by his mother—is that of Sukumar in an oxygen mask still dictating a nonsense rhyme. Satyajit strove to translate it into English, but it defied translation. Translated, its depth of meaning vanished. Sukumar Ray, who brought something new to Bengal's literature, died on September 10th, 1923.

The creditors closed in. Younger brother Subinay's attempts to carry on *Sandesh* were crushed. Upendrakishore's college friend demanded the principal on the mortgage at once. He did not explain that he himself was deep in debt. With no alternative, Subinay hurriedly sold the zamindar land. He failed to receive a fair price. There was only enough to pay part of the mortgage. Other creditors showed no mercy.

Subinay's health was shattered. He continued to look after the withering business as best he could. The oldest and best trained worker in the photo-engraving department left, taking with him other competent men to set up a rival firm. It was this which finally broke U. Ray and Sons. Interest due to the creditors piled up. The firm was liquidated in January 1927, when Manik was six years old.

The case was decided in the District and Session Judges Court.

No purchaser offered the minimal acceptable terms for the Garpar Road house. It was awarded to the largest single creditor, the once friendly mortgagor, on condition that so long as Satyajit was a minor his mother receive a regular monthly sum out of the rent. The agreement was honoured. At least there was money to educate Manik Ray.

Soon after this, grandmother Bidhumukhi died. Subinay found a post with the Calcutta office of the Indian Government's Geological Survey office. He lived until 1945 contributing stories, riddles and articles on scientific subjects to several children's magazines after the close of *Sandesh*. Meanwhile, Subimal never deviated from his teaching at Calcutta's City College School. On retirement he went to live with the grown-up Satyajit, who brought alive again the magazine, *Sandesh*, to which Uncle Subimal now contributes articles.

At the end of 1926, Suprabha took Satyajit to live with her younger brother, P. K. Das. They began a new kind of life.

"So," says his uncle, Subimal Ray, "Satyajit is the Ray who grew up untouched by the zamindari atmosphere."

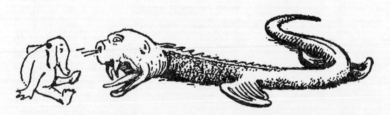

Sukumar (for *Sandesh*)

Satyajit (title-page illustration for
Poems by Naresh Guha)

Chapter 3

THE YOUNG SATYAJIT

SUPRABHA RAY, her relatives of the Gupta and Das families, and
members of the Ray family, conspired, consciously or unconsciously, to shield Manik from all but the vaguest knowledge of
the economic disaster that engulfed the U. Ray and Sons family
printing and publishing business.

Upendrakishore had thought only of the perfection of his work.
He had even overlooked taking out patents on the machines he
had devised for the improvement of half-tone printing and colour
reproduction. People abroad were now making money from U.
Ray's inventiveness. In his lack of business acumen, Grandfather
Ray preserved the reticent shyness of the man who comes from
wealth and is too much of a gentleman to suspect people of
economic ruthlessness, and too inherently courteous to be hard-
headed in his business dealings.

Suprabha accepted the enveloping protection of her own family.
As in the film, *Aparajito*, where Apu's widowed mother is left
with no money and her uncle comes and takes Apu and herself
to his home, so Suprabha Ray went to live with her younger
brother, P. K. Das. But in life the situation was not quite the same
as in the film, for P. K. owed much to his brother-in-law, Sukumar,
who had supported him while he was a student.

63

E

The change in family environment was enormous and Satyajit thinks this affected his life more than the change in financial circumstances. Suprabha Ray had taken her son, who had inherited the main characteristics of the Rays, from a highly conscious intellectual environment, where discussion of everything of creative importance was normal, into the Das family, where no such intellectual awareness existed. They were moderately well-off people immersed in the ordinary affairs of everyday living.

"I was cut off from everything intellectual," Satyajit says. "Even in college I was not aware. Santineketan made the difference. I suppose I observed things without being conscious of doing so Even now in creating I am intuitive rather than analytical."

Having faced the economic collapse of the artistic world of which she had been part, Suprabha Ray became the hub of her own family at the age of thirty-one because "everyone looked up to her".

Manik was planted down and rooted up as his Uncle P.K. moved from one house to another. Sometimes he had to be left for a period in the home of other relatives. Presumably, these shiftings and shuntings intuitively caused him to develop a core so that even now he is a part of, yet apart from, his immediate surround-ings. Sensitive, Ray is yet impervious. Open and frank, he is also introspective and reticent.

At some point it was impressed on Manik's consciousness that some of his maternal uncles and great-uncles were Indian English-men in their dress and behaviour, even though they were descended from the visionary Kalinarayan Gupta who gave up the study of English. This Englishness of the Das family probably explains why Satyajit Ray writes and speaks an idiomatic English without a trace of those twists which have become common in what is termed Indian English.

When asked, "Who is there who knew you as a child?" Satyajit's instant reply was: "They are all dead." Then he corrected himself, saying: "There are my girl cousins. They knew me best. My mother and I spent a holiday with them every year while their father was posted in Bihar. It was wonderful—the games we played!"

Later he recalled that during his childhood and boyhood he had no companions of his own age. The maid's son, who was a Bihari and became his friend, was still a few years older than Manik

"He became one of the family," Satyajit explained. "He ate with us. He became a tailor and we still meet."

His Ray cousins, the daughters of Aunt Punyalata, are older than Satyajit by five years and ten years, and are still known as Ruby and Nini. Their mother was not only Satyajit's mother's sister-in-law but her great friend.

On the walls of the house which the cousins and their husbands share, hang several paintings of Upendrakishore. Ruby's eldest son is already a budding writer, her husband being a publisher. One sister lives upstairs, the other down. The household is pervaded by the speculative and discursive atmosphere which must have been characteristic of Manik's first home at 100 Garpar Road.

Ruby's first recollection of Manik goes back to when he was six. The two sisters, who hardly noticed he was so much younger than they were because he was precocious, played a game of doctor with him. Ruby, taking a box on which she painted 'DR. SATYAJIT RAY', insisted that this was what Manik was going to be when he grew up.

But Manik rejected the idea: he was going to be no such thing. He said: "I'll be a film director and go to Germany and learn and come back!" Cameras came from Germany and his great-aunt Mrinalini's son, Nitin Bose, then—1927—a pioneer director of Bengali films, had been there.

The cousins hoarded the things Manik drew. They kept, among other things a pencil drawing of a bird and a hut. Looked at today, there is nothing in this childish effort to suggest any of his father's or grandfather's artistic talent. It is vastly inferior to the drawings of Satyajit's own son at approximately the same age.

Manik was a humorous child, so little at odds with the world that like his grandfather, no one ever saw him lose his temper. At any time of the year Manik wanted to celebrate Christmas if he was given a present. To please him most gifts had to be presented to him by someone arrayed as Father Christmas.

Within a year or so, he developed an elegantly mature handwriting both in English and Bengali. Writing to Nini, he wrote the address in English:

154/1/1 Bakul Bagan Road
6.12.29

Nini Elder Sister,

I'm very glad to receive your letter. I have written down that long name (floccinausinihilipilification) on a piece of paper.

One day we had been to see a bioscope called "Show Boat". A circus is coming and we go to see that also. I can't find any other news.

Write to me. Take my kisses.

Finished
Manik.

By this time his resourceful mother had gone to work at the Vidyasagar Bani Bhavan Widows' Home founded by Lady J. C. Bose, the wife of the scientist. Travelling from one side of Calcutta to the other by bus or tram, Suprabha Ray taught sewing. She considered her talent for embroidery her greatest gift. It was here that she became inspired to model her heads and figures, a phase which lasted only three years. She sold her work to ease her financial predicament. The figures fetched Rs.50/- each, quite a high price in the early 1930s. When she was not out at work, she taught Manik at home.

Satyajit remembers spending hours of his young life investigating the mysteries of light. There was an intriguing hole in one of the street doors of his uncle's house. Manik would stand in front of this with a piece of broken frosted glass in his hand to catch the reflection of people moving outside on the street. The shaft of light coming through the hole worked like a box camera. Years later, he told his photographer friend, A. Huq, that the images impressed him more when there were sounds along with the images. Thus, he was dimly aware of audio-visual effects at a very early age.

At ten, Manik was given his first box camera. On holiday with his cousins he wanted to photograph them as often as they would oblige him by posing. His father's and grandfather's inclination towards photography had reappeared in him. But his early photographs, like his drawings, revealed no conspicuous talent. Again, his own son's photographs, taken at eight years old, are superior to his.

Bright though he was, Manik could not pinpoint any of his potential talents. His mother's talents were those of a very fine copyist. She was conscious that Manik was creative, but she could not direct his uncertain attempts. She simply wanted him to be an artist like his father.

He developed himself unconsciously, and perhaps by rendering himself oblivious of the trivialities surrounding him. Even today Satyajit Ray absorbs himself in creative thought and works with complete concentration though the greatest hubbub may be going on around him. The Das family did, however, stimulate one thing in Manik which would become a dominant force throughout his life. The love of music first so marked in the Kalinaryan Gupta family was carried over to the Das family and Manik. Though as a man he will seldom display it, he inherited the Gupta singing voice. What he will display, and as if unconscious that he is doing so, is a phenomenally developed whistle which serves him like a musical instrument. His memory for music is exceptional.

Satyajit says that the first tune he learned was the British Great War popular hit-tune, "Tipperary". When he came to make *Pather Panchali*, he included it for the boy, Apu, to hear.

In 1931, when Manik was ten, his mother's half-brother, Uncle Charuchandra Das, died. He left four daughters—Gouri, Sati, Joya and Bijoya—all older than Manik. They came to live with Uncle P.K. Their father had been "a barrister who had been in London a good deal and was a great one for dramatics". Gay, and wrapped up in feminine interests, the girls were stage-struck. Sati became a screen actress and Bijoya, too, for a short time.

Bijoya, the nearest in age to Manik, became his companion. Though she was two or three years older than he, Manik was mentally as old, or older. Of the girls in the two families, Bijoya was the one most attracted to the things that interested Manik. By eighteen, he had fallen in love with Bijoya. To wish to marry one's cousin was a very unusual thing in Bengal, almost unheard of, but marry her he did when he was twenty-seven.

At the age of ten, Manik entered his first school—the Ballygunge High School. He displayed no great brilliance at school, though at home he was a very bright, precocious boy. Between eleven and twelve years of age, he found no difficulty in solving crossword puzzles devised for adults. This rather pleased him.

The only intense passion Manik betrayed while at school was music. Bijoya and he pursued their love of music first by listening to records of popular singers like Paul Robeson and Nelson Eddy. Later, they were absorbed in Western classical music. Neither of them was ever responsive to jazz. He spent all his pocket money on records. Perhaps this passion, echoing his grandfather's absorption in his flute and violin, prevented Manik from realizing there were a great many things from which he was isolated. Music fed the artist within him. He responded to the quality of equilibrium in Western classical music and it influenced his whole character, and certainly his films.

He feels an inward necessity to seek the redeeming or mitigating factor in the character of the least admirable person, or the nastiest situation, holding to a sense that no one, and no situation, can be reduced to the ungraded tones of "all black or all white" —the words he uses to reject a wholly negative interpretation of anyone, or anything.

In line with this attitude, Ray insists: "What the financial crash in my childhood meant to me was only that we travelled intermediary class, or third, on trains instead of first or second. I bought perhaps a book or two a month instead of several. I went to the cinema once or twice a month instead of once or twice a week."

Along with the love of music, Manik was drawn to the cinema in early boyhood. But not in the same intense way as his contemporary, Ingmar Bergman, who developed a conscious passion at the age of five.

"I was a bit of a film fan," says Ray, and reveals his emotions as they were as a little boy, by adding: "I saw *Uncle Tom's Cabin* and I wept and I wept at Uncle Tom's ghost and the death of poor Eva!" He saw David Wark Griffith's film *Way Down East* long after it ceased to be presented commercially in America and Europe. "I remember that fairly well," he says—"the two blood-hounds. There was a villain with three interests in life—women, women and women! I was a regular film fan. But I don't know when it became serious. At some point, I began to take notes in the dark on cutting."

With only a limited awareness of art being fostered in Manik by his mother, his unpromising drawing at six or seven years old had not, he says, become inspired by the time he was thirteen or fourteen. He thinks his draughtsmanship was "good", and that he had a flair for portraits. He had a realistic streak which enabled him to make a balanced estimation of himself.

He had been a very small baby, a rather beautiful but little boy and then, at about fourteen, he started to shoot up in height to becom a very tall and thin adolescent with a sensitive face (Pl. III). By 1936 his mother determinedly sent him to presidency College, the expensive Calcutta institution where his father and grandfather had been students. He was probably taller than any of the tall Ray ancestors, who had for generations been noted as a generally tall family. He did not stop growing until he reached six feet four and a half inches which makes him one of the tallest, if not the tallest, living Bengali.

Yet in his spurt to an unusual height, Satyajit retained the grace of artistically expressive hands, not over large, and in a society where everyone's feet are a known feature—through wearing sandals and going barefoot—his feet remained slim-boned in keeping with his hands. From childhood he has had an inclination to put his feet up on any available object while he works. Today, he writes, draws, paints and reads with his feet on something—most usually the divan in his study—and his knees drawn up. He uses his desk for everything except its intended purpose. He will even have his typewriter on his knees though a table is three inches away from him. (Pl. XXXVI)

At Presidency College, from 1936 to 1940, the economist,

Professor Mahalanobis, a friend of Sukumar's, guided Manik. He concentrated upon Biology, Physics, Chemistry and Economics. Then came the Arts.

Satyajit has the impression that he did not become particularly intellectually mature at Presidency. This is not the impression he made on others. One of his classmates, Potla Sen, the son-in-law of Sukumar's friend, K. N. Chatterjee, says that while Manik was quiet and aloof, he was looked upon as one "of the intellectuals". It is open to question as to whether he had any very intimate friendships. As now, it is difficult to imagine Satyajit opening up to people unless he has constant contact with them during his daily life.

It is still music that looms of great importance in Manik's memory of this period. Professor Mahalanobis's younger brother ran a gramophone shop and presented him with a gramophone along with one record—the last movement of Beethoven's Violin Concerto. This same man had given him a Kiddiphone with children's records when he was four years old. Even now he remains a family friend and drops in at his home.

Before the end of his Presidency College days, his father and grandfather's friend, Rabindranath Tagore, had it in mind (he was to die in 1941) that he must make certain that Sukumar Ray's son, Satyajit, become a student at his art centre and school at Santineketan, some 130 miles from Calcutta.

For several decades Santineketan had served as the hub of a cultural revival based on Indian rather than foreign influences. It paralleled the political awakening which found its expression in the Indian National Congress and the struggle for self-government. Mahatma Gandhi and Rabindranath Tagore, even when they disagreed, drew from a common source of inspiration, and, in turn, served as a united inspiration.

Music, drama, dance, painting, sculpture, and the crafts of pottery and weaving, were studied at Santineketan. Small, beautiful, dark-toned tribal Santhals celebrated their *melas*—fairs—near by. The mystic sect of itinerant Bauls also participated with their dance-song psalms, which had influenced the music of Tagore. They echoed the preaching of Chaitanya, born in Nadia district, a few decades before the birth of Ramsundar Deb, the first recorded ancestor of Satyajit Ray, whose family had lived in the same area as the great saint.

At Santineketan, everyone ate traditionally, with their hands, off banana leaves and lived with the presence of Rabindranath Tagore. For forty years, Santineketan had attracted many people.

It had inspired the dancer, Uday Shankar, the idol of the balle-tomanes of the West. Dartington Hall in England had been founded through its inspiration. The extraordinarily spiritual C.F.—Charlie Andrews—was a moving spirit within it. The doors were open wide to all the human race.

Under the influence of Suprabha Ray and Rabindranath Tagore, Satyajit agreed to go to study at Santineketan in 1940. He adds: "I never had an urge to become a painter. My approach was more literary and I thought of becoming an illustrator."

The head of the Art Department was the distinguished painter, Nandalal Bose, in whose work the indigenous ideals in art may be said to have been successfully interpreted. He had striven to rescue Indian painting from its bondage to Western forms, which had been misunderstood and interpreted in a manner singularly lacking in merit or vitality.

Bose rapidly uncovered certain latent talents in the third genera-tion Ray to become an artist. Satyajit looks back with enthusiasm and gratitude to these days under Bose.

"Bose," he says, "taught me to feel the growth of trees—to con-vey Nature—and the character of living things. Within six months there was a world of difference in my work as a result of Nandalal Bose's pointers. He was amazed by the quick development."

Ajoy Chakravarty, a Santineketan art student at the same time as Manik Ray, vividly remembers a painting of a water buffalo which was included in an exhibition of students' work.

"But Manik never liked his own paintings," commented Chakravarty. "He never wanted to show them. Even though his drawing was always good, he drew very little."

Today there remain a few of Satyajit's paintings at Santineketan. In his Uncle Subimal's room there hangs a pencil portrait of Subimal and a watercolour portrait of Rabindranath Tagore in profile. Satyajit's more recent illustrations for the revised *Sandesh* have matured into greater vitality and variety than those he did at Santineketan.

Possibly Chakravarty's memories of Satyajit Ray as a Santi-neketan student are tinctured by Bengali imagination. He paints a word portrait of an exceedingly aloof student, respected for his personality but held in awe by other students. Chakravarty says he thinks that Manik avoided participating in the dramatic activities because he was self-conscious about his exceptional height.

Satyajit plays down the dramatic in his life. He explains his avoidance of the dramatics on matter-of-fact grounds: "I wasn't interested in acting."

He was for ever being discovered lying reading on his bed, while every evening he followed a routine of playing over and over again his classical music records on his old gramophone. Beethoven, Mozart and Bach were his favourites. He talked a great deal with the art student, Koushik, a good flautist who later became an important painter. Satyajit knew a vast amount about Western music but rather little about Indian which had left him vaguely disinterested.

He browsed extensively in the library, coming across books on the cinema—Vsevolod Pudovkin's *Film Technique and Acting*; Lewis Jacob's *Rise of the American Film* and the books of Paul Rotha. He read them all.

His closest student friend was the erudite Prithwish Neogy who had a fund of information on a great number of subjects. They discussed painting and sculpture a great deal. Prithwish was an admirer of Sukumar Ray's style. They discussed the surrealist elements in it. Manik noticed a face in one of his father's drawings that looked like Groucho Marx. Later Satyajit claimed that Neogy taught him how to look at painting and opened up the world of the visual arts for him.

After his first year there at Santineketan, Tagore died. Because he was so very old, Satyajit had never attempted to approach him closely, despite the relationship with his father. With Rabindranath's death, Santineketan appeared an isolated island too far from realities to suit Satyajit's needs. He looked at it objectively, noticing that all the time he was there he had the strongest urge to go to Calcutta as often as possible "in order to keep abreast of things". He needed to earn money to support his mother who had worked hard for his sake.

In the middle of November 1942, he set off on the first of the two most important journeys of his life. Together with a group of fellow students—all of them theoretically prepared—Satyajit went on a tour of the most important monuments and classical sites in Central India. This tour of one month cost Rs.87/- (£6 10s. 2d.).

"The way we travelled—Third Class!" The tone of Ray's voice conveyed volumes as to the degree of roughing it they endured.

"We cooked our own meals and I was supervisor of the cooking."

The tour took them to Sanchi, the earliest surviving and the most striking example of Ashokan-inspired Buddhist monuments, with its richness of undamaged carving in an intensely humanistic style. It is juxtaposed with some very beautiful ruins of the later Gupta period. Sanchi lies on the trans-country route from Calcutta to Bombay, their destination for visiting the island of Elephanta with its much-damaged caves, but one containing the famous Trimurti with the three heads of Brahma the Creator, Shiva the Destroyer and Vishnu the Preserver.

"Though it is small, Elephanta is wonderful," said Satyajit. "But the first sight of Ajunta and Ellora bowled me over completely," and he went on without breaking his sentence "I realized then I was too much inclined towards Western music."

At Ellora, thirty-four caves sweep in an arc around a ravine The first twelve are Buddhist. From No. 13 to No. 30, the caves are Brahminical with the Kailash Temple hewn out of virgin rock. Only the last four caves are Jain. Many of the carved groups at Ellora have the drama of film stills. Thinking back to Ajunta and Ellora, it is impossible to conceive of any Western music—not Bach or Mozart, Beethoven or Brahms—which could in any way complement the visual conceptions of the caves.

"Ajunta and Ellora made the strongest impressions," Satyajit continued. "We were given facilities with mirrors to reflect light into the caves—there was no electricity then. The frescoes were extraordinarily revealing, not just as to the painting, but in their fundamental Indian-ness. There is a difference between these and European frescoes. In Venice, I went to see everything I could. In European frescoes it is like looking at everything through a window with things receding in perspective. But in Indian frescoes —at Ajunta—everything is coming out towards you.

"I had not realized that classical Indian art afforded such a study in human behaviour. It is so rich in the revealing gesture. The artists knew how to look and see—observe human behaviour." On his divan, where he had his feet propped up, lay a slim book on Egyptian art, and he said with a faint gesture towards it: "Egyptian art is entirely formal—one never sees in it a face in three-quarter view." In Ajunta, the approach is completely human.

The students arrived at Jhansi, one of the nearest railway points for the great complex of twelfth-century temples at Khajuraho. At that moment the Japanese bombed Pearl Harbour. Satyajit immediately decided he was going no further with his fellow students. He was heading straight for Calcutta to his mother. Satyajit never returned to Santineketan as a student. He was determined he was going to get a job.

When he went to Santineketan to collect his things, Nandalal Bose was distressed to hear that the promising young Ray was abandoning his painting. December 1942 saw the end of Satyajit Ray's connection with Santineketan, though he carried what he had absorbed there for the rest of his life. For some reason that he did not understand, Satyajit, who was to fashion the film biography of Rabindranath, had not taken advantage of his family association to gain personal contact with the poet. He had remained at a distance. Much later, he recalled that the ancient man had seemed and looked like an image of God.

It is revealing of Ray's capacity for decision that an aesthetic experience gave rise to determined practical action and not to a state of dreaming contemplation. Satyajit Ray knew that what he wanted was a job that would pay him and he decided to go and find one as a commercial artist. Perhaps Ajunta communicated to his intuitiveness that he did not have it within him to become a great painter. He had always had doubts. Yet his instinctive inclination was to aim for perfection—to, indeed, aim extremely high. He perhaps sensed that he could become the best commercial artist of Bengal. At twenty-one, Satyajit Ray was a responsible man and not a dreamily romantic boy. He had the ability to appraise himself and know what he could do.

Yet in Calcutta, Manik could find no work. He was idle for six months. At last, in June 1943, he went to work with a starting salary of Rs.85/- (£6 7s. 3d.) per month with the British-owned advertising firm of J. Keymer. He was taken on to design book jackets. In due course, Gupta, a member of the staff who became Assistant Manager, and later the owner of Signet Press, invited Satyajit Ray to work for both organizations.

When Ray started to work at Keymer's, the heads of the Calcutta branch—the head office being in London—were a series of Englishmen. For almost a decade these men kept promoting Satyajit's work, increasing his salary, and generally indicating their appreciation. He liked them, even though from 1942 to the end of the British Raj in 1947, the relations between most Indians and most Britishers in India—despite certain very emphatic exceptions—were at the very lowest ebb of suspicion and hostility.

Though Ray was not wholly wrapped up in commercial art and must always have known it was but a stepping-stone, the innate discipline and detachment of his nature enabled him to combine a standard of perfection with hard-working reliability. He had a tranquil pride in craftsmanship. Bengalis are the most artistic group of people in India, people of manifold talents, but frequently they are too easily upset emotionally to be able to apply their talents in an even stream. The exceptions face the group defect and transcend the emotionalism. Satyajit's strength lay in having no feeling that the commercial art he was engaged in was beneath his artistic dignity and potential. He was impervious as to how other people looked at it and talked. Nor did he feel that working for a British firm impinged upon his integrity. He did not consider that employment obligated him to imitate the appearance, or morals, of his employers.

Ray delineates his own attitude, and that of a certain unnamed representative of the London office of Keymer who came to Calcutta to inspect the branch.

"There was a cocktail party for him. You know the kind of thing . . ."; there was a chuckle in Satyajit's tone as he spread his hands, leaving the picture to be imagined of everyone connected doing the expected thing. "You've seen how people drink . . .", but he didn't say that half the people present got drunk, yet he implied they were as drunk as lords. "I drank tomato juice and I was the only person there who came in a *dhoti!*"

As today at a Government reception in Delhi, Ray will come, provided the temperature is suitable, in a *dhoti* which might well remind everyone that this was the garb, and has survived, from the most elegant periods of Indian civilization. *Dhotis* are excessively common as an attire in Calcutta. In Delhi, where there are mixed views about their suitability, the effect of Ray wearing a *dhoti* is like a finger pointing to the fact that the members of the Government, as well as he, are Indians and not Europeans.

Unlike most Indian artists and writers, who rather seldom know how to use a typewriter, Ray's typing looks as professional as a secretary's. He has never acquired a secretary in the last dozen years and it is difficult to imagine what he would do with one since he is conspicuously competent to do his own jobs. He doesn't feel it necessary to his ego to have someone answer the telephone for him and make a show that he is too occupied to speak to anyone. He is never idle, yet he answers his own phone instantly and without irritation.

Of his attitude towards money, his wife, Bijoya, told me: "Anyone can borrow money from him. He'd never sue anyone for what is owed him. But he's ruthless in one way—he'd never be talked into giving someone a job if he didn't feel they were the right person. He gives me money and never asks how I spend it and he keeps pocket money for himself. He seldom has money in the bank!"

Despite the fact that most of Satyajit's personal contacts lay among young Left-wingers, and his political sentiments were, and are, undogmatically towards the Left for humanistic and rational reasons, he could never get worked up over politics as such;

"though," he says, "what I observed might some day be the material for a film for me to make." There are hints of this in his 1966–67 film, *Nayak*.

Satyajit took it for granted that it would be better for British Rule to come to an end. "I'm glad it came in our lifetime. Let us see what happens now."

Taken from the point of view of the series of British heads in charge of Keymer, Calcutta, young Ray was "a gift from the gods". He could be as distant as any Englishman and, like the English, if they were worth their salt, he didn't care a damn whether he was liked or disliked. His sole concern was to keep his work up to a high standard. It was not within the compass of his nature to demean himself for the sake of being liked by Indians or Britishers. Yet he was not arrogant.

This attitude was very clear in May 1961 when he came to Delhi for the private presentation of his Tagore biographical film. That morning, while I was sitting with Satyajit in his room at the Janpath Hotel, Prime Minister Nehru's daughter, Mrs. Indira Gandhi, tracked him down there. She asked me to ask Satyajit Ray if he would be interested to make a film on Social Welfare, because she had been responsible for obtaining the funds for such a film. Satyajit took over the phone and said, instantly and simply, "No, because I'm not interested." He knew Indira Gandhi would understand. Later, he rejected two other proposed films she suggested, rejecting these after considerable thought. The third was a biography of her father, Jawaharlal Nehru. By his capacity to refuse, he earned the increasing trust of Mrs. Gandhi.

Though he may not have realized it, while Ray worked in the early years for Keymer, he had the whip hand. The English recognized what is called a "gentleman" when they saw one. The young Ray fitted into the category. There was something of the magic of "the old school tie" about his reserve and thoroughness. The various heads of Keymer who came out from London were grateful to have found themselves such a staff member as Ray. He was promoted with surprising rapidity, despite the fact that he had made the one cocktail party inspector from London distinctly uncomfortable.

From the start of his employment by Keymer, Ray became increasingly absorbed with the idea of film-making. By the early 1940s, a few better films were being produced in Bengal. Bimal Roy was the cameraman on several above-average films, particularly *Devedas*. When Bimal Roy became a director, his own pictures, *Udayer Pathe* and the comedy, *Manti Mudgha*, had strong and effective scripts. These films inspired Satyajit Ray to think he could become a scenarist.

He kept track of the films based on novels and short stories. Then he set about writing a script of his own as this seemed a way of giving himself practice. His first attempt was a Bengali version of *The Prisoner of Zenda,* on which more than one popular film had been based. Soon he approached Bimal Roy with a script.

But Ray claims that Bimal Roy failed to take him seriously. He was told to come to New Theatre Studios—the studio Ray now frequently uses for much of his work. But when he went there he was left to sit doing nothing. He grew bored and did not return.

Though there was no interest in him, he continued to persist with script writing. After some time he ventured to write two original scenarios, one based on a short story entitled *Williamson,* the other an adaptation of Rabindranath Tagore's *Home and the World.* Both were considered by a producer.

A session for reading the scripts was held, with Ray reading and the producer, Ghosh, and the director, interrupting with such remarks as "Do you know what a fade-out is?"

"It was a horrible experience," Satyajit admitted.

The producer, however, liked the Tagore script and a contract was drawn for the production of *Home and the World.* By this time, Ray was friendly with the Kashmiri, Bansi Chandragupta, who had given up serious painting in pursuit of becoming an Art Director in cinema. As Chandragupta soon discovered, the Art Director's role in Bengali film production was a very primitive one. He even found himself acting a role in a film which Satyajit liked. It was this that brought them together.

As plans progressed for the production of *Home and the World,* Ray expressed ideas totally at variance with the accepted methods of the Bengal film industry. He was insistent that exterior scenes must be shot on location when, by tradition, they were always enacted in a studio set. He was also convinced the selection of locations must be made with the scenario in mind, another concept which had not been introduced into Bengal film-making. To find suitable locations, Ray and Chandragupta went searching during holidays, with Satyajit borrowing a still camera for these excursions. They found a house which Ray thought suitable for the major exterior location in *Home and the World.*

"We also found a carriage—a landau, I think—on one of our searches," Chandragupta told me. "Already Satyajit was considering the camera angles. Once we went to Santineketan where Satyajit decided how the chase scene should be staged in an undulating

landscape of pebbly red earth. On one side was a pond, but otherwise it was barren land," Chandragupta recollected.

"There was another house we looked at," he said, "but in front
of it were electric poles. That made it impossible for, at the time
of the Tagore story, there were no such electric poles. A third
house was in the town of Canning. Later, we thought of this
house for *Pather Panchali*. There was a large artificial embank-
ment—a *bund*—and Satyajit sketched out one of Tagore's characters
—a man walking by the *bund* with a dog."

Even when Ray had first started to write scenarios he had in
mind the casting of non-professional actors. *Home and the World*,
dealing with violent and non-violent methods of resistance, was
originally conceived by Ray with the young revolutionary,
Prithwish Dey, as one of the actors. Dey was to portray a character
akin to his own ideas. It was a remarkable choice, psychologically,
for subsequently Dey was involved in the sensational Jessop
murders in which the British managers were shot at the factory
by a terrorist gang : Dey was gaoled for complicity in the case.
Though *Home and the World* was never produced, it appears that
Ray must have detected the potential to terrorism in Prithwish
Dey several years in advance of his actual participation. It is
feasible to wonder if Dey had been able to portray the role whether
the experience of acting a terrorist would have been sufficient
expression of something in his make-up which was later translated
into reality. His role in the Jessop case was that he wielded the
machine-gun employed. It led to a life sentence. The fact that
Satyajit Ray conceived of the use of non-professional actors in
1943–44 is proof that he did not imitate the Italian neo-realist
movement with its adoption of the method.

The producer and director who had accepted Ray's Tagore
scenarios soon found his ideas completely alien. They made suggestion after suggestion about changes in the script. Ray resisted.
Unable to reconcile himself to these demands, he finally received
the copy of the contract marked CANCELLED. This was 1946. Later
there came a vague suggestion that he should be employed to
design a few sets for a film written by the man who wrote *Udayer
Pathe*. But nothing came of this. *Devedas, Manti Mudgha* and
Udayer Pathe were probably the most important films produced
in Bengal prior to *Pather Panchali*.

In 1945, the year before *Home and the World* fell through, the
Signet Press had asked Ray to illustrate a new and abridged second
edition of the much-loved Bengali novel, *Pather Panchali*. From a
glance at this edition today, it can be seen that only a few of

Ray's illustrations actually tally with the compositions he finally worked out for his film. The idea of a film of *Pather Panchali* kept returning to Satyajit's mind, but he did not write a script at this point, nor did he actually think of attempting to become a film director.

Pather Panchali again came into focus in 1949 when Ray was employed in an advertising campaign organized for the manufacture of ink. The special advertising was built around a series of drawings of authors who used this ink. One whom Ray was asked to draw was *Pather Panchali's* author, Bibhuti Bhusan Bannerjee, a school teacher.

"He was a gentle man," Satyajit recalled, "with a great insight into people." Ray paused, then said, "But he was also as a man quite human. . . . He was quite interested in money . . . but, then . . . at that time, authors were badly paid. Today they are better off. . . ."

While working on Bannerjee's portrait, Ray had in mind that *Pather Panchali* would make a remarkable film. But his ideas were still unformed. He would probably have broached the subject had Bannerjee not given him the feeling that since he had no money to offer, the author might reject the idea.

Following the cancellation of the contract for the script of *Home and the World*, Ray's interest in cinema increased rather than diminished. It was stimulated by the return from Hollywood of Hari Das Gupta who was to become known as a maker of documentary films, and the formation of the Calcutta Film Society.

His fellow founders of the Film Society had little idea of what Satyajit Ray had been doing to prepare himself to work in films. In the summer of 1947, the Screen Writers' Guild of Hollywood sent out a questionnaire which came into Satyajit's hands. He answered it. The Guild's Director of Publications who was connected with the magazine *Screen Writer*, wrote a letter to Ray, saying: "Both I and the Editorial Committee . . . read it carefully, and we all agree you made some excellent points. . . . The article you mentioned as having sent under separate cover has not yet arrived. . . . I hope this article will tell something about the motion picture situation in India. There is little knowledge in Hollywood of this situation or of writers in the Indian Film Industry. . . . If you could write us . . . a letter, say of one thousand words, more or less, we would be very grateful."

By 1948, Satyajit was earning sufficient money from his commercial art work to live more independently. He now desired to taste independence and live away from his uncle's house. After twenty-two years, he and his mother went to live on their own. At this time, an old friend who was also the family doctor had convinced Suprabha Ray that since Manik and Bijoya had been attached to one another for all of nine years, it was only a traditional idea that cousins should not marry. Satyajit was twenty-seven.

Perhaps the doctor had seen two drawings of Bijoya which Satyajit had made in the very early 1940s, drawings which convey where his personal attachment lay. He knew what he wanted for his private life as definitely as he had known what he wanted in terms of his work. (Pl. IV)

Unusual as it was among Bengalis for cousins to marry, it was a matter of indifference to Satyajit whether his choice was unorthodox. He felt no obligation to conform even though, or perhaps because, all his reactions were demonstrations of his inner equilibrium. "It is my placidity", he says.

From the time of his marriage to Bijoya, in March 1949, everything in Satyajit's life accelerated. An important event for him was the arrival in Calcutta of Jean Renoir to make *The River*.

As he wrote for *Sequence*: "Fame invests a man with an aura of unapproachability, and I had all but despaired of a chance of meeting the great director when I stumbled upon Clyde De Vinna," a wizened wisecracking American, who convinced Satyajit of the nightly approachability of Renoir in his hotel. So the enthusiast went to see Renoir and, "as it turned out, Renoir was not only approachable, but so embarrassingly polite and modest that I felt if I wasn't too careful I would probably find myself discoursing on the Future of the Cinema for his benefit."

While Ray was deeply impressed by Renoir, Subrata Mitra, Ray's future cameraman, observed Renoir at work. Satyajit was busy with his job, otherwise he, too, would have been present during the filming. It was at this time that Ray embarked on a correspondence with Gavin Lambert, then editing *Sequence* and soon after to become Editor of *Sight and Sound*. Ray proposed articles to Lambert—"Music in Films", "Orson Welles", "Renoir in Calcutta".

It was Lindsay Anderson who replied, "Write on Renoir." So Ray went to work. The conspicuous feature of this early writing is its liveliness and assurance. Ray might have been an expert hand at interviewing and making friends with famous directors.

Though slowly edging his way nearer the moment when he would plunge into film-making, Ray maintained such a high standard as a commercial artist that in 1950 he became Art Director

F

at Keymer's. This promotion was due not only to his talent for design but to his unhurried methods of getting work accomplished and his ability to maintain order and discipline. While working for Keymer's there was frequent collaboration with the publisher, Clarion, and Ray continued to illustrate books and design book jackets for Signet Press of Calcutta. His designs for jackets were regarded as the best in the country.

The most striking aspect of Ray's illustrations, which range from Westernized comic drawings for the children's stories written by his relative, Lila Mazumdar, to the poems of Heine, is his command of diverse styles. While the period illustrations for Abanindranath Tagore's *Raj-Kahni* have the delicacy of miniatures, other illustrations and designs for covers show a modernity verging on the abstract. He could turn his hand, with ease, to any style.

Satyajit Ray's appreciation and knowledge of the arts in general, and of music and graphic design in particular, gave him considerable resources to draw upon when he finally came to direct films. It was interesting to learn from him that about once a year he formed the habit of going back to the Note Books of Leonardo da Vinci. For Eisenstein, too, Leonardo was his *alter ego*. It seems an interesting coincidence that two men, so different in personality, family history, cultural environment, the one of the West and the other of the East, should be so strongly drawn to the same figure of the past.

While this is an extreme simplification, the three men appear to have a single point in common: their protracted search for exactly the right face and body to convey the essence of a person. Different in period and background, their search was the same in order to discover the perfect physical type to reveal the inner psychology of individual characters. Da Vinci wandered through the streets of the Florence of the Medicis; Eisenstein did the same in the revolutionary Soviet Union of the 1920s; while post-Independence India of the 1950s and 1960s has been Ray's hunting ground. Each was seeking to make visually concrete with the utmost validity the singular from amongst the many.

In 1950, after Ray became Art Director, Keymer sent him to London and Europe for six months. He was to work in the London office. Nothing could have suited him better than a free trip to Europe where he could see films that had not come to India. Bijoya went with him. As soon as they arrived in London, Satyajit met Lindsay Anderson and Gavin Lambert. He and Bijoya became members of the London Film Club.

"In four and a half months, I saw ninety-nine films. That's the exact number," says Satyajit, amused. "In Paris I saw only a few." It was films which most impressed him on this first visit to London. "I was just lapping up films!" Ray recalls. "I saw half a dozen Italian films, including *Bicycle Thieves*. It was a tremendous experience. But I was disappointed with *Bitter Rice*. It was no more than hack melodrama."

Very probably his rejection of *Bitter Rice* stems from the same source as his rejection of *La Dolce Vita*, for all its technical qualities.

"I don't like the sordid and I'm not a part of the New Wave trend of today," he says.

Though Satyajit Ray is not a puritan and his drawings of the Sun Temple at Konarak, done in 1941 when he was a student at Santineketan, prove it, he would probably never devote a film solely to the exploration of sexual exploits. But when he deals with sex, as can be seen in the 1962 *Abhijan*, he establishes very real relations and not artificially "daring" ones.

He maintains, "It is the humanists who don't become stuffy and run out of inspiration."

The sudden, stormy and turbulent expressions that I noticed come now and then over Ray's face appeared in the sharpest contrast to his usual calm. Some of his unit, and Bijoya, were aware that at times—usually of great concentration—he will chew his handkerchief to shreds; also, that at an unusually young age, he periodically—most often when he is not actually on a production—has a sharp rise in blood pressure. It was difficult to believe what people said of Ray—that he has a temperament that lacks the element of temper. It seemed too incredible in an artist. This brooding, stormy expression, which would pass without an explosion hinted suppression of anger.

I thought about the statement of his cousins that as a child he had never been seen to lose his temper. Bijoya says that she "had never seen Satyajit anything but optimistic, even during the most difficult times over *Pather Panchali*". I can vouch for this after being on location for weeks, and being around the Ray house for hours at a time, almost daily for six months; again on location in the hardest conditions, in the studio and the editing room with provocation after provocation. Could one say a man had never lost his temper in his life? It seemed impossible for anyone to have such equilibrium.

One day I felt compelled to tackle the question of Satyajit's brooding, seething, gloomy expression. "You sometimes look like the sky piling up for a storm," I remarked to him. "But it doesn't break loose. Haven't you ever lost your temper?"

He laughed. "I have serenity," he said. "Sometimes I feel like murdering people. But I control it." Then he confessed he had once lost his temper. "It was in London in 1950 when a man in the office there passed my work as his own. You know the kind— bowler hat and rolled umbrella! He thought, 'Here's this native— it's all right to take his work . . .'."

Later, Satyajit reconstructed this London incident with more details.

"X was a bad artist to begin with. He sat in the next room to me. Keymer's were quite a small firm, but they had a commission for a poster from *The Observer*," Satyajit said. "This commission was given to me because I had specialized in typography. It turned out quite a good poster and *The Observer* accepted it. It was being displayed all over the place. In the tubes and elsewhere. . . .

"Then, by accident, I heard X talking on the telephone next door about 'my poster for *The Observer* . . .'." Satyajit did not describe what he said to X when he stalked into the room. He left it to the imagination, as he leaves many things to be imagined in his films.

He said: "I wouldn't tolerate a thing like that!" He walked out and down the street to Benson's Agency and worked there.

"I was deeply affected by X. The unthinkable meanness of doing a thing like that", and Satyajit added: "I had always thought the English in England were better people than the English who come to India. Bijoya and I were staying with a friend of mine. I had a sullen look on my face for days. His mother, who was a nice woman, noticed it and asked me what was the matter. Brougham, who liked me, was very upset about my walking out. But Benson's and Keymer's were under the same management. Now you know I once lost my temper!" he said.

Satyajit leapt over time chronologically—a habit of his—and spoke of two later heads of Calcutta's Keymer where he continued to work after the commencement of *Pather Panchali*—the men Dyer and Nicholson.

"Dyer believed I ought to do *Pather Panchali* and he gave me leave with pay," said Satyajit. "Then he left and Nicholson came. There was the break in time during the production. It was Nicholson I asked to give me leave with pay again to finish the film. He, too, believed I ought to do it. He wrote me a letter about seeing it in London and being moved to tears."

Ray has stressed: "I'm bored with villains." It is a part of his make-up which finds dogmatism about people repulsive. Of his harshly political-minded friends, he has said: "I saw them waiting to learn what Moscow thought. I've seen too many people become befuddled and then swing over to join foreign firms and swing completely over the other way. I remember what happened to Eisenstein at the time of *Ivan the Terrible*. And now he is a hero again!"

"My films speak for what I stand for. They are all concerned with the new versus the old."

Satyajit and Bijoya satisfied their passion for music by buying tickets in London for the Salzburg Music Festival. They went for a week and on to Venice for another week to see the Biennale Exhibition and ferret out everything else in Venice from which there was something to learn. Their last stop, for one week, was Paris.

"Our funds were dwindling," Satyajit recalled. "We did with one meal a day. We walked miles every day to visit museums. I was taking photographs. In Paris, the very important influence photography. I didn't know at the time he had ever had connection upon me was Cartier-Bresson, and the revolution he brought to with films. I first saw his work in *Verve* and then the Museum of Modern Art book. I could see how close to neo-realism Cartier-Bresson was when I saw *Bicycle Thieves*."

The visible record of this odyssey—the prelude to self-realization in the cinema—are snapshots of Bijoya walking along beside the Seine and looking at the river flowing by. This was the city of the warm-hearted Renoir, who was still in Calcutta, and who had said to Satyajit Ray in connection with Indian films: "If you could only shake Hollywood out of your system and evolve your own style, you would be making great films here."

Ray, aged twenty-nine, who had said as a child, "I'll be a film director and go to Germany and learn and come back", had gone and was on his way back. He had learned most from Italian films. During his voyage home, he worked on the script of *Pather Panchali* and thought of ways whereby he could raise money to make the novel into a film.

PART II

THE FILMS

Satyajit (illustration for Lila
Mazumdar's children's stories)

Chapter 4

PRELUDE OF PERSISTENCE

INDIA had been self-ruled for three years when Satyajit Ray sailed
home from England wondering how he could convince any film
producer in Bengal to finance *Pather Panchali*, the film he was
now determined to make.

That year—1950—the international film world received a surprise
as great as that provided by the unexpected film, *Open City*, which
had introduced the style of neo-realism. The surprise was Akira
Kurosawa's film *Rashomon*, the first film to cause immediate international interest in Japanese cinema, although Japan, like India,
had been producing hundreds of movies a year since the 1920s.
For decades, Indian and Japanese films had each annually out-
numbered any other nation's output, including that of the United
States. But quantity bore little relation to quality, although some
very interesting Japanese films had now and then been attempted.

Rashomon, instantly recognizable as an expression of a distinctive culture, was obviously the creation of an original mind. Probably its most impressive aspect was how the working out of the story and the moulding of the cinematic form to embody the story maintained a convincing atmosphere. There was something indigenously Japanese about this film. *Rashomon* conveyed both the violence of Japanese history and the restraint characteristic of Classical Japanese art.

But Japan is a homogeneous culture with a single unifying language, while India is the world's most heterogeneous culture with fourteen major languages officially recognized by the Union Government. Bengali, in which Satyajit Ray intended to make *Pather Panchali,* is spoken by some twenty million people and by scattered Bengalis in other states. Because of the presence of Bengalis outside of their own area, as mentioned earlier, it has been customary for a few Bengali films to be given limited presentation beyond the boundaries of Bengal in order to attract the group-conscious Bengalis to cinemas in cosmopolitan cities like Delhi and Bombay and even towns like Poona. These films had attracted only a handful of people other than Bengalis, although there was a general belief that Bengali films were the best in the country. This was generally true. If Ray's project had any chance of realization, it had a greater likelihood of support within Bengal than in any other state.

Yet it is probable that had Ray been dominated by any approach except the intuitive, his will would have been crushed by his past experience in trying to gain acceptance as a scenarist. He knew the mentality of the Bengal film industry. Logically he might have supposed that if he could not get a scenario accepted in the form he insisted upon, how could he possibly be acceptable as the director of his own script? The only thing he had in his favour was *Pather Panchali*'s popularity as a novel. But then he had not adapted Bibhuti Bhusan Bannerjee's story in a conventional way.

As Ray later explained in an article: "I chose *Pather Panchali* for the qualities that made it a great book; its humanism; its lyricism, and its ring of truth. I knew I would have to do a lot of pruning and reshaping—I certainly could not go (in the first film) beyond the first half, which ended with the family's departure for Benares—but at the same time I felt that to cast the thing into a mould of cut-and-dried narrative would be wrong. The script had to retain some of the rambling quality of the novel because that in itself contained a clue to the feel of authenticity; life in a poor Bengali village does ramble."

In order to explain the style of the film he intended, Ray prepared a book of drawings of the scenes and individual shots to be shown. His scenario was thus given visual form for the prospective producer. This was a radical departure from the customary script presentation in Bengal, or indeed India in general.

As Ray wrote in an article published in March 1952: "In the thirty years of its existence the Bengali film as a whole has not progressed one step towards maturity. Looking over the past three or four years one comes across a handful of commendable efforts . . . a bare dozen altogether, none entirely successful and satisfactory but each containing passages of acting, direction, writing or photography which, if sustained, would make for respectable cinema. As for the others (the overwhelming majority), they bear the same relation to art as do the lithographs in Wellington Square to the art of painting. . . . These films neither stimulate the sensibilities, nor please the senses. It may be argued that in any creative medium, greatness is the exception rather than the rule; that a good deal of painted and printed stuff that passes for painting and literature deserves to go down the drain. . . . There is no director in Bengal whose work even momentarily suggests a total grasp of the film medium in its dramatic, plastic and literary aspects."

Ray presented his idea, script and book of drawings of *Pather Panchali* to about a dozen producers, including "all the top people" in Bengal cinema, and to the owners of New Theatre Studios who were generally considered to have produced the best films.

The repeated reaction of the people approached was: "It sounds wonderful the way you relate it. But you, with no experience, could not realize even fifty per cent of your idea."

At the end of the year, he was still no nearer starting work than the day he returned from Europe.

Yet he had already gathered around him the basis of a unit: only one—the Art Director, Bansi Chandragupta—had some professional experience through his recent work with Renoir. There was also Subrata Mitra, who had been an observer of Renoir's direction of *The River*, especially watching the camerawork of Claude Renoir. Mitra, by nature a cautious soul, slow to be carried away by enthusiasm, and often easily reduced to despondency, had an intense desire to be a cameraman on Satyajit's projected film. Three others joined: Dulal Dutt, as editor; Shanti Chatterjee, as Assistant; and the long and lanky Anil Choudhury who looked rather like a bamboo waving in the wind, but was a tough man with great qualities of endurance. All have stuck to

Ray through the ups and downs. Choudhury is still today Ray's Production Manager.

Among the dozen producers they approached was Ajit Bose of Aurora Films, who later acquired the distribution rights of *Pather Panchali* from the West Bengal Government, and subsequently became the financier of *Aparajito*, the second film of the Trilogy. At the outset, Bose liked the idea of *Pather Panchali*. He intimated he would be agreeable to financing the film provided Ray would accept the supervision of a known director.

This proposal was as unacceptable to Ray as the suggestion of another producer that he should use established film stars in exchange for financing.

"I was not going to submit to anything like that," said Ray. The film was going to be made his way or not made at all.

Asit Choudhury, the man who later financed *Apur Sansar*, the third film of the Trilogy, was also approached. At the time, his reaction was to say to one of the unit that he thought "Satyajit Ray must be a madman".

Ray and his unit had started their search for finance as innocents in the ways of film producers. They had no ideas as to who had money to invest. At one point they noticed that a picture running in Calcutta was "a super hit". This led them to conclude the distributor must have funds. They looked on a poster and found the distributor's name; but they could not trace his address or phone number in the telephone directory. They discovered his whereabouts through the theatre where his picture was running.

Anil Choudhury went to see this man at his office. He approached him in a tone suggesting that his proposal was very important and that Mr. Satyajit Ray was a person of great importance. Surprisingly, Choudhury gained access to the distributor and the man of Kalpana Movies appeared responsive to the idea of a film on *Pather Panchali*.

"He went with me at once to see Satyajit Ray at his home," said Anil Choudhury. There the gentleman questioned and cross-questioned Ray as to whether or not he had already acquired the film rights of the novel. Ray had been in touch with the author's widow but he had not, as yet, paid any money for the rights. Ray's reply that he had not negotiated for the rights led to the gentleman proposing they should all meet again in seven days' time when a contract would be drawn up. Hurriedly the Kalpana man called on Mrs. Bannerjee, the author's widow, to tell her that he would pay whatever she wanted for the rights of her late husband's novel—Rs.7,000/- (£523 3s. 4d.), Rs.10,000/- (£747 7s. 3d.). He

kept on increasing the amount until it reached Rs.15,000/-
(£1,121 1s. 6d.). All the time he added that Mrs. Bannerjee must
not let an inexperienced man like Ray, who knew nothing of film-
making, ruin the book which deserved a well-known director to
transfer it to the screen.

Mrs. Bannerjee, being a devoted and old-fashioned widow, resisted
such blandishments. Finally, she rejected the offers with the
interesting words: "One doesn't sell one's son." She sent the
distributor away empty-handed having judged him as playing false
to Ray whom she immediately informed of what had happened.

After seven days, Ray and his unit went to Kalpana Movies
and Ray confronted the distributor with his trick. "Still he pre-
tended to be interested," said Choudhury. "He offered to distribute
the film." But Ray said he would never permit the finished film to
be distributed by Kalpana.

At this stage the last attempt to raise money came when
Choudhury heard from a man, who had money in an unreleased
film, that he might invest in *Pather Panchali*.

Choudhury went to visit this man in a small hotel in north
Calcutta. "He wasn't very rich," said Ray. "He already had money
in one film. He was genuinely interested in *Pather Panchali*. But
his film opened and flopped. He was scared by his failure. There
was no one else to turn to."

Still Ray could not renounce his overpowering desire to make a
film of Bannerjee's novel, and to create it his way and no other.
He decided to take the only course open to him : finance the start
of the film by raising a loan of Rs.7,500/- (£560 10s. 9d.), against
his life insurance policy. He finally paid this back in 1960. Some of
his relatives then loaned him a little over Rs.2,000/- (£149 9s. 6d.).
This money enabled them to take the first step towards the creation
of *Pather Panchali*.

With Rs.9,500/- (£710 0s. 3d.) in hand, Satyajit hired a 16-mm.
camera and, doing his own photography to test out his approach,
he went to visit the actual village which Bannerjee had used for
the setting of his novel.

"It wasn't photogenic enough; not sufficiently visual," was Ray's
conclusion.

Ray's money was then used up in an unusual way. Two locations
were found, one a field of beautiful white flowers sixty miles
from Calcutta, the other a visually suitable village only six miles
from where Ray lived, a village on the periphery of the Calcutta
district of Tollygunge.

The village of Boral was found by accident—through one of

Chandragupta's friends mentioning he had a small house there. Satyajit and Bansi went to see the village, but it was a monsoon day and impossible to view it properly. So they returned when the weather cleared and searched the village to establish its possibilities. They found a house, no more than a heap of ruins, according to Bansi Chandragupta.

But it was potentially suitable to represent the dilapidated family house of Harihar Roy. Hence they decided that the bulk of the money must be spent by Chandragupta in reconstructing this house as the main location.

"I made additions like exterior walls, doors, a kitchen," Chandragupta related, explaining how he utilized all he had learned while building sets for Jean Renoir.

"For instance, from inside the kitchen, the courtyard and main gate had to be visible," said Bansi. "In reconstructing, we rejected all former methods and materials of set-building here. During work on *The River*, there had been a lot of experiment with materials to gain interesting textural effects.

"As the property must look old and used," Chandragupta added, "I made use of plaster and brick. The reconstruction work was mainly done by plastering over bamboo mats. The use of plaster was something entirely new in Indian film production. It was chosen because plaster makes a very flexible material."

The rest of the money was not spent as other people would have spent it—on shooting a dramatic scene to impress distributors and thus induce them to advance money for the completion. Instead, Ray spent three days shooting scenes of the two children, Durga and Apu, in the field of flowers sixty miles from Calcutta.

The reasoning was: "If we don't shoot this scene now, the flowers will be gone and we can't shoot the scenes for another year."

As one of the unit admitted: "It was a non-professional approach to shoot the field of flowers and have no dramatic sequence to show to a distributor."

The first shots were taken with an old Wall camera and without the children having even been tested.

Ray's theory was that with a set ready in an ideal location and one scene shot, finance would be easier to obtain.

They edged a step ahead when someone found a man willing to distribute the film, a man who had money in several pictures. He advanced sufficient money for the shooting of 4,000 feet. Then, just before he made a further advance, all the films in which he had invested opened and failed.

Ray, his unit and cast had started work. They were shooting out at the Tollygunge village and they had to be fed. On top of the other pressures, Satyajit's wife, Bijoya, had become pregnant.

The dauntless Anil Choudhury had been promised Rs.200/- (£15) with which to feed the cast and the unit. When he went to pick it up, no money was forthcoming. He turned to Satyajit's wife in the hope that she would agree to pawn her gold bangles.

Bijoya gave her bracelets to Anil Choudhury, both of them knowing that Satyajit's mother, still being in certain respects traditional, would be greatly upset if she learned that the bangles had been pawned, these bracelets being objects that symbolized much in Bengali marriage. The pawning of Bijoya's bangles soon created an embarrassing family situation.

According to tradition, at the eighth month of pregnancy it is still customary in Bengal for the expectant mother to entertain her women friends and to array herself for this occasion in all the jewels and ornaments of which she is possessed. If Bijoya failed to put on all her bangles for this day, Satyajit's mother was bound to detect what had happened. Again Anil had a brainwave. He arranged to borrow the bangles of another woman and deposit them in the pawnshop in place of Bijoya's, who received hers back and wore them on the proper day. They were then returned to the pawnshop and the helpful lady was given back her own bangles.

Anil, Bijoya and Satyajit supposed they had successfully hood-winked Suprabha Ray. But when Satyajit went to New York in 1958 he told the story of the bangles and it appeared in an American newspaper. In order to keep the secret, he inked out the reference to the bangles before he sent the clipping to Bijoya. The moment his mother saw the clipping with the inking out, she began to laugh. Then she confessed to Bijoya and Anil that all along she had known what had taken place. But she kept her own secret as to how she had found out.

When the would-be distributor of *Pather Panchali* discovered he had lost money in his other films, his withdrawal forced a halt of eight months in Ray's work. Still there was the 4,000 feet of film. Day after day, Satyajit, Subrata Mitra, Anil Choudhury and others, went to the laboratory and worked on the editing.

They often waited a very long time to catch an over-crowded bus. Except for Ray, the others could push and edge their way into the bus and stand. But Satyajit's height was thoroughly disadvantageous, for his head constantly hit the roof. Therefore he stood on the step. Being without a car, they travelled everywhere this way, even to the location.

To work under such strain would have been hard anywhere, but during the summer months Calcutta has one of the world's most exhausting and irritating climates. It is not so much the heat, which is never excessively high, but the intensity of the humidity which piles up for days on end until the sultriness seems to accumulate into a physical weight. Suddenly there comes the downpour bringing the floods.

Rumours of a man named Ray in search of money for a partly finished film made Satyajit a target for a shady class of broker who announced that they specialized in film finance. Three or four of these characters appeared with suggestions that this or that person would finance the completion of the film. They promised that for a commission they would introduce these people to Ray.

Since there was no alternative, Satyajit took the risk the first time and was cheated. No introduction materialized. He took a second chance and again nothing happened. He was so absorbed in the idea of completing *Pather Panchali* that, though he knew he was taking a risk with such people, he continued. Each of these confidence men insisted on an advance ahead of any introduction.

It became difficult to pay the demanded advances. Having been cheated twice, Ray naturally feared derision for being a fool. How many times would he get his fingers burnt? He no longer felt he could confide in Bijoya as he went on gambling through brokers. Finally he resorted to secrecy to pay the advance to yet another broker. If he paid from his salary Bijoya would know and her intuition would dictate that he was bound to be cheated once again.

"Yet he could not sit idle," said Choudhury. "He could not renounce the idea that somehow *Pather Panchali* would see the light of day."

Ray's passion for the film was so intense that he, an intelligent man, refused to believe that he might well be fleeced a third time, or a fourth, or even a fifth.

He went and secretly sold his only valuable possessions—his art books and records—in the hope that the latest broker might keep his word and introduce him to a financier. Once more nothing happened.

During this period a single ray of encouragement came from an unforeseen quarter. John Huston arrived in Calcutta in connection with the Rudyard Kipling story, *The Man Who Wanted to be King*. The publicity on this visit was handled by R. P. Gupta of J. Walter Thompson, who mentioned to Huston that an interesting film was being made by a commercial artist named Ray. He asked Huston if he would like to see the footage which had been edited.

Kadambini Basu, India's first woman doctor, who became second wife of Dwarkanath Ganguli. The photograph was taken in Edinburgh

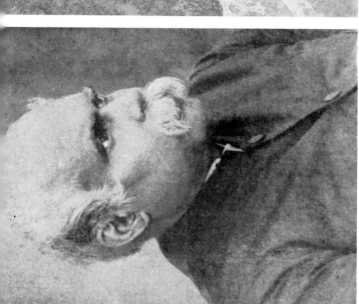

Dwarkanath Ganguli, noted Brahmo Samaj crusader. Father of Satyajit's paternal grandmother

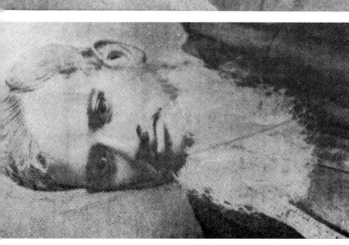

Kalinarayan Gupta, Satyajit's maternal great-grandfather. A famed member of the Brahmo Samaj in East Bengal

1

Sukumar Ray (1887–1923), writer and illustrator. Father of Satyajit and the most talented of Upendra-

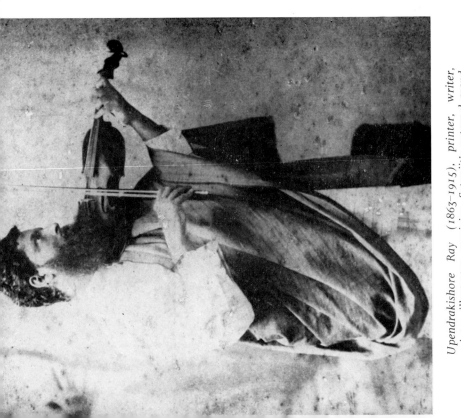

Upendrakishore Ray (1863–1915), printer, writer, painter, illustrator, musician. Satyajit's paternal grand-

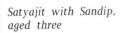

III

Satyajit (Manik) at the age of three

Satyajit with Sandip, aged three

1935—Manik at fourteen with his mother, Suprabha. He composed this photograph himself and devised a means of taking it

The Family

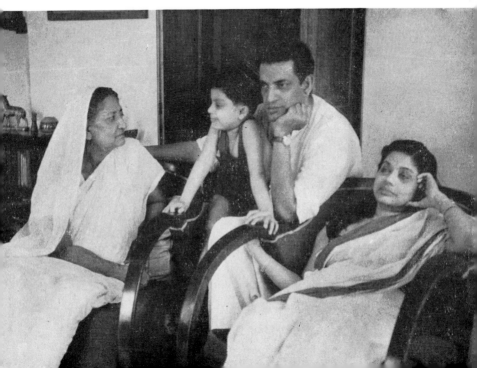

IV 1941—*Brush drawing by Satyajit of Bijoya Das, the youngest daughter of his mother's half-brother, whom he married in 1949*

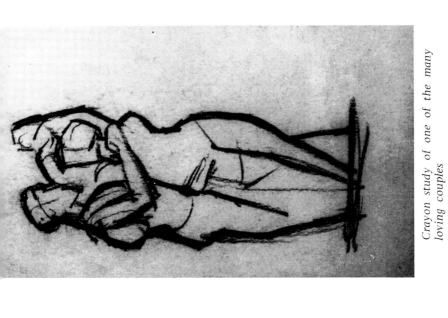

A small figure carved as a medallion on one of the stone chariot wheels. Pencil study

Crayon study of one of the many loving couples

V 1943—Ray's studies from the Sun Temple of Konarak, Orissa

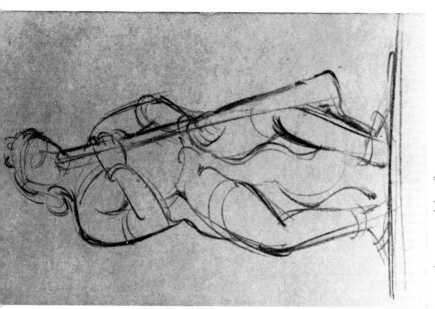

VI Two pencil studies of the large and famous dancer-musician figures which surmount the highest tier of the Sun Temple of Konarak. All his Konarak studies were done on postcard size boards

VII
Pather Panchali
The Song of the
Little Road,
1950-55

A scene between the children, Durga and Apu, which was discarded at the final editing of the fim

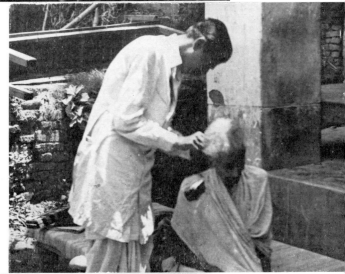

Shanti Chatterjee cutting Chunibala Devi's hair for the recommencement of shooting (p. 103)

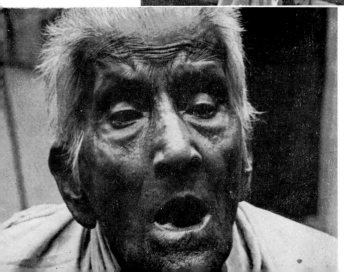

Chunibala Devi as Old Indir

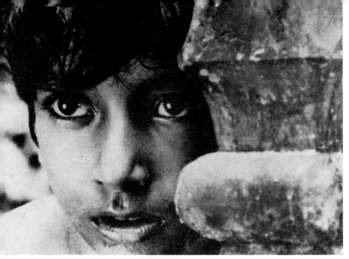

The childhood of Apu to the childhood of his son, Kajal

Subir Bannerjee, the first Apu, whom Bijoya Ray discovering on the next door roof top

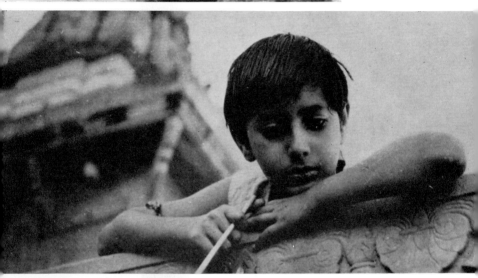

Pinaki Sen Gupta, the second Apu. Apu's curiosity is fed by the curious sights of the Holy City of Benares

Apu's son, Kajal (Alok Chakravarty). Deserted by his father, his play is concentrated upon killing birds

IX
The family in Pather Panchali

Durga at the beginning of the film, age six, already a thief . . . A city man, the village made Ray want to observe and probe, to catch the revealing detail

Karuna Banerji as the mother; professional actor Kanu Bannerjee as the father. "I made additions . . . from inside the kitchen, the courtyard and main gate had to be visible."—Bansi Chandragupta, Art Director

The young girl, Durga, Uma Das Gupta, steals for love of Old Indir, Chunibala Devi

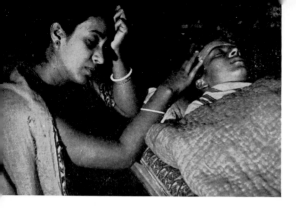

The Death of Durga
The scene "is almost wholly composed of dolly shots— slow, dread-laden approaches in panicky light . . ." —Arlene Croce

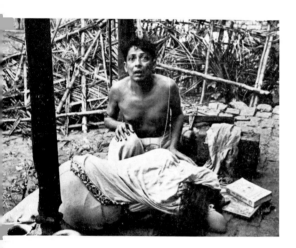

The return of Harihar, the father. A moment before, the mother's anguished cry has been heard in Ravi Shankar's music

The villagers come to bid the family farewell. Characters such as these portrayed by non-professionals appear as a stylistic motif in many Ray films. Compare with Pl. XXVI from The Postmaster

XI–XIV *Sketches for a proposed musical short, 1951*

Ray made a completely visual scenario of approximately thirty-three sketches for a film he wished to make—and may still make—with Ravi Shankar

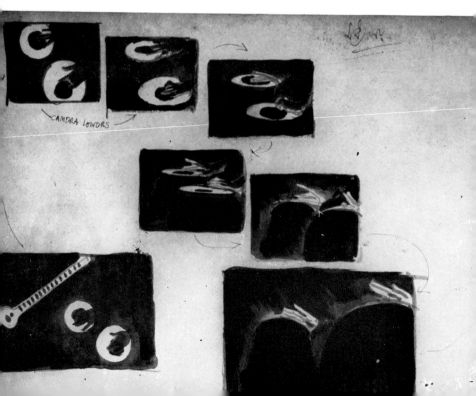

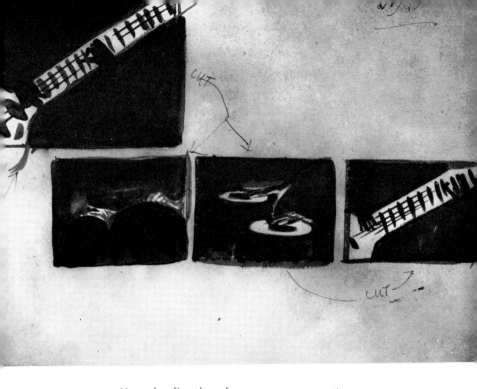

Note the directions for camera movement

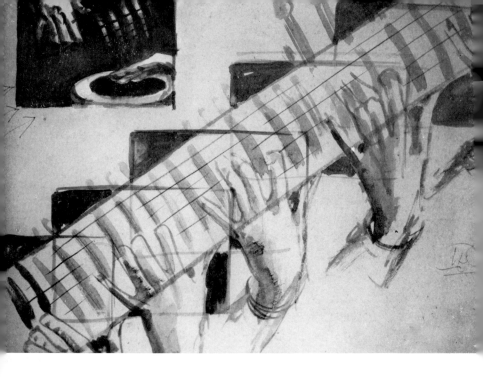

For this book he selected these eight sketches to represent his concept

XV
Aparajito (The Unvanquished), 1956

Harihar reading the Scriptures on the Ghats. The composition with the boats is typical of any day in Benares. Apu, in Pl. VIII, is watching this scene

The death of Harihar, the father. The first takes were more realistic in terms of dying. The scene was modified

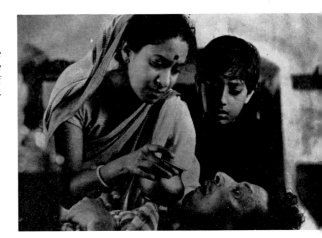

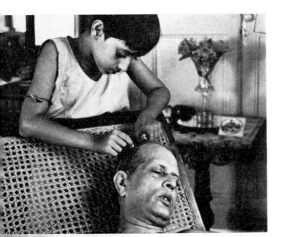

Shot No. 224. The mother, Sarbojaya, watching a subsequent scene where her son is acting like the servant of her employer, decides to return to the village of her uncle

Apu makes painful and un-willing efforts to follow in his father's footsteps as a priest. He longs to go to school and study

The adolescent Apu, Sumiran Kumar Ghosal. Shot No. 323. The turning point. Apu has stood second in the school examinations and can have a scholarship to Cal-cutta University. The globe has been given him by the headmaster

Shot No. 398. Apu has returned from Calcutta.
"Sarbojaya: Now talk to me!
Apu: What about?
Sarbojaya: Well . . . tell me what you have seen in the city.
The gulf is ever widening."

When Huston was shown the footage of *Pather Panchali*, he recognized that here was an example of unusual film-making. He offered to do anything helpful by way of setting in motion the mechanics for the completed film to be sent to an international festival. This was confirmation of Satyajit's faith in his own work. But it did not bring him one step closer to obtaining further finance.

Night after night the unit came to Satyajit's home. His mother could not escape the knowledge of what had been going on month after month. She had never wanted Manik to have anything to do with film making, but she was his mother and she adored him even while disapproving of his unquenchable passion for *Pather Panchali*. She had lived for him, and she alone knew how hard she had worked to bring him up. Despite her distaste for Manik's being involved with the uncertain profession of film production, Suprabha felt she must, if possible, rescue his project after so many months of frustration. She could not endure to watch him making endlessly futile attempts to obtain money that was never forthcoming.

Suprabha had a woman friend, a Mrs. S——, whom she thought might be of help. Mrs. S—— was on very friendly terms with the most powerful man in West Bengal—the Chief Minister, Dr. B. C. Roy. Suprabha thought that perhaps the State Government might finance the completion of *Pather Panchali* if her friend Mrs. S—— was convinced of the film's value and then spoke to Dr. Roy about it. In the past, Dr. Roy had known Sukumar Ray and other members of the Ray family.

Mrs. S—— was asked to see the 4,000-odd feet of edited film. She liked it. Indeed, she must have been much impressed by it in order to be able to convince Dr. Roy, a man with no pronounced love of art and no knowledge of film as an expressive medium. Yet Dr. Roy gave his time to seeing the footage and consider granting Government money to complete it.

It seems that the Chief Minister immediately concluded that the film was the beginning of a documentary film about village life. Dr. Roy's first reaction to *Pather Panchali* was to suggest "Have the family join a Community Development Project."

Satyajit Ray kept silent.

Dr. Roy instructed the State Government to draw up a contract. Long afterwards he spoke about "that documentary". Later he became very proud of "my film", and was an admirer of Satyajit Ray, whom on subsequent occasions he showed a willingness to help. The last film Dr. Roy saw before his death on July 1st, 1962, was Ray's *Kanchenjunga*.

G

The West Bengal Government purchased the film of *Pather Panchali* outright with Satyajit Ray making over all his rights in the film in exchange for the Government investing the necessary money to finish it. The sum it took was about Rs.200,000. There was also a verbal agreement between Ray and the Director of Publicity for West Bengal that should the film ever bring the Government any foreign payments, Ray should receive a percentage of these royalties.

In 1961, Edward Harrison, the American distributor of *Pather Panchali*, told me that he had paid the West Bengal Government $50,000 in royalties, and still owed them more. I asked Ray what percentage of this he had received.

"Not a penny," he replied. "They get the money but I got the fame."

Late in the summer of 1957, just after *Aparajito*, the sequel to *Pather Panchali*, had won the Golden Lion award at the Venice Film Festival, the Film Critic of the *Hindusthan Standard*, published extracts from a Note, allegedly written in February 1954, by an important State Government official regarding the sponsorship of *Pather Panchali*. The extract appeared in a long piece under the headline : *"Story Behind Pather Panchali."* The Note's wording was alleged to be :

> My impression is that even when exploited, this picture will not pay as much as is being invested in it.
>
> *Pather Panchali* is rather dull and slow moving. It is a story of a typical Bengali family suffering from privation and family embarrassments but at no stage does it offer a solution or an attempt to better the lot of the people and rebuild the structure of their society.

The Film Critic, indignant at the content of the Note that had come into his possession, commented : "The official (who had written the note) totally disapproved of the way the author had written the concluding chapter of the book and the Director proposed to follow it, and branded it (leaving of home and village by Harihar) as 'Cowardice'." The critic then quoted further from the Note :

> It is considered that this film along with a supplementary shot of about 2,500 to 3,000 feet depicting the second part of the story, which unfortunately does not occur in the original *Pather Panchali* to represent what would be the shape of the Village Community in the present age with provision of land

reforms, of the Community Development Projects, the National Extension Schemes and an all-round urge in Independent India to rebuild the society for better living and through self-help, rather than resigning to one's present condition to fate, circumstances and certain unknown factors.

Had Ray compromised on a new ending no award would have been made to *Pather Panchali* at the Cannes Film Festival two years later. This award was only the first. There followed the National Award of the President's Gold Medal, which Mr. Mathur, the Director of Publicity, went to Delhi to receive on behalf of the West Bengal Government. There was criticism that Ray was excluded from receiving the award himself. It must have been embarrassing for Mr. Mathur, considering someone in his office had written a Note deriding the film.

Ray had become the hero of Bengal cinema. His exclusion from the Delhi presentation aroused a furore in Calcutta only a month before the 1957 Election. Dr. B. C. Roy, the Chief Minister, ordered that the State Government itself should make a magnificent presentation of medals to Satyajit Ray and the *Pather Panchali* unit. In front of a large conclave of photographers at the Rabindra Bhavan, the State Government did honour to Ray and his technicians and actors.

The arrangement with the Government was that the financing should be paid in instalments. Ray had been given leave with pay by his agency, Keymer. As long as he had money in hand the unit and actors went on working. Then they were compelled to halt while the Government scrutinized the bills Ray submitted. Once satisfied that Ray's accounting was correct, another instalment was issued and again the work commenced.

But as far as anyone knew, there were no distribution arrangements for the film. While they were still at work, Monroe Wheeler of the New York Museum of Modern Art arrived in Calcutta. He was arranging for an art exhibition to be held in New York in the coming April of 1955. After seeing as much of the film as was edited and some of the rushes, Wheeler proposed to Ray that the film be finished in time to be shown as part of the April exhibition.

"It was impossibly hard work to get the film ready in time. I was only able to show Ravi Shankar a few reels for him to get the 'feel' for the music," said Ray. "The whole of the music was recorded in one session of eleven hours.

"Some of the 'primitiveness' and 'roughness'—which some people liked was neither due to intention or anything else. It would not have been there except for the rush to get the film edited to send to New York for the Monroe Wheeler combined exhibition."

In order to finish the film, none of the unit went home for ten days. They worked continuously with virtually no sleep.

"Our beards grew like this," said Anil Choudhury, and made a gesture to show how long the hairs were on his chin.

Actually, Satyajit Ray never saw his film in its complete edited form before it was sent to New York. While Dulal Dutt, working against time, was editing the last reel, Satyajit and Anil Choudhury rushed around Calcutta in search of a trunk in which to pack the tins. They dashed to the Customs authorities to get clearance for that every time there was a pause he fell asleep.

As they hurried from place to place, Satyajit was so exhausted that every time there was a pause, he fell asleep.

"Since he was unknown he got some very odd looks," Anil recalled. "No one could make out what it was all about."

The film had finally been completed against all odds. They all went home and slept like logs. They woke up with nothing to do but wait and see what would be the fate of *Pather Panchali,* granted finance by the West Bengal Government for Road Improvement because *Song of the Little Road* was the meaning of the title.

Satyajit (title-page illustration for *Poems* by
Jibanananda Das)

Chapter 5

PATHER PANCHALI

B U T for persistence, *Pather Panchali* would never have been commenced and certainly not completed.

The most important thing about the Apu Trilogy is not the
honours heaped upon it, but the attitude that went into its creation.
Lindsay Anderson, who had not seen Satyajit Ray since 1950 in
London but had received letters from him, at Cannes recognized
Pather Panchali as made "with humility and complete dedication".

Anil Choudhury, who has continued to work with Ray for
more than eighteen years, made an illuminating remark about
Pather Panchali : "We all became sincere" in the process of creating
the film. Under the influence of Ray's conviction each person
became absorbed into a single aim.

The first to join Ray had been Bansi Chandragupta, the Art
Director. The second was Subrata Mitra, a science student who,
becoming disinterested in his chosen subject, had been striving to
become a photographer. He belonged to a traditional family.
Though his father and mother were not unsympathetic to him
following the profession of his choice, the rest of the family, and
the family friends, were violently opposed to Subrata having any
connection with cinema. They regarded the world of films as
frankly disreputable.

Yet Mitra's father was willing for Subrata to take a job with
Jean Renoir if he could get one. Renoir's Assistant Director, Hari
Das Gupta, could not find work for Mitra, who was only able to
be an observer during the production of *The River*. He met Ray
when he too came to watch the work on Sundays. When the film
was completed, Mitra longed to go to Paris to study camera work
with the help of Claude Renoir. But this idea came to nothing.
Mitra began to visit Ray after his return from Europe in 1950,

Mitra's hope being that if *Pather Panchali* was ever made he could serve as an assistant cameraman.

By the time the first trial shots were to be taken, the suggested cameraman had gone to work in Madras. This left Mitra extremely nervous at the thought of replacing him. He had never handled a motion picture camera in his life. All he knew was still photography. But Ray had faith that Mitra could become a cameraman.

"He kept explaining to me that film photography was only photography in movement and I would be able to manage," said Mitra. Perhaps Ray had over-simplified things for when they made some test shots in 16 mm., something went wrong with the speed which Mitra could never fathom later. "What was shot turned out to be awful."

The first effort to shoot the field of flowers sixty miles from Calcutta was a fiasco. Yet Ray retained his faith that Mitra could become a good cameraman. He instilled confidence into him. Gradually, Mitra became more sure of himself.

"The most difficult shots were those showing night in Harihara's house," he recalled. "I'd been good at daylight photography. But when it came to shooting in the village house with electric light— studio shooting—I found it very difficult.

"But Satyajit had a complete conception," continued Subrata. "Yet often when we saw the rushes, it only looked as if someone was walking away from the camera, for example. His concept only became clear with the editing of the shots."

Many critics, who were later ravished by enthusiasm for the film, failed to observe in any detail how the camera work contributed. Arlene Croce, writing in *Film Culture*, is one of the few who noticed and commented, "Ray's camera is articulate, highly mobile." She gives an example: "The scene in which the mother nurses her dying child in the darkness of the stormed hut is almost wholly composed of dolly shots—slow, dread-laden approaches in a panicky light. . . . The genuinely spell-bound camera is no small achievement, and I wonder what the bug-eyed clod that shoots our supermovies with its Bausch and its Lomb would make of the lowering skies and fading lights of Bengal."

Ray says that *Pather Panchali* is the only film of his where much footage was discarded: "Before completion whole incidents were removed." (A still of such a discarded scene is included: Pl. VII.)

Before Ray could shoot the film, he had to discover the suitable boy to play Apu, who was to emerge as the Trilogy's central character. According to Anil Choudhury, they searched the schools of Calcutta. "Yet Satyajit couldn't find the boy he was looking for.

We put advertisements in newspapers. But none of the boys was the right one." But evidently Satyajit had conveyed the exact image he had in his mind to his wife, Bijoya, for one day when she was looking out of the window at 31a Lake Avenue she noticed some boys playing on the roof of the next house. Among them was Subir Bannerjee. The instant she caught sight of him, she thought of Apu.

Bijoya ran to Satyajit and announced: "I've found Apu!"

"Where?" demanded Satyajit. He must have been intensely excited by even the vague hope that this might be true.

"Just next door." She had spotted the boy Satyajit had been seeking to find all over Calcutta.

Uma Das Gupta had already been discovered to fit into the role of Durga, Apu's sister. From the outset of the project there had been Karuna Banerji, who had acted now and then in amateur theatre.

"Karuna was never very effective in the theatre," remarked Satyajit, "for she is the perfect screen actress. Even her voice was too small to make an impact in the theatre."

Though Karuna Banerji in life is elegant and sophisticated and possessed of a very beautiful walk, she fitted exactly into Ray's visualized image of how Sarbojaya, the stoic wife and often irritable mother, should look. Karuna must have conveyed to Satyajit her extraordinary gift for denuding herself of her own personality and sinking her consciousness into that of the village wife, or any other woman she was subsequently called upon to interpret.

When the work started they had not found anyone to interpret the ancient relative, Indir, a vitally important character in Ray's conception. She is something of a petty thief and it is because of her thieving that the embarrassed Sarbojaya is finally driven to tell her to leave the house once and for all. At the same time, Indir is a very lovable old woman.

Ray first thought of seeking an aged village woman to portray Indir. In search of such a woman they went to observe ancient crones lining up to receive their allotment of rice. They noticed several old women who were right in appearance but they doubted if they could face the camera and memorize the lines.

It then struck Ray that he must seek out some old actress. Contrary to the widespread idea that everyone acting in *Pather Panchali* was non-professional, there was from early on a professional actress included—Rebi Devi—who appears as the rich, betel-nut-chewing neighbour, Mrs. Mukherjee. Rebi Devi mentioned an eighty-year-old former actress, Chunibala Devi, who had been a not very well known player thirty years before when the professional stage was considered a disreputable profession for any woman. In fact, more often than not a stage career had led to prostitution as a sideline.

Chunibala Devi was reputed to live on a street on the north side of Calcutta in a red-light district.

While Anil searched for the house amid solicitations, Satyajit remained in the car. Suddenly, someone they both knew appeared on the street, and confronted Choudhury with a much entertained, "Hello, Anil Babu!" Anil blurted out that Satyajit Ray was waiting in the car.

Finally they found the house, and rang the bell, which was answered by the bent and wizened Chunibala. She immediately impressed Ray as the Indir for whom he had been searching.

Chunibala invited them in, introduced them to a younger woman—a professional actress—who referred to her as mother. They were asked if they would take tea. Soon Chunibala enquired if they would like to see the young girls living in the house.

Satyajit hastened to explain that they had come to talk about a film, not to see the girls; that Chunibala herself was just right for the character of Indir. Thrilled, Chunibala forgot about the girls. She brought forth her long-cherished handbills of the plays in which she had appeared and assured Satyajit Ray that she had acted some important parts in her time.

The meeting was impeccably discreet. Not a word was said on either side as to what salary should be paid to the ancient Chunibala. The next day, Ray and Anil Choudhury again visited Chunibala. Only then did the professional actress who had been presented to them as Chunibala's daughter venture to ask if they could manage to pay Chunibala Rs.20/- a day. Choudhury said they could. In the end she was paid a little more.

Chunibala was asked to cut her hair very short—to one inch. But only a few of her scenes had been shot when there came the enforced halt in production lasting eight months. During that period no one had the heart to tell Chunibala about the difficulties. They feared to dishearten her.

A professional actor, Kanu Bannerjee, was chosen for Harihar, the unacclaimed Brahmin scholar with dreams of being a poet but who spends his life wandering after castles in the air. For Kanu's first day's shooting he manifested the professional actor's approach. He had visited a barber and had his hair cut. The barber's handiwork left Ray askance. He was so shocked by Bannerjee's well-cut hair that he cancelled the day's shooting even though it cost money to do so. Since it was incongruous to think of Harihar having such a hair cut Bannerjee was asked to grow his hair to its former length.

Instead of being offended, Kanu Bannerjee went about Calcutta declaring that at last he had met a real director. Never before had any director asked him to grow his hair to a special length to portray a particular character.

Once the first instalment of money came from the West Bengal Government, Choudhury informed the ancient Chunibala Devi that shooting was to recommence. Every day she worked he would pick her up in a taxi at 3 a.m. Arriving at her home for the re-starting of work, he was horrified to find her hair, which had been cut to one inch, was now eight months long and stood up in a brush all over her head. It was far too early to find a barber, so Anil took her straight to the location at Boral.

Shanti Chatterji, the assistant who looked after the continuity and was one of the first to join Ray's unit, came to the rescue. He had the odd habit, or hobby, of always carrying some needles and thread together with a razor blade. Though it was an excruciating operation, Shanti used his blade to cut Chunibala's hair down to one inch. (Pl. VII)

"Every day but one, at four o'clock," Satyajit recalled, "Chunibala had to have her little pill of opium. It kept her going. The one day she forgot it, she fainted."

Chunibala might take her little pill to which she was addicted; her past life at times had been squalid; but a sense of artistry existed within her. Even though she was eighty years old when she began work on *Pather Panchali*, and eighty-two when she completed it, her sensitivity emerged under the impact of Satyajit Ray. Anil Choudhury gave an example:

"You remember the cloth she wears around her? Bansi Chandragupta had bought the material new, torn it and tied knots in it exactly as it is described in the book. He kept it until it looked like a rag. One day, Chunibala begged me to get her a new cloth for she said this old cloth didn't cover her properly."

Choudhury bought new cloth which Bansi again tore and tied knots in. But when Anil gave it to Chunibala to wear in place of the one she had objected to it was less torn than the original.

"Chunibala never put it on," said Anil. "She came to think that if she did, she would be upsetting the continuity."

According to Bansi, her memory was most acute. "It was Chunibala who noticed that I had slightly fewer bricks for the steps of the replica house built in the studio than for the reconstructed house at Boral."

As Ray had a "feel" for people, so he had for Nature's moods.

This is revealed not only in *Pather Panchali* but equally passionately, though in different moods, in his later films, *Kanchenjunga* and *Abhijan*. His awareness had been heightened rather than blunted by urban living. With the exception of the holidays he spent in his youth in Bihar and his two years at Santineketan, Ray has always been a city dweller. But, as he said when speaking of Santineketan, the painter, Nadalal Bose, had stimulated his capacity to see trees and animals with intensity of vision. Perhaps he has also inherited his appreciation of Nature from his grandfather and this prepared his nervous system to be exceptionally sensitive to "a new flavour, a new texture", when he went to explore the rural scene for the setting of *Pather Panchali*.

Writing later of the impact of the Bengali village, Ray said : "It made you want to observe and probe, to catch the revealing detail, the telling gesture, the particular turns of speech. You wanted to fathom the mysteries of 'atmosphere'. Does it consist in the sight, or the sounds? How to catch the subtle difference between dawn and dusk, or convey the great humid stillness that precedes the first monsoon showers . . . ?"

European critics immediately identified Ray's handling of the village with that of the late Robert Flaherty. Flaherty's widow, Frances, felt this with intensity when she wrote to me : "Bob was a poet; Ray is a poet and understands, as Bob did, that the nature of the cinema is poetry. And both of them follow that nature with pure conviction, and the sure sense of the process involved, with simplicity and directness."

Few scenes set the mood of a film so instantly as the opening shots with the child Durga running through the wood to bring stolen fruit to old Indir. Durga is established as a thief, but a thief for love.

Ray's synopsis picks up the birth of the long-awaited son, Apu :

On a cold night in the month of Magh (December-January) a son is born to Sarbojaya. Harihar is happy.

As if a reflection of the creative work in hand, Satyajit's only child, a son, Sandip, was born, a small baby like his father and an inheritor of the Ray talents.

The brief original Outline of the film given to Bansi Chandragupta describes Harihar pacing "the veranda anxiously, while Sarbojaya is in the throes of labour pain in the 'labour room' (a makeshift affair of straw and bamboo in a corner of the courtyard).

"Luckily enough, a few weeks later Harihar finds a job as an accountant in the zamindar's treasury. As old Indir rocks the new-born Apu to sleep, singing a lullaby, Harihar sits in the kitchen with Sarbojaya and plans for the future. Sarbojaya is infected by her husband's optimism and dreams of better days. . . ."

It was, as "Adib" said in *The Times of India,* Ray's capacity to convey "even half-formed thought or feeling, a passing fancy" which, even before sub-titled, made *Pather Panchali* understandable to people who did not know the Bengali language. People were able to feel the universality of the ineffectual man of optimism always chasing rainbows, or sunk in despondent apathy, and the stoic woman holding things together despite her constant edginess. It was not necessary to understand each word, for the tones in Karuna Banerji's voice spoke for all the world's harassed women.

The eight-months halt in the shooting did not damage the continuity of the film since six years elapsed in the story. The little girl, Ranki Banerji, was succeeded by the older girl, Uma Das Gupta, as Durga. The plant that is watered in the early shots of the film had grown during suspension of work. Thus, it serves as a convincing detail to convey visually the passing of time.

Harihar is still drudging in the zamindar's treasury . . . the house looks more dilapidated. . . . Durga, now twelve, has developed into an expert fruit-stealer. The boy, Apu, pampered both by sister and mother, has just started going to the local school. The school has eight other students and is run by a Pandit who also keeps a grocery store.

The character of this scholar-grocer is visualized with vivid economy. Satyajit cast the professional actor, the late Tulsi Chakravarty, for the part. He would later interpret the central character in *Paras Pathar.* Chakravarty had failed to make much of a mark as an actor; possibly because no director save Ray had seen the effectiveness of his odd face and body. He appears in only a few shots, and he worked but one day.

The thing that impressed Chakravarty was that he was never given just a line of dialogue by Ray, but always some piece of appropriate business to go with the lines. Ray might be a new director but he did not direct as a novice.

One afternoon while Sarbojaya is feeding Apu, there is a sudden invasion by Mrs. Mukherjee and her two daughters. Mrs. Mukherjee demands to see Durga. Sarbojaya, taken aback, asks what has happened. Mrs. Mukherjee accuses Durga of having stolen her daughter, Penchi's necklace that afternoon. Durga arrives, is searched; but the necklace is not found on her person. Mrs. Mukherjee, frustrated, lets loose her tongue and bitterly accuses Sarbojaya and her pettiness, corruption and downright thievery. Then she leaves as dramatically as she came. Sarbojaya, hurt and humiliated beyond words, vents her rage on Durga and literally throws her out of the house. Indir intervenes, only to be rebuked. Apu watches horrified.

It is interesting to note that in the Outline which Ray gave to his Art Director, he had written: "Indir—hard of hearing—remains unaware of the whole thing." Chandragupta stresses that Renoir kept making it clear to his Indian assistants that he didn't agree with a film script being kept "airtight". There should always be room for change.

It has been frequently argued that Satyajit Ray was influenced by Jean Renoir. Here perhaps is an example, for Ray, who is the most careful planner of the general pattern of each shot, is also a most flexible director and has a gift for instantaneous improvisation.

The scene of the frenzied Sarbojaya chastising Durga is an extremely poignant moment of realistic acting. In 1950, Ray had seen Roberto Rossellini's two films, *Open City* and *La Voce Humana*. What had impressed him most was the acting of Anna Magnani. He described it to Bansi as wonderful in the first film, and as "a most amazing performance" in the second. When Karuna Banerji grabs at Durga and drags her out of the gate by the hair, she attains a quality of passion which parallels the outbursts of Magnani. It is a terrifying scene of a mother's fury as a reaction to humiliation by a coarse woman.

> After a while Sarbojaya realizes the extent of her cruelty, asks Apu to go and find Durga and fetch her back, which duty the boy performs only too gladly. . . .
> That night (it is the month of September) while Indir tells a fairy tale to the two children, Harihar returns home with three months' pay (which has been due) and good news: the offer of an Initiation ceremony in a rich peasant family. Harihar, however, is in no hurry to accept it, for he has a sense of dignity. . . .

Few films convey in such a piercing way how poverty frays the nerves. Yet few films are less sentimental in mood or so deeply preserve the authenticity of sentiment. As in life, where the most lacerating moment can be diverted by something unconsciously comic, the moods of *Pather Panchali* pass from one to another so that life is felt in its entirety. Everything is not grim. The lyrical, the amusing and the delightfully real pleasure of youth constantly keep breaking in upon the accumulating spectre of impoverishment, like the sunshine filtering into a dark wood. Rasping quarrels and the grind of procuring enough to eat give way to the repeated visit of the sweetmeat seller with his baskets seeming to dance in rhythm to Shankar's music.

The Puja ('Worship') comes, Apu and Durga, who do not feel the sting of poverty as much as the elders do, enjoy it in their own humble way. Apu's imagination is fired by a Jatra (a village theatre) performance and at home he dresses himself up as a king, having helped himself to knick-knacks and ornaments from his sister's box.

Here Satyajit Ray introduces the property which will subsequently appear many times in his films—the mirror. Ray uses mirrors because he thinks they allow for numerous interesting visual patterns; including conveying perspectives of rooms, for example, as in the Snuggery Cottage scene in *Kanchenjunga*. Perhaps his most symbolic use of the mirror to date is in the opening shot of *Abhijan*, where the jaggedly broken mirror reflects the state of Narsingh's mind during the conversation which establishes his disillusion. In *Pather Panchali*, the mirror is used simply—for Apu to try on his made-up moustache.

Durga discovers the theft (Apu's) and the two have a fight. Durga pretends to be piqued and runs away, out of the village, along the river, across the meadows and the paddy (rice) fields. Apu follows desperately afraid that he will lose his sister's friendship. On the edge of an unknown "Kash" field, the two are reconciled and their long journey is rewarded by their first, totally unexpected and wondrous glimpse of a railway train. . . .

This field of "Kash" was the field of flowers where the first scenes were shot. The train, diminutive as a toy crawling at the edge of the field, is the symbol of the modern world cutting in upon village life. The train and its harsh clatter will form a link in the development of Apu and the important events in his life through the trio of films. Here Apu makes the exciting discovery of its very existence. In *Aparajito*, it will bear him to and again away from Benares to a new kind of life and bring about an inevitable estrangement from his mother. In *Apur Sansar*, Apu will live across the railway tracks; the train will carry his wife away—to death. Left again alone, Apu will be tempted to hurl his life away beneath the wheels of an approaching train.

It is the sequence of the train in *Pather Panchali* which includes the shots which established Ray's acute use of real sounds for his imaginative sound track: Apu's curiosity is captured by the odd noise made by the telegraph wires. We see this curiosity—that quality in him which will play so important a part in Apu's subsequent development—being aroused.

Old Indir, who has been turned out of the house, returns again. This time she is ill and begs that she be allowed to die in her home. But Sarbojaya, incredulous, sternly refuses. So Indir has to leave again, tottering.

Apu and Durga, returning, catch sight of Indir lying beside a bamboo grove. They move close to her, gladdened by the discovery of their beloved aunt. But Durga, wiser and older of the two, realizes with a shock that Indir is dead. . . .

When the film was finally released in New York towards the end of September 1958, Bosley Crowther, in the *New York Herald Tribune*, declared enthusiastically: "Chunibala Devi is fantastically realistic and effective as the ageing crone", while some months earlier, Peter John Dyer, in *Films and Filming*, recognized her as "a fantastic old actress".

In the dusk of her life, Chunibala created an extraordinary character. The most memorable aspect of her characterization is how she conveys the joy of youth still bubbling in extreme old age without suggesting senility, and despite the ravages time had done to her in real life and which was used with such power to image Indir.

Through the love between Durga and Indir, and the juxtaposing of the very young and the very old united by a similarity of spirit—even of fate since one is dead half-way through the film and the other at the end—a visualized philosophic core is presented. Both the old and the young die. But while they live these two have within them the utmost joy of life.

The shooting of Indir's death scene and the carrying away of her body is one of the moments in the production of the film which has remained vivid in the memory of Anil Choudhury.

He regards it as illustrative of his view that "Satyajit is dual in as much as he is ruthless in getting an effect because he is truthful.

He cannot tolerate seeing falseness in his creation. At the same time he is compassionate in his handling of people."

Though Chunibala was eighty-two at the time her death scene as Indir was shot, Ray had her topple over. Having designed such a physically dangerous scene for a very old woman, the instant Chunibala toppled Ray rushed to her and took her head on his lap.

They were all worried about the next day's shooting when it was essential to take the scene of Indir's body being carried away on a bier. Ray felt that at eighty-two Chunibala herself was approaching her own death. Everyone evaded telling her up to the last moment as to the subject of the scene. But those who were evading were young. They did not foresee what old Chunibala Devi's reaction was going to be.

When they explained to her Chunibala laughed, saying: "I am only acting so why have you hesitated to tell me?"

Having crowned the end of her life with a creative interpretation, Chunibala lived long enough to learn that *Pather Panchali* was appreciated.

Indir's death marks the first major climax in the film. From then on there is an intensification of the dramatic element with the documentary envelope becoming somewhat subordinated.

Agrahayah (November-December). As planned Harihar sets out for the initiation ceremony at the rich peasant's. "I shall be back in a week's time," he says, "and with the money I will have earned, I shall get the house repaired. It is doubtful if it will last through another monsoon without repair. . . ."

But instead there comes a long silence on the part of Harihar. At last he sends a postcard to say that the rich peasant has suffered two deaths in the family. Harihar moves on to Benares where, by reading from the Scriptures, he may earn enough money for the house repairs.

Days run into weeks, and weeks into months. Winter comes and goes, but there is no letter from Harihar. The Mukherjee's oldest daughter, the charming and gentle Rahu (a favourite of Durga's) gets married. The wedding touches Durga. Apu finds his thirst for knowledge growing and along with it grows his sense of wonder and curiosity.

But their poverty grows too. Sarbojaya finds herself fighting a losing battle and begins secretly to sell and pawn her possessions. But Nilmani's wife finds out and generously offers to help. Sarbojaya, reluctant at first, is later forced to accept.

In the Outline of *Pather Panchali* Ray attached importance to the time of the year, and to the times of day and night for each sequence. One is reminded of his conversations with the flautist Koushik, in his student days at Santineketan, with whom he discussed the representation of the hours by different traditional ragas.

According to Chandragupta, Ray had already recognized the qualitative differences in the values of light—winter light sharply contrasting with summer glare—during his work on the scenario of Tagore's *Home and the World*.

The contrast between the psychological situation and the external world is revealed when Sarbojaya has no food left and her friend helps her. The Outline notes, ironically, that it is a spring morning. This is life—a desperate situation yet the sun shines.

At last another postcard arrives from Harihar on April 25th. He has collected some money and intends to return soon.

The Bengali New Year's Day comes: as Durga performs the Punyipukur Brata, a ritual for young girls, suddenly without warning comes the season's first nor'wester. Durga leaves her Brata, runs out and meets Apu in the mango orchard. Then comes the rain.

The most lyrical passage in the film is the prelude to the bursting of the monsoon. Waterbugs skip and scamper about the surface of the pond where the lotus leaves begin to flip up at their edges in the rising wind. The tempo increases. Tonal colour is added to this sequence of transition in Nature by Ravi Shankar's marvellously expressive music. It is interesting to compare this exquisite passage so perfect in sound and image with the corresponding transitional audio-visual link shots in the sophisticated *Kanchenjunga*, where the rapidly drifting mist reveals and obscures the vistas of the Himalayas.

The waterbugs disporting themselves epitomize the joyousness of life, the joy being translated into Durga's delirious happiness as she and Apu make for a field. As the rain comes, she whirls round and round to get thoroughly drenched. Apu, less adventurous, shelters under a tree. Sister joins brother and they huddle together.

As every year in the life of India, the monsoon has begun by bringing new life and, at the same time, death and destruction come to many. The dualism of Hindu philosophy may be born from the monsoon.

Durga catches cold which develops into pneumonia. The village doctor does his best—which is really not much.

The storm rises in ferocity and the house itself begins to give way beneath the lashing of the storm—as thousands and hundreds of thousands of houses collapse every year—as Durga's life begins to flicker to its end. On the wall bracket the figure of Ganesh, the elephant-headed god of welcome, shudders. Desperately, Sarbojaya pushes a trunk against the door to prevent it bursting open.

Satyajit (illustration for *Pather Panchali*, Signet Press, Calcutta, 1945)

For six days and nights following Durga's death the mother remains like one petrified, and Apu wanders about the ruins of their home. At last Harihar, the father, returns bringing with him the gift of a sari. He can see the destruction but he knows nothing about Durga. When he speaks to his wife, there comes one of the most inspired moments of the film: Sarbojaya gives a sudden cry of agony. Instead of the cry being the voice of Karuna Banerji, this cry of pain comes in the music, in the solo tone of the stringed instrument, the high-toned *sarange*. (Pl. X)

It has been said that the musical instruments of India are allied in their nature to the human voice. This might explain the unforgettable effect of this passage of sound. In any case, this scene is,

H

perhaps, truly Asian in concept—to lift the starkest realism on to a poetic plane. There are scenes in the Japanese Kabuki Theatre where severed heads are supposedly brought on to the stage; but all the audience is allowed to see is a beautiful jar with a cover. Had Sarbojaya actually cried out in this scene it would probably have been unendurable.

While Harihar, Sarbojaya and Apu prepare to depart for Benares the neighbours sit around giving their advice. The unpleasant Mrs. Mukherjee experiences something of a change of heart. She brings Sarbojaya a gift. Apu then discovers a dish enmeshed in cobwebs. Inside is the necklace his sister had actually stolen from Mrs. Mukherjee's daughter. Yet no one will ever know, for he takes the beads and throws them into the pond. Slowly the scum closes over the forever-hidden secret that Durga was the thief she was said to be. As father, mother and son trundle away in the bullock cart towards what they hope will be a new life, a snake slides furtively into the house. Snakes are believed to move into houses when human beings have deserted them.

Though it is not over-obvious in *Pather Panchali*, nor in the Trilogy as a whole, one of the most vital elements was supplied by the Art Director, Chandragupta.

Bansi had learnt a great deal about the designer's role from working with Renoir and in collaboration with the vastly experienced Eugene Lourie. It had been Bansi's job to devise authentic backgrounds for *The River*. As he later wrote, he came to understand "the probing question of Renoir and Lourie about where, how and why to stage a certain scene in a certain place". He learned to build sets which might easily be mistaken for real locations—a summer house, a jetty, a ruined temple. This experience was of integral importance to the realization of Satyajit Ray's film which was not, as most frequently supposed, shot wholly without studio sets.

It was only after the West Bengal Government allotted the money to finish the film, that the night scenes were attempted. At that point, Bansi Chandragupta set about constructing a replica set of the village house within the studio.

This was a challenge to him. Every crack and detail had already been established in the day shots taken in the location house. It was arduous work to produce each crack and weather-beaten bit of plaster. It had to be done very painstakingly.

The day scenes utilizing the village house were all executed in natural light. Because of this, the *Pather Panchali* project provoked much amusement among professional film-makers. "The bunch of amateurs" to whom the Bengal Government had foolishly given money became a constant butt for cynical jokes and a topic of discussion.

"Waste of money!" was one chorus. "What the Government indulges in!" another.

The cameramen were very scornful of the idea of scene after scene being taken in dull light. They were insensitive to the moods of light. "Do you expect your rain shots to come out?" Subrata Mitra was sarcastically asked. "Why is it necessary to shoot a house on location?"

Yet as the work progressed, projectionists and laboratory people with whom Ray and his unit came into contact began to become sensitive to the novelty of *Pather Panchali*. They felt that something new was being attempted.

But the first screening of *Pather Panchali* in Calcutta's Ordinance Hall was received with disappointment. Nobody knew what to say. This lack of response was due to the very bad quality of the projection. The images appeared dirty and blurred and the sound to be no less poor in quality. Only when the film was released to the public was there an appreciative response. Though the film broke every rule of Indian cinema, an unexpectedly large number of people began to go to see it. They told other people. Word of *Pather Panchali* spread quickly across the country to reach everybody interested in cinema.

Possibly the most apt review written in India about the film, and applicable to the Trilogy as a whole, was "Adib's" comments in *The Times of India* on February 11th, 1956:

It is absurd to compare it (*Pather Panchali*) with any other Indian picture—for even the best of the pictures produced so far have been cluttered with clichés. *Pather Panchali* is pure cinema. There is no trace of the theatre in it. It does away with plot, with grease paint, with songs, with the slinky charmer and the sultry beauty, with the slapdash hero breaking into song on the slightest provocation, or no provocation at all. . . . *Pather Panchali* makes a complete break with the world of make-believe, of a mélange of the impossible. . . . Satyajit Ray has an uncanny eye for the scene and for people. He composes his shots with a virtuosity which he shares with only a few directors in the entire history of cinema. But neither the angling nor the cutting of his shots gives the entire clue to his success. The secret of his power lies in the facility with which he penetrates beneath the skin of his characters, and fixes what is in their mind and in their heart—in the look of the eyes, the trembling of the fingers, the shadows that descend on the face.

"Adib" wrote this several months before the film was recognized at the Cannes Festival as "the best human document" of the year. His enthusiasm is reflected in a letter later written to the *New York Times* by a Mrs. Paul E. Killinger of Bloomington, Indiana. She found the film "one of the most beautiful and sensitive pictures I have ever seen. . . . In addition to its artistry it performs the invaluable function of helping the viewer to understand somewhat a little more deeply, life in a faraway country—something we need so desperately in this country."

No portents heralded *Pather Panchali*. It was suddenly there to create a surprise. Nobody imagined at the time how much planning had gone into its creation. Dr. B. C. Roy was not the only one to mistake it for a kind of documentary film.

Inaccurate stories soon became fixed ideas about the mode of the film's production. The fact was that Ray, though he was experimenting, had a definite theory of film-making. He was, and remains, ambitious from the creative point of view, not the financial. His over-all aim is to depict different facets of Bengal's history. Because he was to continue to keep his production costs low, he would be able to evolve his style in accord with his own will. Had he done otherwise circumstances would have defeated him and forced him to compromise.

I do not know exactly how the decision to send *Pather Panchali* to the Cannes Festival was finally reached. Due to the lack of enthusiasm in the Bengal Publicity Department there was at first no influential backing from the Indian Government for *Pather Panchali*. One member of the Cannes Jury—James Quinn, then Director of the British Film Institute—had seen the film when a copy had on request been sent to him in London as a result of the urgent appeal Ray and I had written to the Institute from Calcutta in December 1955. Quinn was determined that it should win an award.

Ray had written long letters to Lindsay Anderson during the production of *Pather Panchali*. He knew a great deal about the film when he wrote after the Cannes screening: "With apparent formlessness, *Pather Panchali* traces the great design of living. . . . You cannot make films like this in a studio, nor for money. Satyajit Ray has worked with humility and complete dedication; he has gone down on his knees in the dust, and his picture has the quality of intimate unforgettable experience."

Yet even after *Pather Panchali* had gained the Cannes award there remained official hesitation about responding to those people abroad who wished to present the film. There was even a rumour in Bombay that the film would be shelved. To ward off such a fate I sent a letter to Prime Minister Nehru enclosing the letter sent to me from the British Film Institute extolling the film. Jawaharlal Nehru's response was to instruct his Ministry of External Affairs to acquire copies of *Pather Panchali* to circulate to Indian embassies abroad.

London's Curzon Cinema was eager to exhibit the film and a contract was made with the Curzon for *Pather Panchali*'s distribution in England. But there was delay in sending the text of the dialogue for the making of English sub-titles. By the time the film was titled the advantages of publicity from Cannes had been lost. The Curzon hesitated to release the film thinking it would be a failure.

In the meantime, *Aparajito*, the sequel to *Pather Panchali*, had been completed and won the Lion of St. Mark's at the 1957 Venice Film Festival. *Aparajito* was at once taken for distribution in England by Contemporary Films. Only the announcement that the second film would be released in London at the Academy Cinema finally galvanized the West Bengal Government and the Curzon Cinema into deciding to give *Pather Panchali* its first commercial presentation, also at the Academy Cinema. The release finally took place at the end of December 1957, more than eighteen months after its acclaim at Cannes. In the United States, Edward Harrison became distributor of the Trilogy.

Satyajit (sketches from *Aparajito* script)

Chapter 6

THE SEQUEL FILMS—*APARAJITO* AND *APUR SANSAR*

IN the final shots of *Pather Panchali* Harihar, Sarbojaya and Apu trundle in the bullock cart towards Benares. The sequel, *Aparajito*, or *The Unvanquished*, opens with the river Ganges seen from a train as it crosses a bridge. The family have changed their environment. Ray consciously changed his style from its lyrical rhythm to an austere stance in *Aparajito*, a dramatic film concentrating upon the gradual estrangement of Apu from his mother.

In *Pather Panchali*, the central characters—they are plural—are the members of the family, with two eliminated by death. At the close of the third film, *Apur Sansar*, or *The World of Apu*, the idea of the future is conveyed by Apu evolving the mature sentiments of a father. The little Apu is an engaging child in the first film; he is even more interesting as he passes to adolescence in the second film, while his son, Kajal, in his neglected state in the third film is an unusual, difficult child. The Trilogy is not only the biography of Apu. It begins and ends with studies of childhood in two different sets of circumstances and from one generation to the next.

The family stands as of central importance in the majority of Ray's films. It is the angle from which the family is examined that varies. In *Jalsaghar—The Music Room*—which followed *Aparajito*, there is disintegration with the particular aristocratic family involved coming to a total end. *Devi—The Goddess*—explores a family where a tortuous obsession brings disaster. *Kanchenjunga* reveals a rich contemporary family who need to escape from the father's destructive domination. In *Mahanagar—The Big City*—the theme is the reaction of a retired schoolmaster's family to the daughter-in-law going out to work and unexpectedly making a success of a career. *Charulata* studies an 1879 progressive urban Brahmo family's relations and emotions where there is no child.

The prominence of the family in Satyajit Ray's work is reflective of life in Bengal, and in India, where few people's lives become divorced from a family setting. Even in Ray's fanciful comedy, *Paras Pather*, the childless Parash Dutta treats his newly acquired secretary as if he were his own son. Ray's choice of themes involving family relationships is also understandable in the light of his own life. He has never become detached from a family environment.

Satyajit Ray, Bijoya his wife and his only son, Sandip, live in a flat, which since his mother's death in November 1960 is shared with his mother-in-law who suffered a paralytic stroke, one of his sisters-in-law, and his father's youngest brother, Subimal Ray. Such an environment for permanent living is almost unknown as a setting for the life and work of most internationally known artists in the West. The Western artist generally moves away from the family to lead a separate life. Ray has not. The family, starting with his own, has fed his understanding of people.

In adapting the second half of Bannerjee's novel *Pather Panchali* and the first half of the second novel, *Aparajito*, Ray reshaped the book. As he has stressed: "Books are not primarily written to be filmed. If they were, they would read like scenarios; and, if they were good scenarios, they would probably read badly as literature."

In order to make an effective film. Ray eliminated numerous episodes and characters. He concentrated upon "the profound truth of the relationship between the widowed mother and the son who grows away from her. The whole *raison d'être* of the scenario, as, indeed, of the film, was this particular poignant conflict."

At the opening of *Aparajito* in Benares, the family relationship is seen intact. Apu is still a little boy. He is ten years old and interpreted by Pinaki Sen Gupta (who also appears as the young son in *Jalsaghar*). Sarbojaya continues to slave for him, while her husband, Harihar, spends most of his time reading the Scriptures on the ghats leading down to the holy Ganges. By tradition, many Bengalis retire to Benares to end their lives there. Thus, Harihar had a community of his own people to serve even though Benares is far outside the boundaries of Bengal.

In taking his second step—*Aparajito*—had Ray not had confidence in himself, he could have sought to shape the sequel in the same vein of lyricism as *Pather Panchali*. But he felt the need to grapple with new problems. With the exception of the opening sequence in Benares, the essentially 'documentary' elements and beautiful visual passages which served to create such appeal in *Pather Panchali*, become subordinated in *Aparajito* to Ray's handling of scenes in studio sets, and the preoccupation of building up the psychological development of Apu in subtle scenes between mother and son.

The entire camera work for *Pather Panchali* was executed with direct sources of light, natural light for the daytime sequences and direct studio lighting for the night scenes. With the commencement of the second film, Ray and his cameraman, Mitra, began experimenting with the reflected light, which they continued to explore in all Ray's subsequent films, including their first colour picture, *Kanchenjunga*.

Satyajit Ray and Subrata Mitra consider their device of bounce lighting as an important element in the visual effects achieved in the films, and specifically as an aid to the creation of psychological effects. For each of the films where Mitra has been Ray's cameraman, he has read the scenario at an early stage of preparation and drawn up a basic plan to convey the mood and evolve a style of camera work suited to the particular subject.

"But", Mitra insists, "it is not a rigid plan and both mood and style grow during the shooting when the detail effects evolve."

Mitra claims that Chandragupta was responsible for their devising bounce lighting. Bansi's set for the Benares house was to have been built on the studio lot where they would have natural light. But Bansi and Satyajit thought it advisable to build it in the studio so as not to lose days in shooting during the monsoon. The rain might damage the set.

For this reason, Mitra had to contrive a mode of lighting which would convey the character that daylight has as it filters into Benares houses. The sun itself never directly penetrates these houses; only a soft, diffused, shadowless daylight seeps in from the space open to the sky above the traditional courtyards.

They bounced—reflected—the lights on to a large wooden frame fixed above the open top of the set of the courtyard with a stairway and rooms off it. This was covered with cheap white cotton cloth stretched like painter's canvas. In principle, the method was adopted from portrait photographer's studio lighting. It produces effects such as sun filtering through spun glass and "effects suggestive of painting".

When Mitra instigated this method of lighting some film technicians, including cameramen, laughed. They were not at all enthusiastic about such an idea, supposing the results would be flat and eliminate the effects of modelling objects. While bounce lighting has the limitation of being impossible to re-direct on to a given spot, for example, the facial area of the body, it is effective in suggesting daylight for scenes shot in the studio.

Mitra points out: "It is logical lighting. The fact that in life we see direct light with shadows cast in night scenes, but in the day we don't have direct light and shadows of the same kind."

In consequence of his lighting experiments of the Benares house set in *Aparajito*, most people supposed this set was a real house on location. It is, in fact, difficult to detect any difference between the studio shots and the location shots. Take, for example, two shots—the first of Harihar walking along a lane of Benares—a location shot—and appearing to enter his house as if it were a location house in Benares. The quality of light appears to be the same. The continuity is maintained from the shot of Harihar walking in the lane and walking on to the studio set in Calcutta.

Benares heightens imagination. Not the least remarkable thing about the opening scenes of *Aparajito* is the visual richness of Benares which was restrained from flooding out preoccupation with the characters. This indicates Ray's self-discipline. Benares was intoxicating to him, but he resisted this intoxication on the screen. There is only one Benares even if Venice recalls it, as Ray had observed to me a few months before he commenced *Aparajito*. In 1950 he had commented to Chandragupta in a letter: "Venice is a fantastic place—very reminiscent of Benares in some ways, and equally photogenic."

Ray kept a diary of the impressions of scenes in Benares shot on location in March 1956.

> March 1, 1956 . . . In the afternoon the same ghats present an utterly different aspect. Clusters of immobile widows make white patches on the greyish ochre of the broad steps. The hustle of ablution is absent. And the light is different, importantly so. The ghats face the east. In the morning they get the full frontal light of the sun, and the feeling of movement is heightened by the play of cast shadows. By 4 p.m. the sun is behind the tall buildings whose shadows now reach the opposite bank. Result: a diffused light until sunset perfectly in tune with the subdued nature of the activity.
>
> Morning scenes in the ghat must be shot in the morning and afternoon scenes in the afternoon.

For the first sequence Ray sought those visual elements of the teeming life of the extraordinary city which would best reveal the inner processes developing within the transplanted village boy, Apu, who is expected to follow in his Brahmin father's priestly footsteps. As suggested in *Pather Panchali*, curiosity is one of Apu's traits, and Benares, where all of India's eccentricities are magnified, would titillate even the most apathetic propensity to curiosity.

Benares is seen through Apu's wondering eyes: The odd sight of athletes swinging their clubs on the ghats; the boys' games in narrow lanes shot on March 22nd, according to Ray's diary:

> From the ghats to the lanes. Concluding shots of scene of Apu playing hide-and-seek with friends. Clearing the lanes of unwanted elements (animate and inanimate) for long shots a Herculean task. Pack up at 4 p.m. and proceed directly to the Viswanath Temple for shots and recording of Arati.

Apu watching at a distance as his father reads the Scriptures to a group where widows in their white *thans* are dominant—a silent comment on how the traditional widow still devotes herself to religious matters.

The composition of the long shot of this group on the ghat exemplifies how casually Ray embraces within one image the focal point of action by placing his individual characters within the characteristic image of the place where the scene is laid. To the right of the frame, small rowing boats are seen on the river. This is a typical sight at Benares. The shot of Harihar reading in a sing-song voice from the Scriptures, and *including* a stretch of the river with the rowboats etches an intimate impression. In Benares, the devotional scene is constantly juxtaposed with the secular and mundane. (Pl XV)

It is interesting that critics did not draw attention to the dramatic situation introduced almost at the beginning of *Aparajito*—the upstair neighbour's predatory attitude and desire to find an opening for making advances to Sarbojaya. The whole episode, which is hinted at from the early scenes to the moment of Harihar's death, is conveyed in half-tones: especially by Sarbojaya's urgent covering of her head and hastening away at the man's presence.

Though this attempt at seduction is portrayed in half-tones, as more often than not in life, the final attempt, with the man treading barefooted to come behind her culminates in a profound expression of feminine psychology. Sarbojaya is immeasurably shocked when she realizes she is the target of the neighbour's intent to seduce her. Mutely horrified, she is yet prepared to plunge her cooking knife into his swelling paunch. Her reaction is the universal one of women who have always supposed themselves to be sexually identified with only one man, the one who has long filled the entire horizon of their female consciousness. It is an emotion beyond any matter of conscious virtue or concept of fidelity. It is simply disgusting, repulsive, for any other man to intrude himself and express physical desire.

But critics did not notice this revelation of intense emotion within Sarbojaya. It is there, but the attempt to seduce and the reaction are portrayed with so few words and such a subtle play of expression that it is as if this incident may not have happened at all. The flow almost submerges this moment, with the film gliding on to the husband walking falteringly up the steps of the ghats—the shot intensified by the presence of a dividing bar. At the top, he spins around and suddenly collapses. He is brought home.

"In the rushes," said Ray, "Kanu Bannerjee's acting of Harihar's death scene is more realistic than in the finished film."

But the death is memorable with the frightened Apu suddenly awakened by his mother and told to fetch a pitcher of water from the holy Ganges for his father to drink before he dies. (Pl XV)

> March 22 . . . 5.30 a.m. Started with shot of Apu fetching water from the river. The idea was to have a long shot with Apu in the foreground and a solitary wrestler in the far background, and no other figures. But bathers had already arrived and we had a tough time persuading them to stay out of the water, and out of camera-field, until end of shot.

As Harihar gasps to death, birds wheel across the sky:

> March 15 . . . At the ghats at 5 a.m. to shoot the pigeons. Memorable fiasco. The shot was to be of the pigeons taking flight in a body from their perch on the cornices and making enormous circular sweeps in the sky, as is the way with them. We had a fairly potent-looking bomb which we meant to explode to set the pigeons flying. The camera was set up and Subir had set the match to the fuse when, with barely half a minute to go, Nimai started making frantic but indefinite gestures. We could sense something was wrong, and Subir made an eloquently mimed appeal to the bomb to refrain from exploding. The bomb off, the pigeons performed nobly but the camera didn't turn. And then we discovered that the motor hadn't been connected to the battery.
>
> Luckily, after three or four sweeps the pigeons were back on their perch, and with the second bomb (we had four) we had our shot.

With Harihar dead, his wife and child are penniless. Immediately, Sarbojaya's resourcefulness—hinted in *Pather Panchali* when she manages to feed her children by selling her wedding gifts—asserts itself. She becomes a servant in the house of a rich retired Bengali family with its gross, lazy wife and self-indulgent husband. All goes well. Apu has no objections to attending to the employer's hair or running errands for him, as if he were a servant. It is not the boy who reacts, for he feels free. He enjoys himself wandering off into temples and playing with privileged monkeys.

Apu's impressions are marvellously woven into the city's life. Ray's diary contains amusing hints of how the temple scene took shape:

> March 3 . . . Called on the Mohanto Laxminarayan of the Viswanath Temple. The purpose was to persuade him to give us facilities for shooting inside the temple (something which has never been done before). Panday, our intermediary, had insisted that I shouldn't be reticent but should "project my personality" which he was sure would clinch the deal. Two things stood in the way: (a) my lack of chaste Hindi and the Mohanto's lack of any other language, and (b) the chairs we were given to sit upon had been designed for the maximum comfort of bugs.
>
> It seems at least two more visits will be required before the great Mohanto condescends to give a nod of that immobile head of his.
>
> Stopped on our way back at the temple. Were told we were in time for the Saptarshi Arati. A spine-tingling experience. Those who miss it miss one of the great audio-visual treats. Pity I can't use it in any except a decoration manner in the present film.

On the 22nd:

> Durga [sound recordist] sets up tape recorder in a house across the lane opposite the Temple. Mrinal worms his way through milling crowd of devotees with mike and 90ft. cable which just reaches the southern door of the inner niche where camera has been set up. Temple attendants get busy stretching a cordon to keep off crowd who push and crane their necks to get a sight of the image now being decorated for the Arati. We wait, sweating, acutely conscious of the audacious incongruity of the camera.
>
> The time arrives. We hold our breath. The great chant begins. In the deafening crescendo I can just hear myself shouting "Start" and "Cut".

The Arati goes on for an hour. The end finds us—and our raw stock—exhausted. As we are about to pack up, word arrives from the Mohanto that he would like to hear the sound we have recorded. Would we be good enough to have our equipment conveyed to his apartment and the sound played back to him?

It takes half an hour to reach the Mohanto's place with the equipment, another half to install it, and a full hour to play back and pack up. When we finally leave the great man it is a quarter to eleven. He smiles his approval. I almost expect him to tip us . . .

Sarbojaya's moment of discovery of the predicament that Harihar's death has put her in—that Apu is serving her employer as if he were a servant—is one of Ray's most compelling uses of intensified sound followed by tense silence. One can feel Sarbojaya deciding she must return to the village with her uncle—a priest like Harihar—in order to save Apu being trapped into the life of a servant. Sarbojaya, her old uncle and Apu are seen on the train, which symbolizes a new phase in the life of Apu. (Pl. XV)

> Took the 9 o'clock train to Moghulsarai. Ramani Babu (70-year-old resident of Benares we picked up on the ghat) with us to play Uncle Rhabataran; also Karuna and Pinky. Shooting inside third class compartment. Sarbojaya and Apu look out of window. We give the old man an orange but he consumes it before the camera is ready, so we give him another. Shot is O.K. subject to the Tri-X performing as expected.

Though mother and son return to the village and live in the uncle's house—as Satyajit, too, lived in his uncle's house for twenty years—Apu is already lost to a traditional way of life. He cannot fit naturally into the traditional role of the Brahmin though he attempts to prepare himself to follow in his father's footsteps. He is out of touch with such a life even though he is still so young, not more than twelve.

There is pathos in Apu's misfit effort to practise the priestly rituals when he only desires to run off and play with the other boys, and go to school. Endeavouring to perform the ceremonies he gives the impression of an orphaned waif who is utterly lost in the midst of prayers. He is so evidently bright and lively and drawn to the secular world. It is Apu who argues with his mother that if he studies for the priesthood in the morning he can go to the local school in the afternoon. (Pl. XVI)

From this point, the biography of Apu becomes that of the boy who must inevitably go his own way, which is toward the world beyond the village. The transformation which comes to Apu with adolescence becomes intensified when Pinaki Sen Gupta, as the boy Apu, is replaced by S. Ghosal as the youth Apu, who has captured the interest of his schoolmaster, a teacher utterly different in outlook from the eccentric Pandit-grocer interpreted by Tulsi Chakravarty in *Pather Panchali*. The subtle touch that denotes that this teacher is a Christian is the cross on his watch chain and the character of his clothes, the period being about 1925. In an oblique way it is suggested that modern education has penetrated into the village.

Apu has a thirst for knowledge. As a good student who is encouraged, he begins to grow still farther away from his mother who is only half-hearted in her desire for him to develop his intelligence. She ceases to hold interest for him and he, unconsciously, pays less and less attention to her wishes. Sarbojaya is too traditional rather than lacking in intelligence. She can no longer share Apu's feelings which must drive him away to college in Calcutta. When he is offered a scholarship Apu is only too eager to go though it means leaving his mother to loneliness. In any case he reads so much at home that she is lonely even when he is in the house. Shortly before he is to leave for Calcutta, the headmaster asks if Sarbojaya will give her consent for his departure. Apu has not even confided in his mother as to the possibility of his going to college. The globe of the world which the master had given him has fired his imagination. Finally assured of a scholarship, he comes home. He has to tell his mother.

Karuna Banerji poignantly expresses how hard Sarbojaya has tried to do the best she could for her son. But it is her mother-love that floods her as she looks at him, and yet causes her to seem insensitive towards new opportunity for him. In the morning when he leaves, he has his uncomfortable moment of transition when he puts his feet into his first pair of laced shoes and sets off to walk in them to the station.

The globe and the shoes are the symbols of the change which will take place in Apu before his mother sees him again. He boards the train for the metropolis of Calcutta. Apu, the village boy of *Pather Panchali* grew up in the town of Benares. The holy city tilled his intellectual awareness, while the sight of too much devoutness blunted his religious feelings until there arose the unwillingness to become the image of his father. Calcutta, again, is different from the town of Benares. Apu comes to a printer's office with a letter of introduction from the headmaster. He needs a room to stay in. There is the room upstairs (one of Bansi Chandragupta's sets) and the printer allows Apu to live in it. The printer's office and the room are so authentic that they add a documentary element to the atmosphere the film creates of impoverished middle-class Calcutta. Once upstairs, Apu makes a discovery paralleling his discovery of the train in *Pather Panchali*. The room has electric light—a marvel Apu has never seen before. He is intrigued by the light switch. It is from such observations—in themselves trivial— that the convincing picture of Apu's life is built up in *Aparajito* and later in *Apur Sansar*.

Soon, Apu settles into the commonplaces of college life and makes himself a friend. But in the village his mother's loneliness only adds to the intensity of her developing sickness. All she has to live for is Apu's return.

Until Satyajit went to Santineketan, his life was dominated by his mother. Though shy and retiring he was by 1940 in love with Bijoya and she with him. It was the Tagore school which gave him a spirit of independence so that he could reach decisions—in the end the making of *Pather Panchali*—of which his mother did not approve. Like many parents in India, Suprabha Ray at first believed that film-making would have the effect of destroying the morals of her son.

"There's a sequence missing," Ray explained on one occasion. "Apu made friends with a girl—Lila—and the girl hastened his estrangement with his mother. But at the last moment we had to drop it."

"The first girl we found looked right," Satyajit recalled. "But she couldn't act. She had mannerisms which were unmanageable. Then we found another girl with a younger sister who was woven in to be the intrigued watcher of the older girl."

"But we didn't know of the girl's personal situation," said the quiet Subrata Mitra, slyly.

"She had a lover," remarked Satyajit, "and we had hardly taken the first shot when she was called away."

Apparently the lover made a fearful scene and forbade the girl to appear in the film. It was he or the film. She came back and breathlessly explained her predicament. She could not lose her lover for the sake of one more shot.

"Yet he is a film actor himself!" Mitra and Ray chuckled at the memory of the trouble with the jealous actor.

"We just didn't have the energy to find a third girl," commented Ray. "Dropping the girl out weakened the film."

It is probably true that the elimination of the incident of the girl weakens the film's dramatic structure. Yet it is impossible to tell that some link in the development is missing, for Apu's absorption in things beyond his mother's comprehension appears convincing. It is enough that he is absorbed into the college atmosphere that he could never convey to Sarbojaya.

The audience has been made aware of what is unknown to Apu —that his mother is ill. She struggles against it as she waits for his return. With Apu's return for a holiday the change in him becomes acutely clear. Sarbojaya has longed to confide in him and to mother him. But Apu, from feelings of need to make himself independent since he has moved into another kind of life, cruelly —though not intentionally so—holds himself aloof from her. Sitting on his bed the last night:

Shot 398.   M.L.S. *Bedroom: Apu reading.*

        Sarbojaya: The next time you come bring some buttons.

        Apu is too absorbed in his book to answer.

        Sarbojaya: Apu . . . Keep your book aside.

        M.L.S. *Apu does so reluctantly.*

        Sarbojaya: Now talk to me.

        Apu: What about?

        Sarbojaya: Well . . . tell me what you have seen in the city.

        Apu: Oh, all sorts of things . . . The Victoria Memorial, Whiteway Laidlaw, a big departmental store, the Hogg Market, the Zoo. . . .

        Sarbojaya: And the Kalighat temple?

        Apu: Oh yes, we went there the other day. We saw that and we saw Keorotola.

      Sarbojaya: What's there at Keorotola?

      Apu: The burning ghats. (Pl. XVI)

  CUT

399 C.S.   Sarbojaya: What?

        Apu: You know, the place where they cremate people.

        Sarbojaya: I see . . . I hope you walk the roads carefully. I keep worrying all the time . . . I wish you'd finish your studies soon and get a job.

  CUT

400 M.S.   *Apu is dozing off but Sarbojaya is not aware of it*
           and she goes on speaking.

> Sarbojaya: When you get a job I will come and
>   stay with you . . . Will you let me?
>
> Apu (*drowsily*): Oh, yes.
>
> Sarbojaya: Is it ever to be? I wonder . . . I have
>   the strangest presentiments. What if I should
>   fall ill . . . seriously ill? It can happen, you
>   know. I don't feel well in the evenings, I
>   have no appetite. I have often thought of
>   telling you, but somehow I could never bring
>   myself to do it. Suppose I do fall ill, you
>   won't leave your studies to come and look
>   after me, will you?
>
> *Getting no answer from Apu she asks again,* Why
>   don't you answer me? . . . Apu!
>
> *Apu has been fast asleep all this time.*

FADE OUT

There could not be a more memorable depiction of a universal
situation.

Apu will leave in the morning. His mother does not want to wake
him up. She wants to hold on to him. By leaving him sleeping he
will miss the train. As shown quite early in *Pather Panchali*, Apu
hated to get up in his childhood, Durga had to shake him to get him
to move. But this morning he wakes himself blaming Sarbojaya for
failing to awaken him.

He hurries to the train with a seemingly blank indifference to
his mother. Yet, suddenly, he turns and goes back to spend the day
with her before returning to his student's life. He is still unaware
that his mother is very ill. She is now fading out of life for she has
less and less reason to live since Apu has grown away from her.
Neither the one nor the other is right or wrong; they have simply
become two different generations with their roots in different ways
of life.

Sarbojaya wanders about, a listless shadow dreaming away the
last of her days. Exhausted, she sits against the foot of a tree en-
veloped in an inarticulate sorrow. She drifts to the end of her
consciousness—a poetic visualization of death submerging both
energy and all awareness. She simply sits gazing at a pond where
fireflies weave their pattern of light. It is as if the fireflies enter into
Sarbojaya's receding consciousness, or the last of her consciousness

I

detaches itself from her body and fuses with the pattern of the fireflies above the pond. She is gone . . .

The shots of the fireflies weaving over the pond were obtained by the shot of the simulated fireflies being superimposed on the image of the pond.

"The landscape with the pond was shot almost at dark," Subrata Mitra recalled. "The fireflies were simulated in the studio with the unit—in all about thirty people—dancing with torch bulbs which had been painted black save for a pinpoint of light. In the middle, an American, who had come to Calcutta, walked in."

Mitra was amused by this memory, for the visitor had been brought expecting to see Satyajit Ray directing. The man was shocked at the sight of seemingly mad people dancing about with torches. Mitra smiled. He never seems to laugh outright.

It was a good idea. But Mitra thought the execution failed to come up to the idea. "It was not neatly done. On the screen the shot looks dirty, what with the torchlight and additional pinpricks added."

Mitra is probably correct from a technical point of view. Yet the scene gives an imaginative and psychologically valid sensation of passing out of life, a representation of the death visions of an essentially religious nature (as also shown by Upendrakishore's own visions as death began to engulf him). These shots recur in the memory and cause wonder and contemplation.

The two deaths—of father and mother— in *Aparajito* are visualized with a marked difference. It seems right that Harihar's death should come in as unprepared a manner as the whole of his life had been lived, while Sarbojaya should await her death with the same sense of endurance as she has lived.

"People have asked me why there is so much death in my films"; Satyajit Ray made this comment when he first showed me *Aparajito* in Calcutta in 1957. It was the only comment he made during the screening, except to point out that the Benares house was a studio set. He added : "I answer this question with, 'in life there is so much death'."

In 1967, he mentioned to me that his own mother had persistently endeavoured to insulate him in youth from seeing death, his father's death having upset him.

As Sarbojaya dies, Apu receives a postcard in Calcutta to come because his mother is ill. The conventional film would have allowed him to reach the village in the nick of time for his mother to pass away in his arms and, in an oblique manner, provide a "happy" ending even though a weepy one. Such an ending would subscribe to the illusion that the wayward boy had not really grown away from

Ma. Nothing of the sort happens in *Aparajito*, and this is where Ray's film disturbed the Indian traditionalists.

Apu comes by train, walks to the village and meets his uncle. Everything is over and Sarbojaya is ashes. Apu breaks down and weeps. The uncle makes a feeble attempt to persuade him to return to the ways of his father. There is nothing for Apu to do but depart again for the city.

The film failed in Calcutta. Some reviews compared it unfavourably with *Pather Panchali*. This came as a shock and disappointment to Ray, who believed it to be a considerably more mature film than his first. The adverse reviews hurt and angered him. The film's unenthusiastic reception in Bengal led to *Aparajito* being ignored by the State for entry for the National Awards. Ray was once again face to face with the hostility of vested film interests and the obstacles presented by the long-cultivated escapist tastes of Indian filmgoers.

Satyajit's wife, Bijoya, attributed *Aparajito*'s failure to appeal in Bengal—that Apu was not the conventional son.

One traditionalist later insisted to me that Ray's films were morbid and perverse.

Even though most Bengali films remained theatrical and Indian film production as a whole jogged along, trailing its impedimenta of well-worn clichés, it was beyond the possibility of any anti-Ray element in or out of the film industry to influence his international standing.

Aparajito was invited to the Venice Film Festival because of the impact *Pather Panchali* had made at Cannes, though as yet the film had not been given commercial release outside India. Ray went to Venice for a second time.

From Room 41 of the Hotel Riviera on the Lido, he wrote to Bansi Chandragupta on September 2nd, 1957, that

. . . my film comes on in two days time. Strangely enough, I haven't started feeling jittery yet. Main reason is probably that the films so far shown have been bad—almost unbelievably so . . . the films from Mexico, Japan (not *Macbeth*, which will be shown on the 5th—but the film by Tasaka who made *Yukiwarisu*) and Yugoslavia have all been disappointing. The last three films approximate to the standard of the average Bengali production! But the real competition, everybody says, will be between Kurosawa, Zinnemann, Visconti and *Aparajito*. The Soviet film is a "dark horse", but being based on a famous Gorky story, should not be overlooked. The real revelations here have been the retrospective shows of Kenzi Mizoguchi (*Ugetsu*) films from 1938 to 1954—five films in all and no period pieces. Mizo-guchi was one of the great directors—in many ways greater than Kurosawa. There is a great deal of dialogue in his films but the handling of cutting and the movement of the camera is so masterly that theatricality is completely banished. And the photography! The five films we saw were photographed by five *different* cameramen, but the same style prevails and it is the most masterly I have come across. Nearly all the sets (if they are sets) are built outdoors and in all five films there isn't a backdrop or a back projection shot.

"And there is a ceiling to every room", Satyajit added in the margin.

As he awaited the screening of *Aparajito*, the Lido began "bristling with big names mostly stars, of course. Henry Fonda arrived yester-day", and he listed the luminaries and the "starlets vying with each other to attract attention". He speculated that "the fate of *Aparajito* in an atmosphere like this is unpredictable".

One wonders what the big names—the V.I.P.s of the film world —and the starlets thought of the enormously tall Satyajit Ray whose *Aparajito* captured the Golden Lion with Kurosawa's *Macbeth* (*Throne of Blood*) and Visconti's *Le Notti Bianche* completing the trio of major prizes.

Satyajit sent off a cable to Bijoya, which was unconventionally addressed to "Monku"—her nickname.

As someone remarked, the Bengal Regional Awards Committee, who had spurned *Aparajito*, must have had a fit of collective blush-ing over its members' mistake when they read the news of the film winning the chief award at Venice, as well as Le Prix des Critiques Internationale and Le Prix du Cinema Nouveau.

Arturo Lanocito, the critic of the *Corriere della Sera*, who had been carried away with delight by *Pather Panchali*, felt his enthu-siasm vindicated. The amount of space the Italian press as a whole allotted to the film was enormous.

When Ray's B.O.A.C. plane touched down at Dum Dum Airport on a mid-September Saturday (in the interim period between his departure for Venice and his return to India, Satyajit had won the David O. Selznick Golden Laurel Award for both *Pather Panchali* and *Aparajito*), "the news of his arrival having been sufficiently publicized, a large crowd of his friends and admirers as also men from the film trade and industry defied the scorching heat and wended their way to Dum Dum Airport to give a hero's welcome to the film-maker on his arrival from London". On the following

Monday, a public reception was staged in the evening at the Ranjit Indoor Stadium at Eden Gardens to felicitate Ray on bringing such honour to India. At the head of the reception committee, in the role of Chairman, stood the Sheriff of Calcutta.

There is a quaint coda to Satyajit Ray's winning the Lion of St. Mark.

One evening during the writing of this book, Satyajit and Bansi Chandragupta confessed, "Satyajit didn't know what to say during the making of *Pather Panchali*!"

Satyajit chipped in: "He'd whisper to me 'Say—start Sound!' Bansi was the professional!"

"He couldn't say 'Action!'" Bansi chuckled.

"I thought if I did I'd scare my actors!" Satyajit said with his chuckling turned to a laugh. "I was never able to say 'Cut' until my third film. I didn't know how!"

"He only knew how to make a film," said Bansi, "but had no idea what a director was supposed to say. I knew from Renoir who shouted 'Auction!' for 'Action!'"

"But I did know that to get a child to do what you asked, you bent down whispering in conspiratorial tones—just between you and he, and no one else!" said Satyajit with mock reproachfulness.

"Do you know, I've never heard what Satyajit has said to any child in any film," remarked Bansi.

The eventual international success of *Aparajito* must have been perplexing to the Indian film industry and exhibitors who had developed and continued to function in a state of isolation and complacency. It has often seemed that both distributors and exhibitors in India couldn't be bothered even to take advantage of Ray's fame to promote his films outside of Bengal. He was, and to a certain extent still is, as much of an outsider as Rabindranath Tagore was in his day in terms of the commercial Bengali and Indian theatre.

In the late summer of 1958 Ray made a short trip to the United States. Appropriately enough, as an innovator and a humanist he was invited by Frances Flaherty to be the first foreign guest to the Robert Flaherty Seminar, later called International Seminars. Edward Harrison arranged the release of *Pather Panchali* at the Fifth Avenue Cinema to coincide with Ray's visit to New York and the film opened after having won five awards. Evidently Ray went over well—or big—in the States. Howard Thompson commented: "He is no dreaming dilettante. A strapping, swarthy chap, with strong features, he talks like a realistic poet, without the slightest foreign accent, looking fresh from the American gridiron." Here was "no mystic Oriental trailing clouds of wisdom" but "a big rangy Calcuttan in comfortable Western garb". About film-making Ray remarked that Hollywood "rather exaggerated the value of experience. . . . In film-making the problem is having good taste. That's the necessary thing."

Ray was very good-humoured and gentle at his interviews and it delighted his interviewers that he was "completely enchanted by what he had done". On the other side of the continent in San Francisco, *Aparajito* had won the 1958 prize for the Best Film and Best Director.

At the time, Ray was already working on the plans for *Apur Sansar*, the third and last film of the Trilogy.

*   *   *   *

The release of *Pather Panchali* and *Aparajito*, first in England and then in America, paved the way abroad for initial interest in *Apur Sansar*—or *The World of Apu*. The period of this last phase of Apu's biography is the early years of World War II. Apu is twenty-nine years old at the close of the Trilogy, an age which almost corresponds to that of Satyajit at the same period.

Between the release of *Pather Panchali* and that of *Apur Sansar*, Ray's films exerted one notable influence upon Bengali films, and to a lesser degree Hindi films. Other directors were made aware of the value of location shooting. Ray also may have stimulated the more original attempts in film-making embarked on by at least two or three young Bengali directors, notably Ritwik Ghatak, Mrinal Sen, and Topen Sinha. But it was the style of acting introduced by Ray which began exerting a powerful impact on actors. Scattered here and there were professionals of more than average ability, but they had been handicapped in their screen appearances because they had not received the kind of direction which could reveal the extent of their talent for expression in front of the camera.

Soumitra Chatterjee, the interpreter of the adult Apu, though young, had already some theatrical experience. He has now emerged as a star in numerous films made by other directors and he is particularly articulate as to what he has learned from appearing in six conspicuously contrasting roles in Ray films—Apu; Umaprased, the young son in *Devi*; the comic young bridegroom, Amulya, in the Tagore story, *Samapti*; Narsingh, the disillusioned and violent Rajput taxi driver in *Abhijan*; and subsequently, Amal, the thinly veiled portrait of Tagore in *Charulata*, and the uncertain egotist in *Kapurush*. In 1969 he was cast for *Ashari Shanket*.

Chatterjee maintains that prior to *Pather Panchali* and *Aparajito*, Bengali film actors, who, as a general rule, came into cinema from the theatre, had given no serious thought to the difference of emphasis in acting for the theatre and for the motion picture camera. This accounts for the convention of staginess in Indian cinema acting.

"But," Chatterjee insists, "Ray's films brought about a real change from the acting point of view. Actors began trying to be cinema actors.

"I didn't know what to do when Mr. Ray first asked me. I didn't know what was the real difference between stage and screen acting. I wanted," he said, "to be a newcomer. I was afraid I'd overact—that I would project my voice too much, when for film you should under-act. The mike is close. Then there is the detailed movement of your muscles. You have to be conscious of your proportions.

"The film medium belongs to the director instead of the actor being supreme," continued Chatterjee. "The director emerges as the main actor.

"I think", he went on with increasing enthusiasm, "that stage experience helps in building up a character. But the acting must be modified. I had a strange notion, for I always thought of myself as a stage actor. After I saw *Pather Panchali*, all my notions about film were revolutionized."

This was the state of mind in which Chatterjee came to work on *Apur Sansar*. His chief asset was the natural sensitivity of his appearance. Moreover, he had an appreciation of orderly work. Even while a student at Calcutta's City College, he had formed his own amateur dramatic group. For a number of years now, Chatterjee has been publishing and co-editing a Bengali intellectual magazine to which Ray contributes.

As Ray says of the character of Apu in *The World of Apu*, he is of "a somewhat unclear emotional pattern". Adapted from the second half of Bibhuti Bhusan Bannerjee's novel, *Aparajito*, there is little "plot" beyond Apu, now a man, marrying and begetting a son.

Eliminating many of the complexities of the original novel, Ray "concentrated mainly on two aspects. One was the relationship of the struggling intellectual Apu and his unaffected, unlettered chance-wife, Aparna, brought up in affluence but inspired to adjustment with poverty by love for her husband. The second aspect was even more exciting. Aparna dies in child-birth. A conventional writer would have made the father rush to the crib of the surviving child. Bibhuti Bhusan, who often reaches the truth below the surface, makes Apu turn against the child—he reproaches him for having caused the mother's death. The first meeting of father and son takes place after a lapse of several years."

Apur Sansar opens in Calcutta with Apu as a university student who has aspirations to become a writer. He wakes on the morning of October 16th, 1939, without a job. He is driven to sell his best books and seek a job by the arrival of his polite, rapacious and merciless landlord who sits like a vulture in Apu's room demanding his rent. The sensitive Apu is thus forced to go out looking for work he doesn't want. He is not aggressive.

There is no greater problem in Bengal than the educated unemployed and what they feel, and how they resent the frustration of being forced into jobs to which they feel superior and wish to evade. It is as true of Calcutta today as in 1939. Many critics, both in India and abroad, have noted the small details that embroider the simple line that flows; for example, in the opening scene where Apu, asleep in his attic room, has overturned a bottle of ink which has stained the mattress. (Pl. XVII)

Fagged out from looking for an unwanted job, Apu returns to the room in the evening. With nothing to do he picks up his flute until in bounces his friend, Pulu, as an echo from his student days in *Aparajito*. Pulu, in shirt and trousers as if to emphasize his modern aggressiveness, is in the sharpest contrast to Apu in his *dhoti*. How his voice rings out with confidence! He hauls Apu out to a restaurant for a meal—his first good meal for a long time. Across the table, and at the background tables, the two outward strands of India's modern culture pattern are shown facing one another. Pulu waves around his fork as he talks to Apu who eats with his fingers, which is the traditional way of eating and the most general. The touch of Western clothes and the fork are infinitely telling. It is not necessarily true—as subsequent events in the film will show—that the user of the fork is the more emancipated of these two young men. But it is implied that Pulu's home is Westernized.

After eating, they wander the streets with Apu spouting poetry and the two of them talk of art; that Apu will become a great writer, a Tolstoy or a Hardy. But he insists his book will be "like a chronicle. Simple. About simple folk. About poverty. Like life itself, with its ups and downs. . . . Of course, something of my own life will be in it, and my background. . . ."

In Sequence No. 3, they are on the way to Pulu's uncle's house, where the wedding of the daughter, Aparna, is to be celebrated. The next scenes were shot on location with the use of only two sets—the interior of the uncle's home and the bridal chamber.

The whole family is involved in the preparation of Aparna's wedding. Apu enters the house and the mother comes to greet him as she would come to greet anyone. Then something happens with a validity rare on the screen. We see the meeting of the mother and Apu and there is an instant exchange of genuine feeling. The look that comes into the mother's eyes is one of immediate liking and confidence. It is a very small scene, but it stays in the mind. All too frequently the meeting of people on the screen projects nothing but a simulated look, or gesture, which is supposed to suggest some psychic recognition, yet conveys no inward process.

Without the swift establishing of sympathy between Aparna's mother and Apu, the coming incident of marriage as a result of accident, would appear both artificial and melodramatic. This little scene establishes communication. It reflects an instant feeling of liking as it arises in life. The fates of people become interwoven in an instant, resulting from something intangible.

The greatest coincidence in all of Ray's films now drives forward the action in *Apur Sansar*. As the wedding preparations continue Apu recedes into the background. The bridegroom's procession appears carrying the palanquin in which the groom sits. The bearers halt. The camera peers in at the bedecked bridegroom. For a moment there is nothing abnormal. The angle of vision is striking and oblique. (It was a very low angle improvised at a moment's notice and with the camera sunk into a trench dug in the ground). As it lingers, the peering camera reveals a situation that shocks the senses. The bridegroom-to-be is evidently of unbalanced mind. This is the first realization. Suddenly, this imbalance flares into a half-hidden, very short scene of raving lunacy followed by the no less short and emphatic scene of the mother barring the door and protecting her daughter, Aparna, from such a horrific fate as marriage with a lunatic.

This appalling situation could arise more easily in India than elsewhere. Yet it is still a situation that has arisen—or the threat of it has—where families anywhere have been anxious to bring about a marriage either for material reasons or as an attempt to bring balance to an unbalanced man. The peculiarly Indian aspect of this situation is the astrological factor. This particular day has been astrologically cast as propitious when Aparna must marry or else—in the face of this catastrophe—be outcast and regarded hereafter as unmarriageable.

It is this astrological dictum which provides the urgent motive for Pulu finding an immediate solution. Apu offers the solution, if he will agree to marry Aparna. Pulu says to him:

"Listen Apurba, you can save us from a catastrophe."
Apu bursts out laughing.
"That's a good joke . . . a great joke . . . ha, ha, ha. . . ."
But Pranab is not joking. He is deadly serious.
Half a dozen other elderly men come and stand in a cluster around Apu and Pranab.
Pranab says in deadly earnest: "Please try to understand the nature of the crisis. If there is no wedding tonight before the appointed time, Aparna's future will be ruined."
"Yes," adds one of the elders. "The girl will be ruined for life!"

Apu has been slowly moving back, step by step. Now he stops and says:
"Pranab, we are living in the twentieth century."
"I know that, Apu. But you know and I know that certain things have not changed in this country. . . ."
"But I have changed," says Apu grimly.
"I am asking you as a friend. As my best friend."
"Go away, Pranab. I don't want to hear any more of this."

Pranab's hopes are dashed. He turns and walks away, hurt beyond words. . . .

Outside, it is getting darker.
Apu has slowly approached the house.
He seems to be tormented by an inner struggle.
He watches the groom's party leaving, brass band and everything.

Among the other things Apu notices, or senses, is the crying of a child. He sees Pulu, and calls him. Apu agrees to marry Aparna.
In portraying Apu, Soumitra Chatterjee felt Apu to be the image of the contemporary Indian man in the process of becoming modern. He considered that the final phase of Apu's biography epitomized the predicament of young men beset by conflicting problems. It seemed to Chatterjee that the sound of the child crying, which is repeated in different situations in the film, was a very important symbol. He found half of himself in Apu. "We"—meaning his own generation—"can identify with him." He added that plenty of young men who saw the film came to him and remarked "I would like to marry".

Because Apu's feelings were deeply rooted a traditional concept could prevail with him despite his modern attitudes. In the original novel, at the moment of Pulu asking Apu to marry Aparna, Apu was enamoured by a girl he knew in Calcutta. Ray eliminated this aspect from the film. It is, in fact, still not too uncommon in India for a younger brother to step into the place of his older brother if the older brother has been involved in the negotiations for a marriage but later finds the girl unsuited to his taste. The younger one steps in as a gesture of traditional courtesy so that the girl and her family may not feel injured. Such a case was related to me by Prithwish Neogy after we had both seen *Apur Sansar*. The brothers involved were a scientist and an Air Force pilot—outwardly very modern men.

Apu and Aparna, brought together as husband and wife through the forces of astrology, stand arrayed in their bridal attire on either side of their wedding bed. Apu, the man who lives in poverty in twentieth-century Calcutta, has saved the girl. Now he seeks to save her from a hard life for which she is unprepared. He tries to explain his position and suggests she should remain with her parents until he has found work and can support her. Aparna, who is profoundly touched by Apu's gesture, insists that she will go with him to Calcutta. (Pl. XVII)

Sharmila Tagore, fourteen at the time she portrayed Aparna, endowed the girl not only with loveliness but, as the next sequences reveal, a great deal of character. It is the brief episode of love in the dingy Calcutta flat which has evoked much attention. Love is depicted as growing naturally from propinquity. Aparna's gorgeous bridal sari glistens against the tenement staircase walls with the only too visible cracks. A child squats on the landing. The woman at her sewing machine turns a casual eye upon them. They enter Apu's room. While Apu is absent for a moment, Aparna looks out of the window with its curtain full of holes. Her tears well up. Below, near the railway tracks, she notices a woman with a child, playing and laughing. They are much worse off than Apu and herself. This gives her courage. (Pl. XVIII)

Their awakening the next morning, side by side, on the bed with Aparna detaching herself to begin work, and Apu finding her hairpin and fondling it as he speaks to her, is one of the few scenes in cinema where one can believe that these two people have actually had intercourse and come to know one another as man and wife. There is a sense of a bond growing between them. They are relaxed with one another as only those who have come together can be.

The subsequent scenes of Apu and Aparna's married life—brief as they are—radiate a joyousness. She is perfect in her attention to his needs, playfully gay when she bursts a paper bag at him, and rather shames him when she weeps at the grotesquely bad mythological film to which they go together. During the short months, Apu teaches his chance-wife to read and write. Finally, she confesses she is pregnant and they decide she must return home to have the baby. Apu takes her to the station. But the last words she speaks to him from the train are lost in the din.

Aparna's letters come to the love-hungry Apu. They help him to endure the dullness of his office work, though they distract his efficiency. Travelling home to his attic he tries to read her latest letter in an overcrowded tram. The solid stare of a bulky passenger jabs Apu into self-consciously stuffing Aparna's letter into his pocket only to read it, hearing her voice, as he wanders along the railway tracks to reach his flat. Their love play reaches through the words: "You promised me eight notes last month, I had only seven. I can't trust you." He folds the letter tenderly and walks with jaunty steps towards the flat. The child Aparna saw from the window on the first day there strays across the tracks to be saved by Apu who picks him up and restores him to his mother living in a tin hut.

Upstairs, with the joy of Aparna's letter still tingling his nerves, Apu finds Murari, his brother-in-law:

> Apu stops dead. Murari looks unusually tense.
> "Murari . . . ?"
> Murari stares blankly.
> Apu is tense too, and apprehensive.
> "Come here." (Pl. XVII)
>
> Murari approaches, his head lowered.
> "What's the matter?"
> Murari looks up. He is making a great effort to speak.
> "How is Aparna?"
> Murari's lips tremble.
> "What's the matter?"
> "Premature . . . delivery. . . ."
> "How's Aparna?"
> Murari shakes his head, lowers it.
> A violent tremor grips Apu. Shaking, gritting his teeth, he suddenly, involuntarily, gives Murari a stinging ruthless slap which sends the boy reeling.

"I sat for days thinking what Apu would do," Satyajit said. "I couldn't think of him doing anything but hit Murari."

This is the incident which people in Bengal, and India in general, still dispute about. Many people cannot accept it as in keeping with their Indian concept of Apu's character. The slap is not in the novel. Individual objections found an echo in some reviews. *The Hindusthan Standard* critic claimed: "The whole incident too will appear shocking to many, as it runs counter to the author's original conception of the character. In this connection it may also be mentioned that other deviations from Bibhuti Bhusan Bannerjee's novel have hardly improved the film." Virtually, the same words appear in the Bengali language newspaper *Ananda Bazar Patrika*.

The most likely explanation for the disquiet this scene caused in India is that it jolted not only a streak of sentimentality, but the traditional image of Indians as non-violent. Under the stress of great feeling, emotional people—and Apu is—are the people who hit out blindly in life and hurt when they are hurt themselves.

From this point, and for a period of several years, Apu, having pulled back from throwing himself under a train, wanders the country in desolation. He even flings the pages of his novel to the winds. Apu's life has been dogged by death, commencing with that of the loving old Indir. Intense sorrow and loneliness possess him. He saw Durga, his sister die, his father die and never spoke a last word to his mother.

At last, Apu's friend, Pulu, aware of the mournful neglect of the bright but resentful child, Kajal, who vents his frustrations in shooting at birds, hunts Apu down. Here a blasted tree is a background reflection of Apu's arid state. Finally, he is induced to return to see the son he has shunned. Now it is Apu who has to bear the consequences of his own neglect—to have stones thrown at him by the boy who refuses to believe he is his father. Kajal has created his own image of an ideal father. Each nearly loses the other, and a chance for each of a new start. But Kajal is a daring little boy and runs after the stranger to say he will go with him to find his father.

The comment was made that Kajal was largely the creation of Satyajit Ray rather than the author, Bannerjee's. Whatever transformation the boy's character underwent, it can be explained by the unique relationship between Ray and his own son, Sandip. They are friends, almost inseparable, rather than father and son.

Despite arguments about the deviations from the novel, the film was a success in Bengal. That it should win the President's Gold Medal seemed a foregone conclusion from the moment it was seen.

But trouble came from the Venice Film Festival. In 1957, at the time of the *Aparajito* award, Ray had announced that he was going to make *Apur Sansar* as the third part of the Trilogy. A verbal understanding was given that if he did, *Apur Sansar* would be shown competitively. Ray went ahead and completed the film in time. *Apur Sansar* was summarily rejected on the grounds of its similarity to its two predecessors. It seems—a suspicion confirmed by the newspaper reports of the time—to have been the policy of the Festival's director, F. L. Ammannati, to favour Italian films. In fact, Roberto Rossellini's *Il Generale della Rovere* and Mario Monicelli's *La Grande Guerra* shared the first prize, though neither film was actually complete. Rossellini revealed that a week before the awards were decided he had been asked whether he was prepared to share the prize with Monicelli.

The London Film Festival, normally devoted to films which have won festival awards, decided by way of protest to invite *Apur Sansar* as the film to have the Place of Honour, inaugurate the Festival, and receive the largest number of screenings. *Apur Sansar* won the Sutherland Award for "the most original and imaginative film first shown to a British audience at the National Film Theatre".

From this point *Apur Sansar* commenced its international commercial career. While it may not have been reviewed further afield than the first and second film of the Trilogy, the reviews which reached Ray came from more countries. It is the Apu trilogy which has been seen by the greatest number of people both in India and abroad. Though the Trilogy demonstrates Ray's development and ranges from his lyrical pastoral to an urban style, the three films are but an aspect of the body of work which becomes a study in contrasts.

Amita Malik, reviewing the March 1960 Trilogy Festival in Delhi for the *Sunday Statesman*, concluded that "each film has been a growth in directorial stature; if Ray was in love with his first lyrically young film, in the second it was more adult and mature, an altogether far more seasoned director who made no compromises whatsoever and refused to let himself be carried away into the softness which might have tempted another director. The final act, in *Apur Sansar*, is a restrained, deliberate bit of work. it comes firmly to grips with reality, and yet does so with that tenderness and humanity which first moved the international jury at Cannes."

Probably the most remarkable reaction to *Apur Sansar* was that of James Powers, reviewing the film for the tough *Hollywood Reporter*. He said: "It is good for Hollywood to see a film of this sort and of this success. Made with little more than a camera and imagination, it is a reminder that our great technical improvements are often priceless assets. It is a reminder also that they should remain assets, not be treated as fundamentals, and that the chief ingredient of any film is still the intangible genius of its maker."

Finally, Edward Harrison, with his deep enthusiasm for the *Pather Panchali* Trilogy, decided to screen all three films on one programme in New York lasting five and a half hours with two breaks for coffee. This, of course, gave the Trilogy a chance to be seen as a unified work. As someone said, this Trilogy put Satyajit Ray on the level with "the Russian greats". While each can stand apart as a separate and distinctive creative act, each film gains when it is seen as part of the whole.

In 1960, the first American homage to Satyajit Ray was presented at the University of California, at Berkeley, by Albert Johnson. This Ray programme included the United States premières of *Jalsaghar* and *Devi*.

অবনীন্দ্রনাথ ঠাকুর

রাজ কাহিনী

Satyajit (title-page for Abanindranath Tagore's *Raj-Kahini*)

Chapter 7

THE ZAMINDAR FILMS—*JALSAGHAR, DEVI* AND *MONIHARA*

HAD Satyajit Ray been concerned with the financial gain rather than the preservation of his creative integrity he would have utilized the fame the Apu Trilogy brought him to become a 'national' rather than regional Indian director. It would have been infinitely more profitable to him to do so. He could have accepted to direct films with dialogue in Hindi. Had he done so, he would have secured a nationwide commercial release for his films beyond the borders of Bengal. But he rejected this course to avoid the imposition of Hindi film conventions upon his work. He paid for this liberty by accepting restricted release outside Bengal. Alternatively, as a modification of this course, Ray might have agreed to the dubbing of his dialogue into Hindi. This, too, he has rejected except in the case of the two-story film *Kapurush-o-Mahapurush* (*The Coward and the Holy Man*), which he would classify as one of his secondary works.

Ray's rejection of the easy method of capturing a larger Indian audience is due to his essentially aesthetic sense which causes him to dislike the dubbing of dialogue into a different language. Moreover, he has persistently stated that his knowledge of Hindi is insufficient for him to direct a film with Hindi dialogue. The nuances of speech are most important to him: "Film dialogue must have the feel of lifelike speech, as opposed to literary and dramatic speech. Then only can it have the true plastic quality which can enhance a film instead of stultifying it." Ray has insisted that he knows no community except that of his own Bengal with the required intimacy to portray it in depth. Only one story laid beyond Bengal has strongly attracted him—E. M. Forster's *A Passage to India*.

On the basis of the Apu Trilogy many people, especially in India, formed the mistaken impression that Satyajit Ray's predominant concern was the depiction of financially impoverished people. This is an inaccurate view of his work, even if Ray's sympathies veer towards poor and ordinary people rather than the rich. In contrast to impoverishment, the opulent Bengali zamindar society of the nineteenth and early twentieth centuries has fascinated Ray.

This society of landlords on their large, medium or small estates has exerted a powerful and complex influence upon the history and culture of Bengal. Landowners changed with the change of rulers. Whenever land tenure came into a state of flux most land-owners were pressing if not harsh landlords. By the middle of the Victorian era the refined culture associated with zamindar life assumed an ideal image in the Bengali imagination. This was enhanced by the fact that many eminent Bengalis came of zamindar origin; for example, Raja Rammohan Roy and generations of the Tagore family. The famed minority employed their wealth and leisure to further reform as well as patronage of learning and the arts. Satyajit's grandfather, Upendrakishore Ray, was a personification of the ideal zamindar.

Though Satyajit never experienced the life of a zamindari, it is natural that he should be attracted to investigate the psychology of zamindars. He has explained that all his films are "concerned with the new versus the old". This being his point of view, the zamindar is, of necessity, a symbol of the past and not the present.

Ray has explored aspects of zamindar society in three films depicting different periods: *Jalsaghar* (*The Music Room*), represent-

K

ing the 1920s with a central conflict not dissimilar to that in John Galsworthy's play *The Skin Game*. Ray commenced work on this film in 1957 shortly after completing *Aparajito*. *Devi (The Goddess)*, made in 1959, traces the cause and effect of a religious obsession on a zamindar of the 1860s who dreams that his young daughter-in-law is the incarnation of the goddess Durga. *Monihara*, laid in the 1890s, is based on a short story by Rabindranath Tagore called *The Lost Jewels*. Ray made it in the early months of 1961 as one of the trio of stories forming the Tagore Anniversary film, *Teen Kanya (Three Daughters)*. The three films explore the obsessions which dominate and bring disaster to people living within the enclosed world of zamindar society. In two of the films, the situations could not arise outside a world of luxury.

The action in all three films is concentrated within a magnificent zamindari house. Studio sets were almost exclusively used. Western influence by way of clothes and furnishings are powerfully evidenced, for it was the zamindar class that adopted the outward embellishments of European life to enhance the comfort of an excess of elegant repose. Objects, possessions, people these three films almost to the degree of becoming characters.

Though the respective periods of the films are carefully preserved as to detail, the relationships established between the characters has not substantially changed its essence. Indian life in general is multitudinous in effect where there is not much money. People live crowded together; there are relations and friends coming and going. (The neighbours come in to give advice as in *Pather Panchali*.) But, even today, if the lives of the rich are examined their actual mode of living is frequently wrapped about with a subtle sense of isolation. People of status quite often exist in a remarkably cocooned state within a very small circle beyond their own relatives. Isolation surrounded by inanimate objects is shown in Ray's zamindar films to be the setting for ruinous obsessions. No one in these films has any constructive work to occupy them, except for Umaprasad, the intelligent younger son in *Devi* who has escaped the bondage of superstition but is nevertheless powerless to save his wife.

A short story by Tarashankar Bannerjee serves as the base for *Jalsaghar*. The proudly aristocratic Biswambhar Roy inured against the realities of his financial decline is obsessed by the compulsion to compete with the upstart parvenu, Mahim Ganguly, who is impertinently encroaching upon him as a neighbour. Roy drives himself to ruin and death.

The situation has been universal where members of the aristocracy have been unable to adjust to social change. During the 'twenties English prototypes of the zamindar Roy were unwillingly compelled to close up half of their ancestral homes. Everywhere there have been those who lived on overdrafts until nothing was left, while everywhere, except perhaps in communist countries, the repulsively vulgar Gangulys have spread themselves indifferent to all snubs.

In England the thing to do in the 1920s, if you were the *nouveaux riches*, was to get your daughter presented at Court. In Bengal, the holding of a fabulous *jalsa*—musical soirée—still epitomized a similar belonging to, or entry into the class of the élite. Thus, the music room with the three *jalsas* held in it mark three stages in the exhaustion of Roy's financial reserves. While passion for music may appear to Roy as the main thread binding the episodes of his life together, it could be pride in what the grandeur of the music room itself signifies that has exerted a lifelong hypnotic influence upon him. The final culmination is his death through reckless impulse as an escape from penury.

Jalsaghar's first shots establish the atmosphere of decay which has been creeping upon the zamindar, Biswambhar Roy, throughout his life. Aging and dilapidated, he sits mummified on his roof terrace in an ornate chair singularly unsuited to use outdoors. The impression of grey listlessness is conveyed. When the shabby retainer approaches Roy with a hookah (the emblem of pleasure for the old and ineffectual in Ray's films), the zamindar enquires vaguely what month it is. For a moment he seems senile. Then the implication emerges that alone, enclosed by a vast house and the neglected wasteland of his estate, there is nothing alive for Roy to care for beyond a useless elephant and a now unridden white horse. Roy has no anchorage to time or reality except memories which explain the vacuum in which this aristocratic last representative of a profligate line exists in loneliness induced by pride and thoughtlessness as to consequences. His wife and only son are dead.

In flashback he is shown as seemingly a very different man on the day his only son was to be invested with the triple thread of his Brahmin caste. It was to be celebrated with a *jalsa*. That man, the upstart Ganguly, whose family had served the Roys, dared to come with an invitation! The impudence that money breeds! The contest in assertion of status—the inherited versus that gained through business enterprise—commences. Roy and Ganguly become locked in a contest in equal contempt for one another. The coarse Ganguly has lodged himself like a thorn that will fester within the aristocrat who cannot cope with the strident business world trespassing upon his domain.

Behind the glittering façade of the *jalsa* with its classical singer in honour of the thread ceremony, and the company of zamindars lolling with their drinks on comfortable pillows, is the worried steward who has sold a portion of the Roy jewels to pay for this musical embellishment. Roy's wife, patiently waits in her room for the *jalsa* to end, women not being permitted to attend except as performers.

This first performance establishes the music room as the dominating central focus of Roy's inherited way of life in which he is petrified. The vast room itself is the microcosm of the enclosed, leisured, luxurious society of inherited privilege which Ganguly is determined to blast his way into as his lorries hint the ruthless energy of his activities in the distance.

Of the furniture for Chandragupta's very large set—it had been difficult to find the suitable objects, particularly when there had not been the money to buy what was required—an enormous mirror, a magnificent chandelier, and a huge carpet loaned by a Tagore, were introduced as active elements in the creation of atmosphere which would subsequently be intensified with the help of these objects.

The first *jalsa*, visually and tonally, is one of unalloyed delight. It is only when Roy weaves slightly tipsily into his wife's room after the *jalsa* has ended that the shadow we have seen lengthened over Roy at the beginning of the film becomes an anxious hint. The next day his wife is to leave with their son to visit her father who lives across the river. She begs her husband to exert more prudence where money is concerned.

He would no doubt wish to take his wife's advice. But left alone, with his wife and son away, he grows infuriated when he hears that the vulgar Ganguly, now his offensive neighbour, is about to compete with him in the holding of a *jalsa*. This forces him to embark on further lavish expenditure. His steward endeavours to warn him but to no effect. Ganguly arrives offering his invitation. Roy, without thought for his own financial self-interest, flings at Ganguly that he will be holding another *jalsa* to honour those who honour him.

Again more jewels must be sold to pay for this second performance where a classical male Muslim singer will take the place of the woman who sang at the first. The zamindar sends word to his wife to return with their son. Just as he is about to go and receive his guests, he notices that a small ivory boat on a chiffonier has overturned. He stands the ornament upright.

From the first note, the long song has a tone of anguish. The voice ever mounts in intensity as the camera searches the enthralled face of the bearded Muslim singer (or rather that of the actor who impersonates the singer). It is a striking face conveying suffering. The singer links together a mosaic of images constructed both as counterpoint to the song itself and as tension presaging and accompanying the unseen tragedy for Roy which is being enacted beyond the brightness of the room lit by the many-candled chandelier. Beyond in the darkness, a storm is rising over the river.

Engrossed in the music, the guests notice nothing. The huge mirror reflects the avid attention of the gentlemanly zamindars. Only the host becomes conscious of the wind. From his expression, thoughts of his wife and son stir him to unease. He knows they are crossing the river in obedience to his will. The chandelier stirs from the rising gusts of wind heralding a gale. The wind's rising ferocity penetrates into the music room. There is no way to bar out the presence of storms as they lash into the houses of India. The swaying of the chandelier becomes the measuring rod of the storm's violence.

The zamindar glances at his wine glass. An insect is struggling in it. It is both a symbol and a realistic image, for insects rush into the houses of Bengal when a storm arises. They fall into glasses where they drown. Some critics found this too banal a symbol for the son and wife being drowned. But like the ivory boat overturned, the insect would be remembered in India as a premonition. Here is visualization of Indian thinking which seems intuitively true to the most natural thought. With the last notes of the impassioned song, Roy has intuitive knowledge of what has befallen his life.

In the pallid morning light he seeks the body of his son, who loved his father's white horse and elephant. Roy clings to these now useless animals in memory of the boy. He sinks into a deepening moribund state. Those he loved have perished solely because he commanded them to return. Nothing is left to him save his irritated pride. The insolent Ganguly is spreading his presence closer and closer with his damnable trucks and his humming dynamo. Yet Roy is impotent to check Ganguly, for he is becoming ever more impoverished while Ganguly becomes richer and richer. Only Roy's two old retainers remain. The music room is closed up.

The film comes full circle with Roy mouldering away towards final penury. Yet still pride compels him into one last bravado act. He must outdo Ganguly who, in a new gesture of defiance, has arranged a *jalsa* with a famous Kathak dancer.

In the original story, this dancer was the mistress of Biswambhar Roy. Ray eliminated this aspect of the zamindar's life. Some people attributed this to prudery on Ray's part.

"I left it out because it was melodramatic. Its elimination makes the film more austere," was Satyajit Ray's explanation, which seems a valid one.

The obsession to humiliate, or at least compete once more with Ganguly, ignites the will of Roy to hold one last *jalsa* to vindicate all he has ever stood for. The famous Kathak dancing girl must be engaged for the evening.

Carried away with enthusiasm the two loyal servants open up the vast salon, polish the dusty, clouded mirror, unroll the carpet and light the chandelier as of old. Ganguly arrives with his bag of coins, weighing them pleasurably in his hand as the dancer's feet commence their rhythmic pattern on the marble floor.

Faces are watched by the camera, which turns back to the dancer and revolves again to the guests—to Ganguly with his pouch of money; to Roy who leans forward. The camera stares at the mirror which reflects everything. At one moment, the only movement to be seen in the mirror is the faint flutter of the hand-operated *punkah*. The zamindar drinks more and more as the dancer twirls and her feet pat ever faster on the patterned floor in their ever-changing rhythm. The sensuality of the dance with its rhythm of coition prepares for the climax—Roy's absurd purchase of what he supposes to be triumph over Ganguly. He presents the dancer with the bag containing his very last reserve. (Pl. XIX)

The elation persists beyond the departure of the guests, leaving the music room strewn only with the round white pillows traditional to the performance of music. There is only Roy wrapped in the haze of drink and his servant hovering around him. The ancestral portraits call up the family past as Roy lurches about, talking nostalgically of what for him is gone for ever. Finally, he stands before his own picture, on which a spider is crawling.

It is open to question whether this intrusion of a spider, acceptable from a naturalistic point of view, is not too artificial and obvious as a symbol. It was a temptation which should have been withstood when the interpretation of the degenerated Roy by Chhabi Biswas spoke for itself without the need for such a visual aid.

As the dawn impinges upon the psychological dusk shrouding Roy, the candles flicker. Still intoxicated and enmeshed in his illusion of triumph, the zamindar orders his white horse to be saddled for him to ride. Arrayed as in his earlier days when he customarily rode the horse, the half-demented man, who has driven himself to a dead end through divorce from realities, mounts and gallops towards the river. At the sight of an upturned boat the horse rears. Roy falls backwards and his turban rolls and unfurls on the sand.

This shot, powerful and true to the film's style, provided a significant close to a mismanaged life. But Ray allowed a subsequent shot to soften Roy's end to the verge of sentimentalism. The end is that of the two servants lamenting over the body of their master. However true to the feelings of old servants, these shots disturb the austerity of an otherwise uncompromising film.

In the context of Indian cinema, including the previous styles developed in Bengal, the most uncompromising aspect of *Jalsaghar* was Ray's use of the strictly classical music of the noted sitar player, Ustad Vilayat Khan, in place of the more fluid musical approach of Ravi Shankar who had collaborated on the music for the Apu Trilogy.

The concept and presentation of the two long classical songs and Kathak dance which provide the focusing sequences of the film challenged the whole convention of songs and dances in Indian cinema. Audiences in India conditioned to the introduction of songs and dances as entertainment interludes and dramatic and romantic stresses, had never before been confronted with a similiar presentation to Ray's: classical singing and dancing as integral focal points of realistic sequences integral to the development of the story. Ray had not deviated from the re-creation of the atmosphere of the traditional *jalsa*.

Many Indian critics, bewildered by the style, were lukewarm about the film. It was not a conspicuous commercial success. Like *Paras Pather*, Ray's first satirical film which it followed, *Jalsaghar* called for appreciation of a very sophisticated kind. However, it won the year's Certificate of Merit as the second best Indian feature film. The award brought the producer, Ajit Bose, the prize of Rs.10,000 with Rs.2,500 being awarded to Satyajit Ray. The Gold Medal went to another Bengali film, *Sagar Sangamey*, directed by the veteran Debiki Bose. For three years in succession Bengali films had captured the top national awards.

It was not until June of 1959 that *Jalsaghar* could be seen beyond the borders of Bengal. Then it was screened in Bombay only on Sunday mornings. A few months later, the film was sent to the Moscow Film Festival. No Russian reviews reached Satyajit Ray. But someone reporting the Festival for the American *Saturday Review* wrote glowingly of *The Music Room* as "quite simply, a remarkable, even great film, made with subtlety, beauty, and maturity found only rarely in any art form".

Coming early in Ray's career, *Jalsaghar* contradicted many of the assumptions drawn from the impressions made by *Pather Panchali* and *Aparajito* as to Ray's approach. The film indicated that Ray was not as first supposed a successor to Robert Flaherty drawn to lyrical subjects lending themselves to the maximum in location shooting.

There were rather few scenes shot on location in *Jalsaghar*, as indeed in the case of all his zamindar films. It was not realized that Ray was inimical to directing similar films in succession; that his interest lay "in many aspects of life, many periods in history, many styles and many genres of film making". It was too easily assumed that he was hostile to the use of professional actors. Ray, naturally reticent, did not broadcast the ideas that lay behind his film-making. Not until 1966 did he clearly state that he wrote the scripts of *Jalsaghar*, *Devi*, and his own story for *Kanchenjunga*, with the well-known professional actor, the late Chhabi Biswas, in mind.

Ray was able to utilize effectively the urbane star actor atmosphere which was part of Biswas' personality for the central characters in these three films.

Devi (The Goddess) evoked considerable controversy in India. But for Ray's script being based on the story by a Hindu and not a Brahmo author—the late Prabhat Kumar Mukherjee—the attacks made upon the film might well have been more personally abusive towards Ray as a Brahmo. For a time, *Devi* embarrassed the Union Government and resulted in a disinclination to send the film abroad.

Numerous officials thought it distasteful that India's most noted director should choose a theme which the Government regarded as outmoded. That the theme of a zamindar dreaming in the 1860s that his younger daughter-in-law is an incarnation of the goddess Durga was not outmoded was proved about a fortnight after Ray announced the subject. A young village wife in Western India was declared to be the incarnation of a minor local deity. Her parents-in-law were convinced and word of the girl as a *devi* began to spread. Thousands of people, as thousands will flock anywhere in the world at the report of a miracle, streamed into the village to see the girl and take *darshan* of her. A stampede resulted and a number of people were trampled to death.

Ray's theme of the idea of a deity incarnate in spirit within the body of a human being living today or a thousand years ago, has been an engrained aspect of Hindu thought. The dual mother goddesses, Kali-Durga, wives of Shiva, Lord of Destruction, have ever absorbed intense religious emotions within Bengal. Even in the latter part of the last century, the holy man, Ramakrishna, now the deity of a sect, declared his wife to be Kali incarnate.

Those people who were to condemn *Devi* as an attack upon religion itself, as opposed to an examination of superstition, did not enquire about the views of Satyajit Ray. Had they done so, they could have learned that he holds no aversion to celebrating the traditional religious festivals of Hinduism. He is not a strict Brahmo who continues to condemn the worship of deity figures. As an artist appreciative of Indian culture, Ray sees the beauty in such worship. But he rejects dogma.

He has said: "Until Man can create life himself, I am prepared to believe in the Sages and that there is a central Intelligence within the Universe."

The family attitudes which emerge in *Devi* were common in nineteenth-century Bengal when the confrontation of Hindu ortho- doxy and rational reformism was at its most intense. This conflict had entered the zamindar class from which, as the Ray family history reveals, many reformers sprang. *Devi* embodies through its characters the conflict between the acceptance of orthodox Hindu superstitions and the growth of scepticism and revolt. The father, Kalikanker Roy, dominating his eldest son, Taraprasad, represents Hindu orthodoxy which has ceased to be credible to the younger son, Umaprasad, studying in Calcutta and influenced by the rational Professor Sarkar, the advocate of reformist thought. Harisundari, the elder daughter-in-law, is betwixt and between acceptance of orthodoxy and reasoning rejection. She is a rational woman, but her emotional reactions to Daya, her young sister-in- law, are ambiguous in that her child's love for Daya is a cause for some jealousy. Harisundari might be able to accept in principle the possibility of a deity becoming incarnate; but not in the case of Daya who at first is a great deal more lively and human than herself. Jealousy breeds reservation as well as reason.

As the opening shots of *Jalsaghar* established the mood of decay which holds the zamindar in thraldom, so the opening sequence of *Devi* reveals the dominating, fervid religiosity of Kalikanker Roy, a zamindar of the more stable social period of the 1860s. Chhabi Biswas as the zamindar watches the incense-shrouded Durga Puja, the autumn festival, as if in near trance. It is immediately evident that he is an enthralled devotee of the Divine Mother, one intoxi- cated with faith.

Still, today, this festival honouring the Durga aspect of the Divine

Woman, with Durga conceived as the slayer of a demon symbolic of evil, is enacted with intense fervour wherever there are Bengalis. Even in modern Delhi dozens of Kali-Durga figures are carried in procession to the river and there submerged as night descends. Though there is a powerful terror element in both Durga and Kali, and there was a time when their thirst for blood was satisfied by human sacrifice now replaced by the flesh of a goat, the worship is emotionally comparable to the Madonna cult of the Catholic Church.

The *puja* night in *Devi* with its heated sense of expectancy, is succeeded the next day by a villager carrying his sick child to the steps of the Roy zamindar house where he sings a prayer for aid to the image of Durga standing within the Roy household shrine. The goddess dominates the house. But for the moment everything within is still normal, even sweet and gay because the charming young Umaprasad and his sixteen-year-old wife, Dayamoyee, are enchanted with each other. Ray, creating his second variation on the theme of marital intimacy, presents them happily in their bed as the clock strikes one.

Daya says: "The days seem so long when you are away."

"But you shall have plenty to do," says Umapada, "reading my letters, and writing yours. I have addressed all the envelopes for you."

"How many?"

"Fifty. By the time you finish them I'll be back for Christmas."

"Christmas. . . . That's a long way off."

After a little thought Daya says: "Can't you take me to Calcutta with you?"

Umapada knows that Daya isn't serious. He says: "You couldn't live without Prodyumna, could you?" [his little nephew].

Daya pretends to ponder a while and says: "No. I don't think I could. It's a pity that. . . ."

Daya stops.

"Yes?"

"That he isn't our own son. . . ."

The two look meaningfully at each other, and the scene dissolves. (Pl. XX)

But for the young husband (played by Soumitra Chatterjee, the matured Apu) leaving Daya (Sharmila Tagore, the Aparna of *Apur Sansar*), the ghastly fate of Daya could not develop.

Daya is the sunshine and warmth in this goddess-dominated house with the paterfamilias's religiosity turned to drunkenness in his elder son whose wife, Harisundari, despises him. The parrot cheerfully calls "Daya! Daya!" from its perch while the loving little nephew desires to sleep in enchanting young Auntie's bed. Yet for all her liveliness, once Umaprasad has gone, the pliable Daya is seen as the devout devotee of the Durga-Kali image in the household shrine. It is here that her goddess-enthralled father-in-law is first shown in direct contact with Daya. The sound of his lame tread (he is lame from a hunting accident in which he would, he thinks, have died but for the goddess's protection) is heard like a slow hammering foretelling doom, before he is seen overshadowing Daya from behind.

Though the likeness is slight between the soft devout face of the worshipping Daya and the traditional image of the staring Durga, to a goddess-obsessed imagination they could resemble one another. Kalikanker Roy, alone, with a garland strung about the picture of his dead wife, is an entranced father-in-law.

Ray inserts a further subtle scene, termed by him "the Freudian angle", which quietly registers the source of the dream translating the image of Kali-Durga, and imposing it upon the face of Daya.

Kalikanker reclines in a chair covered with a tiger skin, his foot outstretched on a stool. The angle of the camera is suggestive of a vitality relaxed in luxury and the sensual pleasure of ease. Daya, with her head covered in respect of her husband's father, comes softly into the room. Nothing is more common in India than for an older man or woman to have their feet massaged either by a servant or a younger member of the family. Therefore, with the naturalness of her youth, Daya sits down, with her back to the camera, and softly massages her father-in-law's injured foot. There is nothing overt, except perhaps the abandon to comfort of his posture, to suggest that this goddess-absorbed man has any conscious will to worship, possess and dominate his son's wife, no matter how tenderly pleasurable is the massaging touch of her hand. Awake he directs his sublimated passions in worship of the Divine Mother. (Pl. XX)

That night, asleep in the room where the garlanded picture of his dead wife stands below a picture of the Divine Mother, the zamindar's thoughts of Durga and the tender touch of Daya become confused in his dream of Kali-Durga's face. The third eye of the goddess image becomes the *tilak* mark on Daya's forehead; the hypnotic eyes of the goddess transform themselves into the eyes of the innocent Daya. (Pl. XXI)

Half-awake, dazed, unquestioningly convinced that this is revelation of Durga's incarnation in Daya, Roy flings himself out of bed. Staggering towards Daya's room, he mutters "Ma! Ma!"—Mother! Mother! which is a word in Bengali frequently used beyond the conventionally accepted English meaning. Taraprasad and his wife, Harisundari, emerge from their room. Daya comes out to receive the shock of her esteemed father-in-law falling at her feet to touch them in abject worship. Her weak, degenerate brother-in-law imitates his father.

Revolted, instinctively Daya's nails scratch on the wall beside her door, her toes curling away in revulsion. At this instant she knows she is human and possessed by no spirit of a goddess. Yet the next day it is beyond this very young girl to resist the now fanatic will of her father-in-law. No one in this house openly questions the zamindar's dream. He enshrines Daya as a *devi* with his priests obediently conducting worship of her. Only she has some awareness of the appalling predicament her father-in-law has forced upon her. Garlanded, her face is ravished by doubt. Still she is too young, too bound to tradition, to assert a will of self-preservation and escape before the hypnotizing effect of being worshipped sneaks away her sense of reality.

In all religions, women, either with seeming psychic powers or under the dominating influence of men, have been induced to espouse mediumistic stances, or hold themselves out as miracle workers. Communion with the unknown has haunted, and still haunts, certain people all over the world. *Devi* vividly depicts the reason for the struggle against orthodoxy in nineteenth-century Bengal.

Confused, bewildered, churned up by the conflicting emotions within her, Daya pathetically submits to the worship she lacks the power to halt. The overpowering clouds of incense cause her to faint. To the credulous, this fainting spell appears to be a state of trance. A trance is only further evidence of Daya being possessed of the goddess's spirit as the dominating Kalikanker Roy has claimed, trance being much revered by devotees of all religions.

Unhurriedly, with a restraint that is compassionate yet coolly impersonal, Ray unfolds, in shots of compelling beauty, the inevitable doom that has become Daya's fate. (Pl. XXI)

The sensible Harisundari, watching everything with increasing disbelief, makes no overt move towards Daya to aid her to hold on to her sense of human identity, though she can see the process by which from shot to shot, Daya's warmth and expressiveness become submerged by the isolation of worship. Soon Daya's face commences to assume the quality of an enigmatic mask hinting an increasing resemblance to the Durga image. This fearful transformation is marvellously conveyed by a subtle change in make-up. Harisundari, played with a quality of waiting pathos mixed with a standoffish dash of spite by Karuna Banerji, decides at last to write to Daya's husband to come home immediately. Ray breaks the tension by shifting to Calcutta where Umaprasad is living the life of the young Western-educated intellectual. He is seen at a theatrical performance where a scene of drunkenness looks like a madhouse.

Returning in a carriage to his lodgings, his friend discusses his desire to marry a widow and the trouble his parents are creating because this is again orthodox tradition. Umaprasad exclaims: "I'll come to your father and reason with him." Here a single sentence indicates how far he has moved away from orthodox beliefs. Entering his lodgings, he receives Harisundari's letter.

He reaches home one moment too late. Before he is able to speak to Daya, an apparent miracle has taken place because of her presence. The villager, seen at the beginning of the film, has brought his dying child to the feet of Daya. Kalikanker pleads with her to cure the boy. Ceremonial liquid is poured into the boy's mouth. The boy appears to revive. Umaprasad enters the house at the moment of exaltation.

A gulf yawns open between husband and wife. The alleged miracle, the *Sloka*-chanting priests, the crowds of worshippers and the will of his father hold Umaprasad at bay. He is seen waiting and wondering how to extricate Daya from the web of unreality woven around her. It is here that the role of the gleamingly polished opulent furniture plays its suffocating part in building up a claustrophobic isolation. The camera crawls around the young, rational husband hedged about by the massive symbols of the feudal luxury which has bred fanaticism. Religion ornamented by superstition has been the only outlet of the family who, throughout the film, have had no communication with the outside world. Except for Umaprasad, not one member has been seen outside the enclosing walls of the house.

Umaprasad at last manages momentarily to drag Daya from her trance-like state. He persuades her to leave the house with him to go to Calcutta. Only half aware, still isolated from full communication with her husband, she walks with him towards the river. It is a weirdly moonlit night with the vegetation appearing as if in a vision. The unearthliness of the light contributes to Daya's self-destructive reaction. As they almost reach the river where a boat is waiting to carry her away from the bondage of the nightmare created around her, she suddenly stops dead. She has noticed the skeletal structure of the Durga Puja figure submerged at the opening of the film. It has been washed up on the bank. The sight fills her with awed indecision. Perhaps she really *has* performed a miracle; perhaps she really *is* an incarnation of the Mother. She is seized with dread of going away with Umaprasad lest she bring destruction upon him. She pulls away from him insisting she must return to her father-in-law's house. His obsession has taken deeper hold on her than the reasoning of his son. Umaprasad returns to Calcutta, his rationalism defeated.

Daya, rejecting her chance to return to a normal life, sinks into a still deeper entranced state. Her enthronement shrouds her in oppressive isolation as larger crowds of worshippers come to take *darshan* of her, day by day. Between *pujas* she lies inert on her bed. The climax of the captivity of her own identity is the child, Prodyumna's reaction to her. He no longer comes near her, but one day his ball accidentally bounces across her threshold and into her room. The frightened child peeps in, makes a dash to rescue his ball and runs away. The parrot suddenly calls "Dayamoyee! Dayamoyee!"

A faint, reawakened recollection of the past comes to Daya. She rouses herself. She is lying on what had been her marriage bed. Memory of Umaprasad's letters breaks through her inertia. Tears come. The will to find the letters wells up. Filled with a returning normalcy of feeling, Daya gets up and goes to find her husband's letters. She notices the bird on its perch which she has long ignored and turns to speak to it as she did before the night her father-in-law declared her to be a *devi*.

Reading Umaprasad's letters still cannot save her because she does not wrench herself free from the paralysing submission to worship. So she is doomed, for the boy, Prodyumna, falls fatally ill. Harisundari sends surreptitiously for a doctor who, after seeing the child's state, declares that nothing short of a miracle can save his life.

Taraprasad, dominated by his father, grasps at the thought that Daya, having cured the village child, can surely cure the child she has loved. Father and grandfather, deaf to the reasonings of Harisundari, carry the dying child and lay him on Daya's lap, pleading that she perform another miracle.

Stunned, fearful of her own impotence, the girl sits pathetically holding the child. The mother, Harisundari, comes to the bedside. Her anxiety now forces an involuntary question. She asks Daya :

"Do you think you can cure him?" as if she, too, has come to believe that Daya is the goddess their father-in-law claims.

Daya has no power of any kind. She can do nothing for the child she loved. He dies on her lap. But this proof that she is only human fails to shock her back to reality.

Again, Ray breaks the tension. He counterpoints the miracle that does not happen with the cool and rational scene of Umaprasad in Calcutta seeking the opinion of the scientific-minded Professor Sarkar. He takes courage from this conversation and at once decides to return to the zamindari. The son, unaware of what has happened, confronts his father who now has a lost, almost demented look. Umaprasad asks where his wife is, only to be told "The child died. . . ."

"What child?"

"Khoka . . . Khoka is gone."

. . . "The Mother was wrathful. She took him. . . ."

Umaprasad brings all the venom he can into his voice:

"Nonsense! It's a lie! You killed the boy . . . You took his life. Don't blame it on the poor girl!"

"Poor girl? She was the Mother herself. . . ."

"Madness! Madness! . . ."

"But I saw her! I saw the Vision. I heard the words!"

"You saw nothing . . . You heard nothing! She is nothing but a human being!"

Kalikanker Roy collapses. The son looks unrelentingly at the sprawled figure and orders the doctor to be called. He goes in search of Daya and, horrifyingly, now finds her out of her mind arrayed as if she were the goddess. Both the human and mistaken divine image are now disintegrated. (Pl. XXII)

Up to this point, with the exception of the fervid atmosphere created for the opening Durga Puja, Ray's method for creating the strangeness arising first without and gradually within the very young girl unable to resist her father-in-law's obsession that she is a *devi*, was the tightest of control over any element that might suggest the macabre, the horrific, though both qualities are inherent in the situation. Kalikanker Roy is not an evil man; only one who cannot use reason to question himself and is totally unaware of his destructiveness. With deliberation Ray builds up his inevitable tragedy by imposing a dreadful quietness, a melancholy calm, especially in scenes focused on Daya. Her transformation is portrayed through the extinguishing of her animation which was her original charm. Ray used no lighting effects or camera angles, nor any startling cuts to emphasize a situation that is intensely dramatic. *Devi* could easily have become bizarre. Instead of heightening the drama, the camera was employed to contemplate approaching tragedy with accumulating solemnity.

Only for the moment when Umaprasad is confronted by the unbalanced Daya is light used to produce a strange and abnormal psychological effect. As if from the window the light strikes directly into the camera lens. (Pl. XXII)

Ray and Mitra had disagreed about this unusual lighting, Mitra insisting that such bright light streaming into the lens must blur the images of husband and wife. But Ray insisted they must attempt this effect even though it went against the normal rules of camera work. The glare produced the desired peculiar impression just before Daya, insane, runs out of the house and into a field of white flowers to be engulfed in thick white rolling mist.

The original last shot of Daya was to have shown her drowning as a parallel to the submerging of the Durga figure with which the Desserah festival at the opening of the film is climaxed. The drowning shot unfortunately was spoiled and could not be re-shot. In consequence another ending was resorted to—that of Daya dying near the river bank just as her husband reached her. This death scene left unexplained as to cause, was followed by the enigmatic smiling face of a Durga figure, a shot that also leaves speculative questions in the mind as to its meaning. Perhaps it can be said to be the agnostic's answer to questions about the unknown. The smiling goddess leaves the door open to the question, was Daya a form of human sacrifice to Kali-Durga? Or was Daya destroyed by Kali's *Shakti*, elemental energy? Ray seems to say: "I don't know. Perhaps . . . anything is possible. But do not let us have any bigotry about these things."

In 1960, when Ray's American distributor, the late Edward Harrison, arranged for *Devi* to be invited as an entry for the Cannes Film Festival, Ray reviewed the film and removed the shot of Daya's death. Thus revised, she is only seen rushing into the misty field before the final shot of the enigmatic goddess.

The reserve with which Ray handled his subject disturbed at least one Bengali critic. The *Hindusthan Standard* reviewer chided Ray, saying: "Instead of developing this story as a moving human drama, Satyajit Ray has given it a documentary treatment, taking meticulous care to capture the period and the locale in intimate details, but skipping over the dramatic moments in a calculated effort to bypass entanglements. . . . The artists . . . are hardly able to rise above the documentary limitations of the film's characters."

XVII
Apur Sansar (The World of Apu), 1959

Apu, the young man, Soumitra Chatterjee, in the opening scene. The time is early morning and it is the third shot: "The camera tilts down to reveal Apu asleep on a takaposh (wooden bed with thin mattress)." Note the detail of the overturned inkpot. Studio set

The bridal chamber. Apu, persuaded by his friend Pulu to take the place of the insane bridegroom on the astrologically propitious day for Aparna's (Sharmila Tagore) wedding, seeks to persuade her to stay with her parents until he obtains a job. Studio set

Sequence No. 6. Apu returning home finds his brother-in-law, Murari, waiting to tell him of Aparna's death in childbirth. Apu strikes Murari, a gesture that provoked great controversy. The roof terrace is a location shot

*Apu brings Aparna to his attic
room across the railway tracks.
Note the simulation of the wall in
the previous location shot and the
texture of Bansi Chandragupta's
wall*

*They come to the first floor where
the seamstress, Mrs. Ganguly, lives.
Note the use of vistas and compare
with the set for Mahanagar, Pls.
XLIX,L*

*They continue going up to the attic.
Note the use of garments obviously
used and the texture of the supposedly exposed brick on two of
the stair steps*

XIX
Jalsaghar (The Music Room).
1957–8

Chhabi Biswas as Biswambhar Roy the improvident landlord, bereaved and living in the past, at the beginning of the film. There is but one elephant left. The location shots were taken in Mushidabad, where Ray also shot certain scenes for his biographical film on Rabindranath Tagore; also for Devi, Samapti *and* Apur Sansar

The second jalsa—musical soirée—just before the storm rises to its crescendo. The chandelier and mirror are integrated almost like animate characters into the texture of the film

The final jalsa *where the now bankrupt Roy presents his last bag of coins to the Kathak dancer so as not to be outdone by his vulgar and new rich neighbour. This set was the largest designed by Chandragupta for any Ray film up to* Goupi Gyne, *1968*

XX Devi (The Goddess), 1959–60

*Sharmila Tagore as Daya and Soumitra Chatterjee as her husband, Umaprasad.
Sequence No. 1: "A clock strikes one.*
*Daya says: 'The days seem so long when you are away' . . . 'But you shall
have plenty to do,' says Umapada, 'reading my letters, and writing yours.
I have addressed all the envelopes for you.'*
'How many?'
'Fifty. By the time you finish them all I'll be back for Christmas.' "

*Chhabi Biswas as Daya's father-in-law, Kalikanker Roy. Sequence 2, Sixth
Scene: The angle and the posture of Roy suggests a suppressed eroticism as
Daya massages the injured foot of her father-in-law. "He says: 'When you
are in my presence, my dear, I feel a strange exaltation. Your face . . . ' "*
*This scene presages his dream that Daya is an incarnation of the Goddess
Durga. See next plate*

Daya enshrined by her father-in-law as an incarnation of the Goddess. Increasingly, Daya's face comes to resemble the images of Durga

XXI
A page from the script of Devi. Ray's visualisation of Kalikanker's dream. The traditional image of the Goddess Durga becomes the face of Daya

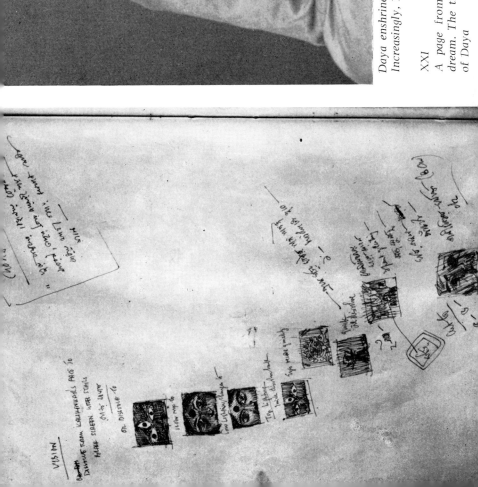

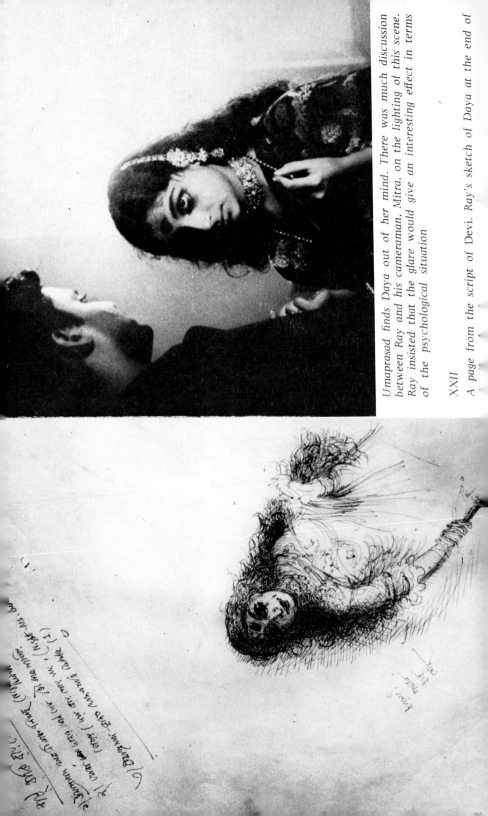

Umaprasad finds Daya out of her mind. There was much discussion between Ray and his cameraman, Mitra, on the lighting of this scene. Ray insisted that the glare would give an interesting effect in terms of the psychological situation

XXII

A page from the script of Devi. Ray's sketch of Daya at the end of

XXIII
Monihara (The Lost Jewels), 1961. One of the three Tagore stories composing Teen Kanya (Three Daughters)

A ghost story, the atmosphere is built up from the start through use of lighting, objects and camera movements. The action is concentrated in this hall, the large reception room (Pl. XXIV) and the bedroom

The indulgent husband, Phanibhushan, Kali Bannerjee, and his jewel-obsessed wife, Monimalika, Kanika Mazumdar, both actors being well known. Subrata Mitra was ill at the time, and the young cameraman, Soumendu Roy, took over to do a superb job. Objects, which early in the film appear perfectly ordinary, for example the vase, later take on a menacing aspect

The element of predatoriness present in the character of the frigid wife, Moni, is projected by the stuffed birds of prey incongruously juxtaposed with the baby doll which this childless woman keeps on the mirrored chiffonier. She, in turn, is the object of the predatory intentions of the mysterious Madhusudan, who arrives and asks for a job. The mirror is a recurring property in many of Ray's films. Compare this use with that in Pl. XIX in Jalsaghar and in Pl. XL in Abhijan

Moni asks Madhusudan, Kumar Roy, to take her with her jewels to her father's house across the river because she is afraid to journey alone. The composition includes the doll, which can be equated both with Moni's childlessness and her own childishness. The birds of prey now shift their connotation to the mystery man. Two of his subsequent gestures leave the visual impression that he intends to murder Moni for her jewels

The husband having returned anxiously waits for his wife to return. The tiger on the table and other objects now begin to become objects of terror

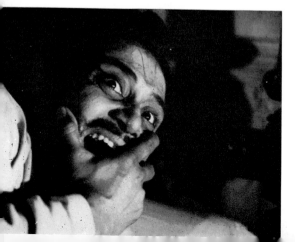

The final shot climaxing Phanibhushan's terror. This is the second place in the film where a hand's movement over a face is used with extreme effectiveness

XXV *Ray at work on the biographical film* Rabindranath Tagore, *1960–61*

Ray making cut-out figure representing Lord Curzon for the sequence covering the partition of Bengal and (above) the burning as it appears in the film

The newly arrived Postmaster, Anil Chatterjee, is visited by the harmless madman, who terrifies him. Ray added this character. The location village

The religious looking poster behind the frightened Postmaster is a warning against malaria. It foreshadows a coming reality for the Postmaster

The musical party interpolated into the story by Ray to visualize the literary description of the snobbishness of the Postmaster. All the players are non-professional. Compare this scene with that of the old men in Pather Panchali, *Pl. X*

The bored Postmaster having nothing to do begins to teach the orphan servant girl, Ratan, Chandana Banerji, a Calcutta schoolgirl of eleven, to read. Note the wall texture, and the effect of lighting suggestive of inspiration drawn from painting

XXVII

Ratan faithfully nurses the delirious Postmaster during malaria. When he first arrived, he hung the picture of his city family on the wall. The composition enlarges the implication of the illness: somewhere far off, the Postmaster is a member of a family. If he should die . . .

XXVIII
Samapti (The Conclusion), 1960–61

Mrinmoyee, Aparna Das Gupta, the village tomboy, watches the return of Amulya, the B.A., who slips in the mud. The daughter of the critic, Chidananda Das Gupta, Aparna, says that before Ray chose her, "I used to act Mrinmoyee in front of the mirror, imagining myself to be her." Playing in Samapti *led to Aparna Das Gupta choosing acting as a career. Note the textural background for the face*

Amulya, at the insistence of his mother, visits the house of a prospective bride. But in bounces Mrinmoyee to retrieve her escaped squirrel. Note how the pictures of King George V and Queen Mary comment upon the social background and attitudes of the prospective in-laws. Compare this use of pictures with the pictures of deities in Abhijan. *Pl. XL*

The bewildered bridegroom. Soumitra Chatterjee's comment on the character of Amulya: "I found I had grown up sufficiently so that I wanted to have a good laugh at myself and my adolescence."

XXIX Charulata, 1964
Page 9 of the shooting script

The opening sequence: Charu, Madhabi Mukherjee; Bhupati, Sailen Mukherjee. The year is 1879 Victorianism is evident in the door panels, the cut and material of Charu's blouse

Amal, Soumitra Chatterjee, Bhupati's cousin, becomes the companion of Charu, her sister-in-law being a coarse bore. "The bedroom scenes were dominated by the huge Victorian bed." Chandragupta

Bhupati, fired with intensity about British politics, and the nonchalant Amal. The decor reflects the acute British influence. "We were looking for a typical adaptation of the Victorian style house to Indian or more correctly to a Bengali style." Chandragupta

Amal, the inadvertent seducer
of his cousin's wife, Charu

Mutual literary competition
breeds love. The third of Ray's
musical motifs here emerges
as the audio correspondence
of love. It is based on the
Scottish air used by Tagore
for his song "Phooley
Phooley". Here it is softly
hummed by Charu

Amal echoes the Tagore song
"Phooley Phooley" as reconceived by Ray. Chandragupta:
"This pattern (for the wallpaper) was first designed and
then screen-printed. The
paper came in 30 in. × 40 in.
sheets and we pasted these on
to plywood finished walls. It
took a whole day and a night
just to stick the paper."

Bhupati's party. The English atmosphere gives way to an essentially traditional Bengali one. In the background, Charu's brother, played by Kumar Roy, awaits his moment to decamp with the contents of Bhupati's safe

In the office of Bhupati's printing works he realizes how his brother-in-law has ruined him, while Amal realizes he, too, has betrayed Bhupati by eliciting Charu's love. Bhupati's despondent disillusion is intensified by both the lighting and Ray's original music. This "motif is first heard with the first hint of the tragic outcome of the story." The motif, written for the lower strings, comes into its own in this scene

Charu's attempted reconciliation with her husband, Bhupati

Satyajit (poster for *Devi*)

This review is quoted because it indicates that Satyajit Ray's specific style which, in accord with his own temperament, is the art of understatement, is frequently misjudged in India on account of the general Indian film custom of portraying emotion with exaggerated stress. The attraction of melodrama, even in Bengal, is a paradox when restraint is customarily exercised among Indians, particularly among the middle-class who are the main filmgoers. It is as if the exaggeration on the screen affords a vicarious escape.

By contrast to this local reaction, Peter Lennon's views of the film in *The Guardian* are interesting: "There are hardly more than a dozen overt pictorial or verbal statements in the film, and yet

L

the characters of the protagonists, their relationships to each other, are unerringly caught. Although Ray's style is finely economic it is never dry. And even in the final agitated moments, when the son implacably accused his father there is no violence—only a quickening of the tempo and a harshness in the pictures which previously had such serene softness."

In one respect *Devi* brought Satyajit Ray to an impasse—in the question of music, which was of the utmost importance to him. Up to the completion of *Devi* only the three most creative musicians had worked with him: Ravi Shankar for the music of the Apu Trilogy and the ironic fantasy *Paras Pathar*; Ustad Vilayat Khan for *Jalsaghar*; and for *Devi*, Ali Akbar Khan.

Great musicians as these three are, none had proved entirely attuned to Ray's concept of music in relation to film, except Shankar in performing the music for *Pather Panchali*. Probably Ray's own knowledge of music, and the degree to which with each film he was developing his own musical ideas, made collaboration with professional musicians increasingly strained. He had become aware that to try to guide composers roused resentment. While Ali Akbar Khan's music for *Devi* cannot be said to be out of place, neither can it be considered to be inspired. Heard again and again, it becomes increasingly disappointing.

Musically, a turning point had been reached. With extensive knowledge of music, a phenomenal musical memory, yet no training as a musician, Ray reached the decision to attempt to compose his own music for his future films. He commenced with tentative efforts for *Teen Kanya*, for which *Monihara* was made.

Monihara, released in May 1961 as the middle film of the three-story Tagore Anniversary film, has had less attention paid to it than any of Ray's films. Up to 1967, the film had received only one screening abroad. On account of length it had been withdrawn from inclusion in *Teen Kanya* when that was sent abroad. *Three Daughters* became *Two Daughters*.

The film is discussed here, but mentioned later in connection with Ray's adaptation of Tagore stories, because, like *Jalsaghar* and *Devi*, the core of the story is an obsession and the society portrayed that of zamindars. The period is the last decade of the nineteenth century. *Monihara* is the only horror film that Ray has so far made and it deviates but slightly from the original story.

The presence of something macabre is introduced in the very first shot. The Narrator of the story, a dishevelled schoolmaster, comes stumbling distractedly through the overgrown garden of a rambling, mysterious house in the village of Manikpur. Nothing is shown of the village.

On sight, this man prompts the question, "Is he mad?" What is the matter with him? This question is given an ambiguous answer in the film's last shot; though the answer only raises yet another question about the horror story within a mystery story.

The schoolmaster, whom Tagore left nameless, begins to read his manuscript while a black-cloaked figure sits hunched up on the old ghat by the river. This figure suggests menace.

Despite these macabre first shots, the schoolmaster's story as it commences to unfold appears entirely concrete. The English-educated and fastidiously dressed Phanibhushan—he wears immaculate Victorian clothes and matching beard—arrives with his elegant and beautifiul wife, Monimalika, to live in the palatial house inherited from his childless uncle.

From the entry of the couple into the house, the camera work of the young and talented Soumendu Roy, replacing Subrata Mitra who was ill during the shooting of the Tagore films, is singularly polished and vivid. Ray's composition for every shot has a calculated quality so that household objects with nothing extraordinary about them at this stage are sharply related visually to the new owners. An ornate European vase serves as a compositional focal point as if to comment upon a certain artificial manner about these people. A tiger is distinctly seen to be of bronze. But later this common-place figure in a rich man's home will emerge again as if it is the repository of some menacing force prowling about the house. (Pls. XXIII and XXIV)

At first Monimalika, who holds her husband enthralled, is merely moody, defensive and complaining that her husband's relatives dislike her. She is glad to have escaped from them into this house. She teases her impassioned husband—a seductive look followed by a petulant or freezing one. The presence of stuffed birds of prey does not immediately become associated with this rapacious woman who is only capable of passion for jewellery. Her obsession is its acquisition. (Pl. XXIII)

Day after day, the good-natured Phanibhushan seeks to please the frigid and increasingly neurotic Monimalika. In return for a diamond she may melt, momentarily, into a simulation of amorousness. But unless she is collecting jewels she wanders about the house uneasily, restlessly lacking human response.

The development of the story of husband and wife is related in isolated scenes by the schoolmaster who, reading his manuscript, becomes increasingly enthralled by what takes place. He remains seated on the steps leading down to the river where the black-shrouded figure remains crouched. There is never a moment when the viewer fails to sense that something appalling will happen in the house where the couple are shown.

The tension of the story itself is tightened with the arrival of a peculiar and suggestive character who has tracked down Monimalika. There is the hint that this "relative", Madhusudan (a faintly drawn minor character in Tagore's story whom Ray expanded), belongs to a period of Moni's life over which a veil of secrecy has been drawn.

Madhusudan, unshaven and shabby, first appears in the doorway of Moni's room. As he stands there he produces a hint of almost overpowering decadence. It is not exactly a threat of blackmail that he makes as he presses for a job about the estate.

This scene is so effective in its undertone of threat because Madhusudan never steps inside the room, only remains standing in the doorway blocking Moni's escape. She retreats as far away as possible from him and fiddles with something on the other side of the room while striving for her words to hold him at arm's length. In this scene it is the man, not the stuffed birds of prey, that embody menace. What is going to happen if this creature achieves his objective—a job in the house? For all his seeming lethargy, and his bad-luck story, he possesses the determination to obtain what he wants.

The emphatic turn of the screw comes when the husband's jute business goes up in flames. Momentarily he is faced with ruin. Crushed, he explains his affairs to Monimalika, saying he must go to Calcutta at once and endeavour to salvage his fortune. He will bring her more jewels.

As soon as her husband has left, the obsessed wife falls prey to anxiety. She panics, dreading that her unloved husband will demand her jewels in order to save his business. In panic she forgets her fear of Madhusudan and sends the old servant to find him.

With his second appearance, Madhusudan has the whip hand, for Moni has formed the wild plan to flee to her father's home across the river taking her jewels with her in order to place them beyond her husband's reach. Madhusudan must accompany her. He listens to her, only too pleased to agree. You can feel her suggested plan circling round and round in his mind. (The genesis can be seen in Pl. XXIV.) Madhusudan's long-fingered hand moves up his face, slowly moving about his nose and to one eye. Monimalika is oblivious of this chilling gesture. This hand feeling his oddly degenerate face suggests murder.

Moni, singularly unconscious of real danger, leaves him to dress for their departure. She reappears wrapped from head to foot in a large black shawl which looks like a cloak. Madhusudan, now holding in his hand a carved walking-stick, enquires if Moni has remembered her jewel box. As reply, she flings open her shawl revealing how she has decked herself with the jewels—for safety— as she explains.

Madhusudan's hand twirls his stick very slightly, looking at its carved handle. It is a second brilliant gesture of innuendo.

Ray later explained that the stick had a double implication: that Madhusudan could now feel prepared to carry the type of stick associated with the wealth of the zamindar class, and also use it for what he intends to do.

"The husband," said Satyajit, "thinks that he hears the cry of boatmen in the night. But when he looks out there is only a boat on calm water. . . . Anyway, Moni dies."

But will she have been killed by Madhusudan?

Kumar Roy, who would later give another brilliant performance in criminality in *Charulata*, combined in his interpretation of Madhusudan with utmost economy of expression and gesture, the paradoxical qualities of indolent good-for-nothingness and a will that *could* kill.

The final level of tension and the onset of terror commences with the return of Phanibhushan bringing with him the new jewels he had promised his wife. Full of anticipation, he finds the house deserted except for the old servant. As the husband, Kali Bannerjee has no further opportunity to speak. His monologue with growing terror is conveyed through facial expression and the movements of the camera counterpointed by realistic sound magnified and music composed by Ray.

Up to this point, objects have remained decorative even if they hinted an underlying meaning. Slowly, relentlessly, certain objects now take on a subjective character through camera angles and lighting effects. The camera becomes an increasingly active participant, stealthily moving about, prying here and there, staring at this, then that—the stuffed birds, the bronze tiger. Objects, though still inanimate, appear to be about to move of themselves. Every shadow holds a threat. The *tanpura* seen lying serene on the divan in daylight is suddenly twanged by unseen hands. The billowing curtain, the lamp beside the bed, all seem to be acting a menacing role. The camera creeps towards the filigree screen guarding the passage beyond the bedroom. A shadow appears; anklets clink chillingly. The shadow enters the bedroom and solidifies into a black-robed figure. There is the face of the terrified yet elated husband crouched in bed.

He has waited for this moment with terror-stricken anticipation. His present is in the jewel box on the table beside him. It is open for the returning wife to see—a gold necklace studded with diamonds that glint. The hand clinking with bangles claws out to take the box. Skeleton fingers clutch at the husband's living hand. Drowned? Murdered? Whichever it was, Monimalika is dead, except her obsession for jewels remains active. (Pl. XXIV)

The schoolmaster is still elated in recounting his fearful tale on the river steps. The black-robed figure, who has been listening, rises, announces who *he* is, or was—the husband—and dissolves. Another ghost! (In Tagore's story, the ghost himself tells the story.) Completely unnerved, the schoolmaster shrieks and stumbles up the steps. Yet a further twist is suggested as he turns pointing as an afterthought to his pipe lying on the steps. Had he been smoking a drug which caused him to experience the hallucinatory story he has told? There may have been no story, no ghosts—nothing.

Tagore had closed his story on a twist. Ray added an additional twist. He delights in open endings which lead to speculation.

Admittedly, *Monihara* seemed somewhat out of place as the middle film composing *Teen Kanya*. It would have been more effective if placed as the third and last film. Seen by itself it gained as a study of a malignantly obsessive woman, the only repellent feminine character to serve as a central figure in a Ray film. Kanika Mazumdar, a star in Bengali cinema, combined the qualities of seductiveness and harshness to lend so neurotic a character validity.

According to Ray, *Monihara* had been completed in a hurry with less thought lavished upon it than on other films. No doubt, from his point of view, this was true; but, as Ray's unit and actors repeatedly assert, there is nothing accidental in his work and he only undertakes to shoot when everything has become crystal clear in his mind.

If this film remains permanently classed with such minor films of Ray as *Kapurush-o-Mahapurush* (1965) or the 1967 detective film, *Chiriakhana* (*Menagerie*), it is still an example of brilliant camera work and a very effective use of inanimate objects as if they were animated personalities. It is also a demonstration of an unsuspected attribute of Ray—his capacity to create suspense and build up impressions of horror.

To critics, and those of the public who have seen Ray's work, his fame has been most generally related to the Apu Trilogy. It has been his observation of people from his particular humanist point of view which has impressed, and his lyrical and compelling use of locations. The zamindar films, representing his work (with the exception of *Paras Pathar*) between 1958 and early 1961, with *Jalsaghar* between the second and third films of the Trilogy, introduce and expand Ray's dominant use of studio sets and the most careful selection of properties.

A letter written in 1950 to his future Art Director, Bansi Chandragupta, about Italian films remains interesting for establishing Satyajit Ray's approach to the approximation of reality in his films. He found "the entire conventional approach (as exemplified by even the best American and British films) is wrong. Because the conventional approach tells you that the best way to tell a story is to leave out all except those elements which are directly related to the story, while the master's work clearly indicates that if your theme is strong and simple, then you can include a hundred little apparently irrelevant details which, instead of obscuring the theme, only help to intensify it by contrast, and in addition create the illusion of actuality better."

It was easy to assume from the Trilogy, as some critics indeed did, that Ray's discernment and artistry was specially responsive to etching conditions of poverty, and at first that he was a "primitive" who succeeded in making a great film, *Pather Panchali*. But the zamindar films demonstrate that Ray's discernment is no less sharp when he turns to examine the neuroses of riches and the psychological pitfalls attending upon those trapped within endless leisure. His examination of economic extremes is pursued with equal sensitivity as to detail.

The zamindar films, set in the past, have all the immediacy of those of his films set in the present. With Ray, the past is a realistic continuum with the present, while the present is becoming increasingly sharpened in his contemporary films, which are discussed later.

The quality of immediacy is partly the result of his handling of his actors, whether professional or non-professional. None of his actors in discussing his methods of drawing out of them a characterization has ever mentioned that he had them picture the character as living in a past period; he only asked them to feel and understand the person. The validity of the sets used, whether in *Jalsaghar*, *Devi* or *Monihara*, or, subsequently, in the small contemporary Calcutta middle-class house in *Mahanagar*, contribute greatly. The work put in in collaboration with Chandragupta on sets and the discovery of the right furniture, the precisely correct knick-knack, has always been enormous.

Chandragupta has explained the role of any set in a Ray film: "A set is not a replica of what already exists, otherwise there would be no need for designers. A film set is built for the camera and for the camera angles only. Anything that is not effective through the lens is waste of good money and effort, however pleasing it might look to the naked eye. . . . Ray has a keen camera-eye and each carefully picked detail helps to build the atmosphere."

So important is the set in relation to Ray's scenario, that for the sake of Chandragupta, who does not read Bengali, Ray writes all his scripts first in English.

Satyajit (costume designs for Amal in *Charulata*)

Chapter 8

THE TAGORE FILMS—*RABINDRANATH TAGORE, TEEN KANYA* AND *CHARULATA*

BY 1789, the phenomenal Tagore family had emerged as merchant princes. Tracing their lineage back to the eighth century, they belonged to a distinctive group of Brahmins who by unusual custom engage in trade. Dwelling as an enormous Joint Family they inhabited the gigantic, gracious, colonial-style palace, Jorosanko, which still forms an architectural oasis tucked in behind the seething merchandising street of Calcutta's Chitpore with its myriad small shops. This is the street which has changed the least in two centuries.

Jorosanko's expansive façade is still painted in its original rosy-red. Though the family has shrunk in size and few members remain residing within the palace, the building itself has become a shrine not only in honour of Rabindranath, but to the family which stood as the symbol of the mid-nineteenth century's Bengal Renaissance. The Tagores epitomized the dynamism of the period which fused a new critical awareness of Indian tradition with acceptance of scientific Western thought. It was here that Satyajit Ray's grandfather, Upendrakishore, was in the habit of visiting the Tagores, bringing his violin with him.

In 1861, Rabindranath was born in this great house, its rooms opening off the four veranda'd buildings surrounding a central courtyard of classical Hindu design. Eighty years later Rabindranath, evolved into Gurudev (Revered Master), died in one of the austerely beautiful rooms. During this span of years paralleling India's sloughing off of centuries of lassitude, the most brilliant creative figure of an artistic family stretched his imaginative urge to experiment in all possible directions.

Author of a first book of poems at sixteen, Rabindranath plunged into a whirlwind of writing plays, performed for his own pleasure and that of his family on the platforms built at each end of the courtyard. Novels and short stories jostled each other to be set down on paper. At an early age acting entranced him while music, according to his own inspiration, absorbed him all his life. Finally, when seventy years of age, Rabindranath commenced to pour forth thousands of extraordinarily provocative and suggestively Surrealist pictures in a last surge of activity. As if to give this individual torrent of creation a wider national and international framework, Tagore espoused political and educational reform, with Santineketan centred in tribal country as his self-created monument to encourage the resurgence of Indian art.

"Rabi" was the fourteenth child born of the famed leader of the reformist Brahmo Samaj, Debendranath Tagore. This son of the princely-seeming Dwarkanath, "suffered social ostracism for preaching the monotheistic faith that he called Brahmoism". To his followers, many of whom excelled in the new branches of learning invading Bengal, Debendranath was Maharishi, the Great Sage. The youngest child of so august a father, awed by the line of older brothers and sister stretching above him was, not unexpectedly, a lonely unhappy little boy left to wander the verandas of the family palace.

In his old age at Santineketan, Rabindranath Tagore had appeared remote, like God, to the young and shy Satyajit Ray, whom he had been determined to bring there. Despite the formidable impression, Ray would become a very free interpreter of

Tagore's stories when he came to translate them into films. Tagore's literary admirers would frequently argue as to Ray's apostasy.

Since Tagore's centenary was due in 1961, a committee was formed in 1959 to prepare the celebrations. The name of Satyajit Ray, as a Bengali, came up during early discussions about the production of a biographical film on Tagore. Overtures came to Ray from the Government's Films Division as to what he would charge per foot for a film. Ray agreed to make a film for Rs.25/- per foot, this being £2 at that time. Though Ray was eager to make the film, uncertainty as to commissioning him set in.

At a meeting of the committee, someone with very vague ideas as to film-making put in the objection that Ray, not being an historian, was an unsuitable person to direct the Tagore film.

The committee member who grasped the fallacy of such a view was Jawaharlal Nehru. He put down his foot, reportedly saying: "We don't need an historian. What we need is an artist!" Having seen *Pather Panchali*, Nehru could speak for Ray and say: "Satyajit Ray is that. I don't think any historian should interfere."

The commission went to Ray but with creatively unfortunate conditions. There were to be two versions of the film. The original hour-long picture with Ray's own self-spoken English commentary. From this a two-reel condensation, not a shorter film reconceived, was to be edited and generally released to theatres outside Bengal. This was to accommodate the law providing that theatres were only required to screen Government sponsored films of two reels. Moreover, Films Division retained the right to arrange the Hindi commentary and that for other language versions. The full-length original version was only shown in Bengal and sent abroad.

Only the original version represents Ray's intentions. The short version has no greater merit than the work of any competent documentary director. The translation of Ray's commentary into chaste Hindi, and other languages, when spoken in a conventional commentating manner, destroys the sensitivity of the images. Consequently, the atmosphere of the film is diminished.

On the day the full-length film was premièred in Delhi (May 5th, 1961) Ray remarked: "I put in as much work on it as on three feature films. My approach to the biography was to stress Tagore as a human being and patriot."

Though Tagore's life was one to inspire an artist such as Ray, after a month's research at Santineketan he realized the cinematic limitations of the authentic material he must utilize. Manuscripts, books, conventionally posed photographs of important events, even Tagore's paintings, were static in character. The problem was to endow this visually meagre material with an illusion of movement.

Ray went to Darjeeling to think over how he could devise a form which, in the face of the obvious difficulties, would bring Tagore's life alive in visual terms. Frequently, Ray's scripts had taken him as little as ten days to complete. For *Tagore* he wrote no formal scenario, but to prepare a visual continuity took him a month. Much of this continuity was written down in the crowded lounge of the Mount Everest Hotel, chosen by Ray because he has sometimes found that to be surrounded by impersonal crowds has sharpened his powers of concentration.

He came to the conclusion that the Tagore film would require more camera movement than any of his feature films; that there would have to be hundreds of opticals each worked out with mathematical exactitude; that this would cost a great deal.

Camera movement used in relation to static pictures and even the most skilful optical work could not provide the kaleidoscopic impression of Rabindranath's genius or the scope of his life. The structure devised by Ray took on the character of a mosaic: the authentic but static material, subjected to camera movement wherever possible, must be edited in conjunction with a certain number of reconstructed or invented scenes to bring to life the history of the Tagore family, grandfather Dwarkanath, father Debendranath, together with flashes from the childhood and youth of Rabindranath.

Ray rejected out of hand the idea of an actor impersonating the mature Tagore because, in maturity, Tagore's face and figure were too familiar. This familiarity did not apply to "Rabi" as a boy or youth. So Ray decided to reconstruct a few scenes from these little-known periods. In the finished film several such reconstructions stand out as memorable: the death and cremation of Debendranath's mother which evoke a profound spiritual awakening in him; the loneliness of "Rabi" as a child; the pressure of incessant learning that is put upon him and the poignant experience of being alone with his father, the Great Sage, in an isolated house in Dalhousie. The Dalhousie episode, shot by Ray at the house where the Tagores had stayed, is in long shot and provides the early signs of the role of music in Rabindranath's life.

Ray also decided to include newsreel material, both footage on Tagore and some that might illustrate the final thoughts of Rabindranath as expressed in his last message to the world—*Crisis in Civilisation*. In order to find the right footage, Ray went to Paris where he hunted down suitable newsreel and documentary shots, Pathé's vaults serving as the most rewarding source. He was helped in this search by Lotte Eisner. From Paris he went to London to collect information and arrange for footage to be shot of Dwarkanath Tagore's tomb, for he had died in England. Ray also arranged for a long vista shot of Hyde Park. This was subsequently used for back projection for a reconstructed scene of Dwarkanath riding in a carriage through the park.

Ray was fortunate in the newsreel material on Tagore he was able to acquire through his patient search. Some dozen shots were visually impressive. Among these were five shots of the dead Gurudev being borne through the streets of Calcutta to the cremation ghat. With the discovery of these shots, Ray reversed the usual chronological method of biography—to begin with birth and close with death. Thus, the film opens with scenes of mass mourning, with a close-up of Tagore's face suggesting his majesty in death. The music—the first to be devised by Satyajit Ray himself —austerely conveys the grief of millions. His own words, spoken with no dramatic affectation, are of the simplest: "On August 7, 1941, in the city of Calcutta a man died. His mortal remains perished, but he left behind him a heritage which no fire could consume."

Flames burn in the darkness until again the sun rises. It does not rise to reveal the youth of Rabindranath, but Calcutta as it was in earlier times as a background to the rise of the Tagore family. Some Indians found this visual account of Calcutta and the portrayal of the Tagore family too pedantic and others felt Ray's approach to be too unemotional. Like all his work, this biography has restraint. The scope of Tagore is captured and presented in chronological order and set within the flow of events of his time. For example, Lord Curzon's partitioning of Bengal and the burning of his effigy as a reaction; or the use of a panning shot of Amritsar and a single reconstructed shot of the 1919 massacre ordered by General Dyer edited together with an expressive photograph of Tagore supply illustrative reason for Tagore's action in writing his noted letter renouncing his British Knighthood. (Pl. XXV)

The film sustains an intellectual interest throughout its sixty minutes; but it is only certain sustained sequences which remain in the memory as essentially cinematic. One such passage towards the end of the film depicts the evolution of Tagore's painting. Ray had made a careful study of the calligraphy in Tagore's manuscripts. This he employed in an inspired way. A printed page is succeeded by a hand-written manuscript with doodles. One after the other, the doodles become more distinct in form until, detached altogether from manuscripts, they emerge as individual paintings which uncover the far from placid imagination of Tagore. Strange birds and forms of men and beast and many mysterious faces of women, timeless and modern at the same moment, express the feelings which words can no longer convey as Tagore is growing older and older and more and more bent.

It is through Tagore's writing that Ray is able poignantly to convey that death is coming near. He shows a page of manuscript with the writing faltering crookedly across the page and slanting off. Fortunately, there existed a number of expressive photographs of Tagore struggling to work during the last days of his life. With the help of these the climax of Ray's film was fashioned into its most memorable sequence, one that makes acceptably evident the idea of Tagore as a universal man who closed his life's work with the book *Crisis in Civilisation*. Ray inserted shots of Hitler's steel-helmeted men marching aggressively to war and follows these with images of the shrivelled corpses flung into concentration-camp ditches. The images of horror give way to the face of a weeping woman. Then comes the face of Tagore who looks, as it were, upon the wreckage and sorrow with a stricken expression in his eyes.

Battling against mortal illness, the old man struggles to set before the world the immortal ideal that the Brotherhood of Man must be reborn out of humanity's suffering. This end is the affirmation of life. It is the logical close for Ray, as a humanist, to choose for Tagore, representing as he did, the humanist tradition. Ray quotes Tagore's words: "I shall not commit the grievous sin of losing faith in Man. I shall wait for the day when the holocaust will end and the world will be rendered clean with the spirit of service and sacrifice." A shot of the sun over water comes, and the camera approaches the sun. Finally, the most compelling shot comes on to the screen—a photograph of Tagore in the act of prayer and appeal.

Due to the film's unusual length, the Ministry of Information and Broadcasting suffered a certain degree of confusion as to what to do with it once it was completed. Prime Minister Nehru's opinion was sought in this matter as in so many others. On March 4th, 1961, a private screening was arranged in the basement cinema of the President's House. As the screening commenced, the Home Minister, Pundit Pant, a friend on whom Nehru relied, lay dying. The rumour went round those assembled that he might not live through the hour which it took to screen *Rabindranath Tagore*.

Nehru entered the small theatre with drawn face and weary steps. Accompanied by a visiting Soviet Delegation, Jawaharlal Nehru looked as if life had become almost unbearable. But, as the lights went up at the end of Ray's film, the affirmation of life and ideals impregnated in Ray's presentation of Tagore's life had wrought a remarkable change in Nehru. His exhaustion was banished and he smiled spontaneously. Two months later when he saw the film again, having presented Ray with a silver plaque on its première, again it evoked a reaction of seeming hopefulness in Nehru.

*   *   *   *

Tagore's stories had attracted film-makers, especially Bengali directors. As the Tagore centenary approached, Ray had embarked on the project of producing three distinctively different Tagore short stories and presenting them under the title, *Teen Kanya*, which means *Three Daughters* or *Three Women*. The three stories were planned to form a film of sixteen reels, the longest of any of Ray's films. A study of women, the first and shortest film presents a portrait of the child-woman, Ratan, in *The Postmaster*. *Monihara*, the study of the neurotic Monimalika, served as the second; the third, *Samapti* (*The Conclusion*), being a comedy of the tomboy adolescent, Mrinmoyee, painfully shredding her immaturity to become a willing wife.

With two of the films, Ray was to try out his capacity for creating a very natural style of comedy, an element that had slid in and out of the texture of the Apu Trilogy and been exercised in the ironic fantasy, *Paras Pathar* (*The Philosopher's Stone*) which he had directed almost simultaneously with *Jalsaghar*. But in the three stories composing *Teen Kanya*, with their women belonging to differing social classes, there is also an underlying irritation at the traditional in each of the films. The Postmaster, resenting his appointment to a remote village which seems too dull for him, is impervious to what it might offer. This is as true of the pseudo-intellectual today as it was in Tagore's time. Amulya, the college student of *Samapti*, is, like many students of today, resistant to his mother's idea of a suitable bride and insists upon his own choice. In *Monihara*, irritation and dissatisfactions have evolved into neurosis.

The Postmaster is only forty minutes in length. Tagore's original story ran to ten and a half pages. Generalizations are made about the Postmaster's character but they are not concretely illustrated by any incidents. The character is never vivid. Ratan, the orphan girl who cannot be paid for her loving care of him, is an appealing waif. The end is somewhat Victorian in sentiment and the two characters, the only two, in the story remain with faces that are in no way visualized.

Samapti (The Conclusion) is a singularly meandering story lacking a focal point either in time or space, with pleasing but blurred characters. They drift from one place to another over an unspecified period of time during which their ill-defined problem of adolescent marital adjustment rocks them to and fro on an emotional stream.

Of the three stories, *The Lost Jewels*, the basis of *Monihara*, required the least additions and subtractions. Without drastic refashioning and sharpening the other two stories, had they been literally followed, would inevitably have resulted in dull and amorphous films.

Working in an atmosphere of criticism of a heavily literary kind, for Bengal is literary minded, Ray had been the target of much literary-minded criticism for the changes he had made in his second film, *Aparajito*. At that time, the Frenchman, Jean Herman, had defended Ray. What he said then was applicable no less to Ray's need to follow his own convictions in regard to Tagore's stories:

> There is a profound specific of the filmic style—which makes it impossible to be faithful to the letter of a literary work, the cinematographic and literary style being very different; the problem does not consist in copying the book—chapter after chapter —but in interpreting the spirit of the author and in organizing the sensation procured by the words in a purely audio-visual context.

This is precisely what Ray achieves in the slim tale of the bored Postmaster who, with nothing to do, teaches his orphan-servant girl to read and write. The sensitivity of the two characters has been heightened and humour, not very evident in the original, introduced.

Nervousness at rural strangeness—a very real trait in urban educated Indians—is almost immediately introduced by Ray's addition of the shaggy-headed, charmingly absurd madman who, on arrival of the new Postmaster, comes hopping and marching menacingly outside the new man's rickety house. He is a deliciously eccentric creation with his dangling soldier's hat and staff concocted of a fishing rod surmounted by what looks like a trowel. He puts the wind up the young man on his first job, so much so that, aping dignity, he reads his book upside down. But really the mad menace is a docile lamb the instant the little Ratan appears and orders no more frightening of the Postmaster who has shrunk against the wall. Nervous as the Postmaster is, his sense of self-preservation is far from alert. Just behind him plastered on the wall, a poster in the popular style of religious pictures (which at first glance has its comic aspect) is, in fact, a Government poster warning against malaria. (Pl. XXVI)

Later, that night, Ray allows new fright to get under the Postmaster's skin. But he employs sound rather than images to do so. The forest sounds, at dead of night magnified, awake nightmare fears in the man who knows nothing of the rural world. Thus the human need of fear compels the urban man to seek the company, as protection, of the child-woman, Ratan, who is sleeping near by. From this there flows the idyll of the waif being taught to read and write and have someone to care for. Self-centred as Nandal, the Postmaster, is, she grows to dote on him. (Pl. XXVII)

Ray had found the eleven-year-old Calcutta schoolgirl, Chandana Banerji, to create his image of Ratan. Intelligent but plain, she understood exactly what he wanted her to convey. Nobody has ever heard him give his directions to children; but he has claimed that though different children require different handling, the secret of his direction of children has been his treatment of them as adults.

Anil Chatterjee, from whom Ray drew an exceptional performance as the Postmaster, has given a vivid account of Chandana Banerji's acting as Ratan:

> There is a scene in which I brusquely ask her questions like —"Why aren't you better cared for? Doesn't your mother wash your clothes?" She replies "No". Well—this scene has to be played with a lot of emotion and in one of her lines there was suddenly a delayed reaction. I assumed she had forgotten her lines and looked up. To my utter surprise, her hesitation and the slow smile with which she gave her reply was just . . . perfect. It was inspired! But it took the wind out of my sails. I fell completely flat in my own responses. When the scene was over Ray understood my feelings and dissatisfaction with my own performance. I didn't even have to tell him. He came to me and said we would re-shoot. He went over to the little girl and said "You were very good, but Anil Dada was a little inattentive. So we'll take it again." Another director may have been so enamoured by the perfect performance on one side . . . he would have failed to regard the response to it as equally important.

Not only did Ray inspire the born actress in Chandana; but by scraping her hair back he revealed the remarkable squirrel-like

M

character of her face. The feature that then made her face so individual were her small pointed front teeth.

In order to stress the fish-out-of-water quality of the Postmaster, Ray introduced a collection of odd-faced old men—human specimens much beloved by him and introduced in other films They sit around and gossip in the shabby little post office. Imagining they are musicians, they invite the new Postmaster for an evening—a friendly gesture even if the singer is grossly out of tune. The Postmaster, suffering from a feeling of his cultural superiority and lack of interest in anyone except himself, does not refuse to go. But he goes in a wincing state of mind which effectively visualizes Tagore's comment: "Nor is the Calcutta boy an adept in the art of associating with others." (Pl. XXVI)

The old men added further flesh to the thin bones of Tagore's story by their concern for the Postmaster when he becomes stricken with malaria. This is the incident where the film shifts from concentrating on the Postmaster to showing the growth of Ratan.

This particular scene with its physical and psychological details perfectly illustrates Ray's capacity for evolving the slightest literary sketch and refashioning it into an exquisite example of cinematic language.

The temporary, casual contact between Nandal and Ratan, the child who is shown verging upon womanhood as she nurses him, emerges clothed with a moving depth of perception. Through the intensity of the girl's patient care it becomes important to the spectator that the not too appealing Postmaster recover. He begins to matter as a human being through Ratan's and the old villagers' concern.

This effect is not achieved, I think, only through the marvellous interpretation of Chandana Banerji, or the sincerity of the anxious men; nor from the effective camera angles or, if it can be so described, the suggestion of urgency which the lighting gives to the scene. It may be due to the manner in which Ray throws searchlights on his characters to give them the dimensions of being people belonging to a real world. Early in the film, at the Postmaster's arrival, Ray hinted how this rather silly young man belongs to a family. He is seen taking out a family photograph and hanging it on the rough wall near to the peg for his clothes. The texture of the wall conveys the ramshackle, cobbled-together quarters he must live in. While Nandal is delirious, this subtly placed picture is seen in the background from various angles to evoke his past connections. Thereby, there is suggested the cause of his inept adjustment to a village job. (Pl. XXVII)

By his blend of humour and genuine emotions, *The Postmaster*, Ray's seemingly most simple film, accomplished the feat of expanding what was rather a flat sketch of a complex relationship into an absorbing study of two credible people.

Where Tagore's story of the self-centred Postmaster was lacking in action and visualization, his leisurely story *Samapti—The Conclusion*—only subliminally suggests the comic and sparkling *Taming of the Shrew* which Ray constructed from it by his drastic subtractions and pointed additions.

He visually stresses three focusing elements first to sharpen the psychological conflict between the student and the girl and, later, to resolve their marriage. These are the mud which Tagore only introduced at the opening of his story; a tree which the tomboy "Beatrice"—Mrinmoyee—climbs down to escape her husband on their wedding night and climbs up again finally to accept wifehood; and her pet squirrel, Chorky, whose death marks her realization of womanhood. The essence of this comedy with serious undertones is the attraction of the untamed, frivolous, untraditional adolescent, nicknamed Pagli, for the bespectacled, dignified Amulya, who thinks of himself as masterful but finds himself a very nonplussed husband. Tagore set the atmosphere:

Apurba had got his B.A. degree and was coming back home to his village. The river, which flowed past it, was a small one. It became dried up during the hot weather, but now in the July monsoon the heavy rains had swollen its current and it was full to the brim.

The boat, which carried Apurba, reached the ghat whence the roof of his home could be seen through the dense foliage of the trees. Nobody knew that he was coming and therefore there was no-one to receive him at the landing. The boatman offered to carry his bag, but Apurba picked it up himself, and took a leap from the boat. The bank was slippery, and he fell flat upon the muddy stair, bag and all.

As he did so, peal after peal of very sweet laughter rose in the sky, and startled the birds in the neighbouring trees. Apurba got up and tried to regain his composure as best he could. When he sought the source of his discomfiture, he found, sitting upon a heap of bricks lately unloaded from some cargo boat, a girl shaking her sides with laughter. Apurba recognized her as Mrinmoyee, the daughter of their neighbour. . . .

Mrinmoyee was the talk of all the village. The men called her "madcap". But the village matrons were in a state of perpetual anxiety because of her intractable wildness. All her games were with the boys of the place, and she had the utmost contempt for the girls of her own age. . . . (Pl. XXVIII)

Amulya, as Ray renamed Tagore's hero, arrives home to be instantly set upon by his mother who announces she has found a suitable bride for him—the daughter of another neighbour family far more desirable than that of Mrinmoyee. Rather grandly he agrees to inspect the girl, but he is not too willing. His vision of himself is summed up by the picture of Napoleon—a Ray addition—which he carefully places on a shelf. Before his visit to the Chatterjee household, he notices Mrinmoyee playing beyond his window with a group of boys. Questioning his servant, the man in a disparaging tone declares the girl to be called Pagli, an absurd name.

All dressed up with his best shoes on and remembering to wear his watch on its chain, Amulya sets off for his prospective bride inspection. Again his dignity slips as he slides about in the mud with the teasing Pagli mischievously watching. Arriving at the Chatterjee house, Amulya's handsome but muddied shoes have to be removed and he is forced to borrow carpet slippers. He is ushered in for the crucial inspection into the primmest of rooms replete with ostentatious photographs of King George V and Queen Mary on the wall under which he and his prospective father-in-law sit. Stone deaf grandfather, added by Ray as part of the incongruously proper reception committee, couldn't care less. (Pl. XXVIII)

Decked out as a bundle, the mute, stodgy prospective bride is propelled in by her *ayah* who periodically prods her in the ribs to show off her dreary traditional charms, including a cracked-toned song. The wicked and vibrant Pagli, all curiosity watching through a window, allows her squirrel, Chorky, to escape into the room. Rushing in like a whirlwind she captures her pet only to cause Amulya to choke up his sweetmeat on to grandfather's bald pate. The die is cast. Though the departing B.A. finds his shoes filched and discovers one of them thrown after him as he struggles home through the mud, this indignity cannot cool the romantic fire that begins to burn for the madcap. Furiously, he recaptures his other shoe from the girl hiding protectively against a tree. She has almost captured him into kissing her there and then, but he's not quite that bold for all his cherished Napoleon picture.

Amulya confronts his mother—he has found his own bride, Pagli. The shocked mother seeks to investigate the girl. Finding her not as awful as expected, she yields agreement. From this point, the film becomes almost entirely Ray's invention, except for the retention of the idea of Mrinmoyee's ultimate maturing into a wife.

Indignant when her own mother agrees to the marriage, she chops her hair off to reduce her womanly attractions, only to be beaten by her mother. Unwillingly married off, she is trapped in the bridal chamber, asserting her will that she only does what she wants. She doesn't want the bewildered bridegroom. Unfortunately for him but fortunately for her, the defeated bridegroom falls asleep. Pagli shimmies down the tree outside the window to spend the night on a swing fondling Chorky whom she kisses rather than kissing Amulya.

Brought back, her mother-in-law locks her in before the duly inquisitive array of neighbours who have gathered. In rage she tears the room apart while Amulya sits disconsolately outside the house. Amulya—Napoleon, at last asserting his authority, goes up to the room only to have his worldly wisdom vanquished by the obdurate Pagli. Gentleman-like, he announces: "You are not grown up enough. We will meet when you are grown up enough. Write me a letter and I will come."

With his dignity saved he departs for Calcutta and Pagli departs home to her Ma. But she begins to mope. Romping around with the boys, even her pet friend, no longer appeals. Ultimately, Chorky's death brings the shift in Mrinmoyee's emotions into focus. She has become so detached from her immaturity that she tells her chief boy playmate to cremate the squirrel on the river bank. She has been weeping for Amulya. Now she wants to love him. But it is not the letter she writes that brings him back; but a letter complaining of a non-existent illness from his mother. Amulya, renouncing his dignity to search for Pagli at the key location—the riverside where mud ignited their attraction for one another—leads to her coming back to give herself up to being transformed into a willing wife.

The Conclusion is a perfect structure in five movements, each with its developing mood. If subtracted from the triple-story film it stands out as the most wholly satisfying and fine-woven short film by Ray. Or, as Ralph Stephenson said in *The Guardian*, it "is a comedy every bit as rich as anything of Chekhov".

The London *Times* made an accurate observation in saying: "Mr. Satyajit Ray is one of those directors whose least works are likely to prove better worth seeing than the warranted masterpieces of many a more pretentious film-maker." It was going to emerge that Ray's interest was in making the films he wanted to make—"for

the love of it"—for he enjoys "every moment of the film-making
process". He was not aiming to create only masterpieces.

Except for a single American screening including the three
films, *Teen Kanya* abroad became *Two Daughters, Monihara* being
left out on account of length. *Two Daughters* expanded Ray's international distribution to West Germany and the Middle East. In
Australia, it won the top award at the Melbourne Film Festival
An English reviewer commented : "This is Ray's seventh film and
it becomes clear that his talent is not going to be quickly
exhausted." Of Ray's films, only *Teen Kanya* was released in India
with English subtitles.

*   *   *   *

Three years would pass before Satyajit Ray would again construct
a film based on a Tagore story. *Charulata* would emerge as his
most elegant film, his chef d'oeuvre in the reconstruction of a
period, the year 1879. As early as 1958 and almost simultaneously
with *Devi*, Ray wrote his first script. Finding it impossible to cast
he threw this original draft away. It is an oft-repeated pattern with
Ray that a number of years pass between the initial conception of
a film and its final realization on the screen. *Mahanagar* was the
film he planned to make directly after the release of *Teen Kanya*
in May 1961. Unable to cast the central character, he patiently
stored away this film for more than two years and in the meantime
wrote and directed the first of his own stories, *Kanchenjunga*, and
Abhijan.

At the time of doing his research for the Tagore biographical
film, Ray came across Tagore's manuscript of the novel *Nastenir*
on which his 1958 script was based. Translatable as *The Fouled-up
Nest* or *The Lost Nest*, Ray noticed Tagore's marginal notations
linking the name of Rabindranath's sister-in-law (who was believed
in Bengal to have committed suicide following "Rabi's" marriage)
with that of Charu, the novel's central character. The notation
suggests a strongly autobiographical aspect. On account of another
film bearing the title *Nastenir*, Ray's had to be retitled *Charulata*.

Despite its delicate restraint, *Charulata* is the most passionate of
Ray's films : Charu, reflective of the intellectual Brahmo woman
of the period, is both the loved and neglected childless wife of
Bhupati, an essentially good and trusting man. Intellectual and
progressive, his total absorption with current politics and newspaper publishing makes him an emotionally unsatisfying husband.
To assuage Charu's loneliness, he brings her brother and his coarse

wife to live with them. Against Charu's advice he trusts this brother-in-law to handle the financial side of his publishing. Then, as if swept in by a storm, his own young, gay and insouciant cousin, Amal, arrives in the house to provide at first delightful companionship for Charu, but, finally, to leave husband and wife to hopeless alienation.

Charu and Amal become inseparable. Encouraging each other's literary efforts they playfully, innocently drift towards an inevitable romantic passion. As Penelope Houston observed, it is Charu's love for a dream Amal "summed up in the sequence where Amal lies writing on the ground, while Charu flies backwards and forwards above him on the swing". In an outburst of emotion Charu confesses her love to Amal who, shocked at this forbidden love and his own sentiments—they are Indian Victorians—hastily departs from Bhupati's house. Unaware of the real situation, the husband is overwhelmed by the grim discovery that Charu's brother has absconded with the publishing funds leaving him only debts. Only inadvertently does Bhupati come to realize Charu's love for Amal. It drives him to leave, but finally he returns only to find communication frozen between Charu and himself. From Bhupati's point of view he's the victim of double betrayal; yet, objectively, his imperviousness to everything beyond publishing and politics invited the fouling up of his private and public life.

If *Pather Panchali* gained in memorability from a degree of roughness that went with its inspiration, *Charulata* makes its first impact by the glowing polish of Ray's technical perfection, as also that of his actors, particularly (as Charu) Madhabi Mukherjee whom he had finally found for the exacting role of Arati in *Mahanagar* the year before. Ray also excelled himself musically.

Even the one day's shooting on *Charulata* which I saw in January 1964 made it clear that infinite pains were being taken to reconstruct the exact period of 1879. The studio was littered with old photographs of that period from which the Victorian blouses beneath the saris of Charu and her sister-in-law had been copied. Ray was thrilled to have found a bedspread on which the camera dwells during Charu's game of cards which looked right even though it was not an antique. He mentioned the difficulties he was having in tracking down the street cries and sounds which would be correct for the 1870s. He realized how greatly Calcutta had changed.

Satyajit and Bansi had visited a number of Calcutta houses before the *Charulata* sets were designed. Their interest was in houses where Victorian style had been adapted to that of Bengal. In *Charulata* there are vistas, specially those that include the veranda, that

hint influences derived from the Tagore house, Jorosanko. Chandragupta was supplied with detailed guide lines by Ray—see pp. 186-7.
   Chandragupta had a floor space of 80 feet by 45 feet at his
disposal. In relation to Ray's first sketch, they built only three
verandas, which gave the required camera angle view of the central
quadrangle and a suggestion of rooms. Three additional major sets
were constructed: (1) Charu's bedroom requiring a view of the
three verandas and glimpses of two staircases. The room and its
veranda was life-size in scale and built on a 6-foot-high platform.
The two other verandas were constructed on reduced dimensions
in order to convey distance and perspective. (2) The drawing room
with the suggestion of verandas. For this set the wallpaper was
specially designed to lend a Victorian flavour and screen-printed in
sheets of 30 inches by 40 inches. It took a day and a night to stick
the paper on to plywood finished walls. (3) Amal, the cousin's,
bedroom. Subsidiary sets included the cluttered-up editorial office.
   The most used and therefore the most impressive and dominating
piece of furniture in *Charulata* is the enormous Victorian bed seen
against pale unpapered walls with a frilly shelf to hold appropriate
ornaments. The first shot of the film covered by the titles reveals
Charu on the bed embroidering her husband's initial 'B' on a handkerchief, which will poignantly reappear.
   Ray has claimed that all his films have been influenced in their
structure by musical forms, the dominant being the sonata and
the symphonic. He told the late Georges Sadoul that he thought
endlessly of Mozart in connection with *Charulata*, for which he
composed four musical motifs, two being original and two being
variations on motifs derived from Tagore. A traditional Scottish
air had served Tagore as the base for one of his songs, "Phooley
Phooley". Variations upon it cement the inseparable pair and
both sing it, but in entirely differing moods.
   A mood-creating passage establishing a character (usually the
central character) in relation to a place appears in many of Ray's
films. But in no film is this achieved more memorably in sound as
well as image than in *Charulata*. Charu, having finished embroidering her gift for her husband, is bored. She seeks a book murmuring
'Bankim' the revered writer of the time—and the richness of the
home is revealed. From some of the verandas the outside world
can be glimpsed through the slatted shutters. Charu, who may
be shortsighted, finds her opera glasses and peers from window
to window watching a fat man in the street as he passes by and
a monkey man leading his monkey on a string. Ray's music is
"used as an evocation of Charulata's loneliness". He uses various

Indian plucking instruments, a throbbing accompaniment for the
thematic range of five notes up and down. This theme will recur
as the link in the musical chain. The husband, Bhupati, stocky,
bearded, chewing on his pipe and absorbed in reading a book,
appears in his shirt-sleeves. He is the image of the Victorian intellectual, pince-nez on a black string and all. He passes Charu standing
in a doorway unaware of her presence. She watches him, sadly
resigned. (Pl. XXX)

Charu's tedium finds no release with the arrival of her brother
(played by Kumar Roy who so successfully conveyed the decadence
of the threatening Madhusudan in *Monihara*) and Manda, his coarse
mischievous wife. The stupid vulgarity of Manda is shown as she
and Charu play cards on the bed. It lays the foundation for Manda's
assistance to her husband when eight weeks later they abscond
with Bhupati's money stolen from the safe.

The house, with its somewhat melancholy grandeur, lights up
with Amal storming in during a gale of wind. In contrast to the
ever prim Bhupati, who even looks tidy in his shirt-sleeves, the
nonchalance of the budding writer-cousin is given a nice touch of
self-neglect by the torn state of his shirt as Charu, delightedly,
watches him throw all his clothes out of his suitcase. Her husband
has all the virtues but his cousin all the charm. Even the dead
serious Bhupati with his Gladstonian views reacts to the charm.
The cousins play at pitting their strength one against the other as,
in the distance, dogs are heard growling. With an ironic flourish
Amal plonks himself down at the piano and very softly plays "God
Save the Queen"!

By tradition, the elder brother's wife (and brotherliness extends
to the cousins and even more distant relations) was accepted as
exerting a deep and intimate influence upon her husband's younger
brothers and the youths of the family until their own marriages
This explains how the constant companionship of Charu and Amal
evokes no jealousy in Bhupati and why, from the start, there is
no wall of inhibition; why, in fact, Charu remains unaware that she
is falling in love with the delightful and playful Amal who takes
her companionship for granted. It is not within the somewhat
claustrophobic atmosphere of the house that Charu realizes the
passion that has been stirred within her, but when the two of them
are liberated into the surrounding beauty of the garden with its
swing.

Swinging higher and higher, Charu is carried into the lyrical
tempo of her idyllic emotions. The camera, which has quietly and
beautifully observed the change in her since she was first seen in

her bored and restless loneliness, zooms to reflect the leaping of her joy. There is this passage of dazzling excitement followed by the swing coming to rest. Amal with his writings is in the background under a tree. The thoughtful Charu, who carries about opera glasses to bring things close, looks around her. She notices off to her left a woman servant with her child. Bhupati has given her no child. She turns and looks at Amal, then barely singing, hums a song based on a Scottish air. To paraphrase Penelope Houston writing of *Charulata* : these two people having discovered the nature of their attachment are absorbed in silence. They cannot speak; they are within the atmosphere of both Indian and Victorian reticence. (Pl. XXXI)

But back in the house the fate of Charu, Bhupati and Amal becomes inevitable. The casually joyful Amal only projects his enthralling charm still further upon Charu's now romantic consciousness of him. He sings the song she hummed but in a lilting tone. Unintentionally, he is playing the seducer. Now in love with him, Charu notices how worn his slippers are. In that instant she's compelled to make him a gift of the slippers she has embroidered for her husband. Amal will leave this clue behind him in his room for Bhupati to find and thus realize that it was his wife as well as his fortune that was stolen from him by two men he trusted.

The richness of the film is aptly conveyed by Penelope Houston's long analysis in *Sight and Sound* :

. . . in *Charulata* the interplay of sophistication and simplicity is extraordinary. The whole small business of Charu's literary competition with Amal, for instance, and the impulses of jealousy, crossness, obstinacy and love which work on her, is very subtle indeed. Her feeling that Amal is writing in *her* notebook, and for her, in those long afternoons by the swing; her irritation when Amal jokingly asks the sister-in-law what magazine to send his story to; everyone's annoyance when Amal bounds in at precisely the wrong moment with the ice-cream that is to celebrate publication, and has to fling his sweetmeats to the cat; out of half a dozen such incidents emerges a motive which isn't apparent to Charu herself. But the incidents are never enough in themselves to break the film's even flow. Nothing, in any direct narrative sense has happened.

As there existed a deep kinship in life between Rabindranath Tagore and Satyajit's grandfather and father, so there appears to exist a particularly strong creative kinship between Tagore and Satyajit, even though in life they hardly ever talked. Ray has said that he will come back and back again to the stories left by Gurudev, even though there are many Bengalis who quarrel with him as to his transcription of Tagore's literary form into film.

Michael ffolkes's cartoon af Chandana Banerji as Ratan and Aparna Das Gupta as Mrinmoyee in *Two Daughters*

PHONE GOPALPUR
Dav. No. 1

CRAM : PALM BEACH
GOPALPUR (GANJAM)

Oberoi Palm Beach

GOPALPUR • ON • SEA

REGISTERED OFFICE : PALM BEACH HOTEL PRIVATE LTD.
17, CHOWRINGHEE ROAD, CALCUTTA-13

BANSI

1) It would be very convenient if the Main Bedroom (Charu's) could be built along with the verandah. There are all sorts of crucial entrances & exits from between the Bedroom and the Verandah, and there's too long a gap in shooting, it might give rise to serious continuity problems. The other two bedrooms (Amal's & Mandakini') need only be in suggestion — although you would need the space for them. The drawing room and the new study need not be built at all — so what you need for this big set is this —

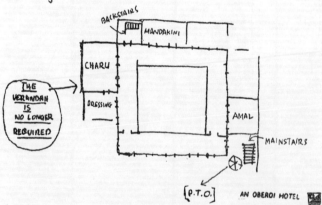

Letter from Satyajit to Bansi Chandragupta with designs for *Charulata*

2) ⊗ This must be the first floor main landing, so that the top of the staircase could be seen from the verandah. This is what a camera set-up would look like —

staircase railing

THIS IS VERY IMPORTANT
FROM THE POINT OF VIEW
OF THE ACTION AS I'VE
PLANNED IT

3) This is the set-up for the last shot of the film —

THIS IS A
VITALLY IMPORTANT
SETUP, AND CAN'T BE
CHANGED

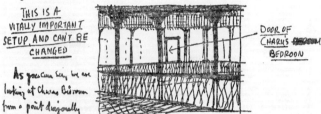

DOOR OF
CHARU'S
BEDROOM

As you can see, we are looking at Charu's bedroom from a point diagonally across, on the drawing room-side of the verandah.
This is a normal eye-level view point.

THE PROBLEM IS — HOW CAN WE AVOID THE STUDIO FLOOR
UNLESS THE WHOLE SET IS BUILT ON A HIGH (6/7 FT) PLATFORM ?
IS IT POSSIBLE TO DO SO ? TO ME THERE SEEMS TO
BE NO OTHER WAY.

We'll talk about it on Monday. My work is proceeding quite smoothly. Best, Manik

Satyajit (for revived *Sandesh*)

Chapter 9

RAY'S OWN THEMES—*KANCHENJUNGA, NAYAK* AND *THE ALIEN*

"IDEALLY, the director should be in control of every creative aspect of film production (including camera work) because he is the only person who knows exactly what is wanted. I do as much as I feel I am capable of doing and I feel is good for the film."

Satyajit Ray was replying to a question as to whether he insisted on controlling all aspects of his pictures.

In retrospect, the year 1961 was one of creative expansion for Ray. Though not a trained musician nor master of an instrument, he had ventured to devise his own music for *Teen Kanya*. He felt compelled to take this step after encountering difficulties in conveying to even the finest musicians the role he wanted music to perform in his individual films. From his point of view music's most important function was to serve to enrich an emotional and atmospheric situation. Ravi Shankar had captured the idea when his music gave an agonized cry as if coming from Sarbojaya in *Pather Panchali*. But subsequently even Shankar chafed at Ray's suggestions. Musicians had their own ideas which did not necessarily reflect Ray's intentions. He realized the inherent problems of finding musicians with a developed understanding of the film medium. This drove him to rely upon himself if he were to achieve the effects he sought.

By May 1961, Ray had completed seven feature films, the trio of short Tagore films and the Tagore biographical documentary. He had accumulated fame rather than money. As Penelope Houston observed in *The Contemporary Cinema*: "Ray came along to recharge the batteries of humanist cinema at a time when neo-realism had sacrificed its momentum. But if *Pather Panchali* was a direct statement, his later films have been a good deal more complex."

Because Ray had wisely refrained from expanding his manner of living, he had attained just that amount of economic leeway to allow him to do what he wanted to satisfy the diversification of his creative impulse. Having grown increasingly conscious of his ancestral heritage, he decided in 1961 to set aside Rs.1,000/- a month to maintain a revived *Sandesh*, the children's magazine founded by his grandfather, Upendrakishore, and carried on to the end of his life by his father, Sukumar.

The original aim behind the magazine had been Upendra's desire to entertain his own children and all others. Satyajit's own relationship with his graphically talented little son, Sandip, had become profound, growing in common interest and communication from year to year. From 1961 onwards *Sandesh* appeared, with Satyajit constantly writing stories for it, including a science-fiction series which has been published in book form. This was cited as the best Bengali children's book of its year. The embryo idea of the film, *The Alien*, was first developed in the magazine while an endless stream of unsigned illustrations have poured forth from Satyajit.

But he has never specifically explained whether, prior to the summer of 1961, he had a settled intention to produce film scripts based on his own themes. There is much about his ideas and work that Ray never feels an urge to explain unless it comes up accidentally, or he is specifically asked a question. This is probably because his thoughts are constantly occupied with what he is either working on or planning. With the practice of film-making, his early passion for theories became less articulated.

No sooner was *Teen Kanya* released in May than Ray was planning to commence shooting the film *Mahanagar* on June 21st in Calcutta. I had the intention to go there to observe him at work Almost at the last moment his protracted search to find the right girl to interpret Arati, the heroine, collapsed. Unwilling to resort to second best the project was shelved until he could find his ideal Arati. It was at this point that Ray's interest in E. M. Forster's *A Passage to India* warmed. He had two copies of the book, one much worm-eaten which he gave me to read on the train between Calcutta and Delhi. Both his thought and mine pounced upon the qualitative perfection of Dame Sybil Thorndike for Mrs. Moore.

(Dame Sybil was destined to play the role in the London TV production of Rama Shanta Rao's play.) During the summer, Ray went to London hoping to meet Forster. Before he arrived Forster was taken ill and Ray felt compelled to retreat. When their ultimate meeting took place in the early autumn of 1965 in Cambridge, the fragility of Forster so overwhelmed Ray that he barely said a word about his desire. He knew of Forster's resistance to the idea of a film being made.

Breakdown in the arrangements to shoot *Mahanagar* plagued Ray. He tried his best to keep his unit at work in order that they should earn a living wage. He was in no position to pay them when they were not making a film. They had been working steadily since 1956. When not at work, Ray feels extremely uncomfortable. It so affects him that his blood pressure tends to rise.

With the completion of *Teen Kanya*, Ray, indifferent to the predictable invectives hurled at him for the changes he had made in his adaptations, had become convinced "that the long short story is ideally suited to the two-hour span of the normal commercial film." He had in mind a story focused upon a group of people out on a picnic. He had thought of a beginning and an end with several embryonic situations suited to the characters he had in mind. His idea was that the film should open with an album of photographs of the family at a picnic.

"The last of several photographs would become animated," said Satyajit, "the photographs having been taken by the son, Anil, during the picnic."

The conclusion of the film was to be the last photograph in the album. It was to have shown a character something akin to the father, Indranath, who became, in fact, the central figure in *Kanchenjunga*. This frozen scene of him was to suggest doubt, doubt was to be seen in his eyes. Ray had found a garden-house that attracted him as the perfect setting for what he wanted to evolve psychologically between the characters. There was a dining-room in which Ray visualized a scene between the elder daughter of the family and her husband. He would retire there to drink and the wife would come in and there would be a revelation of their conflict.

This picnic story was jolted out of further development because the owner of the perfect house refused to negotiate for its use as the location for a film. Upset, Ray could not bring himself to search for a substitute house. Meanwhile, he had been seeking an author to write a short story embodying the skeleton of his own idea. No short story had materialized. The picnic story was in a state of flux when, on August 12th, Satyajit's friend, Bijoy Chatterjee, arrived at Lake Temple Road determined to have Ray read the novel *Abhijan*, by Tarashankar Bannerjee, the author of the short story on which *Jalsaghar* is based. *Abhijan*, discussed subsequently, was thus injected as a subject which Ray agreed to script between his first thoughts of the picnic film and his decision to develop this embryo story into *Kanchenjunga*, his first original scenario.

The outwardly calm Ray had reached a restless point. No doubt a desire to do something totally different stimulated his decision to embark on a theme and a style of film for which there had been no precedent in India: a scenario written, as Ray put it, "densely within a restricted field in terms of time and space".

Ray's three original scripts all have this characteristic. The action within *Kanchenjunga* occupies one hour and forty minutes —the running time of the film. With the exception of a few shots showing two characters walking up from the bottom of the hill town of Darjeeling, the whole action takes place on Observatory Hill. *Nayak*, constructed of action on a Calcutta-Delhi train, flash-backs and two dreams, occupies the twenty-four hours of the journey. *The Alien* action is within a spaceship and the surrounding village where it lands at night. A day and a half later the spaceship takes off for an unknown destination.

The three films close with what Ray calls "open endings": denouements leaving it to each member of the audience to speculate further on the fate of the characters and supply their own interpretative conclusion, if any.

While *Kanchenjunga* concerns the eruption of reactions of a single well-to-do upper-class family and an outsider to serve as catalyst, *Nayak* and *The Alien* portray diversified groups of people reacting in the former film to the personality of the hero, a film star, and in the latter to a sudden, inexplicable situation. A cross-section of those Indians who travel air-conditioned reveals contemporary attitudes, which is the underlying theme of *Nayak*; while in *The Alien*, the attitudes run the gamut from the automatically traditional—that the spaceship is miraculous, as it would be in any village—to the scientifically deductive.

Though *Kanchenjunga* and *Nayak* might be described as conversation pieces, both, and *The Alien* too, contain more than one level at which they can be understood. In essence, the themes, though worked out with conspicuous differences (how can a film of family conflict and a father's domination and a science-fiction situation be in any way akin?), centre upon a recurrent idea found

N

in the three films. This is that power, wielded on the basis of material wealth, produces varying degrees of moral corruption and, if challenged, reveals an unnerved uncertainty. The dominating Indranath Roy Chudhuri (or Indranath Rai Bahadur to give him his British-bestowed title) finds his world shaken in *Kanchenjunga* when the young outsider, Ashoke, rejects his offer of a Rs.300/- a month job when he is earning only Rs.50/- from tutoring. Arindam, the film star of *Nayak*, is bedevilled by a sense of guilt for having sold himself to commercial success and is fast crystallizing into a drunkard. Bajoria, the thinly veiled portrait of a notorious Indian industrialist, is reduced to a state of apparent dottiness when the supposed temple he was about to reclaim for his self-interest, inconveniently proves to be a space capsule from some unidentified point in the universe.

Except for the two dream sequences in *Nayak* and the improved vision of the Alien himself, the films are clothed in realism even though, for those who wish to see another level, all three have allegorical elements. If there is a hero or a heroine, the role goes to the outsider—the non-conformist.

The unexpected aspect of the films is the importance assigned to dialogue in view of the subsidiary place of words in Ray's earlier films. He explains this:

"It is the literate sophisticates who express themselves more through words than through action. If you are dealing with this class of people, you have to use words. This in itself is not a handicap, nor is it basically unfilmic." But he insists that dialogue in film must reject both literary and dramatic modes of speech and have the feel of speech as it is in life. "Then only can it have the true plastic quality which can enhance a film instead of stultifying it. The quality of a good wordy film does not consist in the words alone, but in the way the words are combined with significant action, details of behaviour."

An example is the second passage of dialogue in *Kanchenjunga*: the gentlemanly Indranath Rai Bahadur, who has just been shown to have a polite penchant for Englishmen, meets his bird-watcher brother-in-law, Jagadish, as he is about to leave the hotel terrace. Jagadish is carrying a book about birds. He faces the camera with Indranath angled in profile:

Indranath: What are you carrying that about for?
Jagadish: I'm going to try for the last time today. That bird must be somewhere. I heard it call.
Indranath: Kanchenjunga must be somewhere too!

Jagadish : Here is the bird (*he shows the picture*).
Indranath : Good for roasting? . . . Can you roast it and eat it?
Jagadish : No. But this bird is . . .
Indranath : Then I'm not interested.
Jagadish : But I tell you, this . . .
Indranath : Put that book away and see if they're ready. (*He insolently flips Jagadish's book closed, revealing his high-handed autocraticness.*)

That Ray's upper-class family were going to speak as people do in life, throwing in all the triviality of their thoughts and lack of verbal brilliance, would set off a controversy in highly verbal Bengal. Ray would be charged with making an "anti-film".

But *Kanchenjunga* was for Ray, so he explained, his first attempt to create rather than interpret.

Determined to shape his own picnic idea into a scenario, he had packed up in September 1961 and gone alone to Darjeeling, the Himalayan town to which his grandfather had a habit of retreating for inspiration. But this time, instead of staying at the Mount Everest Hotel, he was the sole guest at the Windermere perched almost on the top of Observatory Hill surmounting this stratified Queen of Hill Stations.

The hotel terrace, destined to become the location for the opening shots of the scenario Ray wrote in ten days, provided a superlative view, when clear, of Kanchenjunga, the tallest peak of the world's third highest mountain. This "most beautiful snow range in the world" provided the symbolic title. The peak remains veiled until the final shot; but the atmosphere of the place affects every character and their reactions. It brings psychological change to a head. Towards the end of the encounter of the young outsider, Ashoke, with Indranath and his family, he explains his own transformation :

"These vast ranges . . . these solemn fir trees . . . now sun, now mist, now cloud . . . everything seems unreal, like a dream! As if I were no longer myself, as if I were somebody—a hero, full of courage, daring, not afraid of anybody. Being in a place like this puts courage into you, doesn't it?"

Almost all the characters in *Kanchenjunga* stand in need of courage at the outset—to resist the domineering will of Indranath. At the end he is alone, facing the mountain. No one has kept their appointment with him. Each has resolved his own problem.

The initial idea of the picnic disappeared. The focal situation to emerge was the waiting of the family for the younger daughter,

Monisha, to return from an arranged walk during which she is supposed to accept the marriage proposal of the stolid Bannerji, "a real acquisition" to the family's prestige. Instead, by the end, she has disposed of her incompatible suitor and is inviting the outsider to visit her. (Pl. XLIV)

For an hour and forty minutes on the afternoon before the family are to leave Darjeeling the following morning at the end of their seventeen-day holiday, simultaneous, overlapping action, weaving in and out of the proposal walk, uncovers the attitudes and conflicts of all the people involved, those embryonic in the picnic idea: the father, Indranath, dominating, cynical, ruthless, the "director of five companies" whom the British in their time honoured with a title, for which he still honours them; his wife, Labanya, whose life has been crushed without obliterating her perceptiveness; Anil, their womanizing son running after two members of the drainpipe set; the elder daughter, Anima, whom Indranath arbitrarily married off to the once eligible Shankar with near disastrous results; Monisha, who musters the courage not to accept her father's choice; her widower uncle, Jagadish, vastly more interested in birds than advantageous matchmaking; and the outsider, Ashoke, nephew of Sibsankar, a former tutor to Anil who is, perhaps, the negative reverse of the Indranath coin.

Aiming to stress the musical structure, Ray introduced the recurrent motif of Anima and Shankar's little girl—the thread to hold them together—riding around Observatory Hill on a pony anxiously watching them when their conflict becomes the second main line of action, commenting, as it were, on what can happen to Monisha if she fails to see where her father's domination is pushing her. Bannerji and Monisha, too, are haunted by a witness—the small beggar boy who interested Satyajit while he was writing the script. The boy himself became part of the unit when direction commenced. Ray's directorial methods are later detailed in relation to *Kanchenjunga*.

Between *Kanchenjunga* (1961–2) and his second original story, *Nayak* (1966), Ray directed *Abhijan* (1962), *Mahanagar* (1963), *Charulata* (1964) and the double-bill picture, *Kapurush-o-Mahapurush* (1965), each of these ventures being in accord with Ray's inclination to keep shifting genres and trying new fields, thematically and stylistically.

Some of Ray's admirers, particularly Indians, were and are dubious about *Nayak*. They were rather mystified by the choice of a film star to stand for the Hero image. It was a central character which directors had explored in other countries and more dramatically and with a fiercer bite. The quietness of *Nayak* spread a certain confusion. Not too friendly speculation also centred around the fact that Ray had written his script with the star Uttam Kumar in mind. The expectation seems to have been that having done so, Ray would surely unveil the sordidness of the film industry and the evils of the star system. Instead, the Hero is revealed as an actor of some talent, some conscience and a good deal of mediocrity.

Apart from the key idea that money is the root of insecurity, not security as popularly supposed, *Nayak* is, as David McCutchion, of Calcutta's Jadhavpur University, observed, "anti-romantic". Ray took a potentially romantic situation and stood it on its head. The young, quizzical woman editor, Aditi Sen Gupta—she now and then takes off her glasses—captures the attention of the hero of every girl's dream while they are on the same train to Delhi, he going there to receive the Best Actor Award from the hands of the President; she travelling with a couple third class. At a moment of crisis she draws forth from him his life story. Both in literature and life, she might dream to reclaim the Hero from his loneliness and inebriation. Nothing of the kind happens. No romance develops because, in reality, Arindam is captive to a vortex from which he has no will to escape. Here is a plausible situation which is true to the reality of life.

The motif of a prison cell comes with the sharp black-and-white design for the credits and the back of the Hero's head in the centre. It is echoed in the mechanical smile on his face in the large close-up with which *Nayak* ends.

There is more to *Nayak* than this central situation. If possible, the dialogue looms of even greater importance than in *Kanchenjunga*. Again, singularly ordinary words are spoken by Arindam Mukerjee and Aditi Sen Gupta, and between the surrounding characters who react to the Hero and to their own situations. This superficially commonplace dialogue, so adroitly constructed sentence by sentence, embodies a second subtle level: the stress embedded oscillates between comments on Reality, which is what we are repeatedly shown, and Illusion implied by the reputation, the public Image, not only of Arindam, the Hero, but also that of the powerful industrialist, Heren Bose, travelling on the same train. (Pl. XXXIV)

In contemporary India, as indeed universally in what is termed free society, the film star and the successful industrialist elicit the reverence, the excitement of legendary figures. For the former, the reverence is romantic no matter how cynically unromantic the real-life figure is. As Ajoy, one of Aditi's travelling companions in third class, comments on Arindam: "He is the modern Krishna—and all these ladies are his secret gopis." For the latter, the spurious servility is in the hope that contact will put one up one rung on the economic ladder. Sarkar, the advertising man travelling air-conditioned in order to hunt down and hook Heren Bose into a contract, tells his wife, Molly: "Just one client like that and I'm made for life." He is even determined to exploit Molly's sex appeal to gain his ends.

With the exception of the two children on the train, whose reactions to Arindam are free of self-interest, everyone he encounters and speaks of in his biographical past, save his original actor mentor, Shankarda, is on the make in some way. His Leftist Trade Union friend, Biresh, whom Arindam lets down, is out to use him if not for himself then for the Cause. Even the attractive and intelligent catalyst, Aditi, who probes to find out what lies behind the Star image, is serving her curiosity as to illusion and reality. Towards the end, the silent, observing Swamiji, who has done nothing but spray his throat throughout the journey, reveals himself to the advertising man as being in the spiritual business. He offers to pay Rs.30,000 for publicity to promote his World Wide Will Workers. (Pl. XXXIV)

Within an exceptionally restrained framework of almost mundane realism, Ray implies a bizarre vortex of unreality in which all his people, with perhaps the exception of Aditi, are caught.

Arindam, reacting to her early query: "Don't you feel there's something missing in your life? Some emptiness somewhere?" explains: "Look, Miss Sen Gupta, it's no good to talk too much. You see, we live in a world of shadows—so it's best not to let the public see too much of our flesh and blood."

Neither Arindam's two disturbing dreams nor his flashback recollections to his past bring forth revelations that he has greatly sinned either against himself or anyone else. The truth, or reality, behind his mask of success and romantic image, is that intelligent, sensitive as he is, his discontent, doubt, even what is becoming his compulsive drinking, is because he is caught up in a whirligig of "business". (Pl. XXXIV)

Within the first few shots of the film, Arindam is shown counting out a wad of hundred-rupee notes and stuffing them into his pocket and wallet. That he should keep so much money in a wardrobe implies to anyone who knows the Indian film industry that he has received so-called "black money", that which is to be concealed from the Income Tax authorities. Yet he refuses to sign a contract with the Mawari producer who comes to pin him down with an advance discreetly enclosed in an envelope. He is not greedy for money. The dream is therefore prepared, and before the dream he has revealed nothing directly about himself beyond the fact that he likes whisky and that his affair with a woman, which has led to a brawl in a nightclub, is pretty unsatisfactory.

Some Indian critics disliked and dismissed the first dream as obvious. This is a rather curious condemnation to be made in a country haunted by endemic poverty. It is to be questioned if these critics actually observed Arindam's dream except in terms of stylized images not hitherto associated with Ray's particular style. The dream does *not* show the obvious—the Hero's dread of losing the money he now has. It shows him engulfed in panic at being swallowed up and lost in the mountain of money that is his. At first he wafts elatedly about above the piles of dream money. Then the limpid light dims. (Pl. XXXIII)

> Arindam [who is later revealed as having perceptive instinct as to what is effective film acting] looks around apprehensively and suddenly stops short at the sight of a hand on an arm devoid of flesh that protrudes out of a mound (of rupee notes) . . . apprehension gives way to fear. . . .

More skeleton hands spring up from the mounds of currency. They hold telephone receivers and phone bells jangle. The dream image creates a valid terror for one who wants to be a good actor. In reality in India successful stars are besieged by offers to make simultaneous films so long as their films prove box-office successes. They are submerged by the number of their roles. Rushing about, Arindam "is caught in a quicksand of currency notes". A figure approaches in a strange theatrical make-up and grins at Arindam who cannot reach the figure's outstretched hand. "Help, Shankarda", cries Arindam. But the figure allows him to sink as he cries "Save me! Save me, Shankarda."

The dream compels Arindam to talk to Aditi and speak of the dead Shankarda, the theatre director, who had tried to convince Arindam that the actor in films is but a "puppet in the hands of the director, of the cameraman, of the sound recordist. . . ." But neither the talking to Aditi nor the flashback come immediately after the dream. Instead, as is evident in much classical Indian architectonic creation, particularly temple façades where major and minor themes are juxtaposed, the dramatic dream introducing the inner panic of the Hero is succeeded by the minor theme of the advertising man, Sarkar, seeking to persuade his wife to keep the industrialist, Bose, company—"smile sweetly, talk softly"— Shocked, Molly walks out of the compartment and locks herself in the train bathroom.

The train slows down and halts at a station which gives the disturbed Arindam a chance to escape on to the platform—to have fresh air to blow away his dream. The dream has shaken the image of the Star he has been so assiduously maintaining. Like any ordinary Indian passenger he buys tea in a small traditional clay cup to be thrown away. Noticing Aditi in the dining-car, he signals the question to her "does she want a cup, too?" She shows him her fork to indicate she's eating. He goes and joins her, asking what does she know about dreams.

Seven flashbacks and another dream reveal the Hero's biography during the journey. The dream with its death motif is balanced by the enactment of Arindam's drunken "scene" where it looks as if he is going to throw himself out of the train in self-disgust. Some critics have complained that this scene is unconvincing. It seems rather unlikely that Ray intended his audience fully to credit that his Hero, the actor, was intent on dying. He is intent unconsciously on further revealing his need to make the cool Miss Sen Gupta understand him. She is perfectly willing to give her sympathy but not respond to his angling that they meet again. She says: "You live in a different world. . . . We're out in the streets, in trams and buses. . . ." He replies: "If three of my films flop in a row, I might go back into that world." Aditi assures him this doesn't appear very likely. Finally, she tears up the notes on his life she has made. He asks her why she tears them up. "I'll keep them in my memory," Aditi answers and bids the Hero good-bye. She leaves him to go her independent way while he is immediately engulfed in the vortex of stardom at Delhi station where, as indicated in the first scene, preparation for his reception has been made—by phone.

In a letter written me in February 1966, when he was working on the sound tracks of *Nayak*, Satyajit explained the relationship between Arindam and Aditi:

> I wanted a relationship to develop between the Matinée Idol and a girl on the train. Romance was out—the time being so short—but I wanted something with an interesting development. The transition from apathy mixed with a certain dislike, to sympathetic understanding, seemed a promising one. So I made Aditi a slightly snooty sophisticate who questions and resists the easy charm, good looks, sangfroid, etc. etc., of the Idol,

until she discovers there's an area where he's helpless, lonely, and in need of guidance. From the point where he begins to unburden himself, Aditi can ignore his façade because she's had a glimpse of what lies beneath. At first he is 'material' for her for a journalistic probe, until the process of unbaring reaches a point where she realizes it would be unethical to exploit it. Sympathy and desire to help is the next step. The bond between the two is tenuous, but real. Intellectually clearly above him, her goodness consists in providing him with the small area of contact that exists between them. Does this make sense? I'm not sure, but that is how it probably evolved, although I wasn't conscious of calculation when I wrote the parts. It just seemed the most interesting way to set them off against each other.

None of Ray's women are overtly what might be called feminists; but the evolution of feminine attitudes is most interestingly revealed from film to film. The evidence from the masculine and feminine characters throughout Ray's work suggests the creative expression of a man who is free of the bondage of a masculine superiority attitude. From 1961 this becomes more pronounced: Monisha in *Kanchenjunga* takes a distinctly independent line; Gulabi, with her questionable moral past in *Abhijan*, proves the moral force behind the reckless Narsingh's final rejection of a criminal career; Arati, in *Mahanagar*, not only makes a success of her economically necessary career and demonstrates moral force, but her independence does not cause her to reject her husband who, under pressures, has not evolved as rapidly as herself. In *Charulata*, set in the period when women the world over were in the process of straining to emancipate themselves, Charu demonstrates both her literary ability and her capacity for passion; while in the contemporary *Kapurush*, the wife, who in her youth was ready to abandon all security for love of the coward, in her maturity has the courage to renounce romance with him and remain with her dull husband even though he causes her headaches.

Some people were scathing about Satyajit Ray devoting time to what they claimed was the trivial theme of a triangle situation in *Kapurush*. He was accused of making too many films, hurriedly one after the other. *Kapurush* was intentionally a short, lightweight film. It is not, and was not intended to be a masterpiece. It is a sketch of a segment of contemporary Indian society, peopled by three characters whose prototypes are on the increase.

Ray confines himself to a brief encounter between two men, both patently ordinary though sharply contrasting as contemporary types: a film script writer (Soumitra Chatterjee) drives his car into the tea planting area in order to absorb at short notice the local colour for a scenario. His car breaks down and cannot be repaired immediately. So the garage man communicates with a local tea planter to have the Calcuttan put up for the night.

The planter, living in a comfortable but ordinary bungalow, is a good natured if rather loud bore who drowns the insignificance of his existence by tippling. As is not too uncommon in this comfortably off planters' society, his wife (Madhabi Mukherjee) is many streets above him in quality and sensitivity. Indeed, she would never have become a planter's wife but—such incidents occur in life in most countries—for the cowardly retreat of the youthful lover of her student days. He lacked the guts to elope with her when she declared herself only too willing to shed family and security for his sake. She had been an art student. Rejected, she settled for a secure if boring life with an ordinary sort of man.

When her husband brings in the scenarist she does not bat an eyelash. Her poise and inadmission of ever having set eyes on him before adds to his own confusion since he recognizes her as the girl he lacked the courage to go away with. There is no dramatic explosion. Only both of them experience an amusingly sleepless night, each in need of aspirin for their shaken nervous systems. The lady politely donates her bottle of tablets to her one-time love.

The next day his car is still unrepaired. Worse still, husband is an everlasting obstacle in the way for the one-time coward to straighten things out with the none-too-happy wife. He does, however, manage to invite her to come away with him; to join him at the train in which he is now compelled to travel to Calcutta. In the final sequence he is shown sitting expectantly on the platform waiting. His rediscovered true love appears. But she has only come to recover her bottle of aspirin. Having decided to remain with her dull husband she requires to relieve her headaches.

Light in touch, gently humorous, the ironic *Kapurush* is far from complimentary to the male animal. It is a small essay in praise to the long-suffering commonsense and sense of proportion of what Ray clearly considers is not to be regarded as the weaker sex. As in the case of Kenzi Mizoguchi, Ray's interpretation of women is a respectful and socially progressive one. Except for the unpleasant Monimalika in *Monihara*, the element of implied evil, and demonstrated stupidity and weakness, has been depicted by Ray as a masculine propensity. There is no hostility towards

women in his films. Their social significance is that they depict
an evolution of women from generation to generation. By the
time *Nayak* is reached, its heroine, if Aditi can be called such,
stands for the universal type of career women who have achieved
an independent identity distinct from that of their husbands or
families, but without the dissolution of their feminine understanding and sympathy towards men. Aditi is herself, not a woman in
competition with men.

Nayak is a difficult film to appraise in terms of its individual
sequences. No sequence can be singled out as intensely remarkable.
If the film absorbs it is because of its paradoxically seemingly
leisurely yet tightknit whole in weaving a tissue of observation in
the working of conscience. As McCutchion observed in a review,
"the delight of the film lies in its structure—the way the themes
are patterned—and the pleasure of recognizing the familiar pin-
pointed by art". This patterning gradually mounts up to an
investigation of the commonplace but with moral depth. Conscience, for Arindam, is a nuisance. Yet it is this element alone
that makes him interesting as a human being.

This was the appeal of an outwardly conventional character for
those critics who ultimately liked the film when it was presented
at the 1966 Berlin Film Festival. Ray's introspective Hero of this
unromantic film gave the audience, as one critic put it, something
to get hold of in a Festival of films strewn with rapists, layabouts,
alcoholics and an assortment of neurotics. Though disappointing
to some other critics, *Nayak* nevertheless won the International
Critics' award and contributed to the Special Award given to Ray
for the whole range of his work.

In February 1966, while still occupied with the final work on
Nayak, Ray began to develop simultaneously two stories of his
own. He described one, still uncompleted: "A family drama involving four generations—8 year old grandson (future), 4 sons (present)
—mystic, businessman, playboy and frustrated intellectual, Father
(idealist—builder of a township—representing immediate past)
and Grandfather (remote past) who is senile but may live to be
100. Father lies in coma with heart attack, sons converge at bedside.
Father vacillates between life and death, while sons reveal their
bitterly clashing values. . . ."

The other story, which was to loom into the foreground, was
The Alien. But it is this clash of values that has absorbed Ray in
each of his original stories. He had written *The Alien* in embryo
as a story for children. It formed part of his science-fiction series
centred upon a Geography Teacher who encounters numerous

Re Aditi — I wanted a relationship to develop between the Nature Idol + a girl on the train. Romance was out — the voine being so short — but I wanted something with an interesting development. The transition from apathy mixed with a certain amount of dislike, to sympathetic understanding, seemed a promising one. So I made Aditi a slightly snooty sophisticate who questions and resists the easy charm, good looks, sang froid, etc etc of the Idol, until she discovers there is an area where he's helpless, lonely, and in need of guidance. From this point he begins to unburden himself. Aditi can ignore his facade because she had a glimpse of what lies beneath. At first, he is "material" for her for a journalistic probe, until the process of unburdening reaches a point where she realizes it would be unethical to exploit it. Sympathy + Respect help to the next step. ~~This bond is tenuous but real~~ ~~The~~ The bond between the two is tenuous, but real.

Intellectually clearly above him, her goodness consists in providing him with the small area of contact that exists between them. Does this make sense? I'm not sure, but that is how it probably evolved, although I wasn't conscious of calculation when I wrote the parts. It just seemed the most interesting way to set them off against each other.

I'm already at work on 2 more stories — both original. One, a science-fiction story involving a space ship – with only one supremely intelligent Martian occupant — landing on the outskirts of a remote village with as little contact with 'civilization' as possible. Martian first taken for a monster, then for a god — + so on.

Two, a family drama involving four generations — 8 year old grandson (future), 4 sons (present) — mystic, businessman, playboy, + frustrated intellectual, Father (Idealist — builder of a town ships — representing immediate past) + grandfather (remote past) who is senile but may live to 100. Father lies in coma with heart attack, sons converge at bedside. Father vacillates between life + death, while sons reveal their bitterly clashing values ...

All the best,

[signature]

From a letter to the Author

adventures. In this one, the Teacher is in a somewhat depressed mood until he comes upon a spaceship which has landed on earth by mistake. The occupant, who was to evolve into the Alien and title the subsequent film script, possessed an extraordinary piece of glass through which amazing things could be seen. The encounter, which proved to the Teacher that all is not what it seems, endowed the Teacher with a new interest in life and ideas. The fact that no one believed what the Teacher says does not matter to him.

It will be recalled that as a small boy Manik Ray would spend hours of his time experimenting with light coming through a hole in his uncle's door and falling upon a piece of glass which he held up to see what would happen. It was the adult Satyajit Ray's lasting interest in magnifying and microbes which pushed forward the evolution of *The Alien* script.

In the early stages of the first treatment, the Teacher in the children's story was eliminated. Ray was concentrating upon "only one supremely intelligent Martian occupant" of the spaceship "landing on the outskirts of a remote village with as little contact with 'civilization' as possible. Martian first taken for a monster, then for a God—and so on." Subsequently, the idea of "the Martian mistaken for a monster" disappeared from the script, very likely because so many science-fiction films had concentrated upon the dread of a monster arriving from outer space.

During the next twelve months and throughout 1967, crisis gradually engulfed the Bengal film industry, and is described in the concluding chapter. This, inevitably, affected Ray's plans.

Early in 1967, a young international producer with reckless ambitions arrived in India and contacted Satyajit Ray because he had heard of Ray's work on *The Alien*. He had connection with Arthur Clarke, the science-fiction writer, whom Satyajit much admired. It was suggested that *The Alien* was suited to international production. Satyajit agreed, for the growing crisis in Bengal's film production had pushed him into a mood to take risks.

He wanted to expand the technical horizon of at least some of his future films. It was evident to him that the trick work required for *The Alien* would add at least Rs.200,000/- to his normal budget. A curious patch in the normally regulated life of the quiet and disciplined Ray soon opened up. In pursuit of international finance, he found himself whirled off for three weeks into panoramas of Hollywoodesque life quite new in his experience. His mentor whisked him to New York, Hollywood and London where, for the first time, he stayed in Hiltonian luxury. Restlessly nervous stars, who appeared to be on edge in their glamorous Hollywood surroundings, lavishly entertained him. The Hippies to whom he was taken were enchanted by him. In New York, Edward Harrison, who had been eager in 1965 to raise finance for *A Passage to India* if E. M. Forster would agree to a film being made, was lifted out of a period of depression by Satyajit's arrival. But Satyajit somehow had a feeling that Ed's end was near. Harrison died suddenly of heart disease in the middle of October 1967.

The outcome of this weird and hectic three weeks was that the solid men of Columbia with assets frozen in India undertook to finance the production of *The Alien*. It was agreed that the whole of the film be shot on location in the area of Santineketan with the sets, including the spaceship, to be built in an Indian studio. The film was to be made in colour. A new phase in the career of Ray was to be opened up, though there was to be a long wait before this phase could take concrete shape. Subsequently, innumerable unpleasant complications developed. Shooting was first scheduled to commence in November 1968, then advanced to January 1969. Further complications have pushed it far into the future.

During negotiations, Ray refined his first scenario for *The Alien*. He expanded certain scenes and revised the dialogue. An increased subtlety in characterization took place. Perhaps the most unusual aspect of *The Alien* as science-fiction is the absence of threat of danger and violence from the visitor from outer space. The Alien is unarmed except for the possession of psycho-physical weapons. These are self-regulated means of special qualities of sight and a naturally potent life force which causes living matter, if looked at intently or touched, to grow instantly. The Alien is a benign force apparently capable of producing miracles. The embodiment of power, as accepted in this world, is G. L. Bajoria, the industrialist, with his self-interested business drive. Like Indranath in *Kanchenjunga*, Bajoria presumes he is in control of people and situations on account of his money. But in the course of the Alien's visit to an ordinary village where Bajoria is having a well dug, it becomes evident that the industrialist cannot control the mind and conscience of either the American well-driller, Devlin, whom he is employing, or the young, scientific-minded journalist, Mohan, who has come to make a study of village life.

Mohan and the Alien share a quality, an element of values, that of compassion. The target of their compassion is the same—Haba, a small village boy who is being pushed by circumstances within the village into the existence of a beggar. The Alien takes this child away to another form of existence at the end of the film.

The only human who is allowed any direct impression of the Alien is this boy, Haba. It is the Alien's capsule that is assumed to be a miraculously revealed temple by the villagers, even by Bajoria. Devlin is in a perplexed position. It is Mohan, newly married, who fits scraps of news and his own impressions together to add up to the conviction that the mysterious object in the village pond has come from outer space. It has arrived just as "civilization" has invaded the village through Bajoria's scheme of sinking a well.

There are numerous fascinating aspects to the script. As mentioned, the dominant theme is the absence of menace in the presence of the Alien, whose motivation is joyous curiosity about life on earth—from the germs, amoeba and minute earthly forms in the pond where the capsule lands, to the cremation of the ancient villager, who, for a moment on his pyre, is revitalized due to the Alien's gaze. The unearthly visitor has "a large head, sunken cheeks, small mouth, nose and ears". In Satyajit's first sketches for the head, the ears had been eliminated. (Pl. XXXV)

"Eyes sunken—with pupils—if they exist at all—lost in the depths of the sockets." The character is descriptively visualized more completely than any other character in a Ray script. The Alien sees by means of different-coloured lights : green for observing telescopically; blue for microscopic examination; yellow for touch and energy; violet for looking into the brain—Haba's; red for examining the stilled respiratory system of the dead villager. When the red stream of light from the Alien's eyes turns to an intense white, the dead heart begins to beat again. The Alien's hearing is adjusted at will, even to the sound of amoebae drifting in the water and to ants swarming. It is uncertain how many fingers Ray will give to this figure.

When it comes outside the capsule, which looks like gold, the weightless visitor "is a cross between a gnome and a famished refugee child; large head, spindly legs, a lean torso". Sex indeterminate. "What his form basically conveys is a kind of ethereal innocence, and it is difficult to associate either great evil or great power with him." It, the Alien, is the constant observer of ordinary human events. The strange and scientifically advanced oscillate with earthly reality. "Yet a feeling of eeriness is there because of the resemblance to a sickly human child."

In *The Alien* script Ray is an amalgamator of his established realist style with sequences of fantasy bounded by scientifically valid images. Something of this combination appeared in *Paras Pathar—The Philosopher's Stone*—his third film.

The inhabitants of the village are caught between the two invading forces—the materialist schemes of Bajoria, who is both a threat and slightly comic, and the Alien with unexplained energy as the corollary of his presence. The spaceship occupant is observer from the start. Only gradually do his surprising powers unfold. A quarter of a mile from the pond where the capsule is concealed, well-drilling is due to commence.

Bajoria has come with a photographer. He explains the project to Devlin:

19   EXTERIOR—*Drilling Site—Day.*

    Bajoria: You have no idea what this project means to me, Mr. Devlin. I'm not only doing this for my own country, but also——

    Bajoria *is interrupted by the young Mawari (Rajini) running up and handing him a round brass box.* Bajoria *takes the box and continues to talk.*

    Bajoria (cont'd): ——but also I'm doing this for my own sake.

    Devlin *gives him a quizzical glance.* Bajoria *smiles.*

    Bajoria: I'm telling you because I think you'll understand. You know India is a poor country, don't you?

    Devlin: Uh-huh.

    Bajoria: And you know I have a certain amount of wealth.

    Devlin *gives a sidelong glance down at* Bajoria's *hand holding the sweet-box. All the fingers except the thumb have jewelled rings on them.*

    Devlin: You got some on yer fingers!

    Bajoria: What? . . . Oh, fingers—ha, ha! . . . But you know what happens to the rich man in India?

    Devlin: Nope. What?

    Bajoria: He sticks out—like a sore thumb. Because he's not a rich man in a *rich* country—not J. D. Rockefeller, G L. Bajoria—rich man in a *poor* country, ha, ha. So he is a sore thumb, and how can a sore thumb *ever* be a popular image, Mr. Devlin?

    Devlin: I get it!

    Bajoria: So what do you think the rich man does?

    Devlin: Takes to the bottle?

    Bajoria: No, no, no! He *bans* the bottle. He builds schools, parks, hospitals, temples—all for public convenience, see?

    Devlin: And gets J. B. Devlin down to drill for water?

    Bajoria: Exactly! The best man for the job! . . . Helps the country, helps his soul, helps his image!

The Alien's energy will cause the mango tree and the paddy field to grow and fructify with miraculous speed. The dead man on his pyre will open his eyes on being observed. Miracles are therefore thought to happen and Bajoria will be the first to seize upon the idea that the golden capsule is a submerged temple disturbed by the drilling.

Colour in which the film is conceived is not a constant. A section of the long sequence when the space visitor explores the village and discovers the hut where Haba sleeps, gives an impression : the Alien peers inside :

45   INTERIOR. Haba's shack—Night (Studio)
     The Alien sees Haba huddled in sleep on a mat. The Alien's eyes now turn a glowing red.

46   Process Shot (Studio)
     This enables him to see Haba's respiratory system, and to *listen* to his regular heart beats.

47   Process Shot (Studio)
     The red in the Alien's eyes now turns *violet*, enabling him to look into Haba's brain, and sink into his subconscious.

48   Haba's Dream (Studio)
     Haba is dreaming, and the Alien becomes part of his dream. We see Haba and the Alien happy, playing hide-and-seek in a strange black-and-white world of geometrical forms.

49   INTERIOR. Haba's Shack—Night Effect (Studio)
     The light in the Alien's eyes now dim, and with another high-pitched laugh, he is gone from the bamboo grove.

50   EXTERIOR. Paddy Field—Night Effect
     The Alien now arrives at the paddy field. The wide open spaces seem to delight him, and he dances around for a while.
     Then he notices the withering crop and examines the paddy plant.
     His eyes turn *yellow*, and he goes whirling about the field while the paddy around ripens and stands aspiring in the moonlight.
     Standing on the tip of a ripe paddy plant, the Alien looks up at the sky.

51   Night Sky With Moon (Studio)
     He sees the nearly full moon in the sky, and seems fascinated by it.

52   EXTERIOR. Paddy Field—Night Effect
     The Alien turns on his telescopic eyelights.

o

53   Night Sky with Moon (Studio)
     The moon is brought close for inspection, so that its gigantic
     orb marked with craters and mountains and valleys now fills
     a good half of the sky.
     Inspection over, the Alien pushes the moon back in place.

Ray's sensitivity in the conception of his Alien is the furthest
cry from the threatening monsters of accepted science-fiction. His
creation is an intriguing creature with the curiosity of Apu translated on to a supranatural plane. In the last scene where the Alien
is seen—the one before the final scene where the spaceship takes
off with a sudden hiss which turns to a hum gliding up "to a dizzy
pitch, and with a sound like that of a high-C *pizzicato* on a hundred violins"—he is sitting inside the space cabin "cross-legged on
the floor in the classical manner of the Buddha, a red disc of sunlight on his face and around his head". The image has a mystic
rather than monstrous element; a quality of innocence along with
wisdom to be accentuated by the sound, for the Alien sings a
simple folk-song about flowers, rivers and paddy fields taught to
him by Haba.
In a state of weightlessness and suspended animation, the boy
floats in the cabin, together with the other earthly specimens he
helped his "friend" collect—a frog, a firefly, a snake, a lotus, a
squirrel and a bulbul bird, all of which are also in a condition of
suspension. Inevitably, the conception of the Alien suggests that
only those who are as little children can enter another plane, or
planetary existence. The Superman is not endowed in Ray's
imagination with the conventional qualities of power.
Meanwhile, there is the second dominant motif, that of G. L.
Bajoria and his assumption that the dominance of money is supreme. But during the course of the story this assumption fails to be
proved. First, he fails to win over the aspiring journalist, Mohan,
who gradually fits scraps of information into a pattern which causes
him to realize that a visitation from another planet has taken place.
At the beginning, it might appear that the silent but shrewd Devlin
is Bajoria's man, having been employed by him to well-drill. He
makes no obvious protest to Bajoria's suggestion that he carry a
gun to the pond, nor to using it if necessary. He uses it to no effect
except to be mistaken for a hero. Then he throws it into the pond.
Bajoria is totally pooped by circumstances beyond his control. His
own standard of values appears to rebound on him, reducing him to
helpless idiocy.
Satyajit Ray claimed himself to be an optimist while at work on

Kanchenjunga, saying that Ashoke was the embodiment of optimism. In *The Alien,* optimism in regard to individual human behaviour and the possible development of intelligence on other planets is even more emphatically optimistic. This is an attitude of mind hardly reflected in the work of other major directors. It is against current trends of despair and violence, even though Ray is working in a city saturated with uncertainty, despair and a considerable undercurrent of violence.

Quiet as Ray's three original stories are, they make a calm onslaught on the damaging effect of power through money. The financial accumulator is shown as undermining himself because of his vaunted ideas about money. Get on to the treadmill of acquisition in a poor country and you will be damned as a human being. Where, as in *Nayak,* there is some talent and it is sold, the conflict is seen and felt in terms of an uneasy conscience. Arindam is not quite strong enough to escape.

There can be no conclusion except that when Ray embarks on his own story, his thoughts run along a philosophical track. Fascinated for years by his grandfather's fantasy, *Goupi Gyne,* by the time Satyajit had finished adding his own touches to it, the story evolved into a fantasy about the absurdity of war.

PART III

DIRECTOR AT WORK

Satyajit (for revived *Sandesh*)

Chapter 10

RAY AS SCENARIST

IN "An Estimate" of Ray written in October 1957 for *Amrita Bazar Patrika*, Ray's old friend, Chidananda Das Gupta, observed:

Scripting is the beginning of film-making; editing the end. Direction is something built on these two pillars—for Satyajit Ray at any rate. By exercising complete control of these two stages Satyajit integrates his work and makes it the complete translation of the picture in his mind. . . . It is the detail that makes cinema, for all it is something you cannot "see" in any other art. . . . Satyajit's sense of detail is closely linked with his keen observation of life, his memory of the character of the scene. It is, on the other hand, linked also with his study of

213

human character, his interest in revealing the essence of a character and in showing its relationship with other characters.

During the early days of Ray's film-going he was almost exclusively exposed to American and British films. In his early-1940s attempt at a Tagore script, *Home and the World*, which he says he will still some day make from a new scenario, the human relations and political ideas were presented in a style differing little from the script-writing of American and British films of that period. In this script, the characters are shown behaving in a conventional and melodramatic manner little connected with Ray's later approach. But, here and there, his own style for which he was groping was suggested in the details of a camera movement, a sound, or an object mentioned in the scenario. There come sudden flashes of "atmosphere".

In *Home and the World*, a story largely told through flashbacks, two antithetic modes of film-making were detectable. One was in the line of current commercial cinema; the other was striving in the direction of the style which would become idiosyncratic of Satyajit Ray. At the opposite extreme, and during the struggle to realize *Pather Panchali*, Ray produced an entirely visual script without the inclusion of a single word. It still exists in an old drawing book; a visualization of Ravi Shankar playing his sitar, interspersed with almost abstracted images of the accompanying *tabla*. Possibly, some day, a variation on this audio-visual experiment may be made.

With the duality of the first *Home and the World* script in mind, it is interesting to trace the evolution of the 1961 script of *Abhijan*, the adaptation to the screen which could easily have developed as a strictly commercial entertainment film.

The chief influence Ray had absorbed from Renoir was the idea of scenarios being kept fluid. Worked out in illustrated detail as to basic composition, Ray has left room for improvisation. In the case of *Abhijan*, dialogue and business were frequently subject to improvised changes.

When Bijoy Chatterjee came to discuss his idea of producing a film from Tarashankar Bannerjee's novel, Chatterjee had the notion of venturing to direct the film himself. Having read the novel over two days in August 1961, Ray advised Chatterjee to acquire the film rights immediately. Chatterjee acted with such alacrity that the rights were settled within a few hours. His enthusiasm was such that he wanted to start the film at once. But he had no script. Satyajit's interest was so captured by *Abhijan* that he agreed to assist Bijoy with advice and to write the screen play, despite his determination to push ahead with *Kanchenjunga*, his own idea.

There is one point of similarity between *Kanchenjunga* and *Abhijan*, though in all other respects they are strikingly in contrast. In both films a financially successful middle-aged man attempts to buy over a younger and impoverished man. Both Indranath and Sukhanram, who is overtly shown as a trader in opium and women in *Abhijan*, adhere to the same standard—that money can buy anything and, more particularly, people. Both men discover there are exceptions to this ruthless operator's rule.

Tarashankar Bannerjee's long novel is laid on the Bihar-Bengal border, in the general area of Tagore's Santineketan, where Mawari businessmen—a powerful community of entrepreneurs much disliked throughout India—and Rajputs of warrior—*chhatri*—caste from Rajasthan have settled. They speak a dialect of Hindi. The Bengalis in the film speak their own language. The central character of Narsingh, a disillusioned, frequently drunken Rajput reduced in status to an ill-educated taxi driver, was based upon a real man who was still alive. Satyajit visited him after he decided to direct the film from his own script. The author, who had been a political worker in the national and peasant movement, had set his novel in the period of 1942–43.

Ray shifted the period forward to 1961 on the grounds that the essential sociological role of men like the Mawari, Sukhanram, had not changed in rural areas in twenty years. There were still reports in the Press of similar opium smuggling and of white slave traffic.

Ray's adaptation is focused upon Narsingh's reactions and conflict as to whether, having failed in everything honest, he will or will not engage in criminal activity—the delivery of opium in faked tins of *ghee*—in order to make money. In the novel, Narsingh's background was given in great detail. His much-loved wife had died. Ray replaced the dead wife by a wife who had deserted Narsingh and deepened his disillusion. The past life of Gulabi, the young Bihar village widow, and the rape that had loosened her morals, was also detailed. Her parents sold her to Sukhanram to save their reputation. Ray made drastic deletions. Only in one poignant scene with Narsingh does Gulabi attempt to explain her past life.

Without identifying his long opening sequence of *Abhijan* as a Prologue, Ray set out to establish the psychological condition of Narsingh prior to his first encounter with Sukhanram, at which point the main story commences. The first sequence shows his resentment towards women; his aggressive recklessness which re-

bounds upon himself; and yet his innate courage even if his character is too weak to support either his anger or his pride.

The following is a condensation of the scenario, which begins, as
the film itself does, in the village of Imanbazar.

SEQUENCE I

The public vehicle stand showing the taxi of Narsingh (Singhi), and
his helper, Rama, waiting for fares. This shot was eliminated and
the opening shot shows a man questioning Narsingh about the
desertion of his wife. Narsingh's reflection is seen in a jagged,
broken mirror. He is drinking heavily. (Pl. XL)

He lurches out of the wine shop to find that the fares in his taxi
are a wedding party. Disgusted by women, he turns the party out.

Dissolve

Narsingh, with elderly nervous passengers and Rama, drives recklessly to catch a train. He deliberately plays upon the passengers'
nerves. (In the film, the credit titles come over this scene and end
as the level crossing gate comes down.) "There goes my train",
says one of the nervous passengers. The gate rises and the journey
continues. Narsingh races the train and beats it by a hair's breadth.

Slow Dissolve

A lapse of some hours.

The taxi is parked beneath a tree. Narsingh lies on the ground
with a book while Rama fills the radiator. They continue, with
Rama driving. Narsingh dozes. The honk of the horn wakes him
and he sees a car in front. He takes over the driving; but still the
car in front refuses to move out of the way.

In it is a sour-looking official—the Sub-District Officer. Narsingh
twists his taxi off the road, into a field, and passes the car.

Dissolve

The S.D.O.'s room. The confrontation of the bullying S.D.O., who
is determined to revoke Narsingh's taxi driver's permit for reckless
driving, and a diffident Narsingh ready to apologize until, threat-
ened with a riding crop and a savage "GET OUT", he is seized with
fury. But, faced with the bully in authority, he finds himself helpless. . . .

Dissolve

Narsingh's car parked under a tree. Brought to rock bottom
humiliation by the S.D.O., Narsingh flings a chunk of brick at the
car he cherishes. Nothing is left for him but to go back to his
village of Giribraja. The faithful and good-natured Rama will tag
along too.

Fade Out

The contradictions in Narsingh's character have been hinted at. He has nothing to look forward to. The main story is about to unfold. The theme underlying the action, which carries a more formal plot than any other Ray film, is that of temptation, accommodation and redemption. During production, Soumitra Chatterjee, as Narsingh, commented that he felt Ray was constantly encouraging him to uncover the latent spiritual conflict within the character; that the Narsingh of the film was more complex than Narsingh in the novel.

SEQUENCE 2

Opens with a "long stretch of metalled road with paddy fields on either side". Night descends. Change of objects along the road emphasizes distance. Suddenly, in the glare of Narsingh's headlights, a man is seen waving. Behind him a bullock cart has overturned.

The man is the Mawari, Sukhanram. He asks if Narsingh will drive him to Shyamnagar. "No." The man pleads. They bargain on price. From the shadows a girl appears—Gulabi—whom Sukhan identifies as a "maidservant". Narsingh protests. Sukhan offers him Rs.50/- for the journey. On arrival at Sukhan's house, Narsingh is invited in to rest. He goes reluctantly, with Rama remaining outside.

The exterior wall of Sukhan's house and the inside courtyard shown in the gray light of early morning was later shot on location at a genuine Mawari house in the town of Dubrajpur. The next scene, a set, was Sukhanram's Room, also used as an office. Several subsequent scenes take place here.

Sukhanram, "all kindness and hospitality", begins his tempting of Narsingh by ordering a sherbet for him and declaring "we need a man like you here". (He sees possibilities in the collaboration with a man owning a taxi.) He offers Narsingh a cigarette from a gold case and passes him a fancy-looking lighter, while pursuing his idea about the usefulness of a taxi. Narsingh, intrigued by the lighter, is offered it, but resists taking it.

Sukhan says: "After all you were a great help to me today—and you can be of help in the future too."

"Future?"

"I want to make you an offer."

"What offer?"

"I want you to set up as plying trade between here and Panchmati—seven miles away . . ."

He will advance money to repair the car. Suspicious, Narsingh wants to know how would this help Sukhan. "You can transport some of my goods from time to time. A car is much quicker [than the bullock cart he has been using]. It'll help my business and you'll have no difficulty in getting a permit here. The S.D.O. is a good man." He invites Narsingh to stay and look around. (Pl. XL)

When it came to production, Chandragupta and Ray devised a set concentrating upon atmosphere which reflected not only the sociology of this Mawari set-up, but the psychology. The entrance hall of Sukhanram's house was given a fanlight window, a detail which is repeated in the construction of Sukhan's room-cum-office. It allowed for patterns of lighting which illuminate the inner conflicts within Narsingh. (Pl. XLI)

With the possible exception of the 1879 drawing-room in *Charulata* and the primly modest room of the prospective bride in *Samapti*, no set evolved by Chandragupta and Ray is so indicative of the mentality of the occupant as Sukhan's room. It reflects the dualism of Mawari psychology, which is also examined in the characterization of Bajoria in *The Alien*. While serving as the greatest money-lending and business caste throughout India, and with an exceedingly powerful grip in Bengal, Mawaris are hall-marked by a superstitious religiosity. They pray intensively, as if to ward off retribution for their worldly activities. They are notable as donation-givers to temples. This ironic but not incongruous aspect is prominent in the habitat of Sukhan, the rural dealer in opium and women. The whole back wall of his sanctum is cluttered with popular prints of protective deities. A large cherubic Krishna, all mischievous innocence, serves as obscene comment that Sukhan cherishes the sight of this holy horror of divine infancy. And the sly reminder: Krishna enlightened the milkmaids through love. Sukhan trades in "milkmaids", or "gopis", as Gulabi will breathlessly reveal. (Pl. XL)

SEQUENCE 3

The next morning at the vehicle stand of Shyamnagar, with Narsingh and Rama a centre of interest to the bus-drivers. It is here that Narsingh first meets Josef, the good-natured and upright Christian driver of the S.D.O. when Josef strikes up a conversation. He elicits the information that Narsingh is on the way to Giribraja This delights him for this is where he, too, comes from. He asks: "May I know your name?"

"Narsingh."

"Are you the famous Singhs of Giribraja?"

Narsingh smiles and says: "Yes".

Josef is astonished. He says: "My name is Josef."

"Josef?"

"Josef Ranjan Das."

Josef points to a little crucifix around his neck. Then he says: "I think my grandfather knew your grandfather—my grandfather was Prankrishna Das."

"Then originally you were. . . ."

"Yes, low caste. My grandfather was converted."

"And now . . .?"

"And now we are Christians and I drive the S.D.O.'s car."

Josef also suggests that Narsingh open a taxi service.

Once representative of family social extremes, Narsingh, whose *chhatri* ancestry is an important psychological factor—it is referred to several times and a lion is tattooed on his right arm which he looks at each time he meets defeat—has sunk in the social scale, while the low-caste Das family have risen.

Brought together, it would appear that Narsingh is a degenerate and reactionary personality, while Josef, as subsequent scenes reveal, is apparently more progressive in outlook and certainly far more conscious of moral standards. He will seek to restrain Narsingh from becoming Sukhanram's tool. But as Ray estimated these two characters, he later explained to me that Josef, the consciously virtuous man, was a relatively static personality while Narsingh, being at bottom a good man, had greater capacity for growth and undergoes a marked degree of change.

In view of the social implications of the meeting of the two, the casting of Josef appeared as an example of marked perceptiveness. Ray selected a stage actor, Jnanesh Mukherji, with an interesting and strong face conveying integrity. But in contrast to Chatterjee, Mukherji is decidedly dark. This is most apt for Josef since it is noticeable that, apart from Goan Christians, darkness of complexion is often a characteristic of Indian Christians. This darkness is not always because they are South Indians of Dravidian origin; but because relatively recent converts—like Josef's grandfather— have often been drawn from among dark people of former low caste or Untouchables. The explanation as to why people of the fourth caste, *Sudras* and the Untouchables should frequently be dark is that the conquering Aryans, whose descendants are so visible among the Brahmin and *Chhatri* castes, pushed down the dark aboriginal and Dravidian people and locked them into servitude in a caste-dominated society. (Pl. XXXIX)

The next scene—another part of the town where Josef, his mother and his sister, Neeli, a school-teacher, live—underwent drastic change from scenario to the film. Instead of Josef driving

Narsingh to his home in the S.D.O.'s jeep, Josef walks Narsingh through the area of rocks on the edge of Dubrajpur (the location which made such an impact on Ray that he decided to direct the film; this is explained later). Narsingh is instantly attracted by Neeli (who, as shown later, is in love with the clergyman's son) The mother offers Narsingh tea and cakes. Narsingh is silent—from awareness of Neeli. This is mistaken by Josef for caste consciousness. He says: "It's all right if you feel you shouldn't touch our food . . . after all, you were a *Chhatri*—and we were . . ." The implication is they were Untouchables. Narsingh is flustered and says "Oh, no, no, no . . ." To cover his embarrassment he puts a whole piece of cake into his mouth and chokes.

This, and the previous scene, are the only ones in a Ray film where caste is introduced.

Josef promises to arrange a taxi permit if Narsingh will set up business in Shyamnagar. Josef would like to go into business with him.

Narsingh goes to Sukhanram to discuss the taxi proposition. This time Narsingh accepts the gift of the fancy lighter, and the loan of Rs.200/- for the repair of his car. A stranger sitting in the room adds a sinister touch.

Rama is delighted to stay. He points out the presence of Gulabi, who is watching them from a window. Rama approves of her.

Dissolve

SEQUENCE 4

At the wine shop. The bus driver, Rameshwar, a dangerous type, envious of Narsingh's lighter, attempts to provoke him.

Dissolve

To a restaurant where Rama expresses his dislike for the bus drivers, but his liking for Gulabi.

Dissolve

To Narsingh's room. Situated in an outbuilding of Sukhan's compound, it became the most important set. Costing a little over £175 to construct, the small set aimed that the simulated texture of brick walls with a broken window, barred as the great majority of windows are in India, be as visually effective as possible when lit either for day light or the murkiness of night. (Pl. XLI)

Sounds of music and a noisy party reach Narsingh lying awake on his bed, a *charpoy*. Suddenly there's soft insistent knocking on his door. Opening it, Narsingh finds Gulabi, in a state of near collapse and with her blouse torn, anxious to be let in. She begs him to let her stay for the night to escape from "the new man tonight . . . He [Sukhanram] forced me into his room—to spend the night . . ."

Unwillingly, Narsingh finally agrees to let her stay. (It is because, despite his rough ways, he does not touch Gulabi, treating her as a human being and not a whore, that Narsingh captures her affection and later her love.) He simply goes to sleep.

Slow Fade Out on the girl's face.

SEQUENCE 5

Next morning: Narsingh drives to Josef's house. Josef, having done a little mischief to the jeep, has arranged for Narsingh to drive the S.D.O. to Panchmati. On the way to the Officer's house they drop Neeli at the house of the Rev. Bannerji, her excuse being that she has to collect a book; but it is to meet his one-legged son.

Before they arrive at the S.D.O.'s house Josef warns Narsingh of Sukhan's shady deals. The Officer, in the sharpest contrast to the one at Imanbazar, is friendly. It turns out that he once served in Giribraja while Narsingh lived there. Narsingh is now a model of the careful driver. He refrains from even overtaking a bullock cart.

Dissolve

To the vehicle stand of Panchmati where Narsingh rejects taking any fares until he has a licence.

Dissolve

To evening at Sukhan's house. Sukhan informs Narsingh that he has been to see a lawyer, Ukil Babu, to draw up the papers for the repair of the car. He adds: "A lot of people say a lot of things about me. I don't pretend to be a saint. I am an opportunist and I am bold enough to take risks. . . ."

Narsingh leaves, thoughtfully, and goes to his room. In the script, he found his bed neatly made—and not by Rama. (In the working out of direction, the context in which Gulabi makes Narsingh's bed was altered, placed later, and made significant of the change in their relationship. It comes after they have spent a night together making love)

Fade Out

SEQUENCE 6

Sunday. By a wayside pond Rama cleans the car while Narsingh, responding to his brighter prospects, trims his moustache in a mirror. Josef joins him until Neeli arrives on her way to church; that is, in the scenario. For lack of finding a suitable Church, the next scene was altered for Narsingh to walk with Neeli to her school. They talk, until Neeli asks:

"Don't you believe in God?"

"Oh, . . . I've never thought of it. Perhaps I do. I make a sign when I pass a temple . . . any temple . . . Hindu, Muslim, Sikh . . ."

"But not a Church?"

Narsingh thinks. "I don't think I've ever done that while passing a Church."

There is silence. Then Narsingh says: "But I think I will—from now on."

"Why from now on?"

Neeli is half amused, half intrigued. But Narsingh says with simple sincerity: "Because *you're* a Christian."

Neeli is touched, and also slightly embarrassed at this sudden confession of weakness on this man's part. But Narsingh has suddenly become serious. He says:

"Does your God punish sinners?"

"Yes. We have a saying in the Bible . . . 'The wages of sin is Death'."

This was to become a motif and associated with a particular rock. Ray's resolution of this romantic symbol is discussed later.

In directing the following scene, Ray introduces a notable instance where Nature becomes an embodiment of a human psychological state: Narsingh, sitting at the foot of a tree with a tangled growth of roots, tries painfully to teach himself English in order to acquire the embellishment of "a gentleman" in accord with his ancestry. It picks up the idea of what he has confessed to Neeli during their walk: "I'm only a driver. At least if there were a big company, with trucks and taxis and buses, and I was a partner, then that would be something. But now there's only one taxi and I am the driver. . . ."

Mixes to Montage

Of Shyamnager vehicle stand. Rama keeps honking the new electric horn on the overhauled car.

Dissolve

To a typical trip with Narsingh again driving recklessly with alarmed passengers.

Dissolve

To Narsingh honking outside Josef's house. Neeli comes out and he drives her to school.

Dissolve

To another trip. This time, Narsingh sees the S.D.O.'s car reflected in his mirror and respectfully moves to one side to let Josef pass.

XXXIII Nayak (The Hero), 1966.
Aditi and fellow travellers. Ajoy (Subrata Sen) and Shefali Purnandu, in dining car which serves as focal point of the action: They are discussing Aditi's magazine—
"Shefali: Do you make a profit?
Aditi: We could—with a few more advertisements.
Shefali (addressing her husband): You know a lot of people. Why don't you help her out?
Aditi: You could begin by taking out a subscription for your wife.
Ajoy: Gladly! What's the damage?
Aditi: Ten rupees a year. In these matters I am completely business-like."

Production photograph of the first dream, with Uttam Kumar centre

Arindam, Uttam Kumar, meets Aditi, Sharmila Tagore, and tells her his life story

XXXIV Subsidiary themes.

The Hero feels compelled to drink from compulsive conflict over his memories and what success and money have done to him

Haren Bose, Ranjit Sen, the industrialist, his wife, Monorama, and daughter, Bulbul, who share the compartment with Arindam on the train to Delhi. The Mother and Daughter idolize the Hero.

Compartment B. Morning and nearing the end of the journey. The Swamiji, silent throughout the journey, finds his tongue along with his interest in Sarkar, the advertising man:
"Swamiji: . . . You're in advertising, aren't you?
Sarkar: Yes, up to now.
Swamiji: Do you take on religious organizations?
Sarkar: Religious organizations?
Swamiji: Yes.
Sarkar: Advertising?
Swamiji: Have you heard of W.W.W.W.?"

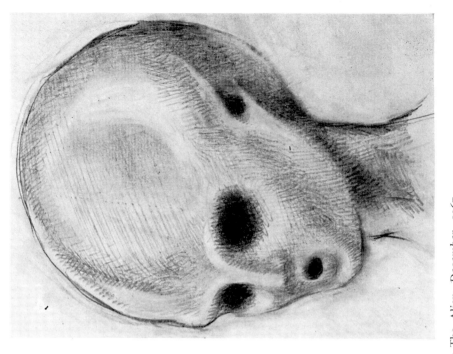

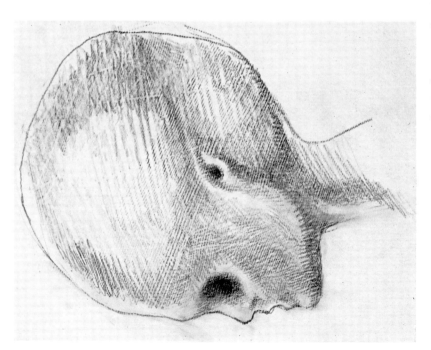

XXXV *Ray's first two drawings for The Alien, December, 1967*

His most characteristic pose at home

XXXVI Director at work

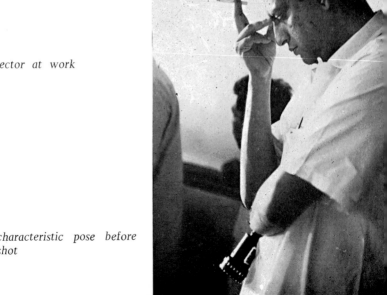

His most characteristic pose before directing a shot

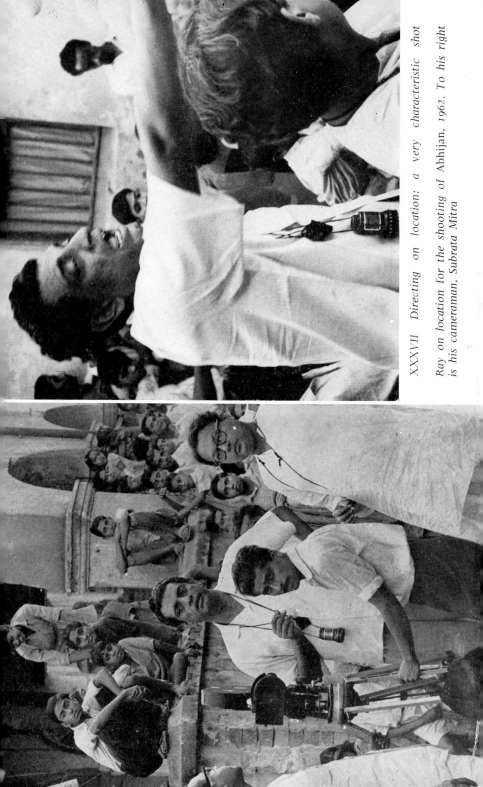

XXXVII Directing on location: a very characteristic shot

Ray on location for the shooting of Abhijan, 1962. To his right is his cameraman, Subrata Mitra

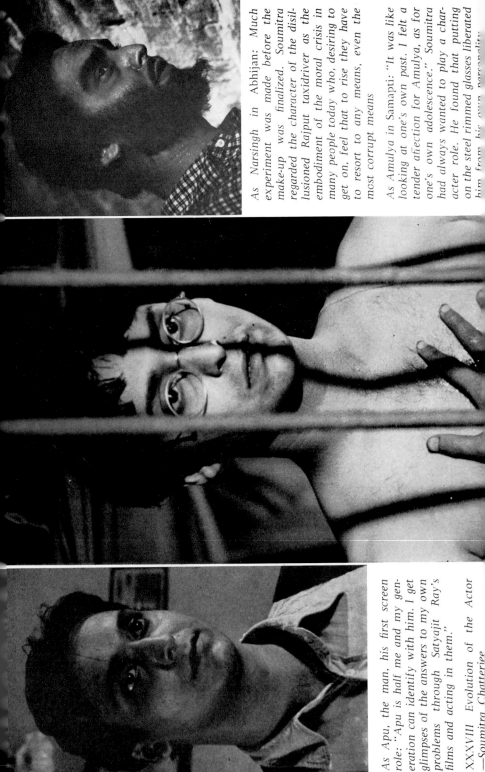

As Narsingh in Abhijan: Much experiment was made before the make-up was finalized. Soumitra regarded the character of the disillusioned Rajput taxidriver as the embodiment of the moral crisis in many people today who, desiring to get on, feel that to rise they have to resort to any means, even the most corrupt means

As Amulya in Samapti: "It was like looking at one's own past. I felt a tender affection for Amulya, as for one's own adolescence." Soumitra had always wanted to play a character role. He found that putting on the steel rimmed glasses liberated him from his own personality

As Apu, the man, his first screen role: "Apu is half me and my generation can identify with him. I get glimpses of the answers to my own problems through Satyajit Ray's films and acting in them."

XXXVIII Evolution of the Actor
—Soumitra Chatterjee

Two of the many photographs taken by Ray of the Dubrajpur rocks.
These rocks so captured his imagination that he decided to direct
Abhijan, the script for which he had written for Bijoy Chatterjee

A particular boulder at Dubrajpur inspired two symbolic scenes. The first (left) was where Narsingh,
Soumitra Chatterjee, pits his physical strength against
the rock which comes to signify the Wages (or
Burden) of Sin. The rock defeats him. Towards the
end the same rock reminds him psychologically of
his corruption and of his violence towards Josef. Both
scenes were finally deleted as a falsification

XXXIX Abhijan. 1961–62

Narsingh with Josef, Jnanesh Mukherji, just after they
have met. The physiognomy of the selected actors is
very perceptive, Narsingh being of aristocratic Rajput
origin and Josef of Untouchable origin, his grandfather having become a Christian convert to escape

The opening scene of *Abhijan. The jagged mirror reflecting Narsingh projects the state of his m*

XL

Sukhanram, interpreted by Charu Prokash Ghose, the amateur actor who played the would-be seducing neighbour in Aparajito, commences his enticement of Narsingh who has driven him to his village. End of Sequence No. 2

Sequence No. 3. Study in dualism. Deity pictures, especially the most sentimental are commonly found sanctifying business premises. An atmosphere of veiled evil permeates this scene. The 'business associate' in the chair is never identified by name or occupation, but the implication is that he is a dealer in women

Sukhanram's house. In all the scenes within this set, the lighting creates interesting effects. Here the reflected patterns exteriorize the psychological vortex within Narsingh

Narsingh, the hater of women, is captivated by Josef's school teacher sister, Neeli, Rama Guhu Thakurta. Sequence No. 6:
Neeli is on her way to church
"Narsingh: . . Does your God punish sinners?
Neeli: Yes . . . We have a saying in the Bible . . .'The wages of sin is Death.'
But why do you ask? You have not sinned, have you?
Narsingh: Oh no, not I . . . at least, not yet, I think . . . Will you teach me English?
Neeli: Why?
Narsingh: I want to learn it . . . I want to be . . . to be . . .
Neeli: To be what?
Narsingh: To be respectable.
Neeli: But who says you are not respectable as you are now?
Narsingh: . . . But . . . But . . . I'm only a driver. . . ."

Sequence No. 9. Disillusioned by Neeli, Narsingh has spent the previous night with Gulabi, Waheeda Rehman, the girl Sukhanram has bought and will sell again
This scene in Narsingh's room is psychologically the most important in the revelation of Gulabi's life and character
The room was the most important set in the film, used both for daylight (here) and for night scenes

Scene No. 2: The roof top of Kaventer's Dairy and Cafe.
Ray discussing the scene with Anil, the playboy son, Anil Chatterjee,
and his first girl friend played by Darjeeling college girl, Vidya Singh.
Note the lustre-finished dark glasses in which Lily is reflected

XLII
Kanchenjunga, shot entirely on
location at Darjeeling during 26
days of November, 1961

Ray explaining the character of
Monisha to the Calcutta college
girl, Aloknanda Roy. Her expression here and as she appears in
scenes in the film are almost identical.
Ray "takes his actors completely
into his confidence and explains to
them fully what he wants them to
convey."

Guine, the real beggar boy of D
jeeling who inspired the boy
plays. The boy serves as the w
ness of what takes place and c
stitutes one of the two musi
motifs in the structure of the fi

Scene No. 9: The Snuggery Cottage of the Windermere Hotel where the few interiors were shot with the help of reflectors.

Monisha is warned about arranged marriages by her brother-in-law, Shankar, Subrata Sen:

"Shankar: Moni, just a minute. Do you like him?
Monisha: Who?
Shankar: Now, don't pretend.
Monisha: I don't know.
Shankar: Shall I tell you something?
Monisha: What?
Shankar: Never marry without falling in love. Eligible means nothing. I was once eligible too."

Scene No. 28: The marriage of Shankar and Anima, Anuba Gupta, comes almost to breaking point.

The yellow plastic basket carried by Anima is a shade brighter than the golden rod growing behind the seat

Tulku, the child of the unhappy Anima and Shankar. Riding round and round Observatory Hill she images the second musical motif of Ray's structure

XLIV

Scene No. 15: *The Mall, Darjeeling, where action converges from time to time.*

Enter the catalyst, Ashoke, Arun Mookerjee, when Indranath, Chhabi Biswas, and his wife, Labanya, Karuna Banerji, are waiting for Bannerji, Monisha's prospective bridegroom.

Sibsankar, Ashoke's uncle, was once tutor to Anil. He obsequiously greets his former employer: "I suppose you wouldn't remember me. I was your son's tutor—in 1951—Sibsankar Roy."

Scene No. 35: *Bannerji, N. Viswanathan, finding Monisha with Ashoke, accepts his own rejection, saying: "If you ever feel that security is more important than love, or love might grow from security, let me know."*

All the scenes between Bannerji and Monisha were played in shadow or mist. Here, only, is there a hint of sun

Scene No. 38: *shortly before the last shot. Monisha has invited Ashoke to visit her in Calcutta. All the scenes between Monisha and Ashoke are shot with a hint of emphatic sunshine*

XLV November, 1961, Darjeeling. During the shooting of the Children's Park scene, Pl. XLIII. The young porters sit at the foot of the
tree. The boy with blue eyes is the furthest left. Extreme left, half
of Babu Krishnaswamy, then collaborating on Indian Cinema with Eric
Barnau (right foreground). Centre, Bijoya and author

The Mall, tea break. Satyajit gets his cup. Edward Harrison, Ray's
American distributor, with cup and stick. On bench, Bijoya, author,
Joya, Satyajit's sister-in-law

Apu teaches Aparna to read in Apur Sansar

XLVI *Intimacy: Masculine—Feminine in Ray's films*

Amulya and Mrinmoyee on their wedding night in Samapti

Gulabi and Narsingh in Abhijan. Sequence No. 8. Narsingh, to Gulabi's disappointment, mumbles in sleep "Neeli, Neeli . . ."

Later when Gulabi has spent the night with Narsingh, the following morning the change in relationship is signified by her fingering of her heavy silver bangle

Subrata and Arati in Mahanagar: End of Sequence No. 1

They are in bed. Arati has been gently pushing Subrata to wake him. He asks, sleepily:
"What is it?
Listen, I'll apply for a job.
What? (still sleepy)
I'll apply for a job.
What job? What are you . . .
Any job. I must work. We both must work.
You wake me up in the middle of the night to tell me this?"
He rolls over still half asleep

Abhijan was the first film
which Ray had to create tou
and violent characters. Here
the hostile bus drivers peering
Rabi, Rabi Ghosh later to be c
in Goupi Gyne. An assistant
Ray's (with cigarette in mou
remarked: "At first we did
know how to create su
characters."

It is characteristic of Ray never to use a location landscape for itself,
or its beauty. Something always happens humanly within the landscape. This may be a trait of Indian art where, traditionally, landscapes
are peopled with human beings, or deities

Satyajit Ray explains a scene in Abhijan
to Waheeda Rehman in the New Theatre
Studio, Calcutta. The set is Narsingh's room

Mahanagar, 1963. The scene is a cafe where Arati has come in to have
a meal with a casual acquaintance. Subrata, her husband, who is also
in the cafe, hides behind a newspaper.
   Ray's analysis of the shot with his cupped hand is very typical of
his way in judging a shot before it is photographed

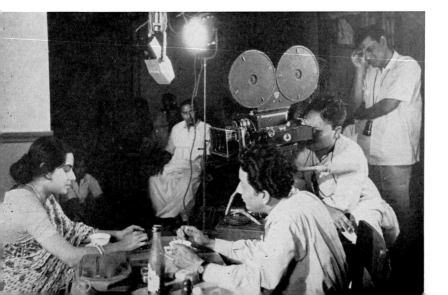

The Montage ends after Narsingh is grimly stared at by the bus drivers when he buys wine in the wine shop.

Dissolve

To Sukhanram's house where Narsingh brings a bag of money to repay, with interest, the Rs.200/- for his car repairs. Sukhan does not wish to take the money. Flattering Narsingh, he broaches the subject of a partnership:

". . . Mr. Narsingh, you're a *chhatri*, aren't you?"

"Yes."

"*Chhatris* are spirited people, aren't they?"

"Yes."

"They like adventure?"

"Yes."

"They take risks?"

"Yes, sometimes."

"Good. I have need of someone who likes adventure, who takes risks, who is brave . . ."

"Why?"

Sukhan goes to his safe and brings out a harmless-looking container. "Do you know what this contains?" Narsingh sniffs the tin and says it smells like *ghee*. But, in fact, it contains opium. "All you have to do is to transport such tins to an address I'll give you in . . ." Narsingh wants to know what's the risk. "Don't get caught, and there's no risk." To encourage Narsingh, Sukhan talks about a partnership and a nice girl to marry. He tells Narsingh to come back in half an hour, reminding him he has left his bag of money. Narsingh collects it. Sukhan suggests "If you should feel the need of female company, just let me know. The bazaar women are no good here."

Dissolve

Narsingh finds Gulabi in his room. Much upset, she says: "If you should ever decide to go away from here, take me away with you and drop me at my native village. It was bad enough there, but here it is a thousand times worse. It is like a living death . . ." She leaves him with an imploring look. Bewildered, Narsingh shakes her off his mind. He orders Rama to get the car ready.

Fade Out

SEQUENCE 7

This sequence was to have opened in a Shyamnagar cinema during a stunt film. But when the film was being shot at the main location of Dubrajpur, a tent cinema was operating there, also the impoverished Tara Circus which was grounded for debt. Ray utilized both as setting for subsequent action.

P

The conversation between Narsingh and Josef—about a partner-ship in a transport business which Josef is so eager for—was set in the circus tent. Direction of this scene is described in the next chapter.

They then go to the wine shop. Narsingh is wearing new trousers. Leaving Rama and Josef outside, he goes in to buy a couple of bottles. The resentful Rameshwar, and several others, taunt Narsingh: "We'd need such pants too if we were to mix in such good company . . ." ". . . and Christian girls too . . ." "You know the girl we mean . . . the one that's so friendly with the lame man, but pretends that she's your girl. She's . . ."

Narsingh knocks out the drunken driver and leaves the shop. A horde of drivers follow him and a fight breaks out. Narsingh is badly beaten up and taken by Josef and Rama to Josef's house.

Ray was to shoot a greater number of shots for this scene than for any other throughout his work. The editing is later described.

At Josef's house, Neeli is very sympathetic. Josef asks what it was that made Narsingh lose his temper. Josef's mother has come into the room. Narsingh, hesitating, then admits: "Oh, something about the lame boy and . . . and . . . her . . ." He points to Neeli.

Josef's mother says: "I wouldn't have fought for *his* sake. He's a no good boy all right . . ."

Josef says: "Oh mother—you don't have to talk like that . . ."

Mother says sternly: "I know what I'm saying . . ."

Neeli leaves the room abruptly without saying a word. Narsingh determinedly gets up to leave, puzzled by the domestic "scene".

Dissolve

To Sukhan's compound. Rama has driven the car. Gulabi is watch-ing from a window. Narsingh collapses on the bed in his room. His pride in his strength is as much hurt as his body: "There were six of them. That's why they dared to do this to me. . . . The cowards. Jealous . . . the whole lot of them . . . jealous."

Rama interjects: "They are a bad lot, Guruji . . . there are too many bad people in this place . . ."

"But I'll show them—the bad ones . . . I'll make them ten times more jealous . . . Wait till the company is formed . . ."

"What company, Guruji?"

"The big transport agency . . . with me as partner . . . I'll let you drive a bus then . . ." His voice becomes thick with drowsiness.

Gulabi has come anxiously into the room. Rama, who cannot speak her Hindi dialect (Narsingh can), instructs her in sign lan-guage to look after Narsingh. Rama leaves her alone with Narsingh. She sits by the *charpoy*, her fingers passing over his hair. Her expression denotes her love. He stirs, moves restlessly but does not wake. He mumbles in his sleep, "Neeli, Neeli . . ." Lines of pain and disappointment show on Gulabi's face, yet she patiently waits.

Fade Out

SEQUENCE 8

Narsingh calls for Neeli to take her to school. She asks him if he will do something for her. He will gladly do anything. "Do you think you could come with your car and meet me in front of the cemetery at about ten this evening? It's very important."

"Of course," says Narsingh with no suspicion of what is involved.

The cemetery became an area of the rock formation on the edge of Dubrajpur.

Leaving Neeli, Narsingh passes a pond. In response to what he supposes to be Neeli's interest in him, he decides to "drown" his wine bottle. Rama takes it to throw away. Instead, he pockets it and throws in a stone.

Dissolve

To the vehicle stand. Since Narsingh is a little late his regular passengers are restive. Josef intercepts him to say he's worried about Neeli and the attitude of the bus drivers. Narsingh says no harm can come to her while he is around.

Dissolve

To the taxi on the way to Panchmati. Narsingh is driving fairly recklessly.

Dissolve

To a change of landscape with Rameshwar's bus in the distance— half a mile ahead. Rama gets excited. Narsingh impassively begins to overtake the bus. The distance begins to shorten. Narsingh sounds his new electric horn three times. Rameshwar keeps to the middle of the road. Narsingh comes right up against the bus. Then he performs his special feat of miraculously swerving off the road, into a field, and he passes the bus.

The original concept of Bijoy Chatterjee and Satyajit Ray was that this race should be shot from a helicopter. But after protracted negotiations and repeated delays to secure a date, Ray had to think of an alternative means of shooting the scene.

Rama throws the bottle on to the road to puncture the bus tyre. The bus stops in a cloud of dust.

Dissolve

To cinema (tent cinema) with typical sequence of Hindi film dance. At 9.30 p.m. Narsingh gets up, giving Rama money for a meal.

Dissolve

A place near the rocks (to which Ray transplanted the cemetery scene). Narsingh picks his way through boulders and comes to one where Josef, Neeli and he have scratched their names. He waits, then hears irregular footsteps. Neeli appears. Behind her is the man on crutches. Narsingh reacts with incomprehension.

In the film itself, an additional emotional dimension is given by Ray's music intensifying over this scene.

Neeli, pleadingly, explains to Narsingh that they have waited ten years to get married. Now they are running away from her mother's objections. She asks Narsingh to drive them ten miles to the train.

Narsingh is almost hysterical. Yet he agrees and savagely drives them as Neeli begs of him.

> *Dissolve*

To Sukhan's compound to which Narsingh returns drunk. Gulabi is watching from a window. Seeing her, he mumbles: "Women are only good for one thing . . ." and asks Rama to tell Gulabi to come to his room.

Narsingh, flinging himself on the bed in his room, says: "What happened to your blood, *Chhatri?* What happened to your blood?" He begins to scratch himself on his veins.

"Why didn't it boil? You could have killed that man . . . that puny man with one leg and no courage . . . Why didn't you do it? . . . I know why . . . You are respectable, Narsingh . . . too respectable, for a *Chhatri* . . . but not enough for her . . ."

Rama brings Gulabi, who gazes at him lovingly. He says to her: "God knows what kind of a woman you are. Tonight I don't care." He pulls her towards him.

> *Slow Dissolve*

When the dawn comes they are still together. She is sitting beside the *charpoy*. Gulabi has removed her heavy silver bangles as symbolization of their having made love. She fingers one of them gently. Narsingh smokes.

In the original scenario, a long scene followed with each of them telling the other about the past. Ray omitted this. It only becomes clear that Gulabi would never leave a man she loves. Again, she asks Narsingh to take her away. Narsingh mentions the partnership with Sukhan, to which Gulabi replies that Sukhan will sell her

> *Fade Out*

Having completed the eighth sequence, Satyajit ran out of inspiration as to how to continue and conclude the scenario. He had made numerous deletions and changes. He had convincingly resolved the situation where Gulabi becomes the stimulant for Narsingh's moral regeneration. But he was not ready for the last lap of the writing. His interest switched away to his own picnic story which became *Kanchenjunga*. The moment he finished *Kanchenjunga*'s scenario, he went resolutely ahead with the direction. Arrangements for the production, his first in colour, went with great speed. He had persistently rejected the idea of directing *Abhijan* himself.

Bijoy Chatterjee, in preparing to direct *Abhijan*, tested Soumitra Chatterjee for the character of Narsingh. Since Soumitra's natural appearance was far too refined and gentle for him to look anything like the rough, uprooted Rajput, the make-up expert went to work radically to alter Soumitra's appearance. The first test photographs indicated how far his personality could be changed. He was eager to play such a character part.

Even while Satyajit was working on the first eight sequences, Bijoy Chatterjee was concerned to find the right location for *Abhijan*. He had the town of Dubrajpur in mind and induced Bansi Chandragupta to go and see the place with him. The town and its surroundings titillated Bansi's imagination. They were impressed by the photogenic aspects of the massive rocks near by.

During the shooting of *Kanchenjunga* in Darjeeling, Bijoy Chatterjee spent almost the whole period of direction there. But he was discretion itself in refraining from pressing Ray to complete the script. Indeed, he spent a great deal of time letting off his pent-up enthusiasm about *Abhijan* in explaining every detail of the original novel to me. While Bijoy supposed he would have to direct the film, he still had hopes that Satyajit might change his mind and take it on.

Back in Calcutta after the shooting of *Kanchenjunga*, with a wait for the bulk of the rushes, Bijoy and Bansi took advantage of Satyajit's disquiet when not at work. They persuaded him to drive with them to look at the Bihar-Bengal border town of Dubrajpur. The scenario was still unfinished. Though Dubrajpur is only some twenty miles from Santineketan, Ray had never been there. They went directly to the rock formation on the edge of the town.

These rocks, forming roughly a mile square in area, are grim, scarred and humped. They are reputed to be a geological mystery. The rocks appear as if they had been flung down from the heavens rather than heaved up from the earth. Boulders mount up like magnified piles of stones uneven in size to form a wall against the sky. Suddenly, single palm trees spring from crevices, while the floor of this mysterious natural amphitheatre is scattered with giant chips of rock smoothly rounded as if pebbles had expanded their size a millionfold.

A legend exists to explain this enigmatic cluster of stones. It is said that when Hanuman, the Holy Monkey of the Ramayana, was flying southward from the Himalayas to bombard the Demon King Ravanna with a mountain—Ravanna had abducted Sita but, nobly, had not raped her—Hanuman was carrying a second mountain perched on his second superman (or supermonkey) shoulder. Finding the weight too great, he tossed it off. The discarded mountain shattered into fragments on the edge of what is now Dubrajpur.

Hanuman dropping a mountain, or a landshift eons ago, no cinematic-minded artist could remain coolly indifferent to such a dramatic landscape. The impact on Satyajit was immediate. He was captivated by the rocks. At once he visualized them as an alternative to the cemetery location he had introduced into *Abhijan*'s scenario.

"You didn't tell me what a tremendous thing they are," Satyajit said to Bijoy. "This must play a bigger role. It can't be passed over so easily. It's one of the best locations I've ever seen."

Turning about to view the shots which might be devised within this bizarre expanse of stone, Ray began to snap photograph after photograph (Pl. XXXIX). The other two kept quiet while he repeatedly clicked his camera, absorbed in his enthusiasm.

They stayed the night in Dubrajpur. Bansi and Bijoy waited about, talked, slept, conscious that Satyajit, who had shut himself up in his room, had become enthralled with the rocks. So affected was he by them that he went to work with furious haste to complete the scenario which had lain unfinished for several months. The last two sequences took shape. At five o'clock in the morning, Satyajit strode out of his room, announcing: "I must check up on the lighting!" He returned to the rocks and photographed them at different hours throughout that day to have a record of the play of light.

Possibly it was the first sight of one particularly huge, rounded and isolated boulder which struck him as a powerful symbol for the idea of "the burden of sin" which weaves its way through *Abhijan*. At some point this boulder emerged as an individual motif introduced when Josef and Narsingh first walk across the rocks area to Josef's house. It dominated Ray's imagination throughout the making of the film. He went so far as to create two symbolic scenes around it. The first walk. Then the symbolic boulder is sighted and the camera moves forward in the rhythm of walking. Narsingh climbs up and pits his strength against the immovable monolith only to discover his own weakness on the physical level (Pl. XXXIX). In the second scene towards the end of the film, the boulder suddenly confronts the distraught Narsingh who has blindly knocked Josef down for trying to restrain him from smuggling the opium tin. Here the rock became symbolic of spiritual force. It shocked Narsingh out of his state of corruption.

These two initially symbolic scenes should be kept in mind, for what Ray finally did with them serves as an insight into his character as a man and as an artist.

At this stage, they discovered several other locations in Dubrajpur —the Mawari house as mentioned earlier; the wedge-shaped façade for the wine shop and the vehicle stand; also a thatched building near the rocks which became the location of Neeli's school. Here there were swarms of children to incorporate into a scene with the one-legged Bannerjee.

On the drive back to Calcutta from Dubrajpur, Ray probably began to notice the arresting visual features of the road as they reared into view of the car's headlights. The roads round Dubrajpur were to become, both by daylight and after dark, a vital feature of the taxi driver's story.

Before they reached Calcutta, Bijoy Chatterjee ventured to ask Satyajit if he would be willing to direct *Abhijan*. Ray now agreed and Bijoy's ambitions as a producer soared. Outwardly casual, an inner conviction about the story had driven Bijoy with a dogged patience. From start to finish he had enormous faith in *Abhijan*. He celebrated its financial success in Bengal by getting married.

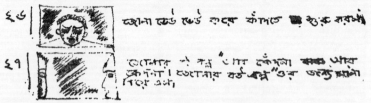

Sandip (sketches from a film script of a Rabindranath Tagore story drawn at the age of eight)

Chapter 11

RAY AS DIRECTOR (I): *KANCHENJUNGA*

WHILE writing the scenario of *Kanchenjunga* and drawing his sketches for the continuity in Darjeeling, Satyajit's cousin, Dilip Bose, the Darjeeling correspondent of *The Statesman*, helped him to obtain the necessary permission to shoot at a number of Darjeeling locations and also to rent, when necessary, the Windermere Hotel's Snuggery Cottage for the few interior shots called for by his completed script. *Kanchenjunga* was the only film of Ray's which did not require the construction of a single studio set.

He followed up his letter to me saying that the shooting of *Mahanagar* was cancelled with a second to say that he was going to start shooting an alternative film—*Kanchenjunga*—in colour in Darjeeling and I could come there any time between October 28th and November 27th, 1961. The shooting would actually take twenty-seven days and I would be present for twenty-three. His letter amazed me for I was unable to imagine Satyajit setting a film in "the Queen of Hill Stations". Darjeeling was solely associated in my mind with atrocious Victorian architecture, English tea planters and retired English types better suited to Bournemouth, yet clinging to a dying mode of life in this outpost of English enterprise.

Ray's American distributor, Edward Harrison, who considered Satyajit a great director, suddenly arrived in Delhi for six days. He had come to India to view all of Ray's films. He was on his way to Calcutta. Then he was returning to Delhi for the opening of an International Film Festival. He planned to go to Darjeeling to watch Satyajit direct. Harrison told me that he had already collected over $50,000 as the West Bengal Government's share of the royalties on *Pather Panchali* alone.

By the time Ed reappeared for the International Film Festival, he had signed a contract for the American release of Satyajit's controversial film *Devi*. It had overwhelmed Harrison so much that he repeatedly said : "It's a great film, one of the greatest I've ever seen Don't you think it's marvellous?" I don't know if he realized that his signing of the contract would help to remove official doubts about *Devi*. He was also nearly certain that if he liked what he saw of *Kanchenjunga*, he would sign a contract for the film with-out seeing it completed.

An hour after touching down at Calcutta's Dum Dum airport, I was off again on another plane for Bogdogra in the north of West Bengal, and on the far side of East Pakistan. This flight of some ninety miles saved a roundabout railway journey of some thirty-six hours. Bogdogra was furnace-hot when the plane landed, for it lies in a plain with the Himalayas shimmering mistily on the northern horizon.

Not until I was on a hunt for transport to carry me the remaining sixty-two miles up to Darjeeling did I realize that Chakravarty, one of Ray's producers for N.C.A. Productions, was on the same plane. We shared a taxi up to the town built on different levels of the 7,000-foot mountain. He, too, had no conception of Darjeeling's magic until the taxi began its stolid climb up the twisting road.

At one moment, the drifting afternoon mist which was to be a visual motif of *Kanchenjunga* seemed to bring the whitened sun so close that you could pick it from the sky. At another, we were overwhelmed by the unexpected appearance of a tall but bending dahlia tree suspending its orchid-mauve blooms over the road so that they gleamed as the only touch of colour against the gliding mist. Ray was to use an almost identical dahlia tree as a back-ground for the first conversation between Monisha and the outsider Ashoke.

The atmosphere of the mountains both heightens the perception and at the same time induces a sense of calm. It was a valid setting for *Kanchenjunga* with its theme of a group of people undergoing a subtle change in consciousness. The film was to con-found by its quietude and perplex because of the muted quality of its dramatic element.

Shortly before sundown we reached Darjeeling, where almost Stone Age Tibetan nomads meet such contemporary examples of the drainpipe set as the local college students who appear as Anil's girl friends in *Kanchenjunga*. All stages of humanity between these two extremes flowed up and down the paths connecting one level of the town with the next. As in Venice, the roads, except for one, and the paths, are closed to motor traffic. The alternative to walking is to ride a pony led by a Tibetan woman or boy on Observatory Hill

Prohibition on motor vehicles meant that Ray, his technicians, the actors and, for the first week, Ed Harrison, moved everywhere on foot. The equipment was hauled by hand from location to location, sometimes as much as a mile for the shooting of a few takes. This constant moving was accomplished with the help of five young local porters—three expressive girls, not related to each other, and two of their brothers. One boy was in his teens, tall and with startlingly blue eyes, presumed to have come from his alleged Kashmiri ancestry. The other boy, though less than twelve, always seized the heaviest object to carry. A sturdy and Mongolian-featured Nepalese, he was known as Giant. As the days passed, the five young porters took on more and more jobs in connection with the production, as well as feeding the entire unit whenever work happened to be when mealtimes came around.

Chakravarty and I went in search of "the film people". We scoured Observatory Hill and could find no trace of anyone. Finally we tracked Satyajit down to the Mount Everest Hotel. Sandip, then eight years old, Bijoya and her sister, Joya, had come for a holiday. Sandip and a servant had formed themselves into a team already known as Second Unit since they spent all their time shooting with Sandip's 8-mm. home movie camera. He was making his first film in a serious effort to follow in father's footsteps. Yet Sandip did not seem to mind when his mother kept him at lessons in the mornings as a substitute for school.

The next morning before shooting commenced, two of Ray's assistants summed up why they liked to work with him : "First, we are making some contribution to films which, if not commercial, have prestige. Secondly, there is Mr. Ray's behaviour and our understanding with him man to man. Thirdly, all of us have common aims. We are making good films expressive of new thought. This is why no one has left from the beginning." I wrote it down word for word.

Ray's handwritten scenario for *Kanchenjunga* was ever present during shooting. It commenced with a carefully drawn map of Darjeeling dotted with seventeen circles each marking a location. He had prepared several additional maps showing the layout of the main locations. As mentioned in a previous chapter, the only locations away from Observatory Hill, were sections of the steps and path leading upwards to The Mall from the teeming market located at the lowest level of the town.

The scenario noted the exact time of day when each group of shots was to be directed in order to capture the particular lighting effects Ray wished to achieve. For example, with the exception of the first scenes culminating on The Mall when Ashoke runs into

Indranath and the family and Bannerji takes Monisha for a walk, all the scenes including Labanya, the mother, had to be shot in dull light, and when there was mist. Scenes between Monisha and Bannerji were to be shot in the afternoons, so as to catch the mist and shadow, except when the day was dull. But scenes between Ashoke and Monisha were to emphasize sunlight. All foreground action and composition for every shot had been sketched in the original script. No formal shooting script had been prepared.

Each pair or combination of characters had been allotted their specific location span, except for Ashoke who traverses the town from the bottom to the top and wanders about the Hill. Monisha and Bannerji, and also Ashoke's plan of movement, was to be concentrated at points along the east side road of the Hill—facing towards the peak of Kanchenjunga. Here the scenery altered from one end of the road to the other. Anima and Shankar's special location for the revelation of their conflict was, ironically, the pleasant Children's Park on the west side of the Hill. Overlooked by the Church, its clock was to mark the passing of time. The flirtatious activities of the playboy son, Anil, were set in the roof-top café of the dairy produce establishment of Kaventer where, in actuality, Darjeeling's young socialites gather to sip chocolate milk through sterilized straws within sight of the exclusive Planter's Club. Visible far below is the market.

The character of Indranath Roy Chudhuri had been written for Chhabi Biswas. Karuna Banerji was cast as his wife, Labanya; while her brother, Jagadish, was to be played by the well-known actor, Pahari Sanyal. Anil Chatterjee, who had made a mark as Tagore's Postmaster, came from Calcutta to act Anil. He was already rigged out with a pair of specially tailored tapering slacks and a natty wind-breaker jacket in grey leather slashed with red. But, before he arrived, Satyajit had seen the two Darjeeling college girls, Vidya Singh and Nilima Roy Chudhury, in their black drainpipe slacks and identical heavy hand-knitted cardigans. Vidya's was canary yellow and Nilima's a gorgeous pink. Their get-up's were exactly what Ray wanted. Fortunately the girls—both of them very bright students—possessed highly contrasting faces for Anil's girl friends. Ray encountered little difficulty in persuading them to appear wearing their own eye-catching clothes.

Juxtaposed with their clothes, Anil Chatterjee's Calcutta-acquired attire appeared too toned down. He was hurried to a Mall tailor and measured up for a new pair of drainpipe slacks in silver-grey corduroy which were ready in twenty-four hours. In the next-door shop, Satyajit found a grey Karacol hat which he put on Anil's head at a raffish angle with a forelock of hair pulled forward. Both Anil and Vidya Singh were equipped with reflecting sunglasses. (Pl. XXII)

Ray's casting for his five remaining major characters—the elder daughter, Anima, and her husband, Shankar; Monisha and her suitor Bannerji; finally, the outsider, Ashoke—epitomizes both the care he takes to find the right person and the risks he is willing to chance with every character visualized in his mind. Three of his five selected actors had never before faced a motion picture camera.

For the husband, Shankar, Ray had persuaded Subrata Sen, the left-wing trade union leader and former member of the Calcutta Corporation, to interpret the upper-class eligible gambler. They had met late in July, Sen having visited Ray as Vice-President of the Cine Technicians of Bengal. Sen had become an active organizer of this new union. They had several times discussed the erratic payment policy in the film industry and the extent of unemployment among technicians. There were plans for a hunger strike outside all the studios. During these meetings, Ray observing Sen, decided that he was photogenic. Sen's face expressed a variety of emotions and he had a most agreeable voice. What Satyajit did not know, at the point when Sen appealed to him as an ideal Shankar, was that Sen now and then engaged in amateur dramatics.

Sen agreed to appear as Shankar. When the first rushes of *Kanchenjunga* finally arrived, it was evident that Sen's face and voice was no less exactly attuned to the audio-visual demands of the screen than Karuna Banerji's for *Pather Panchali*. Sen also appears most effectively in a small part in *Nayak*.

For Ashoke, the representative of a new generation and a different class from the rich family, Ray took the chance of selecting Arun Mookerjee who had appeared in several theatre productions of the semi-professional group headed by Shembu Mitra, one of the most talented of Bengal theatre directors.

But Ray told me he had never seen Arun's stage performances, because a stage performance was no indication of how an actor would appear on the screen. He went on to explain that in casting a character, major or minor, he is guided by appearance rather than by any proven capacity in a person to act. Once he is interested in anyone for a particular character—and he can be first interested by a photograph—he seeks to talk to the person and watch the mobility of the facial muscles. He leads them to talk and observes their reactions. He favours people who are intelligent. He does not show an actor how to portray the character, instead he encourages them to interpret the character in their own way.

Arun Mookerjee's highly individual face was not in accord with the Indian conventions of good looks. He looks puckish. His smile conveyed whimsicality due to his eye-teeth being rather long. He had a kind of independent, devil-may-care look when juxtaposed to Chhabi Biswas's Indranath. Without it being intrusive, Mookerjee also endowed Ashoke with a physical appeal which must intensify Monisha's awareness of the heavy-handedness of Bannerji, her eligible suitor. Ashoke attracts her at first sight and then she finds him lingering in her thoughts.

Ray chose the Bengali-speaking Tamil, N. Viswanathan, to play Bannerji. Combining a career of university lecturer with screen acting in both Tamil and Bengali films, the florid histrionic tradition of Tamil cinema had lent Viswanathan's style of acting that touch of pomposity which Ray wanted Bannerji to suggest. In order to em-phasize heaviness and stiffness in Bannerji, Viswanathan wore a heavy pullover under his jacket to contrast visually with the agility of Mookerjee as Ashoke. On sight, a potential situation was created which lends substance to Bannerji's last remark to Monisha : ". . . if you ever feel that security is more important than love, or love might grow out of security, let me know."

From Labanya's comments on her younger daughter, Monisha— "she has so many good qualities"—and from Monisha's own dia-logue, it can be gathered she possesses warmth of personality, is intelligent and sensitive, while the most positive trait she reveals to Bannerji is her desire to be honest.

Ray had a definite image of Monisha in mind. Moreover, he wanted an entirely new girl—a fresh face and an untried personal-ity—to convey Monisha. He had thought of numerous girls he knew of and had studied many photographs. None fitted his image. One day, Bijoy Chatterjee mentioned a girl called Aloknanda Roy, a Presidency College student who was appearing in a college production. Bijoy, not Satyajit, went to see the performance. The description of this girl interested Ray. She came from what is called "a good family". Therefore, since the cinema is still suspect as a profession for such girls, Satyajit had to proceed with the ut-most diplomacy.

Being the very soul of tact, he telephoned Aloknanda's parents Her father was an engineer and prejudiced against film-making partly because one of his brothers' experience when connected with New Theatres Ltd., the studio which Satyajit frequently used, and uses. Fortunately, it was not Mr. Roy who answered the phone but his bright wife, herself an amateur actress and translator of modern novels into Bengali. When she heard why Ray was phoning, she made up her mind that her daughter, nicknamed Bulbul, was going to act Monisha. But father would have to be handled with care. As a dutiful wife, Mrs. Roy summoned Mr. Roy to the phone. At Darjeeling he gave me an hour-by-hour account as to how he had come to agree. For five days Ray's proposals created a flurry of discussion within the Roy family. Fortunately for Satyajit, they also turned out to be members of the Brahmo Samaj.

The day after his phone call, Satyajit ventured to visit the Roy house where he managed to get a glimpse of Bulbul and make a few casual remarks. He also managed to extract a photograph of the girl on the promise to return it within an hour. The family discussion went round and round. They were astounded as to how much Satyajit Ray knew about them. He explained this by saying: "I have my scouts all over Bengal!"

Mr. Roy's fear was, as he put it, that of a normal family man: Bulbul's standard of values would be changed if she appeared in a film. (His fear was really not unfounded since both Sharmila Tagore and Aparna Das Gupta were destined to become Bombay film stars as a result of being "discovered" by Ray.) For Bulbul to act in a film "was not buying a packet of cigarettes". Mr. Roy had to have time to think it over. His answer would have been an emphatic *"No"* had the proposal come from anyone other than Satyajit Ray.

Mrs. Roy supplied little shoves in favour of Satyajit's proposal while Mr. Roy argued with himself that the middle-class and educated Bengalis much respected Ray, who had not taken the beaten path of glamour or romance in his pictures.

Having studied Bulbul's photograph, Satyajit phoned up to say she was ideal for the part. He invited Mr. Roy to visit his home. No doubt the family atmosphere impressed the cautious father. Nevertheless, he kept his wife up discussing the fate of Bulbul until 2.30 a.m.! Father chatted with daughter the next day. Daughter discreetly threw the matter back to Father to decide. It was all very disturbing since Roy had carefully planned the pattern of his family's life. Bulbul had been given the best education with the understanding that she aim to become a commercial artist.

With much feminine diplomacy, Aloknanda said that, as she had learned from her aunt, the life of a film star could prove disastrous She craved no such life. Father's enthusiasm began to grow with the thought that, after all, it would be a happy experience for Bulbul to see herself on the screen; to have something outstanding to remember for her lifetime. As he put it, "middle-class life is uneventful, dull".

Only one last "but" remained: how would his second brother,

his eldest being dead, feel about Bulbul, his pet, acting on the screen? Since it was Satyajit Ray's film, Uncle thought it all quite proper. A contract was therefore signed at the end of five days. Aloknanda came to Darjeeling accompanied by her father, mother and younger sister. Her elder sister in the film was the well-known screen actress, Anuba Gupta.

The morning after I arrived in Darjeeling—rather little shooting had as yet taken place—I noticed that it was only the two film sisters who wore any make-up. They were precisely the kind of girls who would use cosmetics. Before that day's shooting was far advanced, I noticed a further interesting detail: that Anuba Gupta had two small moles near the lobe of one ear and that when looked at closely Aloknanda Roy could be seen to have a small mole in the centre of her nose. I asked Satyajit had he thought this out, so that the two sisters on the screen should have physical marks to heighten the notion of their physical relationship to one another and that they had inherited moles.

"Just fortunate accident, not design," Ray replied. But the extent of his pleasurable grin suggested how pleased he was that such a subtle physical coincidence could have arisen.

Another detail struck me : how Ray had incorporated the two different styles of jewellery most widely sold all over Darjeeling— the dull silver pendants and ear-rings embossed with deity figures almost looking like abstract designs, and the gay gilt rings, brooches and ear-rings set with turquoise and coral. Anuba Gupta as the sophisticated married Anima, had been given a pair of the deity design ear-rings to wear, the tone of the oxidized silver perfectly harmonizing with the dark grey stripe of the light purple sari she wears in *Kanchenjunga*. A matching brooch was pinned to her coat. In contrast, Aloknanda Roy was wearing the gilt jewellery to blend with the borderless marigold-toned sari she wore as Monisha The shade of her lipstick and the *tilak* mark on her forehead was of an orange tint to match the coral stones.

Using colour for the first time, it became rapidly clear that Satyajit Ray had thought a great deal about the clothes tones in relation not only to the characters but to the locations. The most vivid colour of all—bright red—was being worn by the child playing the little girl riding round on a pony as a motif. The red was very visible In absolute contrast, the beggar boy, as witness to Monisha and Bannerji's walk, was no less emphasized visually by the most emphatic monotone—his own greyish cardigan too big for him.

Colour values loomed into importance in the first scene Ed Harrison and I watched : the first in the Children's Park between Anima and Shankar. The focal point was the homely green bench, a dullish green, in front of a clump of golden-rod. Beneath the pleasant trees on the far side of the Park, children were see-sawing. Shankar in a brownish jacket sat on the seat. Anima, with a black coat over her grey-and-purple striped sari, carried a yellow plastic shopping basket, a tone softer and brighter than the golden-rod.

The charm and pleasantness of the setting served as a direct paradox to the grim mood of the content for this scene containing the greatest number of ugly innuendoes and undertones in *Kanchenjunga*. The "first movement" of this sequence, which follows the imaginative exposition about the migration of birds which the bird-watching Jagadish gives Ashoke, is the most emotion-charged passage. It took two mornings to direct.

With the free movement of children in the background (the children who were playing by chance), the movements of Anima and Shankar were cramped up around about the garden seat. (Pl. XLIII)

Anima comes with her shopping basket towards the seat:

Anima: Shall I go away?
Shankar: No. Sit down. There's something I want to say . . .
    (*His back is turned to her and he switches to English.*)
    Marriage is a noble institution.

Facing him is the Church on a slight hill. Inevitably, it has a meaning to them since they are the class of people who were probably educated in a Christian school.

Anima (*whose expression is hard*): What do you want to say?
Shankar: The daughter of a top society man, gets married to
    such a perfect choice ... the flowers rain down from Heaven
    . . . picture in the *Onlooker* . . . and ten years later, the
    worm has eaten right into the heart. Who's to blame?
    Who's responsible? Don't you think this needs looking
    into? It seems to me this is the right time and the right
    place? Walls may hear, but not mountains. Anima . . .

Subrata Sen had never faced a motion picture camera before. Subrata Mitra, as cameraman, had never worked in colour before. The rehearsal and shooting of these first shots of the scene were composed with meticulous care. For a medium shot of Shankar's last words, the leaves scattered on the grass were kicked nearer together just sufficiently to be visible at the feet of Shankar, who had risen from the seat on which Anima now sat down.

Anima : You tell me whose fault it is, then.
Shankar (*again speaking in English*) : Foolishness, trust, gullibility
   —if these are faults, then I'm to blame.
Anima : What do you mean?

The camera movements were unobtrusive. Now and then, Satyajit exclaimed "Fine!", "Wonderful!". He was utterly engrossed although a considerable number of onlookers had gathered to watch a slight distance away. (Pl. XLV)

> Shankar : That your feelings were already engaged and would continue to be even after marriage, I could hardly have foreseen. I was a fool, and you were the accomplished actress. If any more of my speculations go wrong and I end up bankrupt, there'll be no need for us to starve, because you will be snapped up by the films, and I'll live off you!
> Anima (*who has already been seen receiving a letter from her lover*) : You've been reading my letters!
> Shankar : What a crime! Under what section of the Penal Code does that come?
> Anima : I know you've been reading them. I've suspected it for a long time. (*She bursts into tears.*)

More and more onlookers had collected, pressing closer as the climax was built up under the calm, orderly, yet enthusiastic methods of Ray. The scene was potently lifelike.
"Cut!" shouted Satyajit. He was so carried away with enthusiasm that he clapped his hands. His applause was picked up by those observing.
Edward Harrison, who was fascinated by Ray's methods, turned saying : "I never saw a director do a thing like that before. Did you?"
Following lunch, shots for the second section of the sequence were to be photographed on the other side of the Children's Park, at the foot of a tall tree where Shankar sits sombrely. The scene called for cloudiness and mist. The mist did not appear, instead the sun shone. We waited and waited. Finally, Ray decided it was hopeless and he ordered a move to be made to another location. His normal unit of eight had been expanded for *Kanchenjunga* to sixteen. He strode out of the Park. Some few hundred yards along Mall Road, he suddenly stopped and looked up at the sky.
"We can shoot!" he exclaimed, and turned about and hurried back.

Q

The clouds came but not the mist. By now he had made up his mind to do the shots he had intended. Though he would not choose to simulate an artificial mist, he decided to try to. Several of his assistants quickly set small fires in round metal baskets which they placed behind trees beyond the central tree to be shown. The smoke was fanned to disperse it over the area of the Park. One assistant waved a basket about behind the focal tree itself.

The first shot of this scene is one of the most beautiful, a panning shot down the tree. When edited, this pan emerged as a striking example of visual continuity. It followed the last shot of the scene between Indranath and Ashoke, when Ashoke, refusing Indranath's offer of a job, suddenly laughs, throwing up his arms in astonishment at his own audacity. His arms then drop in doubt—pan down the tree revealing Shankar sitting despondently at the foot.

Now it was the tones of Shankar's jacket which took on a new and subtle importance in a colour film. His tweed jacket and the browny-red scarf about his neck blended, but not obtrusively so, with the bark of the tree. When Anima appeared, her yellow basket, first seen in relation to the green of the garden seat and the golden-rod on the other side of the Park, harmonized in a brighter tone with the yellowish tints in the tree's bark.

Shankar proposes a divorce. In the background, children were rising and falling, up and down, on the see-saw. Ray had not arranged for this. It was simply happening. But it added a dimension to his scene—how in life when something urgent is happening between two people there is casual, unconnected activity going on all around.

The simulated mist blurred the scene corresponding to Shankar's inner mood. He does not really want his marriage to break up despite the other man. Ray, wishing to convey more definitely a sense of autumn and the seeming end of something, thought that a leaf falling from the shedding tree was the right symbol.

But the leaves, even as the mist that afternoon, were stubborn No leaves were falling. Shaking the branches failed to dislodge even one. Finally, Ray's assistant, Sailen Dutta, climbed up the tree to aid Nature. He gathered a handful of leaves for the medium close-up where Shankar first speaks suggesting divorce.

Dutta dropped a leaf as Shankar began to speak. He dropped a second leaf further on and a third where Shankar said to Anima, "I will let you go." After the first "take", Ray decided three leaves were too visually distracting. The second "take", used in the film, showed only a single leaf falling at the beginning of what Shankar had to say.

With part of the long three-section Anima-Shankar quarrel shot (to be counterpoised with the Monisha-Bannerji and Indranath-Ashoke motifs), Satyajit Ray, Edward Harrison and I went off to Glenary's ye olde English tea-room. What Ed had seen confirmed his decision to distribute *Kanchenjunga*. But having fallen in love with the scenic splendour of Darjeeling, he was intensely anxious to convince Satyajit that if he would only add in one more shot of the stupendous surrounding beauty, *Kanchenjunga* would make Darjeeling the most famed beauty spot in the world.

Satyajit said hardly a word to discourage Ed's hopes. But, as shooting proceeded, he refrained from adding a single shot, his argument being that his film was concerned with his characters and what was happening within them. He kept to his original concept that there should be but a single scenic passage with no dialogue but music—Ray's "Mist Music". This transitional passage of five views of the mountains with drifting mist is as if seen by the child, Tuklu, as she rides her pony around after seeing her unhappy parents quarrelling. The last shot contains a bare tree followed by a shot of Labanya, who seems to be contemplating the tree as expressive of her own desolate anxiety that her daughter, Monisha, will make as unfortunate a marriage as herself through Indranath's demands. (Pl. XLIII)

At Glenary's we sat at a table near the window with a view of the trafficless road below. Suddenly, Satyajit exclaimed: "There he is! He's come back!" He pointed out of the window at a small boy in a huge cardigan who was begging off a European woman with a child in a pushcart. "I thought I'd lost him! He's one of the recurring musical motifs. At the end, he gets the bar of chocolate from Bannerji." (Pl. XLII)

The next day, the boy had been incorporated into the unit. Every morning he went to breakfast with the technicians. Up to the end of the shooting, when he was not acting in various scenes, he busied himself in assisting in carrying this and that around.

Ray told Ed and me that he was thrilled by finding two perfect types of Englishman to serve as his English motifs. His cousin, Dilip Bose, who knew them, was trying to persuade them to appear. One was the oldest English inhabitant, aged eighty-four, who daily rode around Observatory Hill on his horse. He finally agreed.

The other was a planter, Derek Royals, whom Ray required to interpret Ellis, the tourist, in the opening scene on the terrace of the Windermere Hotel. When Royals finally agreed, the scene was directed and shot, starting at eleven o'clock on the morning of

November 18th. The time on the screen was supposed to be 4 p.m. and, according to the dialogue, the peak of Kanchenjunga was shrouded in mist.

At the moment of shooting the peak glistened visibly in the sunlight. To create a cloudy effect, the composition within the frame of the shots composing the short scene avoided including too much blue sky. Throughout the whole shooting of *Kanchenjunga*, Subrata Mitra's problem was, on the one hand, to gain contrasts between those scenes where sunshine and shadow are integral to the scene, and, on the other, to contrive as much unity as possible for the dull and misty scenes which had to be shot partly in genuine shadow, partly in bright light toned down with filters. This was a difficult set of conditions for Mitra who had no experience of colour film.

Bijoy Chatterjee commented on Derek Royals as they rehearsed : "He has a kind of Victorian look about the face." Royals's youthful personality, in spite of his silky grey hair and moustache, could well have fitted the image of a nineteenth-century Empire Builder, the type of man who once developed the town of Darjeeling. This was a pointed touch since Indranath is shown at the end of the film as looking back nostalgically to the days of British Rule. This last sentiment is hinted at the moment he first appears and says "Good afternoon" to the tourist (Royals) who is seen walking down the path from the top of Observatory Hill.

The tenor of this first scene—seemingly no more than two hotel guests chatting about the weather and the invisibility of Kanchenjunga's peak—could not be more casual, yet it introduces the main symbol—the peak—the unveiling of which marks the change in Indranath's family and reveals that, psychologically, Indranath belongs to British days.

Royals had never faced a camera before his scene with the professional Chhabi Biswas. Yet, Ray merely explained to Royals what action he required, what was to be conveyed and the tone of voice he wanted. During the first rehearsal, Ray, very casually, made the suggestion that Royals should move to the terrace railing. Putting his own foot up on the bar, he suggested a similar action to Royals.

It was evident that Royals was enjoying himself. He did not tense up. It flashed through my mind how interesting it was that the enormously tall Ray was able to tower over the totally inexperienced man acting for the first time and yet in no way appear intimidating. I tried to analyse how this could be and concluded that it was Satyajit's animation while at work that tended to reduce the effect of his height.

Mitra's camera went into action with Indranath saying "Good afternoon". Royals, walking down the slope, replied : "Afternoon. I've been on top. No luck. Cloudy. It's a pity. It [Kanchenjunga] looks wonderful in the photos." Everything had gone according to rehearsal. The shot was half finished when, suddenly, a man on horseback, utterly oblivious of what was going on, rode into the scene crossing between the camera and Biswas and Royals.

If Ray was furious he failed to show even a trace of irritation. He merely said there would have to be a second take. They all started again. The whole scene, with its several shots, was completed in just over one hour.

Satyajit Ray never appeared to hurry over anything; he never relaxed his meticulous care even for the smallest shot. Yet his average number of takes was two with an occasional three for a variant to be decided during editing. He could say each day what the footage to be completed was likely to run to. Invariably, his estimate was correct. On one day as much as 2,000 feet was shot without a trace of hurry. The planning of work was as complete as a jigsaw puzzle, even though the shift in location frequently involved walks from one end of Observatory Hill to the other—from beyond the Windermere Hotel to Jalapher Road for the scenes between Bannerji and Monisha. Day by day it grew colder and colder in the afternoon.

It was Bulbul—Aloknanda Roy—who had envisioned film-making as a glamorous path of dalliance, who now found acting a hard, chilly job. She found herself having to wear an unglamorous woolly under her marigold-tinted sari. Privately she said that, in contrast to Monisha, if she had to choose between romance and security, she'd choose security any day. But cold as it became, she, as everyone else, worked hard.

The opening scene, followed by Indranath's curt order to his brother-in-law, Jagadish, to go and see if the family were ready to go to meet Bannerji, led to the only interior shots in *Kanchenjunga*. While writing the scenario in the hotel, Satyajit had examined its separate Snuggery Cottage to see if he could utilize it in lieu of a studio set. The front room of the cottage provided a perfect setting for Labanya's packing to leave; Shankar and Anima beginning to reveal their conflict and Monisha popping in to borrow a pin in preparation for her momentous walk with Bannerji. Satyajit thought that if they shot during the sunny hours of the morning they could manage to reflect sufficient light into the room.

N.C.A. Productions rented the cottage for a period of four days at the cost of Rs.150/- per day (£11). The hotel curtains with their floral pattern of marigold-tinted flowers seemed suitable back-ground for shots of Shankar reading in bed after his afternoon nap. The colour scheme was only added to by the introduction of a red-and-black check blanket.

The two problems presented by the cottage bedroom were how to trap the maximum amount of light in order to photograph the scenes without the introduction of artificial lighting, and how, with a very limited space, to give the actors room to move, the camera adequate space, and a minimum leeway for Ray to be able to judge what he was creating by way of visual effects. Everyone, except the actors when needed, Satyajit, Mitra and the camera assistants, had to keep out of the room in order that not an inch of space was lost. Would-be watchers were condemned to the back room, poking their heads round the door now and then to peek at what was going on.

Outside in the playground which the cottage faced there was activity: Durga Das Mitra had trailed his sound-recording cables into the room, but it was very awkward to handle the mike in such a small space. To add to the other objects which needed to be there, the room had to hold an easel to support the large board draped in a white sheet, one of the complex of reflectors employed to bounce the outside sunlight on to the actors.

Members of the unit were utilized at one or another point in the playground to hold the reflectors. They literally formed a cordon around the bay window of the room. At no time were there less than three long mirrors in use and always the two reflector boards which were constantly used. One was covered with silver and gold paper arranged in checks, the other was covered with a plain sheet of silver paper. Since the reflectors were always hand held, they could be adjusted for reflecting at any place or at any angle.

It was instructive to compare these very mobile reflectors mani-pulated by hand with the vast silver-coloured reflectors which had been transported the whole way from Bombay by the Shemmi Kapoor unit which had arrived in Darjeeling to shoot five song-and-dance routines for a Bombay film. These Bombay film industry reflectors set up as massive screens looked immensely more profes-sional than Ray's improvised tatty-looking screens. But the in-dustry's impressive screens lacked all mobility.

One of the attractions of the Snuggery Cottage bedroom in place of a set was that through its windows a children's swing could be seen. Whether by accident or design a child was cheerfully swing-ing at the moment the shot of Shankar in bed was taken. (Pl. XLIII)

Feeling hungry before the end of the first morning's shooting, I went into the Windermere restaurant to have a meal. A man and wife—hotel guests—who looked very English, came in. They were photogenic, particularly the man. With the cottage shooting for the day, I mentioned the couple to Satyajit.

The next day, the interior shooting finished early, well before lunchtime, and Ray turned his attention to the interlocking scenes that take place in the hotel garden not far from the cottage. This was the scene of Indranath and Labanya walking down a steep flight of steps leading to Mall Road. On all sides there was a blaze of flowers with every shade of dahlia and marigold dominating the garden in November.

Karuna Banerji had been standing near by dressed as Labanya in a red-bordered white sari and a black shawl faintly embroidered with threads of red. The continuity called for her to walk from the cottage and join Indranath, Biswas being dressed in a grey suit with a wine-red tie and matching handkerchief in the breast pocket. I had several times watched Karuna waiting for one of her scenes to be directed. Some time in advance her normally animated personality underwent a change; she would cease talking to anyone and submerge herself in the anxious, suppressed Labanya dominated over by the callous Indranath. Her face became bleak and her own elegant walk was replaced by the melancholy steps of an unhappy woman. I noticed the expressive tilt of Karuna's head when she finally walked towards the camera with Indranath demanding to know "What kept you?"

"I was packing your suitcase. Oh"—and with a half-turn—"I forgot your muffler."

Between the rehearsal and the shooting of the medium shot of Karuna Banerji and Chhabi Biswas on the steps, Ray recognized the hotel guests I'd described. Unaware of what was going on, they had begun to climb the steps leading up from Mall Road. In a flash, Ray decided to include the couple in the shot. Running down the steps he stopped them and asked them to walk towards the camera when they reached the top of the steps and then walk on to the hotel.

As they came towards the camera, Mitra went into action. The couple were whisked, as it were, in and out of the pattern without any change of movement being given to Biswas and Karuna Banerji, who moved as pre-arranged to the top of the flight of steps. They paused. For the next shot the camera had to be carried down the steps to a ledge in the descent.

The shot upwards to Indranath and Labanya at the top of the steps was interesting: it contained a key nuance in revealing Indranath's character. Eager to reach the Mall and meet Bannerji, his choice for a future son-in-law, Indranath suddenly notices a man walking along Mall Road below—the long shot was cut in. The man sneezes—an unlucky omen in Bengal. Indranath spits out the word "Idiot!" In this single word Chhabi Biswas concentrated all the egoism and viciousness of which this seemingly gentlemanly man was capable when caught off guard.

As the first take was completed, Ray noticed two more hotel guests who had appeared to watch on the terrace just within the top level of the frame, the camera being tilted upwards. Striding up the steps, he called to them "Don't move! Go on talking, you'll be all right!"

He turned to me on the path below announcing with pleasure : "I'm getting a wonderful international cast, aren't I?" However, when he came to edit this scene he finally chose the first take where no one is seen on the terrace above. His reason was that two additional figures in the background would distract attention from Indranath and Labanya in the foreground.

The most interesting and important instance of improvisation in *Kanchenjunga* took place almost at the climax of the long sequence of Monisha and Bannerji taking their walk, with Monisha hedging to keep Bannerji's proposal from being made. Serving as the film's central core, the sequence runs in the film as a thread seen in five sections and overlapped by Anima and Shankar in the Park; Jagadish talking to Ashoke, and to Labanya; and Indranath revealing his thoughts and life to Ashoke thus producing the revulsion which causes Ashoke to reject the offered job.

The direction of the crucial walk took place after midday and and in the afternoons at various points along Jalaphar Road running south from Observatory Hill from the Mall where action constantly converges. Jalaphar Road on the east side of the highest level of Darjeeling is relatively bare with an awe-inspiring view of the mountains. On November afternoons it is invariably shadowed and often obscured by drifting mist. The view, the shadows and the mist formed an integral element with the dialogue and the composition of the shots. As the sequence develops, section by section, the view and the mist become increasingly interwoven with the depiction of the psychological mood of Monisha. The blunt insensitivity behind the well-meaningness of Bannerji become ever more apparent.

His intention to propose to Monisha is, in the context, only the contemporary form of the arranged marriage. Only a moment after their meeting in the Mall (Ashoke has been inadvertently introduced to Monisha barely a minute before), Bannerji compliments her on

.the jewellery she is wearing, failing to recognize that it is what he has given her himself! (Pl. XLIV)

Their subsequent walk is pregnant with meaning in terms of current Indian society; though there remain many college girls of intellectual as well as well-off families (the prototypes compounded in Ray's Monisha) who still accept the traditional system of arranged marriages negotiated by both families, and will enter into them without apparent conflict, an increasing number of girls in the upper strata of contemporary Indian society are experiencing a sense of revulsion at the notion of meeting a man on an arrangement basis. Some have gone as far as agreeing to an engagement but found the man after meeting him several times so incompatible or repellent that they have refused to go through with the marriage, despite all the traditional arguments. Monisha's predicament is juxtaposed in *Kanchenjunga* by the peril in which Anima's marriage with Shankar has now been put through her acquiescence in marrying the man she did not love because her father wanted it. Anima and Shankar make their free choice to attempt to salvage their marriage while Monisha employs her free will to choose not to marry her father's choice. The subsidiary theme providing gay relief from the intensity of the sisters is the randy efforts of Anil on his hunt for girl friends. He has rejected tradition but has found no better standard to replace it.

The whole of the dialogue between Monisha and Bannerji is a muted fencing match. Bannerji's first attempt to propose is staved off because a friend comes running after him asking him to join a game of bridge at the Club. Satyajit's cousin Dilip enacted this bouncy figure. At the same time, Ashoke comes walking along and joins them. Uncle Jagadish, doing his duty, takes Ashoke away, Bannerji then begins to talk a great deal too much. In the process of edging around to present himself as a desirable husband he alienates Monisha, for their wavelengths stretch further and further apart. Indranath's choice reflects himself for he, too, in seeking to impress Ashoke only produces revulsion against all he stands for.

Watching the direction of the Monisha-Bannerji walk sequence it was possible to detect how subtle the undertones and overtones were in Ray's characters so closely duplicating the types of Bengalis living in or visiting Darjeeling. Then one Sunday afternoon the simmering situation between the local Nepalese Hill people of Darjeeling and the Bengal minority exploded like a firecracker in the middle of the shooting of a walk scene. Numbers of youths from nearby villages had apparently gathered to watch the film-making by the Bengali group. Catcalls and anti-Bengali epithets suddenly were rained down on Satyajit Ray. There was such pandemonium that shooting had to halt.

Up to that moment, Satyajit was totally ignorant about the local resentment towards the Bengali minority, who were only too free in expressing colonial-minded views about the hill people. Satyajit then discovered that his cousin, Dilip, was one of the few Bengalis who was striving to create a better relationship between the two groups. Anti-Bengali sentiment was never again displayed towards Ray or the unit; but the undertones remain. After this episode I felt the presence of Tibet sixty miles away as the crow flies as an enormous question mark.

At midday on the day the last section of the Monisha-Bannerji sequence was to be shot at the far end of Jalaphar Road, Satyajit Ray and the unit packed up from an Observatory Hill location and started to walk. Reaching Jalaphar Road, Satyajit noticed far ahead a long trail of donkeys being driven by two or three nomadic Tibetan families. The bells worn by the donkeys had many tones. In an instant, Satyajit decided he wanted to include this donkey-train in the scene he was intending to shoot.

Sailen Dutta and another Assistant Director dashed along the road to halt the Tibetans—if they could. Brian Brake, who had come to do a series of direction photographs for America, ran after them. I, too, ran. Brake and I got in the midst of the loaded stream of animals. Dutta had wormed his way to the front and was shouting and gesticulating to make himself understood by the Tibetans. These cheerful nomads and their wives just laughed at Dutta's offer. They thought everyone quite mad to want to pay them money to drive their donkeys back to be photographed! It must be a trick! They refused. Five, ten, fifteen minutes, the argument and bargaining went on. Dutta offered Rs.20/- (£1 15s.) if they would just turn the donkeys around. Still they hesitated. But when an advance of Rs.10/- was pressed upon the oldest man, much amused, they all agreed.

Ray could have simply inserted a single shot of the pack animals to lend audio-visual atmosphere. This was not, however, his intention. On seeing the donkeys he reconceived his entire handling of a crucial emotional moment in the Monisha-Bannerji sequence. While leaving the foreground composition and dialogue between Monisha and Bannerji intact, the Tibetans and their animals became integrated as a background movement with the distinctive bell tones serving to italicize Monisha's emotions.

Improvisation added a double line of action—the original planned scene, plus the unforeseen audio-visual element. As Bannerji seeks to pin Monisha down and commit herself with the query, "So much depends on what you think," she answers, "I think—" her words cut off by the donkeys in the background driven by the Tibetans. "What do you think?" asks Bannerji pressing towards his goal. The donkeys were then driven back with only the sound of their bells being recorded. In the editing, the most *powerful*-toned bell sounded as Monisha put out her hand to touch—as if for support—a post of the railing in front of her. She gazes at the view contemplatively, then comments: "It's going to be misty. I love mist!" Bannerji leaps in: "So do I. It's so healthy." Monisha has gained power over her own will and says: "Mr. Bannerji . . ." "Yes." "Let's just walk for a while, without speaking, do you mind?" "As you wish."

What follows becomes a commentary upon the *qualitative* difference in personalities. Monisha's uncle, Jagadish, is talking to the young Ashoke, who is absorbed, about birds. It is implied that these two men have a common sensibility that is completely lacking in the well-meaning Bannerji.

And the next and last time that the symphonic movement returns to the Monisha-Bannerji theme—the whole scene was shot in a real swiftly drifting mist through which there filtered a faint sunshine to create a very extraordinary effect—Monisha is suddenly caught up with absolute determination to escape from Bannerji. "Father must be waiting—" and she hurries away from Bannerji towards the Mall. In the editing, sound became a dominant factor.

As Monisha hurries from Bannerji, the bagpipes and drums of the Gurkha Police Band playing in the Mall grow louder and louder. The rhythm changes three times against the imagery of Monisha hastening to the Mall, where the band is seen. (The band shots were taken very early in the morning and also captured the real mist.) Monisha suddenly weeps against a tree as the Gurkhas play. Because of the mist, Bannerji, seeking her, does not see her. The band having changed to its third rhythm, a third Englishman appears walking towards Indranath on the path east of Observatory Hill. The rhythm appears to be hurried and, somehow, jagged. Ashoke brings Indranath his muffler. Indranath, thinking about the Englishman who has just passed by and with whom he has exchanged yet another of his polite "Good afternoons!" is prompted to let himself go to Ashoke: "You're not one of those who have the effrontery to belittle the contribution of the British in India? You know who built this town of Darjeeling? You come here for a change of air, and so many others? Once it was just a Lepcha village . . ."

Thoughtlessly he expounds on the motive of self-interest which has dominated his whole life. How wise and clever he thinks he has been. He concludes: "I'm sixty. Too old to care. Whatever comes out of Independence, is for my children to worry about, and for young men like you. What I say is—I live, I exist . . . and I have a title—the gift of my ex-rulers—I cherish it; I'm proud of it." As if tossing a bone to a dog, he tosses the offer of a job to Ashoke, who rejects it. The rejection marks the end of Indranath's power to dictate his standard of values. Shaken with doubt he finds himself left alone facing Kanchenjunga. None of the family have turned up to meet him as he directed them to do.

It took several days to shoot the long scene between Indranath and Ashoke which was intended to mark the change towards something new psychologically in all the characters, except for Indranath. When Ray commenced direction, he commented: "Indranath is not a villain in the conventional sense. Villains are boring. He's highly cultured and civilized. But all the same, his actions have the same effect as those of a villain. The character of Indranath calls for a professional actor. No non-professional could give the subtle inflexions required for what he says, or sustain his 'big scene'."

For the ten-reel *Kanchenjunga*, Ray used twenty-six rolls of stock —a ratio of three to one. Shooting was completed two days ahead of schedule. For twenty-three days I watched Ray constructing the visuals, detail by detail, of what on the surface a number of people in Calcutta later called a banal subject. A tremendous and protracted controversy arose over *Kanchenjunga* because, at the superficial level, it appeared just like life as spent for one hour and forty minutes by a not very interesting group of people wrapped up in their own unhappy concerns.

Ray had employed a Western form such as had not been used previously in a Bengali film. At least some of the reactions were probably due to a lack of familiarity with simultaneous action in time. During direction, Ray made it clear that his method of constructing *Kanchenjunga* had intentionally several levels at which it could be appreciated. It seemed immaterial to him whether the film was immediately a success or a failure. What mattered was that he wished to express in his own way an idea that had been tantalizing him.

চিত্রনাট্য, সঙ্গীত ও পরিচালনা সত্যজিৎ রায়

Satyajit (title for *Abhijan*)

Chapter 12

RAY AS DIRECTOR (II) : *ABHIJAN AND MAHANAGAR*

WITH the last two sequences of the scenario of *Abhijan* completed overnight on the visit to Dubrajpur, Satyajit and Bijoy went to work with whirlwind speed to whisk together a cast while Bansi concentrated on designing the sets described earlier. The decision was to concentrate on the shooting of some scenes on location at Dubrajpur before the work of editing and recording of music for *Kanchenjunga* had to take place. These were scenes of the taxi drivers; the first scene among the rocks with Narsingh and Josef; and scenes between Narsingh and Rama.

From the script, the character of Rama appeared distinctly comic. If played by any actor with the engrained mannerisms of Indian film acting, then Rama would be a stock comic. Ray selected the dynamic stage actor, Rabi Ghosh, who had only appeared in one film. Ghosh was so impressed by Ray's methods that he not only endowed Rama with most engaging human qualities, but developed the habit of coming to observe Ray at work on scenes in which he was not personally involved.

As mentioned, Bijoy Chatterjee had already signed Soumitra Chatterjee for the character of Narsingh and make-up test photographs had been made. These he had shown me at Darjeeling. Once Ray had agreed to direct the film, Soumitra's make-up was revised again and again. Finally, it took two hours a day to achieve. Even at close quarters and in the brightest sunshine, his wig made of hair far coarser than Soumitra's own looked genuine. Satyajit added to the wigmaker's skill. He noticed that the red dust of the Dubrajpur area caked the skin and gave a rusty tone to hair. Therefore, this red dust was brushed into Soumitra's wig. He was also given a convincing beard and moustache, and his sensitive personality wholly submerged in the mature and roughened image of Narsingh. I experienced a shock every time I saw him without his Narsingh make-up.

When it came to casting Josef's sister Neeli, Satyajit pocketed his disinclination to cast members of his own family. He chose Bijoya's niece, Ruma Guha Thakurta, who had married his one-time assisant. I first saw her in Satyajit's home where her silence was intriguing, her looks fascinating and slightly enigmatic. She had her two small sons with her and behaved like an average housewife. But a tape recording was being played of an alluring velvety contralto voice.

"Ruma!" remarked Satyajit with a tone of pride.

So this was the kind of voice that had been inherited for four generations from Satyajit's great-grandfather, Kalinarayan Gupta, and his wife. This was a Das voice.

Following the release of *Abhijan*, I remarked to a Ray relative that Ruma was extraordinarily beautiful. The remark evoked a look of astonishment.

"Beautiful? You think Ruma beautiful"—the tone was disapproving, as if I didn't know what I was talking about. "She's so dark . . ."

No one had been cast for the Hindi-speaking Gulabi when the unit and Ray went to Dubrajpur for the first eleven days of shooting. Bijoy had rented a palace-like habitation for Rs.100/- (£7 10s.) a day, where everyone was housed in rural splendour. There was a verbal understanding that they would rent it again for the second phase of location shooting.

An idea generated on location was that it would be interesting to cast a Hindi-speaking actress as Gulabi. Everyone, except Satyajit who had never seen her, favoured the young star, Waheeda Rehman, who originally belonged to Hyderabad, the junction where the northern and southern cultural strains of India meet. Though the Muslim world to which Waheeda Rehman belonged had decayed, its legacy remained in the presence of lovely women and girls. Bijoy Chatterjee was enthusiastic and promised that when they returned to Calcutta he would arrange for Satyajit to see several of her films.

As soon as Ray saw Waheeda Rehman on the screen, he declared she was just the girl to play Gulabi. By this time in her career she was receiving something in the region of Rs.250,000 (£18,797) for each of her films. This was equal to the cost of any of Ray's films until *Kanchenjunga*. Still, a letter was sent to Miss Rehman on the off-chance that she might be responsive. Anil Choudhury and Durga Das Mitra visited Waheeda Rehman in Bombay and were astonished by her saying that Mr. Ray could offer anything and she would gladly accept because she was so keen to be directed by him. Though she was noted as a dancer, no dance sequence had been added to *Abhijan* to entice her.

In the first days of March 1962, Satyajit came to Bombay to check the first colour print of *Kanchenjunga* which was being worked on for colour tones at Film Centre. He met Waheeda Rehman and offered her Rs.5000/- (£375 18s. 9d.) a day, this being what she normally received each day she worked for a Bombay producer. Satyajit had already estimated that he would require only ten days work with Waheeda Rehman in Calcutta.

It was at this time in Bombay that I saw the first rough copy of *Kanchenjunga* minus any opticals, without music and with half the dialogue still requiring to be dubbed in on account of the background noises on the sound track recorded in Darjeeling. This copy was a distinct surprise on account of the immense importance of the dialogue in conjunction with the overlapping action. The engrossing aspect of the film in this raw state was the variability of its continuity: sometimes the double-meaning of the seemingly ordinary conversation threw out a clue for picking up the threads of thought carried forward in the next scene involving another pair of characters; at other times, the flow from scene to scene came from the inner emotions of the characters as reflected in their movements.

Within a week, on March 12th, I arrived in Calcutta to begin work on this book. I found Bijoya and all her sisters seated on the large bed in the room adjoining Satyajit's work room. They were playing cards. Their mother watched cheerfully from her wheelchair. Satyajit was then concentrating on his music for *Kanchenjunga*. He would pick out the notes on his hired piano. Bijoya never mentioned she was helping Manik transcribe the themes for orchestration. Someone else commented later that her musical knowledge was of great value to Satyajit. (Pl. LII and LIV)

Over a period of two months Satyajit's frail and bearded uncle, Subimal Ray, commenced to have long meetings with me. These were usually in the evenings when this meticulously careful retired schoolmaster relayed the jigsaw puzzle of the Ray family. The history of the Brahmo Rays was mirrored in the figure of Uncle Subimal. He seemed to embody the family ideal of restrained probity. The twentieth century, with its awareness of inner conflicts and external flux and violence, had not apparently impinged upon the pristine sense of virtue rooted in Upendrakishore's youngest son. He could not say an evil word of anyone and endeavoured to discover some virtue to balance and soften every fault in the people he told me about.

Uncle Subimal sat crossed-legged on his austere bed while I sat at the small neat table by its side. His room, as might be expected from the family-cherishing turn of his mind, was the flat's museum. The galaxy of family photographs was gathered around the enormous enlarged photo of Satyajit's mother, Suprabha. Close to the anniversary of her death two years before—1960—many garlands of fresh flowers were strung about her picture. Yet nobody said a word about her death. One evening, almost under his breath, Uncle Subimal expressed the wish that Satyajit was a more orthodox Brahmo. Manik did not observe the staid festivals. I went to one. It resembled an old-fashioned vicar's tea-party for his congregation.

Waiting to continue shooting *Abhijan* and the last work on *Kanchenjunga*, Satyajit filled his time with odds and ends. He decided that a Tibetanized Bengali script was best suited to the credit titles of a film laid in Darjeeling. He had bought a Tibetan grammar. For several days it lay open at his toes propped on his divan. With his drawing-board against his knees, he worked on handmade Tibetan paper. People strayed in and out, talked, drank tea; but Satyajit went on with his work on the credit titles wholly undisturbed. The phone, as usual, often rang. Out went his hand to pick it up. He never sounded irritated. Once he had completed the lettering of the credit cards, he went back to the first and began decorating each with an amusing little scene somewhat in the style of recently developed Tibetan painted greeting cards. "Scenes I thought to incorporate in *Kanchenjunga* but never got around to," explained Satyajit.

By the concentrated care he gave to this work one might have thought he was working out the film's most crucial sequence. When the job was completely finished, he let himself fly into a spate of enthusiasm over something he had spent a whole day recording on tape. It was bird calls, including the love call of two birds he had caught in a flying visit to Darjeeling to shoot a re-take of Kanchenjunga's peak. Excitedly he confessed that his recording was not that of the real bird's call. Background noises had ruined the original sound. "Listen! There I am!" he exclaimed.

Still the sounds appeared to be produced by a bird and not a man. What Ray had done was to play the tape of the bird's whistle over and over again whistling to copy the bird's tone. He found this unsatisfactory. Then he worked out a whistle a whole tone lower and held it twice as long as the original call, in order to make it sound effective and distinctive. He was later—in 1967—to do a great deal of experiment of this kind with a variety of sounds in preparation for the sounds he planned to use in *The Alien*.

In all, fifty-five days were allotted to direction of *Abhijan*.

While *Kanchenjunga* had the fewest number of shots in any Ray film, *Abhijan* had the greatest number of shots up to that time. Ray used between 40,000 and 46,000 feet of stock. The editing of certain scenes is later described.

The instant Waheeda Rehman arrived for her ten days shooting in Calcutta, she charmed every member of Ray's unit. She lacked star airs and graces, never behaved in a pretentious manner and was content to go about off the set in her own face without make-up There was an unspoilt quality about her personality and she was conspicuously receptive to Ray's direction. She was pliable, with few ingrained mannerisms. In order that the plan of ten days work be kept, Ray permitted very few people to observe Waheeda on the set. I went several times but not every day.

The first thing I noticed was how expressive Waheeda Rehman's feet were as well as her hands. Her hands had interest because of their expressiveness rather than their elegance. A tattoo mark widely common among north Indian village women had been made-up on the back of Waheeda's hands for the role of Gulabi. This accentuated the character of her hands. A triangle of three simulated tattooed dots was added to her chin, also a common custom among girls like Gulabi. The dots served to focus awareness on the exquisite structure of Waheeda's face. (Pl. XLVIII)

By April 17th, Ray was able to view the rushes of Waheeda Rehman's most important scene—where she comes to Narsingh's room the day after they have made love. Having at last conquered the man she wanted, Gulabi is gay and teasing. Flaunting her femininity, Waheeda, as Gulabi, breaks into the snatch of a folk-song and almost into a seductive dance. Bossily she tidies up the bed. Chattering on about how her grandmother taught her to cook, she gives Narsingh the sweets she has made for him, assuring him she had been prepared to be a good wife.

Suddenly, the moods—half-moods—pass into one that builds up in intensity. Gulabi tells Narsingh that her grandmother "was the only one I had. My mother died giving birth to me. I wasn't aware of this, but they told me on that day—the terrible day—when the . . . the thing happened to me. They said they knew all the time that I was going to ruin the good name of the family because my mother died in childbirth . . ." (Pl. XLI)

It would have been impossible for a non-professional to slip from mood to mood building up the scene as Gulabi feels compelled to confess the truth about herself to the man she passionately loves With the mounting of the scene, Narsingh stands unmoving by the barred window, listening.

R

"They pulled me by the hair, beat me, threw me into the room like a sack of coal and locked me up . . . And all the time I kept thinking of taking my life." Waheeda moved around the room as if back in the room into which she had been locked. "There was a hanging shelf in the room—up near the ceiling . . . I took off my sari and tied it in a knot round my neck . . ." Waheeda's gesture with her hand reaching up to hang herself had a sharp poignancy because it was awkward rather than graceful—a real girl's gesture. The gesture served as apex to the emotion within the scene.

It was evident from the rushes that the rough editing was done in the camera. The composition was simple with Waheeda Rehman as the dominant figure. There was no attempt at clever direction of this scene, no interesting camera angles, or movements, to add to the drama. The humanistic elements of the subject had been emphasized; the "depth content" rather than the action drama of the original novel.

Except for three or four shots taken in Rasjasthan to be cut into the final sequence of *Abhijan*, the end of the story—the redemption of Narsingh who determinedly fights Sukhanram to prevent him selling Gulabi—had to be shot at Dubrajpur. But for the actors and unit to return to the palace-like habitation which had been rented, the daily rent was suddenly increased from Rs.100/- to Rs.1000/-. Though there was no other rentable or habitable place in or near, Dubrajpur, Ray refused to submit to these blackmailing tactics Bijoy went hurrying off to find a solution to the housing problem Ray, the unit and the actors packed up and headed off, leaving Bijoya and myself behind, because it was very uncertain how they were going to house themselves.

In the midst of this upset in the third week of May, Edward Harrison, who had been to the Cannes Film Festival where he had presented *Devi*, arrived in Calcutta. He had a project to propose— that Satyajit Ray should make a feature film on Indian art. He was desperately keen, and so was I, to go on location at Dubrajpur Finally, Audy and Chakravarty, the N.C.A. producers of *Kanchenjunga*, took us both in a small car for the night drive of 140 miles from Calcutta. Ed discovered on that drive what a tropical night can be like at the end of May when one is used to air conditioning!

Dawn revealed parched red earth. At one point a signpost pointed towards Santineketan. But we headed for the District Town of Suri where Ray had been forced to make his headquarters. It was some twenty-two miles from Dubrajpur. Part of a house a stone's throw from the Circuit House where Ray was, had been rented. This wasn't a very happy arrangement though it gave him a room to himself with two beds and a mosquito net.

Rather conspiratorially, since Satyajit isn't one with a natural inclination to violate regulations, he arranged with the servants to allow Ed Harrison and myself a bed each for one night. We had no authorization from the District Magistrate that we were fit and proper people to be housed under a roof intended for officials. Ed shared Satyajit's room while I had the adjoining one.

Soon after 8 a.m., Satyajit left to take shots of a level-crossing gate (the end of the credit titles as mentioned previously). This location was situated where a narrow-gauge railway line crossed a road running parallel with the side of the railway. The track and the road had been selected for the race between Narsingh in his taxi and the local train.

The landscape was harsh. The only glimpse of shade near the level-crossing was a meagre tree under which everyone clustered for refuge from the blazing sun. Soumitra Chatterjee, dressed for winter, was stoically uncomplaining. This was location shooting under gruelling conditions for the climate was about as cruelly exhausting as it could be. We had to go all the way back to Suri for lunch, after which I went to look at the rented rooms crowded with the unit and cast. There was a grey and grim-aspected Christian chapel between the Circuit House—named for the judges who make their rounds of District Towns—and the house with an unshaded veranda. It was housing too many people for the size of the available rooms. Soumitra and some half a dozen others were resting on beds festooned with their washing. No one seemed the least irritated.

A small rainstorm suddenly blew up. The monsoon was coming. Around five o'clock, we drove some twenty miles, this time to Dubrajpur, with its wonderful rocks. Although it was 5.45 p.m. when the shooting of the last Narsingh-Josef scene commenced, the boulders were roasting hot. The sun was beginning to dip behind the dramatically isolated palm trees towards the monstrous craggy wall of stone. Every instant the rocks became an increasingly unearthly spectacle.

Inquisitive and handsome children led by pioneering little girls began to gather. Soon a constant stream of spectators, including schoolboys, arrived. People from the town climbed up the boulders to form an audience. They showed an intuition to avoid getting in anyone's way. The sky turned orange and a deepening murky, smoky hue. Someone remarked that the unit had been waiting six days for this exact effect.

Satyajit utilized the sky effects with astonishing speed. Nothing could have been more organized than his rapidly-taken series of shots to show, towards the end of the film, Josef catching sight of the opium tin and Narsingh following him through the rocks to hit him. There were more camera set-ups than could be kept count of. Action was far more violent than in any previous Ray film. Yet one shot contained a lyrical undertone: Narsingh hurls Josef against a rock where he sinks down amidst two small delicate bushes. The minute flowers were yellow and there were many such feathery tufts clinging about the rocks contrasting with the harshness of the boulders.

With the sunset deepening and night swiftly descending, white reflectors and lights were brought. Urgently, Ray, his actors and the crew hurried from one cluster of boulders to another. In the span of two hours twenty shots were taken. Then they took seventeen in just over one hour. It was almost totally dark when, with a rush back to the road, the last shot of the sequence was caught—that of Narsingh stumbling back to his old Chrysler car.

This was not the end of the day's work. Satyajit said he must do the scenes he had switched to the Tara Circus huddled in a corner of Dubrajpur unable to move further. They owed Rs.50/- (£4 10s.). Their receipts at their pitiful box office had been only Rs.7/-.

Someone remarked that the tent cinema was killing off the circus in rural areas; that it could no longer attract. The all-purpose 1931 vintage Chrysler which Bijoy Chatterjee had bought as the star property for *Abhijan*, now served as transport for holding the lights to shoot the scene of Narsingh and Josef purchasing admission tickets.

What remained of the kerosene-lamp-lit Big Top was hanging in parched earth-coloured shreds of canvas. Those who had come to watch Ray film-making became free extras without knowing it. They were asked to sit in the eight-anna seats and Soumitra Chatterjee commented that it was a pity they hadn't come to the circus and paid their annas.

In a box cage placed in the arena with the traditional red barrier surrounding it, shakily paced one of the two performing leopards. I wondered how the meat for feeding it had been paid for. Outside, the crickets had set up a clatter of chirping as the indefatigable Satyajit first recorded and then took a shot of the out-of-tune band. This was followed by a shot of Narsingh and Josef taking their seats and talking.

The leopard's trainer, or tamer—a woman with a recently born baby on her hip—came and leaned on the cage. At the sight of her the big cat became no different from any well-cared-for household tabby. She tickled its nose before ambling away. I went closer to the cage noticing that now things were going on, the leopard was content to sit, stretch out its paws beyond the cage and watch as if it understood there was to be a performance.

Ray sat down in a spectator's seat to decide what turns to use. The turns, mainly performed by the growing children of the troupe, were far from talentless. It was the third item, too slow in unfolding to be suitable for inclusion in *Abhijan*, which was genuinely exciting. A very small girl climbed up a pole wobbling, yet balancing, on a man's hand, then shoulder. Presumably he was her father. That child on the top of what appeared a very uncertain bamboo pole was a marvellous acrobat.

It was the second item Ray selected—a woman trick-cyclist with numberless acrobatic children and clowns. She wore a pink ballet skirt and her face was heavily whitened. Out tumbled clowns echoing, like the acrobats, the costumes and tricks allied for centuries with European clowning traditions. Or are the clowns of all traditions the same? Ray rehearsed the act so as to fill the arena with action. Mitra then shot, the source of light being three spotlights plus the circus's kerosene lamps. On the last take, the camera panned upwards to capture the image of the slowly disintegrating tent. Mercifully for the Tara Circus, it was now free to move on and try to capture an audience elsewhere for Satyajit Ray insisted on paying Rs.150/- (£11 5s.) to pay the Tara people's debts.

When Edward Harrison at last found an opportunity to discuss his idea of an art film with Satyajit, Satyajit was momentarily enthusiastic. When he returned to Calcutta, he told Ed that he had thought about a film laid at Ellora. He persuaded Harrison to go there before returning to New York. But the film Satyajit had in mind was not an art film. It had evolved as a result of working with Waheeda Rehman and concerned a dancer who, appearing in a film, visited Ellora. Ray thought of it as a story which could have dialogue in several languages. After a few weeks he came to the conclusion that his enthusiasm for Ed's project of an Indian art film was not sufficient for him to sustain interest, at least not in the immediate future. He was occupied with thoughts of a film based on his grandfather Upendrakishore's fantasy, *Goupi Gyne Bacha*. Sandip had been complaining that his papa's films were too tragic and he wanted a film to make him laugh. But this project, which Satyajit hoped to do following the release of *Abhijan*, was far too

vast an undertaking to embark on in the face of a national crisis.
It was fated to be delayed until the middle of January 1968, and
to prove almost as difficult to proceed with as *Pather Panchali.*

In October 1962, external events developed and moved with
frightful rapidity. After several years of border tension, the Chinese
made a sudden thrust to penetrate further N.E.F.A., the Himalayan
belt along the northern frontier of the state of Assam, and to the
far west in Ladakh. On October 21st, the two first Indian posts fell.
A country where the overwhelming majority of people only wanted
peace faced war with defeat. For almost six weeks there was an
agonizing period of shock for every thinking person in India
Except for the habitually anti-Nehru politicians, no one had seriously believed that the border dispute would come to open war
with China. Like almost every other creative person, Satyajit Ray
went through, as he put it, a few weeks "fraught with all manner
of doubts, despondency, etc." The emotional atmosphere in Calcutta was more intense than anywhere else, though it was whipped
up against the local Communists rather than the local Chinese, of
whom there were considerable numbers in the city.

Fortunately Satyajit could recover his composure and resume
work; he commenced work on the long delayed *Mahanagar—The
Big City.* He had at last found his perfect image of Arati, the young
wife forced to go out and work. This was Madhabi Mukherjee, who
had played the wife, though not particularly expressively, in Mrinal
Sen's film, *Baishey Sravana.* Even after two meetings with Ray
when he talked to her about the character of Arati, Madhabi Mukherjee had no expectations that Ray would select her. Later, having
proved ideal as Arati, Madhabi Mukherjee said: "I did not feel I
was acting. The character was so real. I seemed to know her. She
was like someone I had seen."

Based on two long short stories by Narendra Mitra, the development of the characters and the dialogue in *Mahanagar* were Satyajit
Ray's. To a great extent, *Mahanagar* is an urban *Pather Panchali* set
in the 1950s, for it depicts the pressures of impoverishment upon
the family of a retired and traditional-minded schoolmaster. Father,
mother, son, schoolgirl daughter, daughter-in-law and a little
grandchild are crammed into a three-roomed house in a lane in
Calcutta's overcrowded lower middle-class district of Bhowanipore
where "the neighbouring radios keep on playing".

In both *Kanchenjunga* and *Abhijan* a man and a woman exert
their will to make a fresh start, the implication being that each will
help the other. The two sisters, Anima and Monisha, and Gulabi,
are a distinct contrast from the more traditional Indian women in

Ray's earlier films. But in *Mahanagar*, Arati is not only the central character but a woman, as Chidananda Das Gupta observed, who "is awakened to the possibility of determining the course of her own life. Typically enough, the awakening comes from the husband, for men have been traditional liberators of women." This is markedly true in India, as demonstrated by Dwarkanath Ganguli, and later Mahatma Gandhi.

The old school is defeated in its will to dominate the family in the character of the father in the contemporary upper-class film, *Kanchenjunga*, and equally so in *Mahanagar* where the conservative retired schoolmaster father's insistence that he must have new glasses is a force in compelling his daughter-in-law to seek a paying job. Whereas the rich father, Indranath, is arrogant in his ignorance of what is really going on in the minds of his family, Preogopal in *Mahanagar* is selfishly cantankerous in his would-be preservation of past standards.

Mahanagar is the most significantly contemporary of all Ray's films in that it touches upon the socio-economic problems of the extensive impoverished Indian middle-class. Many are Brahmins. The film presents a world of difference in the face of poverty between Harihar's wife, Sarbojaya, in *Pather Panchali* of the 1920s period, and Subrata Mazumdar's wife, Arati, in the big city of the 1950s. Ray set the story in 1955, at the point of the last Calcutta bank crash. As in Ray's other films it is not the plot as such that is of prime importance, but the form and the credibility of the behaviour of his characters. The whole family in *Mahanagar* are seen in a state of growth.

A tram moves behind the credit titles carrying Subrata Mazumdar, a young bank clerk and the only earning member of the family, to his cramped home. His father complains he is going blind from lack of glasses (his pride in tradition does not impede his scrounging from his former students later in the film); Bani, the young sister, admits her school fees are unpaid; Subrata has to tell Arati he has been unable to borrow from his friend—"he's developed a heart ailment and can only work part time at half pay." He mentions that his friend's wife has gone to work.

That night, in bed, Arati thinks what work she can do when she has been trained for nothing. Subrata is too sleepy to concentrate on what she tries to say to him. But the pressure of economic circumstances drives Subrata to help to find his wife a job. He answers several advertisements for her. One employer of salesgirls for a knitting machine responds. The totally inexperienced Arati goes for the interview and lands the job. Bani, her schoolgirl sister-in-law, is thrilled. But Subrata's confession to his father that Arati is going out to work causes a crisis with Preogopal. He simply refuses to recognize that times have changed: "Let them change. I won't. I hold certain views and they have held good for centuries. No woman of my family will go out to work as long as I'm alive." (Pls. L and LI)

Subrata decides his wife is going out to work; that he must disregard his father's traditionalism. His mother weeps. Their child, Pintu, is unhappy at his mother going out and leaving him. On her way into the job, Arati meets her seemingly pert and tough fellow sales-representative, the Anglo-Indian girl, Edith Simmons. She is friendly and very soon introduces Arati to the use of lipstick on the job; but Arati conceals the lipstick at home. The shy Arati expands her personality as she finds she is a success at selling. Edith fights for the rights of all the girls when their employer, Mukherji, tries to reduce their commission. Hence, he is determined to get rid of Edith while favouring Arati. Just as Arati is finding her confidence, Subrata insists she resign the job. A second before she does, he phones to say his bank has crashed. To add to the disaster, which makes the husband dependent on the wife even for his cigarettes, there is the embarrassment of Arati's father's loss of Rs.3000/-, he having opened an account at Subrata's bank.

Preogopal, who visits a former student now a doctor, has collapsed with heart failure at the head of the stairway, his stick clattering down. The doctor brings him home. He will not die, but laid low, the obdurate old man begins to soften towards Arati as a working woman. But suspicion and jealousy seeth up in Subrata who, having found Arati's lipstick, orders her not to use it. She throws it out of the window. Then, in a restaurant, where he has gone for a sherbet (Arati having given him money for cigarettes) he sees her with a strange man. Hiding behind a newspaper he overhears their conversation, innocent enough; but it drives him to visit Mukherji, Arati's employer. His suspicions evaporate and Mukherji promises him a job. No triangle develops as it probably would in a Western film. (Pls. LI and XLVIII)

Meanwhile, Arati, in Edith's absence, takes on Edith's sales schedule. She goes to Edith's Anglo-Indian home where she lives with her mother to give her the commission of five per cent she has collected. Edith is in bed with a cold. Next day she goes to work and finds Edith crying in the ladies' toilet (Pl. LI). Edith has been sacked Mukherji having accused her of being off the job not from illness, but for immoral purposes (many Hindus believing that Anglo-Indians are of loose morals). Arati, infuriated by such injustice since she knows Edith was ill, bursts into Mukherji's room demanding to know why she has been dismissed:

> Mukherji makes a face showing incredulity and contempt: "Don't tell me you've come to fight for a cheap Feringhee?"
> Arati steadies her voice with great effort. "Mr. Mukherji, I've known Edith fairly closely these last five months. We have worked together, we've become friends, I've been to her house. I was there yesterday and saw her lying ill. And now you say . . ."
> Mukherji interrupts. "Mrs. Mazumdar, what I say, whom I dismiss, and for what reasons are my own concern . . ."
> "You insulted Edith and cast aspersions on her character, did you not?"
> "You are presuming too much Mrs. Mazumdar. It's dangerous to overlap your limits."
> "Are you prepared to withdraw your remarks and apologize to her?"
> "No. Let me tell you . . ."
> "Then please be good enough to accept my resignation."

Arati brings out her old resignation letter withheld at her husband's plea, and hands it to Mukherji. This protest against an unjust employer and a prejudiced society leave both Arati and Subrata jobless. She runs down stairs, flight after flight, "panic catching at her throat", for what has she done? On the ground floor, Subrata is waiting. Outside it is raining. They walk out, Arati crying, but her husband says: "Don't worry. We'll pull through, the two of us . . ."

According to Ray, Narendra Mitra was a very modern writer, one who ended his story on a totally pessimistic note. Ray, being an optimist, changed the ending so as to suggest there is hope for the young Mazumdars.

Incredible as to irresponsibility, some Anglo-Indian politico in Calcutta accused Ray of anti-Anglo-Indian sentiment. The complaint went to the Central Board of Film Censors in Bombay so that the film's censorship certificate was held up. Next, the appointed Anglo-Indian representative in the Rajya Sabha, Frank Anthony, not having seen the film, raised a storm. A letter of complaint against Ray was sent to Prime Minister Nehru. Indira Gandhi had the job of finding out whether the charge was true or false. It seemed incredible to her for, by now, she held Ray in very high esteem on account of his integrity.

Before the actual shooting of *Mahanagar* commenced on January

5th, 1963, at the Technicians' Studio in Calcutta, Ray had a meeting with Prime Minister Nehru : the eruption of the border dispute into actual fighting in October 1962 raised the question of the use of films for national defence. In this connection, Gopala Reddi, the then Minister of Information and Broadcasting, who had known Ray as a student at Santineketan, approached him on the strength of a Memorandum on films for morale given to the Prime Minister. This Memorandum suggested that Ray's humanistic style would be effective in the concept of a documentary film somewhat changed in aim from one already suggested by Indira Gandhi to be made by Ray for the New York World's Fair. Ray explained to me in a letter that this new suggestion would be "nothing very elaborate, something simple and effective, and something which—very important this—directly helps Panditji [Jawaharlal Nehru]. To me this is the only worthwhile subject for a short at this juncture. My own wish is to see Nehru, talk to him, and get him to appear in the film."

Shortly after this letter reached me in Delhi, Jawaharlal Nehru decided to go to Santineketan over Christmas 1962. His reaction to Ray's letter, which I took to him, was "send Ray a telegram and tell him to come to Santineketan any time either day [December 25th or 26th] and I can see him". In response to my telegram, Ray drove to Santineketan and had a very pleasant meeting with Nehru and Indira Gandhi—"They held up lunch." The perceptive Ray could sense how severe had been the experience that Indira Gandhi had passed through since he had last seen her. A film might have resulted from this meeting, but events moved too swiftly. The next time Indira Gandhi contacted Satyajit Ray, it was to ask him to come and shoot the immersion of her father's ashes in the river Ganges.

Ten days after his last meeting with Prime Minister Nehru, Ray began direction of all the interior scenes for *Mahanagar* laid in the Mazumdar family's home. It was a "long unbroken schedule" working every day until January 29th, by which time over half the film had been shot. "Lovely set—three rooms, courtyard, veranda. The smallest rooms ever built!" commented Ray after the first five days. This main set, built by Bansi Chandragupta for around Rs.2000/- (£149 9s. 6d.), turned out to be more inclusive than Satyajit's description. Though small, it allowed for a considerable range of visual effects and imaginative lighting. In addition to the rooms and veranda, there was an alleyway formed by an outside wall and the façade of the upper part of a house purporting to be across the street. There was a background view of other houses. Instead of this being a painted backcloth as commonly used in Bengali and

Indian films, it was a photograph of Calcutta houses enlarged to the size of a large screen and it was set at an angle. (Pls. XLIX and LI)

The properties assembled in the three rooms denoted extreme care in selection so as to create the atmosphere of such a house. One of the innumerable calendars from Ray's huge collection hung on a wall. In preposterous chocolate-box style, it pictured the awesome Shiva of the Dance of Destruction with Parvati and their elephant-headed offspring, Ganesh transmogrified into as sweetly saccharin a feminine figure as his competitive spouse. It looked innocently perverse in such a respectable family dwelling as the Mazumdar's. In the living-room—"Father's room which looks like a man's room"—there was a table lamp. Subrata Mitra, who had just completed work as the cameraman on the Ivory-Merchant film, *The Householder*, employed this lamp as his source of light. It was a new idea. (Pl. L)

More than half of *Mahanagar* was shot by the time I reached Calcutta; but casting and set-planning was still in progress. On January 25th, the day before Republic Day, Ray went in search of a girl to interpret Edith Simmons, whom he had conceived as inwardly "quiet, unaggressive to explain her contact with Arati who otherwise would not become friends with her". This search led him to Bandwagon, the only agency in India placing singers and bands, a field in which Anglo-Indians are numerous. This thriving enterprise turned out to be run by the most unlikely person ancestrally connected with Satyajit's paternal and maternal ancestry—K. C. (Bhaya) Sen, the great-grandson of Keshubchandra Sen, who had initiated Kalinarayan Gupta into Brahmoism, and against whom Dwarkanath Ganguli had rebelled on the grounds of Sen's reactionary views on the education of women. Through Sen, Ray now found Vicky Redwood, a professional singer in restaurants and nightclubs. Moreover, he conducted Satyajit to some Calcutta Anglo-Indian homes for the purpose of accuracy in constructing the set for the Simmons's home.

Satyajit returned home, declaring to members of his unit who had gathered, that the area where Sen and he went was no better off economically than the one where the Mazumdar family live—Bhowanipore. He had noticed children roller-skating.

"I want to show how similar are the conditions of living," said Satyajit. "This brings the girls closer."

Bansi Chandragupta, Anil Choudhury, Subrata Mitra and Bhanu Ghosh were all present. They discussed which restaurant they could use for the scene where Subrata sees Arati with a man. Someone suggested Neera, because this restaurant had not been done up and streamlined since the mid-fifties. That was decided.

Attention shifted to Mukherji's—the boss's—room, with Bansi saying that that would have to be a studio set.

Satyajit interjected that the set should have a photographic background, one overlooking the incredible sight of the Esplanade. "We can select the telegraph structure. You can save trouble by having the shutters Venetian blinds. It doesn't have to be a very big room. We can use a wide angle lens. It has to be an import-export business. We must show the contrast between the ramshackle bank where the husband works and the office where the wife works. It has to be a small Indian bank."

Someone added that there was a need for having a letterhead printed for the business. Satyajit agreed, for the letterhead was most important. Files, and file covers, too, were needed, remarked Bansi.

At that moment, Satyajit's friend, David McCutchion, put his head around the curtain at the doorway. He often came in the evening. Discussion about locations and sets ceased because McCutchion had been out of Calcutta hunting nineteenth-century terracotta temples in villages all over Bengal. He produced a folder and, removing two folded sheets, handed the first sheet to Satyajit who, inspecting it with pleasure, passed it around. There were four fascinating pencil rubbings taken from folk art style engravings.

McCutchion passed the second much-covered sheet around for inspection. He regularly brought accounts of, or photographs of, his discoveries to Ray, who was in the habit of giving him the necessary film. They bounced the names of temples back and forth in this village and that one until McCutchion quietly picked up his bicycle lamp from the table and took his leave.

When studio shooting recommenced, the assistant, Bhanu Ghosh who, being of a fiery temperament, had kept the crowds in check at Darjeeling during the shooting of *Kanchenjunga* (and who acts an aggressive role in *Abhijan*), went out to find an old man to appear as a friend of Preogopal in one scene. Bhanu rejected all the extras congregated round about the studio. Somehow he got on the track of an old man reported to be a refugee from East Pakistan —East Bengal—from whence, it is hinted in the dialogue, the Mazumdars originated. Ray and Mitra busied themselves lighting the set.

Satyajit was still enthusiastically proud of Heren Chatterjee and his interpretation of the cranky father. An elderly singer, Heren Chatterjee had long been on friendly terms with various members of Ray's family. But he had never acted. Indeed, Satyajit had originally cast Kanu Bannerjee, of Harihar fame, as Preogopal. Then finding the conservative-looking Heren Chatterjee, he realized the 'rightness' of Chatterjee—his physical type, and the tones of his voice exactly fitting the image of a cultivated schoolmaster. He felt that Chatterjee would arouse understanding if not sympathy for the man a small and now jealous cog in a society crumbling away. Far from admirable, even at moments despicable, Chatterjee could make Preogopal also pitiable. Feeling he was doing a nasty thing to drop Bannerjee, Satyajit had talked to him, and Bannerjee had been very understanding about Ray's desire to change.

Bhanu Ghosh, greatly puffed up by his success, reappeared with a very tall, very dignified old man who walked majestically with a stick.

"He was resting in his own house," said Bhanu, enigmatically. Then he grinned mischievously, as if extremely pleased with his discovery, whose withered face resembled nothing so much as, paradoxically, a handsome and lively skull.

The ancient man sat himself down on a *charpoy* and was soon joined by a conspicuously solemn scholarly-looking friend—unidentified—of Ray's. He wore a beard only around his jaw line rather in the likeness of great-grandfather Kalinarayan, only with the hair cropped shorter. He was studying the scenario with unapproachable concentration. His intentness was so great that he hardly said a word to anyone, not even to Satyajit.

Sandip, acting a belligerent scene with the ever-playful Bhanu Ghosh, took up a piece of chalk intended for the clapper board. He wrote dramatically on the stone floor I WILL KILL YOU! The studious-looking man took no notice. He continued reading the script. Thinking better of this "comics" dialogue, Sandip rubbed it out and drew a round face with big round ears and an odd-looking decoration sprouting up from the head.

The old man, waiting to become an actor for the first time in his life, tucked his feet under him and watched Sandip with smiling eyes. They were hazel eyes, or perhaps they were brown eyes faded.

Tired of the round face, Sandip erased it and in a twinkling produced a new and quaint figure of a man seemingly stabbed to the heart by a sword. The solemn, scholarly man still took no notice.

Chandragupta, who is fond of Sandip, came and made a comment. Sandip decided he was sick of his stabbed man. Using his foot, he rubbed it out. Again he drew, using up more of the clapper board's chalk. This time his imagination ran to a head and arms and, to the side, horizontally, a second head and what looked like a floating body. He added wings behind the first head and body, and above both figures he drew a blazing sun.

Satyajit had almost completed supervising the lighting of Preogopal's room. The scene with the old man and his cronies was to convey sunlight streaming in through the window. I watched the exceptional care taken with the placement of the two light sources with their glare being bounced.

Sandip executed a new head and wrote under it "American Soldzzer" and signed it Sandip Ray! Bhanu, who had always served as the unit's comic, acted a scene of hypnotism with Sandip who responded until, with an agile dancing motion, he emerged from his trance to stage a mock boxing match which was climaxed by him being swung over Ghosh's head. The old man who had been sitting like the pottery Lohan figure in the Victoria and Albert Museum, smiled, rose majestically and betook himself to watch Ray at work on a close-up of Preogopal with his dictionary where the window curtain cast a faint shadow. This was the shot before the old man was required to visit his "friend".

The third and then the fourth round of tea appeared. They were working later than usual in order to complete as much as possible before the Saraswati Puja which would mean yet another holiday in Calcutta the next day.

Saraswati, the Goddess of Learning and the third of the feminine deity trinity, might be called the "teenager's deity". Before the goddess was carried to her immersion, her worship brought an unholy din from loudspeakers blaring film music for forty-eight hours. There was even a version of "Waltzing Matilda". All work stopped. Satyajit remained at home wearing a similar style of long shirt to that he wore when I first met him in 1955.

I went to see him and it was the only time I ever heard him complain. He had had to put up with the blare until midnight and it had started again at 5 a.m. "That", he added, pointing out of his window, "is not the nearest one. Just wait till the nearest one starts!" Soon there came an ear-splitting blast, with Satyajit raising his voice almost to a shout: "It's hard on traditional drummers. Film music is putting them out of work!"

Equally suddenly there descended a moment's blessed silence. But not for long, for there came the beating of a drum. Satyajit and I both looked out of the windows to see a family of street acrobats down below. The tall, thin father was beating his hand on an enamel dish which also served as begging bowl. His khaki shorts were patched behind with a blue-patterned material. His most minute child turned a sudden somersault to be followed by her slightly older sister in a pink net frock and surprisingly clean white panties. The mother, as thin as the father, stepped from the kerb holding a long bamboo pole to which the barefooted parents tied their toddling child.

"Oh!" exclaimed Satyajit and held his breath as the mother hoisted the pole on to her shoulder and clapped her hands. The family, collecting hardly any money, strayed on their way.

I was very curious about Satyajit's scholarly-looking friend who had been immersed in the scenario on the set the previous day. "Didn't you meet him?" Satyajit asked, to which I had to answer no.

He asked me didn't I know about the Jessop case since it was a famous one. I had never heard of it before. "There was a strike, or something—I can't tell you all the details—but several people, including Prithish Dey, the man you mean, went in and threw bombs and used a machine-gun. The English manager was killed, and I don't know who else. Dey was given a life sentence. He became a model prisoner and six months ago he was released after fourteen years. I knew him slightly before, but a friend of mine knew him much better. It was at the time I was working on *Home and the World*. I thought Dey could be an actor and play Sandip."

It struck me as extraordinary by way of insight that Ray should have connected Dey with Tagore's story concerning a terrorist. He went on to explain that Dey had now come to him with a letter from their mutual friend asking if he could do anything to help Dey start off his life again.

"Now he's observing directing. I think," said Satyajit, "he may have changed a great deal in prison. Sometime I may use him as an actor. He needs what you might call rehabilitation."

The irony was that when Satyajit Ray later tried to use Dey as an actor, he proved totally devoid of acting talent.

Satyajit (for revived *Sandesh*)

Chapter 13

WORKING TO COMPLETION—MUSIC AND EDITING

IN March 1962 Satyajit Ray was absorbed in preparing his own music for *Kanchenjunga*. For days on end he was rooted at home working out his twenty-nine passages for recording. He kept picking out the tonal notations on the piano. But also, and more frequently, he worked on it by whistling, with his entranced son, Sandip, imitating father's whistle with excitedly devoted zeal. Both of them went on whistling the music for months; indeed until they transferred their attention to *Abhijan's* music. (Pl. LII)

As soon as the recording commenced, it became evident that Bijoya Ray was a great assistance to Manik. On the first day she came with Sandip in the afternoon and Satyajit constantly asked her opinion. Her presence brought a kind of confidential air to the work which was not present in the morning when she was absent.

The surprising thing was that Ray never showed a foot of *Kanchenjunga*, nor of *Abhijan*, to his musicians. Nor can l recall seeing his musical assistant, the flautist, Alokenath Dey, who had worked with him since *Pather Panchali*, at any screening of the films before their completion.

As the composer of his own music, Ray had been impressed by Sergei Prokofiev's scores for Eisenstein's *Alexander Nevsky* and *Ivan the Terrible;* also by Cicognini's music for *Bicycle Thieves* and *Miracle in Milan*. He thought that the best film music was that which was simply scored, and he liked the use of single instruments

Abhijan, on location at Dubrajpur. Ray explaining the set-up of a shot to Soumitra Chatterjee and Ravi Ghosh. The reflectors, covered with silver paper, or white sheets, generally used by Ray are seen in the background to the left

XLIX

Mahanagar: The kitchen is on the veranda, which is a section of the total set encompassing the house. Note the integration of the characters' movements with the set itself

L
Mahangar (The Big City), 1963

The search to find Arati a job. Subrata, Anil Chatterjee, his schoolgirl sister, Bani, Joya Bhadury, and Arati, Madhabi Mukherjee. The set is the section of the house used as Subrata and Arati's bedroom. Behind the mosquito net there is a garish calendar

Arati prepares her father-in-law's medicine. An interesting touch to show that she is not "Anglicized" is that she wears her ring on the middle finger of her left hand, not on the wedding ring finger which is very general among those people who speak English

Father, Preogopal, Heren Chatterjee. His room is on the other side of the curtain made from a sari. This was the first time Subrata Mitra used a table light as a lighting device

Subrata breaks the news to his father that Arati has taken a job

The fact that Arati proves a success at her job selling knitting machines begins to disturb Subrata and evoke jealousy—

"Woman's place is in the home." He demands that she resign the job

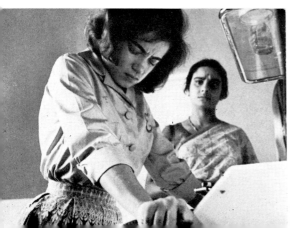

Arati finds Edith, Vicky Redwood, the Anglo-Indian salesgirl, has been sacked

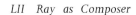

His first stage in composing is to whistle; his second to pick out on the piano, which is hired when he requires to compose

Ray studying his orchestration for Kanchenjunga music recording, March 14th, 1962

Sound stage for recording, New Theatre Studio, Calcutta. "He often went off to a distant corner during rehearsals . . ." He directs his musicians as he does his actors and edits sound as he edits picture

LIII

Ray recording music with James Ivory (left), for the Ivory-Merchant film, Shakespeare Wallah

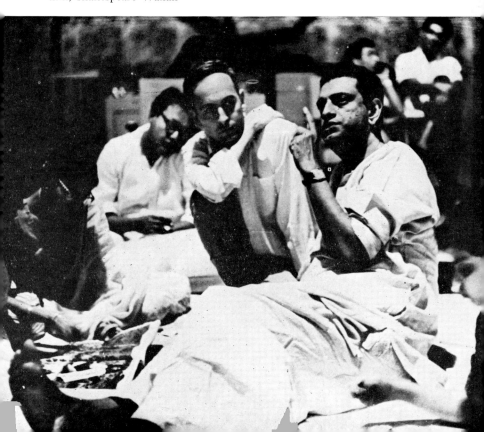

Bijoya with Satyajit during pause in Kanchenjunga music recording session

LIV

"The expressiveness of his hands in explaining . . ." Sandip is all attention. The musician with the Gothic face is in the centre

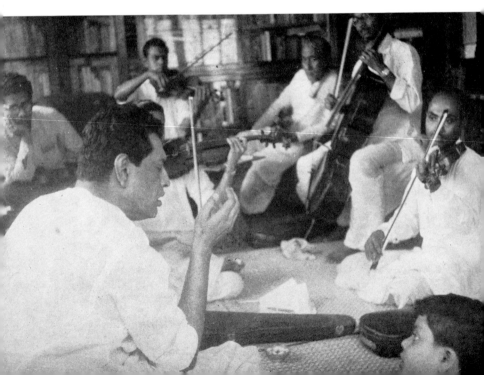

1963—recording a discussion with the author for the BBC in the author's London flat

LV   *Ray Abroad*

1966—with Akira Kurosawa in Tokyo

1965—with Mrs Indira Gandhi, then Minister of Information and Broadcasting, and Mrs Kawakita of Japan at the International Film Festival, New Delhi

LVI

1962—with James Quinn of the British Film Institute as juror at the Berlin Film Festival

LVII Satyajit and his own shadow, like the shadow of his father and grandfather

LVIII

Paras Pathar (The Philosopher's Stone), *1957–8*

Tulsi Chakravarty as Parash Dutta with the magic stone

The Duttas have grown rich

Kapurush-o-Mahapurush (The Coward and the Holy Man), *1965*

The "Saint" discourses to his disciples

LIX
Goupi Gyne and Bagha
Byne, 1968–9

*Sketch of Halla Army
arrayed for the battle
that never takes place.
Halla is the city of the
Bad King. "We have
camels now instead of
horses!"*

*Ray directing the above
scene in Jaisalmer with
the camels instead of
horses*

*Goupi, Topen Chatterji,
the singer, and Bagha,
Rabi Ghosh, the drum-
mer, arrive at Halla bent
on preventing the war*

Ray's Goupi Gyne *sketches*

LX

Satyajit decorating a clay pot for film in Rajasthan

The boys have the first of their magic meals— by their power to wish

Ray directing Santosh Dutt as the Bad King of Halla and Jahar Roy as his Prime Minister

Musicians wait for the singing contest to start

Goupi and Bagha in the Palace of Shundi. Black on white serves as the decorative motif throughout the Shundi Palace

The Bad King of Halla with his Prime Minister, Jahar Roy, who is a great deal worse and the real villain

The Good King of Shundi with Goupi and Bagha, who have become his Court Musicians, and promised to save him from the Bad King of Halla

Goupi and Bagha sing and drum to the soldiers of Halla—and they cannot move to fight

Aranyer Din-Ratri (Days and Nights in the Forest), 1969–70

In April, 1969, Ray commenced to shoot this erotic-centred film entirely on location in Palamau in Bihar, using a bungalow in lieu of a set.

Framed by a Prologue and Epilogue, four young city men out for a holiday in the woods—Ashim (Soumitra Chatterjee), the executive; Sanjoy (Subhenda Chatterjee), a jute mill's labour welfare officer; Harinath (Samit Bhanju), a sportsman, and Shekar (Rabi Ghosh), an amusing parasite—find themselves emotionally confronted in the woods by three embodiments of femininity—the elusive and sophisticated Aparna (Sharmila Tagore) who poses moral questions to Ashim who thinks he can win any woman; her widowed sister-in-law, Jaya (Kaberi Bose), who fails to seduce the conventional Sanjoy, his inhibitions being so inflexible; and Duli, the uninhibited tribal girl with whom Harinath makes love and recovers from having been jilted in the Prologue by a jet-set girl.

The men arrive at the bungalow unconscious that they will leave it with their attitudes shaken.

The next morning, forming the Epilogue, the friends prepare to leave for Calcutta. They conceal from each other their experiences of the previous evening: They are too private and too affecting for disclosure.

A comedy with serious undertones, Aranyer Din-Ratri, based on a light novel by a young writer, follows a somewhat similar pattern to Kanchenjunga, where the natural surroundings sensitize the thoughts and feelings of the characters, turning them inwards to give expression to their deep-seated problems. It is an examination of modern men and women.

LXIV

Pratidwandi (Siddhartha and the City), 1970

Ray's first film to be concerned with the contemporary political scene, this is again based on a novel by Sunil Gauguly and concerns two brothers in 1970 Calcutta

as in *The Third Man*. His liking for the use of a simple ballad, or folk-song, is illustrated in *Kanchenjunga*, later in *Charulata*, and in grandfather's fantasy, *Goupi Gyne and Bagha Byne*. In *The Alien* an American ballad hummed by the well driller, Devlin, is planned as counterpointing the Bengali folk-song sung by Haba, the village boy.

Ray conceives the character of his music early in the development of his films—sometimes during the writing of the scenario. The ideas evolve during direction. For example, while we were at Darjeeling for *Kanchenjunga*'s shooting, an evening was spent recording local music sung and played by a man who had made a special study. This, as Satyajit said at the time, would serve him as a base. Interesting local instruments were tried out. But the final work of scoring was only undertaken when the final editing had taken place.

As Ray later told Georges Sadoul, Western classical music had exerted a great influence on him. While in secondary school he had discovered a record of Beethoven's violin concerto which so fascinated him that he had read and listened to everything he could discover of Beethoven. During the creation of the Apu trilogy, Satyajit had used the motif of the train "for its visual and sonorous elements like the theme of a symphony". He had thought of the rondo structure introducing elements which return again and again in making *Kanchenjunga*.

As soon as the recording session commenced, Ray approached the evolution of his musical tones and rhythms in such a manner as to achieve an exact emotional correspondence with the visual scene for which the music was to serve as background. It was intriguing to watch his direction of the musicians when one had seen him directing his actors. His hands gained expressiveness in explaining. Whenever he listened to the playing, or the playback, he invariably covered his eyes with his hand. He frequently retired to a distant corner of the studio to assess the volume of tone from the position of a member of the audience seeing the film (Pl. LIII). A passage finally recorded brought him back to his customary reclining position somewhere in the centre of the large white sheet that covered a section of the studio floor. (Pls. LIII and LIV)

The sheet lent the studio an Indian appearance since wherever Indian musicians perform such a sheet is on the floor and littered with sausage-shaped pillows dressed in white cases for resting an elbow. As always, the *chappels*—sandals—of those sitting on the sheet had been discarded at its edge. There were ashtrays and the inevitable plate piled up with triangles of fresh green *pan*. Only

S

the unit, visitors, and the musicians performing on Indian instruments, occupied the sheet.

The performers on Western instruments—violin, viola, 'cello and double bass—sat formally on a block of chairs. One elderly violinist had a strikingly Gothic cast to his face (Pl. LIV). There was a marked degree of Indian tradition and Western convention among the musicians. Three of the violinists wore the traditional *dhoti* and they tucked their legs up crosswise under them. Those who wore cotton trousers, or Western-style pants, sat with their feet on the floor. But everyone had kicked off their *chappels*, with the exception of one man who wore black dress shoes.

Thirteen passages of music were recorded on the first day. The original Darjeeling folk-music had undergone a process of transformation comparable to that which is evident in much European classical music. Ray had taken the melodic elements of Western music and fused this with the rhythmic traditions of Indian music. Hence, the use of instruments both Indian and European.

The second day's recording started at 11 a.m., with work on the music designed for the scenes between Anima and her husband, Shankar, laid in the Children's Park—the scene of which the direction has been described earlier. Satyajit said that this was his most complex orchestration in *Kanchenjunga*. I made notes of the immediate impression of the music:

Strings (Western) with 'cello string plucked.

Violins—plucking 'cello alone like the striking of a clock. Then strings picking up same sombre rhythm with plucking as undertone. A dirge on strings as if each moment—heart beat or tick of time—is poised, sorrow laden.

Then in comes Indian flute (played by Alokenath Dey who carries a family of different sized and toned flutes in his box) for the next section.

Satyajit's aim is to inspire the musicians to draw forth from their instruments a *feeling*, something that mere technique cannot achieve, that which is complementary to the expression of human emotions manifested by the characters on the screen; akin, somewhat, to the musical accompaniment of Peking Opera, which Satyajit admires. (This might be essentially Asian, for there are parallels in Kabuki Theatre and in Kerala's traditional Kathakali dance dramas.)

Two flutes (the second played by a young musician) echoing three notes; drumming of plucked strings combining with Indian sarod and 'cello; swelling up of strings.

"Don't attack, please," Satyajit interrupts and picks up a stop-watch. "Once more through . . ." and he says: "Taking!"

Dey, speaking to the recordist in the booth through the mike: "Music No. 14!"

"Da-de-de-de-da!" from Satyajit.

"Ready!" comes the voice from the booth.

"Ta-ta-te-ta"—Satyajit.

The fans overhead are stilled.

The passage is not quite right.

"Cut!"—from Satyajit.

Again —"14 by 4!" and once again, for the fourth time the short passage is recorded.

"I think it's all right," says Satyajit. "Play back!"

On go the fans with their soft whirring sound to flutter shirt tails, *dhoti* ends; collars and trousers stir. The *sarod* player, who plays a multitude of instruments, plucks at his strings. The lament for the lack of communion between man and wife comes through the mike. Not perfect. The fans slow down. It must be done over again in pursuit of perfection.

"Pa-pa-pam!"—from Satyajit. He raises his arms with the finger lifting up the flute's tone. The flautist tries once more.

"Lovely!" Ray makes the motion of an arc with his arms. "Taking!" He picks up a triangle of green leafed *pan* and munches it. Finishing it, he puffs on a new cigarette, sitting cross-legged with his score on the floor. His posture—left arm and hand dangling over his knee and right arm raised holding the cigarette—has a sculptural quality.

It was on the first afternoon of recording rather than during the days of shooting at Darjeeling, that the unique relation between Satyajit and "my son", Sandip, came into focus. They were collaborators in the game of creation rather than father and son. Their inseparability was sharply etched when Sandip, then only nine and yet already a man in his artistic receptivity, sat down back to back with Satyajit. They seemed as if spiritual Siamese twins. While Sandip would play around with members of the unit, it was only to his father he would really talk.

When the music track was edited with the visuals of *Kanchenjunga* the most effective corresponding musical *crescendo* came as the despondent Shankar slumped down in the farthest corner of the green garden seat edging as far away from his wife, Anima, as he could.

Throughout that first day, Ray had some difficulty in breaking through to the feelings of his musicians. By the second day—*Kanchenjunga*'s music took only two days to record, but four were given to *Abhijan*'s—the musicians were in a more receptive mood.

During the whole of the recording that first day, there came an intermittent click-click of a camera. A thin-faced, small-boned man whose name was A. Huq—a classical Muslim name—hovered perpetually around the edge of the sheet and prowled about with devastating spendthrift abandon in taking photographs. I felt he must starve for his photographic passion. Later, when I saw the range of his work and experienced the extent of his selfless generosity in giving away prints, I realized that Huq was the creator of great photographs, yet an exile from the world of practical exploitation. Little by little, he revealed in half-sentences the touching trust Satyajit's mother had put in his friendship during the last months of her life, and shortly before her death when Satyajit was abroad. He had only just reached home in time.

One day, Huq revealed the poignancy of their friendship. Now by nationality a Pakistani, Huq had returned to West Bengal after Bengal was torn apart by Partition. He told me how the descendants of the zamindar, Harikishore Ray Chowdhury, had lost all that remained of the Ray estate in Mymensingh when it became part of East Pakistan. He told me many other things that had happened on the zamindari, which Suprabha Ray had confided to him.

During the second day's lunch break, David McCutchion appeared. He had become Indianized in dress since he came from Coventry. Satyajit's friendship with David was based on common appreciation of the arts, especially music. It grew and grew with time, with David dropping in on Satyajit in the evenings. Frequently they would listen to Satyajit's records. Sometimes they went to concerts together.

On April 17th, Ray worked in the editing rooms of New Theatres in preparation for the re-recording. His editing team under Dulal Dutt were busy in one room cutting the dialogue track for the colour print, while Satyajit in the other room concentrated upon editing the music track with the Anima-Shankar scenes in the Children's Park. He commented on his music: "Emotional ups and downs, physical up and downs, visual ups and downs."

Sandip, humming *Kanchenjunga* music, put in an appearance. Satyajit began whistling. The boy roamed from one editing room to the other searching for clips from the film. I found three colour frames on the floor and passed them on to him. Pocketing them, Sandip waited by the editing table with bright eyes ready to pounce on whatever he could grab. Father remarked that he took these home and framed them in pasteboard so he, Sandip, could analyse them. "He usually knows why I choose one take rather than another."

The re-recording was due to start at 6 p.m.. When the time came the three reels for working on were ready. But another unit was still in the sound studio. They were still occupying it at seven o'clock. By eight they had still not left. Not a word of complaint came from Satyajit Ray. He continued working as if oblivious that his work schedule had been delayed. The clock on the sound studio wall pointed to 8.55 p.m. when Ray was finally able to enter. He had been working since 10.30 in the morning yet he remained lively and laughing. The sound recordist promptly vanished, presumably to have something to eat. Sandip hopped and ran round the studio until, tired, he curled up on a seat and fell asleep to be later picked up and carried off home.

Philosophically, Satyajit decided we had better have something to eat, and a delicious meal made its appearance on banana leaves, brought from a nearby café. At half past nine the recordist returned and out went the lights, three and a half hours later than Ray had planned. Half an hour after midnight we left the studio with only two instead of three reels completed. Satyajit had made no murmur and next morning when I telephoned to find out the day's schedule, he was, as usual, sitting beside the phone at 8 a.m. He was there every day without fail.

Only in the last days of August 1962 was the music for *Abhijan* recorded. Ray had been giving thought to the music for two months before he began actual work on it. There was considerably more music than for *Kanchenjunga* and it seemed that his orchestration had developed a great deal.

The introductory passage was to begin with the first block of credit titles and end with the clang of the level crossing gate closing. The music for this title sequence was based on folk-music Gay in character for the first drive with the nervous passengers, distinct tones of comedy appeared in the music. Considerable use of drums was made and this first passage, lasting three and a half minutes, employs the instruments in the following order:

1. *Tabla* (drum).
2. Western string instruments, commencing with 'cello.
3. Western drum.
4. Indian flute.
5. *Khamuk* (a two-string instrument used by the mystic sect of Bauls who frequent the area of Santineketan).

6. *Sarod* (string instrument) with a variety of drums.
7. Mandolin (the instrument which becomes associated with Gulabi).
8. *Sarod* together with Western strings.
9. Indian flute comes in once more.

The rhythm increased throughout the passage. There was a notable advance from *Kanchenjunga* in Ray's boldness in orchestration and his use of instruments. He often moved his instruments from one position to another to find the tone and volume he sought. Individual instruments assumed greater importance, particularly the viola, mandolin, flute and the Santhal drum, the Santhals being the tribal people of the area in which *Abhijan* is laid.

The music for the night drive culminating in Narsingh being stopped by Sukhanram seemed to contain a distillation of the range of moods which subsequently unfold during the film. The mandolin, which comes in towards the end of this passage—at Gulabi's appearance—emerged as a distinct motif for Gulabi. The flute's tone suggested the ultimate solution expressed in the film. A special theme also emerged as suggestive of the evil inherent in Sukhanram. Ray explained that "the change of key at the end means going to a new place". During this recording it was evident that Ray was applying to sound the combined methods of his direction and editing.

Yet even during the recording session he was aware that appreciation of his music was limited even among his own unit because they had an inadequate knowledge of Western music. They admitted to being somewhat confused by his attempts at fusing Western instrumental timbres with the rhythms produced by a wide range of Indian instruments. For example, he was using a number of drums with conspicuously varying tones.

Critics and musicians alike had taken little or no notice of Ray's own music for *Teen Kanya*. Rather more notice was to be taken of his music for *Kanchenjunga* and *Abhijan*. There was some grudging admiration that for a "non-musician" the efforts were not bad. But among professional musicians there lurked the suspicion that Ray was composing his own music to satisfy his ego. This lukewarm response subsequently abated with the release of *Charulata*, where the music was so excellent that it could not be ignored. The musician, Vanraj Bhatia, wrote, "it is in *Charulata*, where the drama is more subtly psychological, that the superiority of Ray's approach to others who have worked for him becomes noticeable". *Charulata* was followed by a little-seen ten-minute television film,

Two, made for ESSO, a film without words, only sound and music. To evoke the mood of an afternoon in the life of a discontented rich child with many toys and a poor child with only one kite, Ray composed an indefinable melody, a strange refrain played on a univox as the background to an unequal struggle in childish pride. It was a *tour de force* in simplicity.

Kanchenjunga's release took place in Calcutta in the first week of May 1962. For weeks before I noticed the contrast between the highly coloured and usually melodramatic posters of the current Bengali and Hindi films, and Ray's own poster designs. Ray's looked challengingly provocative in their quiet difference. *Kanchenjunga* was announced as about to open in four central Calcutta cinemas. The producers seemed to have it in mind that they were about to make a fortune.

On the opening day, I went with the unit and Ray to the first show at the Bharati Cinema for the 3.30 screening. There was an overwhelming preponderance of men in the packed audience, probably as high as thirty to one. Satyajit said there were likely to be a crowd of rowdies from the University in the front rows. They made a habit of coming to openings to pass judgement on films, and thus seek to influence audiences. In the balcony where most of us found seats, even if it was on the steps, there was a sprinkling of quizzical people from the film industry, including some younger directors.

After a restless start, the scenes between Monisha and Bannerji riveted the attention of this first audience. But, in general the audience could not make up its mind how to react to Jagadish's bird-watching, and the reactions to Karuna Banerji's scenes, as the mother, with her brother played by Pahari Sanyal, were insensitive to the point of coarseness. Standing apart from Ray's previous films, it was the importance of the dialogue in revealing the characters and the overlapping simultaneous action which appeared to confuse a section of the audience.

At the end it could be heard as well as sensed that opinion was sharply divided. The second screening drew a more sensitive and critical-minded audience. Throughout the week-end it was House Full in all four Calcutta theatres. (One cinema on the South Side seated men and women in a segregated manner, and it soon appeared as if women were rather more receptive to *Kanchenjunga's* style than men.) Every day for more than a week Ray regularly checked at each theatre to ascertain what the bookings were.

Even before the reviews began to appear, it became clear that the film held little appeal for suburban audiences. The reviewers were, as could be expected, sharply at variance with each other. Some appeared genuinely bewildered by what seemed to them a total change in Ray's style. Others wrote pretentious and openly spiteful reviews. A critic reviewing for *The Statesman*, but not that newspaper's regular reviewer, remarked quite justly: "I think a serious film should at least receive reviews that are serious." Controversy raged for the whole nine weeks that *Kanchenjunga* ran in four Calcutta cinemas. Endless letters appeared in newspapers and magazines. A non-Bengali writer, but one not concerned with cinema, wrote a diatribe denouncing *Kanchenjunga* as an "anti-film". I was asked to write an answer to this outburst since I knew the film well. But Satyajit put his foot down, saying I should not write an answer—I was suspected of being biased in favour of *Kanchenjunga* on account of having been present during its direction and much of the subsequent work on it.

The intensity of the controversy, much of which centred upon the colloquial character of the dialogue—did upper-class people really talk so trivially?—brought out the objective fact that it was a risky undertaking to endeavour to break new ground even in the Bengali cinema. As time went on, the more inquisitive-minded members of the audience tended to see *Kanchenjunga* a second time in order to make up his, or her, mind about the film. In many cases people who had been in doubt ended by liking the film better. People who had seen an Antonioni film frequently felt some connection with Ray's film; but at that time he had not seen a single picture directed by Antonioni.

Throughout the lambasting controversy, Satyajit remained stoically detached. It was as if he pulled in his horns. When the second week-end showed House Full he was pleased. But as the weeks went by it was noticeable how the producers of *Kanchenjunga* came less and less often to Ray's home. Outside of Calcutta and Bengal they set about exploiting the film according to their ideas, not Ray's. They were eager to recoup their investment as quickly as possible, consequently they did not wait for English subtitled copies before releasing the film in non-Bengali-speaking areas. They unwisely permitted a copy to be sent to Paris and then to London without subtitles. Such mishandling went against understanding and appreciation of *Kanchenjunga*. Thoughtlessly they wore out the colour prints without recognizing that good colour prints had to be made with care in India. A totally faded copy finally reached the Film Institute of India at Poona for preservation. Just one already somewhat worn print reached Edward Harrison who subtitled it himself. What could a distributor do with only a single copy? Finally, the producers themselves disappeared. Enquiries to them remained unanswered. Every interest in the film ran into a cul-de-sac. All Satyajit Ray knew by the end of 1965 was that the negative lay in a Bombay laboratory. Edward Harrison persisted and finally acquired two new prints through the efforts of M. D. Bhat, the former Chairman of the Central Board of Film Censors, who was now in charge of the Film Finance Corporation. It was Mr. Bhat who had done most to gain *Pather Panchali* the President of India's award. Harrison only released *Kanchenjunga* belatedly in the United States. He was already an exhausted and dying man.

With the Bengal release of the film in the first week of May 1962, Satyajit Ray still had much work to do on his highly contrasting film *Abhijan*, the longest film—16,000 feet—that he had made. Finally, editing commenced on June 7th, this being the biggest editing job of Ray's career up to that time. On the first day 1,500 feet of film was edited. This was possible because the general editing scheme had been thought out and rough editing was done in the camera. But it was only at the moviola that Ray decided on the opening frame and closing action on which to cut. For *Abhijan*, he favoured cutting on half-finished movements. As the editing proceeded much short cutting was employed throughout the film. I made copious notes of the first day's work :

Narsingh is reflected in broken mirror which cuts across his face. (The jagged mirror reflects his state of disintegration.) In foreground (close-up) a man, never seen again later. The two talk during one long take with no change of angle or movement. At the end the reflected Narsingh moves out of frame on the word "Singhi", said with an upward inflexion. There were four takes. Ray used No. 4 of approximately 300 feet.

Cut to exterior with Rama ushering a party of fares, including bride and groom, into taxi.

Narsingh, walking unsteadily, stops Rama. He refuses to carry a woman fare. His zigzag movements and the sharp cutting of his hostile gestures externalize his mood.

Sharp cutting on Narsingh's arm gesture in contrast to the flowing editing in *Kanchenjunga*.

Narsingh comes into frame left and crosses towards car.

Front view of Narsingh, coming forward.

Close-up with Rama and Narsingh in profile—highly visual.

Satyajit commented : "Sequences with Gulabi will be leisured, flowing cutting."

The joining of the shots was done by hand with no use of a splicer, the assistant wearing no gloves. He used a razor blade to clean the edges of each celluloid piece before gluing them together. The rushes were not hung up but rolled up for use. Additional shots lay in two bins.

In car: shot begins with trunk of tree visible by roadside.

Pan to Narsingh's photograph framed in car and flanked by picture of historical heroes, Pratab Singh and Sivaji.

Ray remarked: "The first titles will appear over these pictures —5-foot fade in and three titles—producer, name of film and author. Then the action continues":

No. 1. Long shot of car on road.

No. 2. Close-up of old men in front seat and rear, the background being passing palm trees.

"That's some of my back-projection," Satyajit interjected. "I use it perhaps a dozen times." (Later I watched his careful effort at shooting back-projection for the shots where Josef intercepts Narsingh with the tin of *ghee*, which he knows to be opium.)

No. 3 To back seat passengers with a clump of trees on the horizon.

No. 4. To Rama on running-board of car, shouting at bullock cart.

Ray interrupted work to say this was the wrong shot. It was he, and not one of his busily searching assistants, who found the correct one.

No. 5. Back to front seat. Cut on flip of hand.

Ray grows more animated, absorbed by the relationship of Rama's hand to passengers.

No. 6. Back to passengers bouncing in back seat.

No. 7. Passengers in back seat begin to talk, shouting at the deaf one.

No. 8. Close-up of surly Narsingh being talked to by passenger with booming voice. (He is the same amateur actor who appeared as the persistent singer in *The Postmaster*.)

All these shots included back-projection. As Ray went along he kept teaching his assistants the art of editing—where to start a movement and at what point, and why, it should end. Very often he would run a shot through several times to study it. Later he would again check the entire editing and revise it here and there More than two months later, when Ray was making a recheck of the early episode of the night drive, he felt that the sense of time passing was inadequate. He hunted for an additional shot to add in and selected a shot of the road with a number of winding turns; the turns and objects revealed by the car's headlights would tend to extend the impression of miles being eaten up by Narsingh's reckless driving.

Sandip arrived in the afternoon for the first day's editing. Enjoying himself immensely, he climbed up on his father's chair and acted scenes over the top of his head. Now and then, he drummed a tattoo on Satyajit's shoulders. But father's concentration was in no way disturbed by Sandip's antics.

By June 11th, when Ray reached the editing of the scene where Narsingh takes Josef's sister to school, he claimed that the fairly rapid cutting was dictated by the content. There was an overlap from the front to the back seat of the car. Suddenly, at four o'clock, someone rushed into the cutting room, announcing "Accident!" Ray, his unit and I went out to the veranda of the building. In the compound below a man from the studio's office was saying that Chhabi Biswas had just been killed in a head-on collision, his car having been run into by a truck. Satyajit turned grey—"My God! —Chhabi Biswas!"—and he covered his eyes with his hand. He walked to the end of the veranda with Sandip following him.

After a few minutes when everyone from every editing room had come out to hear what had happened, Satyajit came back along the veranda saying that work must pack up. He slipped his feet into his *chappels* lying outside the cutting-room door and was off down the stairs.

The compound was now flooded with distressed people, those who had worked with Biswas and those who never had. All work ceased in every part of the studio lot, for death in India is everybody's concern, not just the affair of close relatives and friends. Ray, and as many members of his unit as possible, piled into the only means of transport—one jeep. Satyajit, who had drawn out the creative reserves of Biswas in *Jalsaghar*, *Devi* and *Kanchenjunga*, looked very grim. His young driver drove more carefully than usual, slowing down as he never normally did at the sight of each oncoming truck.

"What a ridiculous thing," muttered Satyajit with indignation— "that fate should play such an ironic trick just days after Biswas' performance had been seen by international jurors and critics"— he was referring to *Devi*—"and just when he had the biggest role of his life!" *Kanchenjunga* was still running in Calcutta after five weeks.

Editing recommenced the next day. It was the fight sequence.

For the action leading up to this, the jagged, fragmented dialogue serves as counterpart of the zigzag images of the antagonistic drunken bus drivers. Once the fight broke out, cutting was frequently resolved on a six- to eight-frame basis. As the fight proceeded, the number of frames per shot was decreased. Variability of sun and shadow was an important element as the camera had nosed into the midst of the action.

Sandip darted in for this editing. Amused, his father remarked: "The rest of the film will be an anti-climax for him."

Rolling up his fist and hanging on to his father's chair, Sandip shadow-boxed in the likeness of the scenes running through the moviola. Exhausted by his own enthusiasm, he slumped on to Satyajit's chair, avidly watching the splicing of shots.

In relation to this sequence of the fight there would later be people who would feel—indeed I would myself—that Ray's direction of the fight in *Abhijan* fell short of the realism of a brutal beating-up such as has come to be accepted on the screen; that it comes too close in quality to mock fighting. After seeing *Abhijan* many times over a period of five years, at the end of 1967 I mentioned these comments and my own doubts about the validity of the fight, to Satyajit Ray. His response was interesting: he did not think that the depiction of violence was beyond his scope; but he thinks that violence in the contemporary world is of a mean and petty variety; that it was this he was showing in *Abhijan*; that only in the distant past was there violence on an heroic scale. He said he thought he could handle the violence in the epic of the *Mahabharata*, which had interested him as the basis of a film for a number of years. He still hoped he would some day make the epic in two parts if he could only get the money to do so.

Over the years there had been much talk in India about Satyajit Ray's puritanical attitude, talk which had always sounded as if a bit too glib. Refinement of mind should not be confused with puritanism. What is true, is that Ray is unlikely to depict the sordid in a sensational manner on the screen. On the day Ray came to have breakfast with me at the Alipore government hostel in 1956, he spoke about the limitations of Indian censorship in choice of material for films.

At that time there was a novel that interested him and but for censorship he would have liked to make a film from it. Laid some time in the past, it was the story of an elderly and dying man whose family carried him to the cremation ghat in expectation of his death. There, in order to prolong his life, he was hurriedly married to a young girl. He revived a little. The young wife, waiting for the old husband's demise, is passionately attracted to the man who attends to the ghat. Their intercourse does not cause the husband's death. They plan to kill him. Interest in such a story does not indicate a puritan view. Ray said this novel impressed him by its honesty.

The scene in *Abhijan* where the drunken Narsingh calls for Gulabi and has intercourse with her in the most desperate and cynical mood, would almost certainly have evoked an 'X' certificate if handled by another director. Yet the primmest of censors would have a hard time to complain of any hint of obscenity in this scene. The point is that conventional erotic detail is not dwelt on. But there is no romance involved though subsequently the sexual urge between Narsingh and Gulabi evolves into something more. Gulabi comes to love him in such a way that she stands up against his smuggling opium and threatens to leave him: "You're not my master that I should obey you. I take orders from the same man as you do."

During production, Ray saw Fellini's *La Dolce Vita*, and though he admitted its visual force he did not like its theme. But he, and his whole unit, were excited by de Sica's *Two Women*, which had been rather drastically cut by the Indian censor. They did not think that the cuts destroyed the meaning of this film. Just when Ray had completed his first working schedule on *Abhijan*, he wrote a long letter to the Singhalese director, James Lester Peries, relating his views:

. . . The *exterior* of a film is beginning to count for more than ever before. People don't seem to bother about what you say so long as you say it in a sufficiently oblique and unconventional manner—and the normal *looking* film is at a discount. As if being modern for a film-maker consisted solely in how he juggles with his visuals and not in his attitude to life that he expressed through the film. I don't imply that all the new European film makers are without talent, but I do seriously doubt if they could continue making a living without the very liberal exploitation of sex that their code seems to permit, and without this fashion of extolling and patronising the obscene and the unconventional. I would like to see *one* so-called experimental film that can dare to do without this element. So far I've met only one—Trauffaut's *Les Quatre Cent Coups* and I admire it immensely.

As *Abhijan* neared completion, the epic of the *Mahabharata* re-curred quite frequently in Ray's conversations. He gave Edward

Harrison a rough idea of the costing for the two-part film. His idea
was to have an international cast including Mifune, the actor of
Rashomon. The epic called for colour and cinemascope and eighteen
solid months of work for the two films. But finance was hard to
find for such a giant venture. Meanwhile, Ray was seriously thinking of his grandfather's fantasy, *Goupi Gyne*, with songs and
dances. If he could, he would like to make it in time for Upendrakishore's centenary due on May 6th, 1963. He thought of shooting
part of this film in Rajasthan and part in the pink-red long-deserted
city of Fatahpur Sikri, built by the Emperor Akbar some twenty-
five miles from Agra. Then the chance finally to make *Mahanagar*
loomed up when Ray found Madhabi Mukherjee. He planned the
film for the summer of 1963.

It was only two and a half weeks—September 25th, 1962—before the onslaught of the Indo-China war, that Ray screened the
completed *Abhijan* for his unit, the actors and a Hindi distributor.
There was a proposal to dub the whole of the dialogue into Hindi
following the film's run in Bengal. At that time, Indira Gandhi's
personal secretary, Usha Bhagat, had come from Delhi with a suggestion that Satyajit Ray might undertake a documentary film of
contemporary India. He thought about it, but rejected the idea
on the grounds that he was not a documentary director. Then, as
mentioned earlier, he reconsidered the matter in terms of a film
which could help Panditji—Jawaharlal Nehru.

Before the special screening of *Abhijan*, Ray remarked that he
had not had time to view the completed copy. At the end of the
screening he was totally immersed in thought. The next morning
when I phoned him to find out the schedule, he said he was going to
the editing room to take out a few shots at the end. He asked me
to come to Lake Temple Road around 6 p.m. When I entered his
room he looked excessively pleased with himself.

"When I saw *Abhijan* through," said Satyajit, cheerfully, "I
found the two boulder scenes, symbolizing 'the burden of sin', false,
out of keeping with all the rest of the film. I came back here and sat
thinking for five hours. I could no longer believe that Narsingh
could be affected by the boulder as a symbol of sin. He had out-
grown superstition. The boulder was too esoteric a symbol for
everyone to accept. I felt Narsingh could only be shocked by Josef,
by a strictly human situation. I decided to cut both scenes out, also
a shot at the end. The unit were shocked this morning to hear this.
But Bijoya knew what I meant. She felt the same way as I did. I've
had an obsession about those two scenes all the way through
Abhijan. They're out of my system now!" He laughed and looked

even more jubilant, though he had sacrificed two of the most dramatic and visually compelling scenes in the film.

I remembered Anil Choudhury's statement. "Satyajit cannot tolerate falseness in his creations."

Two days later, *Abhijan* opened in four Calcutta cinemas and a number of suburban ones. Instantly it became a huge success with the Bengali public. At the end of many weeks it was still showing to crowded houses. Yet as soon as the film caught on with the general public (and Ray had time and time again said he was not making films for the *élite*), a section of Calcutta's intellectuals —mainly those who had carped that *Kanchenjunga* was "obscure" or "trivial"—commenced to carp that Satyajit Ray had demeaned his talent by making a commercial film.

One writer of film criticisms bitterly complained that Ray had drained out the picture of society which had made the Narsingh of the novel powerful. Ray's Narsingh "is not representative of the working people skirting the abyss of degradation. We feel pity that he should have been born only to be a taxi-driver. *Abhijan* may have established Ray's fame as a commercialized artist; but it has proved him neither an artist who satisfies persons of a finer sense and sensibility, nor a commercialized film maker who pleases people going to see Waheeda Rehman."

"I don't care a damn what the intellectuals think!" exclaimed Ray, momentarily irritated by the habitual stance of finding fault no matter what he did. I'd never heard him swear before.

On February 5th, 1963, he finished the editing of the first 6,000 feet of *Mahanagar*. He mentioned that his editor, Dulal Dutt, was an indispensable member of his unit, and the best cutter in India because of the creativeness of Dutt's suggestions.

This rough cut of *Mahanagar* only covered those scenes laid in the Mazumdar home. When projected, despite being unfinished, these scenes suggested that a decade after he commenced work on *Pather Panchali*, Ray might have captured the essence of Bengali urban middle-class life with the same haunting validity as he had captured in his portrait of the village family of Harihar in his first film.

The vistas achieved on the *Mahanagar* studio set were amazing. It was a feat to create film poetry from the commonplace and unbeautiful. The lighting was conceived with a suffused and glowing imagination. Though there was included a great deal of camera movement in the very small rooms, this was so subtle that it was hardly noticeable. The editing, largely done in the camera, emerged full of life and unexpectedness. The dismalness of the

Mazumdars' life was brightened by a sprightly and tender under-current of humour.

Yet once more, with the release of the film, Bengalis picked holes in *Mahanagar*. To give two examples:

> The pity is that such a director should, from time to time, turn to bank failures and street beat-ups—externalia which others can handle so much more forcefully without achieving an iota of Ray's ability to express events in the mind.

> The theatrical scenes of the old man falling sick, scenes by his bedside, the most unnatural last few scenes of the heroine's valour and passion are too bookish and cliché-ridden to be in pace with the setting created earlier in his film.

It began to seem that for some perverse reason, Bengali critics in particular were determinedly denigrating Satyajit Ray as if they disliked the international fame that had come to him. Later, I was told a story in Bombay that when *Mahanagar* came up for consideration for the national award, someone arranged with the projectionist deliberately to jumble the reels so that the film was difficult to understand. It may or may not be true.

When *Mahanagar* reached the Berlin Film Festival, it carried off the highest award. In 1967, when Edward Harrison released it in the United States not long before his death, Richard Schiekel was allotted an entire page in *Life* magazine in which to review the film. He said:

> It is always a trifle embarrassing to set down, in an un-adorned outline, the story of one of Satyajit Ray's films, for in that form they generally seem too small, too simple to support the critical enthusiasm which they generate. . . . Life for him, in Apu and in all his films, is a series of small surprises; unexpected consequences flow from small thoughts, linking them in odd patterns. Wonder and woe are the result, and they tend to balance each other over the long run, producing a profound art that is neither purely tragic nor purely comic in outlook. We have come to treasure the wisdom and gentleness with which his films remind us that decent, ordinary, sad, funny, inconse-quential life goes on. . . . The real substance of his films lies between their plot lines, in the interaction of his almost Chek-hovian characters. . . . I imagine that Mr. Ray sees the emergence of this character [Arati] under travail as symbolic of India itself,

emerging into the modern world after the long, personality-crushing ordeal of colonialism.

Abhijan was to be presented for a regular run in Bombay on February 8th, 1963. Anil Choudhury and Durga Das Mitra went on ahead by train several days in advance. Satyajit, Bijoya, Sandip, Soumitra Chatterjee, and I, were to go by plane. Bijoy Chatterjee, having celebrated *Abhijan*'s Bengal success with the public, had got married and he decided to take a honeymoon in preference to going to Bombay.

We set off for Dum Dum airport at five o'clock in the morning in Ray's station wagon. It was still dark. Calcutta was wrapped in haze. Nothing moved on the streets except trams, buses, bullock carts, and rickshaws, some carrying vegetables to markets. Many streets glistened from having been douched by street cleaners wielding hoses. On a corner we skidded and almost ran down a shadowy figure pulling a rickshaw. At a crossing further down the narrow, congested road leading to the airport, a huge bus nosed across and we collided with it. Out leapt Satyajit's driver to face the glaring bus-driver who began to shout while passengers alighted to surround him. The driver was no less ready to shout. Seconds ticked away. There were still miles to go. God would have been unable to help us in reaching the plane if the police had arrived on the scene.

"*Shonoton!* Come!" Ray directed, very firmly. "Come!"

He returned and climbed back in his seat with a fight just averted. Snatches of country landscape wreathed in mist were strung out along the overcrowded, brightening road. The driver commented on the sight of the mist and we all agreed it was beautiful.

Bijoya warned "Drive carefully", for Soumitra was nursing a bumped toe. Satyajit kept quiet and Sandip said nothing. We reached the airport only five minutes after the stated time for checking in, and took off five minutes late to allow the mist to lift as the red sun rose, rising higher and higher as we soared into the air.

T

Satyajit (for revived *Sandesh*)

Chapter 14

RAY'S NEW TREND

EVEN as the plane soared up as the sun rose that February morning in 1963, three months after the shattering experience of the brief war with the Chinese, the gloom of financial uncertainty was attacking Bengali film production. Two years earlier the cut in the import of film stock had made it very difficult for Satyajit Ray to obtain the colour stock he required for *Kanchenjunga*.

Over the next five years and throughout 1967, Ray's independent position would have suffered a more drastic assault than it has but for the foreign distribution of the majority of his films. The area of this distribution gradually expanded with *Mahanagar* being the first of his pictures to be released in the Soviet Union. This resulted from his being a juror for the Moscow Film Festival when, after much controversy, Fellini's "8½" won the top award. From 1963, when Ray was invited to Berlin, international invitations were showered on him. There were more than his schedule of work allowed him to accept. But late in the summer of 1965, he made

what has to be described as a dash to Mexico to attend the Aca-
pulco Film Festival. It was on his way back that he finally met
E. M. Forster and had lunch with him in Cambridge. The next
year he at last went to Japan. (See Appendix II.) In May 1968, he
took ten days off from the production of *Goupi Gyne* to visit
Australia, where his films had always been appreciated.

But no matter how great the international prestige of Ray and
his films, this could not rescue film production in Bengal from its
financial crisis which developed in stages. Independence in 1947
inevitably reduced the distribution of Bengali films when East
Bengal was transformed into East Pakistan. In due course Pakistan
prohibited the import of all Indian films. This loss of a large
Bengali-speaking market in what had been East Bengal was a
serious blow that almost coincided with the release of *Pather
Panchali*. No Ray film has been released in Pakistan, although
Pather Panchali influenced the concept of the East Pakistani picture
Day Shall Dawn.

It is impossible to think that the East Bengal market has been
replaced by the national distribution of Bengali films in the non-
Bengali-speaking areas of India. Although Bengal's films, and particularly Ray's, are screened in India's larger towns (though rather
seldom in the Dravidian-speaking States of the South), their national
exhibition has been mainly restricted to Sunday showings to attract
Bengalis. Only one of Ray's films, the comparatively minor work,
Kapurush-o-Mahapurush (*The Coward and the Holy Man*), has had
its dialogue dubbed into Hindi. Though the appeal of Ray films is to
English-speaking Indians, none of his films has been released in
English subtitled versions within India, except *Teen Kanya*. Consequently, vastly more Indians have read about Satyajit Ray's work
than have actually been able to see his films. Festivals of his films
and film societies presenting them have always drawn crowds.
The policy adopted towards Ray's films, and Bengali films in general, has been curiously limited and unadventurous on the part of
Indian exhibitors outside Bengal. It is open to question whether
exhibitors, who make money from Hindi films in particular, have
not deliberately sought to discourage wider audiences for Ray's
films, regional films in general, or any picture breaking away from
long-established conventions.

At the same time, Bengali films, possibly from lack of dynamic
promotion, have failed in making an appeal to overseas Indian
groups. This applies to East Africa, the Middle East and the increasing number of Indian groups in England. All these groups have
given increasingly enthusiastic support to Hindi films. The return

from this distribution field has constantly grown to the benefit of Bombay production.

Bengal producers have also had to face a distribution crisis within their state. This has been caused by the encroachment of Hindi films which are now making a strong appeal to youth. Fan magazines have constantly glamourized Bombay production and Hindi stars. Bengali actors able to speak Hindi have eagerly accepted roles in Bombay films. For example, Sharmila Tagore's success in Ray's *Apur Sansar* and *Devi* led to her becoming a big star in Hindi pictures. Gradually a number of cinema houses in Calcutta and throughout the state changed over from screening Bengali films to those in Hindi. Rise in cost of production has been complemented by theatre rentals soaring to exorbitant heights.

As far back as 1961, Satyajit Ray had it in mind that he should develop a pattern of production which alternated a low-budget film primarily made for Bengal with a more ambitious film of wider appeal. *Ashari Shanket,* a novel set in the period of the 1942 Bengal famine and by the author of *Pather Panchali,* greatly attracted him. He has thought about it frequently with intent to use it as the base for a film. It was still in his thoughts in 1966, but he did not feel in the mood to wrestle with it until the beginning of 1969.

Since 1963 marked the centenary of his grandfather, Upendrakishore, and Sandip was critical of his papa's films as too sad, Sandip sparked Satyajit's imagination into adapting a fantasy of his grandfather's for the cinema. Ray began to think about the story *Goupi Gyne Bacha.* He conceived it in colour and that would add to the costs. Entirely different from any other film he had ever thought about, grandfather's fantasy became a rooted plan. None of the subsequent difficulties could deflect Ray from making this film.

Once Satyajit had found his long-searched-for heroine for *Mahanagar,* Madhabi Mukherjee, he began to work in conjunction with a new producer and distributor, R. D. Bansal, who financed *Mahanagar, Charulata, Kapurush-o-Mahapurush,* and *Nayak* for which a substantial loan was made to Mr. Bansal by the Film Finance Corporation, a Central Government body. It was later alleged to me that Mr. Bansal asked Edward Harrison such a very large down payment on *Charulata* that Harrison could not reach a decision to distribute it in the United States.

Quite a large number of film producers in India, including Bengal, have been amateurs. Having made money in business and often illegally, they speculatively invested in a film or two and then vanished from the film world. But for Mr. Bansal film has been his business. Though Ray never stated that Bansal was going to finance

Goupi Gyne and Bagha Byne, as he titled his grandfather's fantasy, he had every reason to presume that Bansal would. But the intensification of the economic crisis in the Bengal film industry induced R. D. Bansal to decide that in future he would invest his money in Hindi films. Ray's films were not sufficiently profitable an investment in a time of economic uncertainty.

For the first time in ten years, Satyajit Ray's production schedule was catapulted from exceptional certainty to uncertainty. Those who had felt that he should not have made one film immediately after another had not grasped how Ray felt about his unit. As mentioned earlier, the tightness of his working schedule was based on providing a livelihood for the unit. It was probably the best technical combination in India and it would disintegrate if the members could not earn enough to live working with Ray. His unit was devoted to him. By arrangement with him, Subrata Mitra and some other members had been loaned for the Ivory-Merchant productions, *The Householder* and *Shakespeare Wallah*, films Ray wished to aid. He composed the music for the latter in 1965. (Pl. LIV)

With grandfather's fantasy suddenly held up for finance—this was the latter part of 1966—when the Bengal film industry was falling to possibly its lowest ebb, Ray's assistants asked him to supervise a film they wanted to make—*Chiriakhana* (a Hindi word meaning Menagerie), based on a well-known detective novel with a strong Bengali flavour. For some time Ray supervised and went on location with his assistants. Although the character of the detective was played by the star, Uttam Kumar, there came a point where the financiers insisted that directorial credit must be that of Satyajit Ray. Though he had no part in the choice of the story with its "whodunit" structure, he agreed. It was its Bengali quality that induced him to accept. The major clue lay in the use of words characteristic of a particular Bengal region. He liked a story that compelled participation from the audience to follow the clues. Ray undertook the completion of the film, regarding it as one that he, at least, considered outside the scope of his "opus".

Though *Chiriakhana* afforded less imaginative scope than any story chosen by Ray, the result was a competent detective film. But it demonstrates what I had always suspected to be true of Satyajit Ray: that for him to create an inspired film it is essential for him to select his own subject and be wholly captivated by it. He is not a director whose creativeness responds to a commissioned work. In this film, it is Ray's technical ability rather than his subtle imagination which is dominant.

In taking on the director's role for *Chiriakhana*, Ray incurred

troubles not of his own making. Some four days before the scheduled end of the shooting Uttam Kumar suffered a heart attack.
Production was forced to lag for three months in the spring and
summer of 1967. Ray was still editing the film late in July. It finally
opened in Calcutta late in September.

Although Ray was quite pleased with the detective film, he
thought it unsuited for export, "because the vital clue is a matter
of semantics which is untranslatable". He was not sure whether
it might not be rather too subtle and introspective to appeal to
mass audiences. "Certainly not for Bond-addicts!" Yet early in
November it was still running successfully, though some of Calcutta's reviewers had considered it belittled Ray's reputation. This
first run was cut short by the upsurge of extreme political unrest
and uncertainty in Calcutta.

November and December 1967 were crisis months throughout
Bengal. Many cinemas cancelled their night shows because people
were fearful to be on the streets after dark. As the situation became
worse, Ray's film was withdrawn. His difficulties at that time, and
those he can incur in the future, are inevitably linked with the
political and economic crisis within Bengal and India.

So long as Dr. B. C. Roy, the powerful Congress Chief Minister,
who had rescued *Pather Panchali*, lived, restlessness within Bengal
had been fully under control. After his death, his successor, P. C.
Sen, never attained an equal respect. During Sen's tenure from the
middle of 1962 up to the General Election at the end of February
1967, Congress opponents increased their influence, partly because
much odium became attached to the figure of Atulya Ghosh, the
Bengal Congress "boss". Prior to the 1967 Election, a splinter Congress Party formed a United Front with an assortment of parties,
including both the Right Communists, who took a nationalist
position, and the Left Communists, who are Peking-orientated.

This combination defeated the Congress Party in the February
General Election. The new United Front Government in Bengal at
first spurred hopes within the film industry that it might take a
dynamic interest in film production. Ray held such a hope. But the
hope soon petered out. Within a very few months political conflict intensified. Reckless actions on the part of the Left whittled
away some of the United Front's general popularity. Most film
producers, distributors and exhibitors became uneasy and hostile.
They dreaded a revolution. In contrast, according to Ray, a large
number of the younger generation of film people shifted sharply to
the Left. An increasing number of film technicians were caught up
in the wave of overwhelming unemployment, for fewer films were

produced in 1967 than in any previous year. Some film stars made substantial financial contributions to groups furthest to the Left. Congress enticed defections from the United Front and the threat of chaos mounted. The state's Governor dismissed the United Front's government, though this brought no solution. By spring 1968, film workers had gone on strike to draw attention to the Hindi film's threat to the survival of Bengali film production. Their specific aim was to force legislation to protect Bengali films by the setting up of a state quota of screening time for films in Bengali. If the Bengal industry is finally destroyed, Satyajit Ray's career as a Bengali director can be ended.

R. D. Bansal's withdrawal as producer for Ray, combined with the intensification of economic instability and political explosiveness, complicated Ray's plans for the production of *Goupi Gyne and Bagha Byne*. In the summer of 1967, the only plan that appeared definite was that Columbia British would finance *The Alien*, with shooting contemplated for November 1968.

For months, Satyajit's efforts to replace Bansal and raise the necessary Rs. 400,000/- had come to nothing, though he was ready to shoot immediately on *Goupi Gyne*. An idea that the Film Finance Corporation would grant a loan fizzled out. His plan had been to commence shooting in November 1967. That month of acute crisis arrived with nothing arranged. With all sources of finance within Bengal in a state of total uncertainty, Ray decided to go to Bombay. Several years earlier a famous Hindi producer and star had assured him of a gargantuan willingness to invest in any picture Ray might like to suggest, giving the impression that no production conditions would be attached.

I arrived in Calcutta just as Satyajit had decided to go to Bombay. My intention was to see the first shooting schedule of *Goupi Gyne*. While he was in Bombay seeking finance, I went for a week to Assam. On my return, Satyajit was nightly sitting by his phone awaiting a decision.

By this time—the third week in December 1967—people in Calcutta had become somewhat accustomed to tension, demonstrations, and not knowing whether, if they went out, they could get home. Consequently, the second run of *Chiriakhana* commenced. Dodging the area of the now daily demonstration, I went to see the detective film at the afternoon show. The theatre was full. I was due to go to dinner with Satyajit and Bijoya.

When I arrived at Lake Temple Road, Satyajit commented he was back where he was in the *Pather Panchali* days, except "I haven't had to pawn my books and records!"

The Bombay call had come at last. Ray could have the necessary finance provided a particular Bombay star, his brother and his father played the leading roles in *Goupi Gyne*. Satyajit had turned this offer down. He could not imagine what his grandfather's fantasy would be like with these three actors. Already he had cast Rabi Ghosh (who had given a delightfully comic performance in *Abhijan*) as the drummer, Bagha. Ghosh could not be ranked a star. Satyajit could not be forced to compromise on a film he loved the thought of.

Upendrakishore (illustration for a Japanese folk-tale)

He betrayed no irritation nor was his determination to make the fantasy undermined. Though at that moment he had no idea where finance might now come from, he seemed to know with certainty that in the end he would succeed in getting the money. He suggested he play the tapes of the six songs he had composed and already recorded for *Goupi Gyne*. For many months he had been preparing the production. He had a sketchbook full of designs for the costumes so that these could be made immediately (Plates LIX and LX). Another contained his detailed drawings of sets. They were more elaborate than any of his previous sets and they were conceived in colour. We discussed which drawings should be used in this book.

Two lines of thought were uppermost in my mind. Had he and Bijoya been carried away to expand their personal way of living, the pressures upon them now would almost certainly have forced Ray to compromise on the casting of *Goupi Gyne* as the price of obtaining finance. It now seemed proved under this pressure of interminable waiting to go ahead that the paradoxical combination of fame and adulation mixed with some spiteful and negative carping mainly lurking among fellow Bengalis envious of Ray's success, had not gnawed away his solid sense of perspective. It also seemed that his months of waiting and his difficulties might, in the long run, prove beneficial. He had been forced to think a great deal, read, study, plan, as never during the years since *Pather Panchali*. He had had no time on his hands. Money had come easily for every film he wanted to make though he had not made money. Now he had had to assess himself. It looked as if he was being as persistent in regard to his grandfather's story as he had been in regard to Bannerjee's *Pather Panchali*. No film that he had planned, or made, was as experimental as *Goupi Gyne*, with its numerous technical effects largely due to a pair of flying slippers. With this musical fantasy as with his plans for *The Alien*, Ray was setting himself a new direction.

Completely unforeseen, this period of frustrating dead-ends was about to end without Satyajit Ray making any further effort. The next morning—the day before Christmas 1967—one half of the Rs.400,000/- budget was offered to him by the producer-distributor Nepal Dutta, who knew someone willing to invest the second Rs.200,000/-. Apparently, Dutta was influenced by his twenty-six-year-old daughter-in-law, Purnima, who had one rather good film, *Chhuti*, to her production credit. Ray's sole concession was that *Goupi* would be in black and white.

In 1962, when Ray had gone to Rajasthan to take a few shots for the concluding sequence of *Abhijan*, he had instantly decided that this state offered him wonderful locations for part of the action in *Goupi Gyne*. The ancient forts and palaces had enchanted him as settings for the dual kingdoms in the story.

On January 6th, 1968, Satyajit, Bijoya and Sandip flew to Delhi, spent the day there and took the night train for the Rajasthani city of Jodhpur to decide the exact locations to be used. He had set his heart on picturesque Jaisalmer. Between Christmas Day and that day, he had made a sortie to the Birbhum district of Bengal to settle the location for the entirely realistic opening of *Goupi Gyne*, for which the costumes were now being made. The shooting schedule was to be a long one—from later in January to the middle of July, with release optimistically planned for the middle of September 1968. Further difficulties delayed release to 1969.

Over the twenty odd years Ray has worked to create his "opus" it has become increasingly discernible how attracted by and attached to the creative inheritance of his father and grandfather Satyajit really is. Inadvertently, he revealed obliquely how as a little child he had sensed an affinity with his dying father: once when we were discussing Indian intimacy with the process of dying, Satyajit suddenly said that throughout his youth his mother had protected him from this familiarity with death because at three he had been so upset by the death of his father which he could not remember. In consequence, he had only become intimate with death as an adult. It was through his mother and other relatives that the imaged personalities of his grandfather and father were projected upon Satyajit. The impression he received was that of high-minded idealists dreaming to change so many things. They were singularly lacking in suspicion of others and, seemingly, uncorrupted by self-interest. And there remained the "opus" of their literary-graphic expression, which has appeared to exert an intensifying attraction for Satyajit.

His affinity with the creative pattern of the Ray family, and the evident affinity of his son, Sandip, as the latest distinctive development, appeared to come into focus and sharpen in 1961 when Satyajit revived *Sandesh*, the Ray family children's magazine. Since its revival in a different and far harsher period, Satyajit has been expressing himself through this magazine with the same individuality as grandfather, who had founded it, and father who had expressed himself through it up to his premature death. Like the magnanimous-minded Upendrakishore and the surrealistic-slanted Sukumar, Satyajit has developed as an author-illustrator with this sideline activity feeding his dominant role as film director.

It is worth mentioning that Ray, who has conveyed facets of childhood on the screen with possibly more authenticity than any other director, has never manifested a sentimental interest in children. When working with them he had drawn out their imaginations by treating them as intelligent people. Presumably this was his grandfather's attitude when he took his own large family to exhibitions and passed on knowledge to them. An intense concern with creating for the young has been a marked family characteristic even in members who are peripheral and therefore have not been mentioned.

When Ray first selected a number of his own illustrations, together with examples of his grandfather's and father's work, and gave them to me to illustrate the Ray family graphic style, I could see a link. But it was only when Satyajit chose an illustrated film script by Sandip of a story by his great-grandfather, Upendraki-shore, and his own drawings for the film of *Goupi Gyne*, did the aspect of a family "school" embracing a century from father to son become vividly illustrated. (See p. 306 and Pls. LIX and LX.)

Sukumar (for original *Sandesh*)

The closer the Ray family and the character of Kalinarayan Gupta are studied in relation to traits and attitudes of mind embedded in Satyajit Ray's films, and vice versa, the stronger becomes the evidence that Satyajit's character and talent, and his liberal, humanitarian attitude towards human frailty and virtue is the contemporary evolution of the idealistic and reformist Brahmoism which Upendrakishore espoused and Sukumar preserved when Brahmoism began to lose its pristine dynamic force. As they served this once progressive creed, and it in turn served to give their talents a moral base, Satyajit, an unorthodox Brahmo, has added to his inheritance a conscious awareness of both Freud and Marx.

Though highly socially conscious, as in their time his grandfathers were, this consciousness has never been expressed in direct propaganda terms. Satyajit depicts the clash of values, old and new, in the pattern of human relationships.

Two qualities strongly developed in Satyajit's father and grandfather find renewed expression in him: humour is woven as a natural thread through the texture of all Ray's films with the exception of *Jalsaghar*, *Devi* and *Monihara*, where the inclusion of any comic element would stand out as vulgarity. The use of the fantastic appealed to Upendrakishore and Sukumar for, as a form, it served as envelope for ideas. Two of Satyajit Ray's films, not as yet discussed, are motivated by these same elements: his third film, the fantastic comedy, *Paras Pathar* or *The Philosopher's Stone*, and the 1965 satiric farce, *Mahapurush* or *The Holy Man*, the second of the dual-story film. Lastly, to date, grandfather's story *Goupi Gyne Bacha*, as expanded by Satyajit, carries the qualities of fantasy and the comic on to a more complex level. Ostensibly a fairy tale, the dual heroes, two young musicians, bring, by their tricks, an end to the disease of the ages—War.

Laughter is employed in *Mahapurush* to expose a couple of confidence men and the gullibility of the superstitiously devout. One trickster, promoting soul-saving balm, masquerades as a saffron-robed Guruji, while his scheming partner (Rabi Ghosh) apes discipleship. Travelling on a train, "Guruji" encounters a seeker after Wisdom with more money than brains and captures him with tall tales of his heavenly powers. Through this asinine patron the team build up a profitable business with a bevy of devotees. Devotee-in-chief's daughter and her loving boy-friend set to work to rout the salesmen of Enlightenment. The climax is slapstick with the large and fat and small and cheeky mountebanks just escaping with their skins on plus an armful of lady worshippers' handbags weighting them down. (Pl. LVIII)

Even today *Mahapurush* can appear as blasphemy to the superstitious and gullible would-be devotees who cannot conceive of themselves as decoy-ducks for artful dodgers arrayed in saffron robes and holding themselves out to be Holy Men practising magic powers. Some critics in India have extolled Ray for exposing the irrationality that persists. Others found the film too trivial. Still others were disturbed, echoing the earlier objections to the serious examination of superstition revealed in *Devi*. Not only does orthodoxy run deep in India of the 1960s, but there is evidence to suggest that this orthodoxy is increasing in militancy and intolerance of Free Thought.

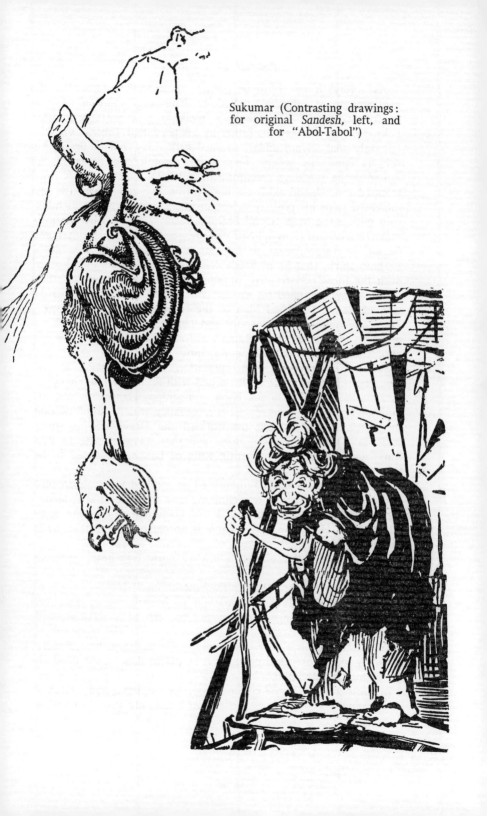

Sukumar (Contrasting drawings:
for original *Sandesh*, left, and
for "Abol-Tabol")

As a Ray, it can only be natural to Satyajit to question the assumptions of religious orthodoxy. The Ray tradition of non-conformity goes back without a break to great-great-grandfather Loknath, who enraged his father by his persistent Tantric worship. His only son, Shyamsundar, strained orthodoxy and incurred censorious comment when, keeping his promise of approval, he attended the wedding ceremony of a virgin widow. In his most talented son, Upendrakishore, both rationality and progressiveness increased with his positive rejection of idol worship and membership within the most liberal Brahmo Samaj group led by the militant Dwarkanath Ganguli. Nor can the good zamindar, Kalinarayan Gupta, be forgotten as so far out in expression of the liberal Brahmo spirit, that he overrode class as well as caste and shocked even the more conservative Brahmos. But it was Satyajit's father, Sukumar, who applied his mischievous wit to question the perfection of Rama, the Ideal Man of the revered epic of Hinduism—*The Ramayana*—with its godly and heroic monkey-genius, Hanuman, inventively rescuing Rama's purest wife, Sita, from the not altogether ignoble demon king, Ravanna.

Sukumar's irreverent reinterpretation was performed at the Nonsense Club before 1911. It opened with Rama, or Ramchandran as he was called, with his boon companion, Hanuman, and his monkey army and devotees. (It is now fairly widely supposed that the epic's Aryan authors transformed the Dravidians of South India into monkey collaborators, and that Ravanna, the Demon King, was, in fact, an authentic King of Lanka, presumed to be Ceylon.)

The hero, Ramchandran, announced he had had a strange dream : "I dreamed that Ravanna was climbing up a palm tree and suddenly slipped and fell down and died. I told Hanuman to cast the body into the sea. Hanuman said : 'There is no need of doing that, he is completely dead.' "

Off stage, at that moment, a mighty noise was heard growing nearer and nearer.

Someone enquired : "What's the row about?"

Another asked : "Is it Ravanna coming here?"

In dashed a messenger to announce the arrival of Ravanna and his demon host.

To soften the blow to Ramchandran, whose dream has so sadly misfired, and whose ideal pride must be placated, someone piled all the blame on Hanuman.

In another scene of the comic *Ramayana*, Sukumar had a character enquire of Hanuman "What sort of a man are you?" to which the Monkey God retorted, indignantly: "Why do you call me a man? Why do you so abuse me?"

When the terrible-aspected, many-headed Demon King appeared, his famous club was replaced by a pillow. A gramophone horn served one of Hanuman's army as a weapon.

Yet Sukumar, like his father, cherished rather than scoffed at what they held to be true. Shibboleths carried no weight with them. Even in supposedly unchanging India, the shibboleths attracting reverence have shifted. Wealth, which once was little respected in comparison to wisdom, now wields more power over the imagination than it ever did before in India.

Satyajit, who counted the pennies throughout his youth, seems to have equated wealth with impecuniosity of spirit, if not active evil, in all his films. *Paras Pathar*, based on a ten-page satire by the scientist Rajshekar Bose under his pseudonym "Parasuram", jolted Ray's admirers early in his career as film-maker. The Calcutta audience were wholly unprepared for the creator of *Pather Panchali* and *Aparajito* to discard the style they accepted as his and present them with a film of fantastic situations—a satiric fairy tale—and magic as if strictly commonplace and part of everyday life.

A childless, middle-aged clerk, Parash Dutta, to whom nothing exceptional has ever happened, leaves his dreary office, shelters from the rain, dozes and opens his eyes to find a black stone in front of him—the Philosopher's Stone of legend which transforms base metals into gold. He emerges as the boundlessly rich and bountiful Rishi Chakravarty and, in due course, causes panic on the Calcutta stock exchange. D. P. Bhattacharya, writing about the film, sums up the challenge it presented when released in 1958:

> The very improbability of a man's finding a "philosopher's stone" that turns every metal into gold becomes secondary in the light of the social exposure that it brings in its wake. Politics, culture, economics, philanthropy, law and order—all become victims of Ray's social satire and the significance of the title of the film becomes doubly and unexpectedly powerful when it suggests a reassessment of the entire social structure faced with such a phantasy. One recalls that in *Miracle in Milan*, de Sica attempted an identical theme that blended phantasy with realism. Ray uses the improbable situation only as a catalytic agent. Some foreign body must be inserted into the dubious social values that have been accepted as the norms to test their merit. Once it is there, the whole absurdity and preposterousness of the values become evident.

This black-white motif is incorporated into the early long over-head shot establishing Dutta in the city of Calcutta. Clothed in the

As a poor hard-working clerk going from shabby office building to shabbier lower-middle-class home, Dutta had been a good husband and kindly to children. For respectability's sake the impoverished Duttas kept a servant who goes up the ladder of notoriety with them as a result of the wealth the magic stone brings. The mysterious wealth draws in a romantic young secretary with a love affair at the end of a telephone. It throws the new philanthropist into the social whirl where he does not fit in; it lands him with threats of blackmail and into the hands of the police. The Duttas' escape from criminal prosecution to renewed obscurity padded with some promised material comfort is no less magical than Dutta's emergence into wealth. (Pl. LVIII)

A stylized format framing the purported realism of ordinary life where extraordinary "happenings"—in the current meaning—occur quite naturally, appeared in Ray's own design behind the credit titles—a cubistic pattern of violently contrasting black and white. All Ray's visuals for credit titles—unfortunately often removed in foreign sub-titled versions—add their integrated point to his films. traditional white *dhoti*, he is seen scuttling across a starkly defined zebra crossing, the white lines intensified by the street's dampness. These hints of stylization dissolve into strictly realistic visuals. None of the scenes of the magic stone pinging mundane metal objects into seemingly solid gold are presented in a stylized or fantastic manner. The fantasy takes place within the idiomatic frame of Calcutta in the mid-1950s when a real bank crashed. The emphasis of a stylized black-white motif only reappears in the décor of the set for the climactic episode of the Dutta couple's interrogation in a police station.

In truth, no couple could be more innocent of fraud in the acquisition of an unaccountable fortune. Their only guilt may have been subsequent pretentions not open to criminal prosecution. At this point Ray abandons the satiric and comic vein. Though the set is visually sharpened to a black-and-white pattern beyond the fringe of realism, the emotions portrayed by the couple are intensely real. Ray's unlikely, undistinguishable hero is moved to the depths of his essentially commonplace being. He emerges as a human being from whom comicality and pretentiousness are stripped.

In the whole range of the remarkable performances in Ray's films none surpasses in subtlety of emotional variation that of the late Tulsi Chakravarty as Parash Dutta. This previously little known actor created the memorable cameo of the pundit-grocer in *Pather Panchali*. At that time he appealed to Ray as a potentially great actor if given an opportunity. His own life had been an unusual one. In his early teens, Chakravarty had run away from his Brahmin home and joined a travelling circus as an acrobat. In time, his unusual face, suggestive of both the clown and the magician, had drawn him into films as a player of bit roles, usually minor comics. He had never achieved a marked success until *Pather Panchali*. Thanks to Ray's insight into Chakravarty's untapped talent, the culmination of his career was an interpretation of Dutta reminiscent of the rich performances of Michel Simon in its combination of comic, serious and pathetic elements. The poor man on whom fate thrust the Philosopher's Stone emerges in depth as a real human being caught up in a web of fantastic circumstances.

Paras Pathar was, as a whole, a somewhat unappreciated film. It has been too little seen. Yet it has grown upon people who have seen it more than once despite its intensely idiomatic Calcutta character. Three sequences remain remarkably sharp in their lasting impact. The first is where Parash Dutta, fearful of the supernatural, only wishes to dispose of the magical stone—throw it in the Ganges—but his wife, Garibala, prevails on him to use it on household utensils which he takes to sell to a bullion merchant. Ray found a real merchant to play the role and he exactly duplicated a goldsmith's shop in central Calcutta. Testing the assortment of objects the merchant is amazed. Never in his life has he seen nutcrackers and scissors made of solid gold. Assuming an air of indifference, Parash Dutta laughs and says "They are heirlooms. Belonged to my great-grandfather. You know how these old aristocrats were . . . whimsical . . ."

The word whimsical then becomes appropriately audio-visualized in a wonderful sequence of delightful and ludicrous day-dreaming: Dutta, his pocket full of money, takes a taxi probably for the first time in his life. Ray employed a real cab he found with fanciful decorations. The taxi, with Dutta, drives through central Calcutta traversing the Maiden, with its scattered statues of the long-demised Great. Emotions flit over the face of the newly-rich Parash. He is incredulous yet believing, subject to anxiety, doubt, excitement, fear, elation, and shrewdness. Wonder and satire are supplied by the music and sound track.

Statues of long vanished British dignitaries rise up within his range of vision. Parash pictures himself on a pedestal transferred into bronze—all except his head which peers above the garlanded statue of himself. The legend reads: "Great Son of India". He sees

U

himself elevated into a V.I.P. inspecting a Guard of Honour and orating a speech with an umbrella held over his head. Noticing the steel skeleton of a new building he realizes he could turn this structure to gold. This gives him a sense of what he can accomplish.

Suddenly, the taxi passes a scrap-iron dump. Dutta halts the cab and excitedly totters into this treasure trove of metal debris. There is so much to choose from on every side. He looks and looks about until he spies the perfect object for his purpose—a pile of ancient cannon balls. He picks one up but drops it guiltily when someone appears. It clatters along a girder making a terrific noise to indicate its weight. Sounds—a dog barking, a child crying, voices praying, the chirp of crickets, a child's bouncing ball—are important components of all Ray's films; but it is not always easy to isolate their effect as in this sequence. There is no shot of Parash acquiring the cannon ball. He is seen driving off in the taxi with two cannon balls lodged on the ledge behind his head. This shot serves as transition to his recognition as a V.I.P. in "reality". Philanthropy has made him famous as Rishi Chakravarty. He is shown occupying a dais as Guest of Honour spewing forth noble clichés: "Traditions!" intones the secret possessor of the magic stone. "We must uphold tradition", and so forth and so on. On the table in front of him he has a box full of gold medals.

He has acquired a car, a posh house, a romantic secretary of implied Christian persuasion, while his wife has developed a love of jewels. Their rich furnishings are in atrocious taste and out of date since they suggest Victorian. Not unnaturally, wealth has opened the doors of cocktail party society to him. (Pl. LVIII)

The sharpest satiric sequences come with Dutta's arrival at a smart cocktail party. The scene called forth the note at the film's beginning that all the characters are fictitious! The leading lights at the party were portrayed by well-known actors such as Chhabi Biswas and Pahari Sanyal. The smart Calcutta drinking set parade upon the screen with the satirical spirit building up. The set is the kind of smartly decorated room where such parties actually take place in Calcutta. The taste is showy rather than elegant. A muted stylization can be seen in a pattern of black and white as a stepping-stone to the more emphatic stylization of the culminating police station scene.

At first Dutta is distinctly a fish out of water in this society cocooned in "youism", the intimate "in" talk that shrouds the absence of any intimacy at all. The women are overdressed and overblown. The drinks circulate. Parash imbibes to aid himself in trying to circulate. The drinking types are absorbed in themselves: from the moon-faced elderly boyish "English" type to the supercilious no less "English" Government officer who wants to look as if there is nothing in the world he does not know. Hovering around with a fixed stare is a pipe-chewing executive, obviously a member of a British business house. He never utters a word, only looks askance at the innocence of Dutta. Parash, inspired by his fifth drink, lets out an unbecoming yell. What he wants is a little music. Really! Even though somewhat tight the sophisticates preserve their stony view that this interloper doesn't know the rules. Dutta entertains them with a song. Goaded by sneers he becomes belligerent. After all, it is *he* who holds the trump card to enforce their attention. Discretion demolished, he rips off his elegant coat, produces his stone and announces he's a magician. Ping! He taps the stone upon a metal ornament. The bronze turns to glittering gold, and out he stalks forgetting to take his coat. Next morning, his intrigued host arrives at breakfast bringing with him not only the coat but the threat of blackmail. Parash and wife are well on their way to find themselves in the police station. They only escape the clutches of the police because the stone, swallowed by the love-lorn secretary in order to kill himself, fortunately mysteriously dissolves in his stomach and all the Dutta gold turns back to what it was. There is no fraud to prosecute although the stockbrokers nearly run mad and the public run around in a panic.

As an interesting footnote as to sources of influence upon Satyajit Ray: the brother of Rajshekar Bose, the author of *Paras Pathar*, had been the Ray family physician and in his time he had been close to Freud.

In 1957, the year that *Paras Pathar* was made, Chidananda Das Gupta wrote: "I consider Satyajit Ray perfectly capable of producing a better fantasy than all other Indian directors put together. I do not think his special predilection is towards tragedy either. I should not be surprised if he produces a first-class comedy one day."

These elements of the fantastic and comic cemented by pungent social satire found no further evolution after *Paras Pathar*. Comedy with serious undertones was explored in *Samapti* and to a lesser degree in *The Postmaster*; while in *Mahapurush* satire breaks loose into farce. Ray's interest in the fusion achieved rather unevenly in *Paras Pathar* did not dissolve like the philosopher's stone within Dutta's young secretary's intestinal tract. It remained dormant while his attention was occupied with other ideas. But it was again activated in 1961 by the approach of grandfather Upendrakishore's centenary due in 1963. The fairy tale, *Goupi Gyne Bacha*, offered many possibilities for Satyajit to try directions he had not explored, including location shooting outside of Bengal. He could not get grandfather's story out of this thoughts.

He described the form his film was going to take to Georges Sadoul in January 1965, during the Third Indian Film Festival for which he served as Chairman of the Jury: "It will be a musical fantasy with gods, demons, singers and comic actors trying to

Upendrakishore (for *Goupi Gyne Bacha*)

prevent war between two nations. I will use many technical effects in this experimental film in which there will be a Good King and a Bad King, both of whom an epidemic has made mute." As revised in script form, the Good King of Shundi's subjects have been struck dumb by a plague. The king escaped, having been away on holiday with his family. But as a gesture of sympathy their virtuous king, a lover of music, only acts dumb. The Bad King of Halla, who turns out to be the long-lost brother of the Good King of Shundi, is not the antithesis of the Good King. He's a personality split into opposites when administered a drug by his villainous Prime Minister. In his natural state, he doesn't even want to be a king, much less to conquer his neighbour's country. But drugged he bellows "Chop off their heads!" A pair of magic slippers to carry them anywhere and the power to wish three wishes, wished on the boys Goupi and Bagha, singer and drummer, by a kindly cheerful parody demon deity, turns them into peacemakers without a shot being fired. When they sing and drum they transfix their listeners, even soldiers ordered off to war. (Pls. LIX–LXII)

Reversing his previous methods with music where the music itself evolved along with the shooting, Ray evolved six of his eight songs before he had money to start production. He tape-recorded them. The songs are sharply different in tonal character : for example the fourth, where the Bad King in a bad mood orders, "Chop off their heads" (the heads of those who do not want to fight), the song's style is a parody of the South Indian classical song. The last song, the one that freezes the war, has two distinct moods, the first that the soldiers ordered to fight are in reality famished; the second, that it is useless to fight battles. Again, rooted in the texture of this fairy tale, there is Ray's philosophy : that excessive wealth is the cause of misery. Palace and prison are synonymous.

The scenario of *Goupi Gyne* (Gyne means "singer") is of exceptional interest. Its quality of fairy tale calls for camera tricks (magical changes of clothes, hair standing suddenly on end, a meal appearing from nowhere). Its crowd scenes verge on spectacle. Much knockabout humour and some parody is preserved throughout. The characters of the two boys and those of people they encounter, plus the compound of natural wit and wisdom in the dialogue, endow grandfather's story for children with undertones of allegory for adults pertinent to today when national leaders of opposing sides declare they don't want war and are aiming at peace.

In the light of the mass appeal in India of the mythological film, of songs and spectacle, it is a pertinent comment on Ray within the context of Indian cinema that he should have such a grinding time to obtain finance for *Goupi Gyne*. Had he shifted into the foreground the denouement of the two boys marrying the daughters of the two kings, the romantic element would have taken precedence and money would have been easier to get. But Ray's uniqueness is, in part, his inability to compromise. This has set him apart from the general trend of Indian film-making.

Sukumar (for "Abol-Tabol")

That he has inspired some younger directors to aim to direct better films is undeniable; but few of these films are free of compromise. This is their weakness when compared with Ray. But Ray does not seem to have provoked any fundamental change in attitude of professional producers, distributors or exhibitors. They remain mainly indifferent to film as an art (though Ray himself has never claimed that he makes films for an élite group). They continue to judge the merits of a script, or film, by its conventional box-office standards.

Ray's films have very definitely raised the hopes of the youngest film-makers, some of whom have managed to raise money for short independent pictures, and students at the Film Institute of India at Poona where several experimental films have been attempted. Some of these students may find a way to develop a type of film that avoids compromise. Through his use of locations, Ray has exerted a wide influence on this aspect of Indian film production. He has had the effect of liberating film-making in India from the confinement of studio sets.

It is true that Satyajit Ray has exerted a strong influence upon the style of film acting. This influence seems to have extended beyond Bengal. At the same time, this influence has its individually painful aspect. All the actors directed by Ray have experienced a measure of frustration when they have found themselves under the direction of another director, or appearing in other directors' more conventional films. Not even Soumitra Chatterjee has ever seemed to be as talented an actor when appearing in the films of other directors.

It is difficult at the end of more than fifteen years not to draw the conclusion, at least for the present, that Satyajit Ray stands unique and alone in the context of the Indian film scene. This is not an easy or desirable position to be in if it continues indefinitely. Under difficult conditions, Ray has pushed forward in his will to expand his style. *The Alien*, though as yet unproduced, and *Goupi Gyne* are the expression of his driving will to experiment.

Since the total aim of Ray's work is to create "a document of Bengal", and thus to picture its history and culture, past and present, he is unlikely to abandon return to modest budget films. He still intends to make the famine film. He is interested in a biographical story of the Bengali who mapped Mount Everest but whose name was not given to the mountain; also one of the nineteenth-century classical novels by the much-loved Bankim. Ray says he will always return to stories and novels by Rabindranath Tagore and his intention is to write a new version of his early scenario of *Home and The World*.

The creative spirit of Tagore and of his own family stand as highly personalized shadows, in fact like guardians, behind Satyajit Ray's shoulders, exerting an influence upon though not necessarily dominating his creative endeavours. In a quiet way he is aggressive, even masterful, in the pursuit of what he wishes and intends to do. Beneath the serenity of his manner and his mode of working, Ray has an immense toughness. He is a most singularly disciplined member of one of the world's most temperamentally volatile groups.

Though seemingly such a far cry in form and content from *Pather Panchali*, *Goupi Gyne and Bagha Byne* could never have reached the production stage but for the phenomenal persistence of Satyajit Ray. This persistence forms the impregnable base of a cinematic style that evokes understanding and appreciation beyond India, but is still not of the West. Penelope Houston caught the essence of Ray's cinematic expression when she wrote: "Ray has an unmatched feeling for the moments when a situation catches people unawares, and minds perceptibly expand or contract when confronted with some infinitesimal stress." This quality permeates both *Goupi Gyne* and *The Alien* script. It is Ray's particular signature.

As a person known for many years, Satyajit remains an enigma in one respect: his capacity never to dwell upon his troubles or difficulties. He remains serene. It appears that this is an inherited characteristic. Grandfather Upendrakishore was possessed of it and so was father Sukumar. Manik is the reflection of an ancestral personality and the creative urge that continually intensified in his branch of the diligent and imaginative Rays with their strongly independent moral bent.

POSTSCRIPT I — FROM SATYAJIT RAY

Two extracts from letters to the author

(*December 12, 1968*)

Goupy has turned out to be quite a film. The 6½ minute dance of the Ghosts is surely the most striking thing ever done in cinematic choreography. Topen Chatterji is fabulously good as Goupy, and Rabi Ghosh and he make a wonderful pair. The film is packed with ideas and a lot of people I know have seen it twice and are waiting to see it again. I am very happy with the film, although I can see that many of the concepts in the second half may be too unconventional for the mass audience. But the last 20 minutes have a gaiety and simplicity which should satisfy everybody. . . . *Goupy* will follow Topen Sinha's new film which opens on Friday—which means we'll open sometime in March. I've decided to make the famine story with Soumitra and Sharmila, starting in mid-January. I feel it's good to come back down to earth after the fantasy;—at least, I feel in the mood for something deadly serious and utterly realistic.

Best,

SATYAJIT

P.S. You'll be tickled to know that I won the State Award (Rs.5000/-) as the best director—for *Chiriakhana*! There seems to be a great dearth of prize worthy directors in India!

(*January 18, 1970*)

The new film* opened two days ago. The infamous Samity Mantid hired hoodlums in the theatre at the opening show—their misbehaviour nearly wrecked the films for the audience—quite the worst experience of its kind I've ever had. But subsequent shows have been OK—and I've heard some extremely favourable comments. Personally I think it's one of my most satisfying films—subtle, complex (but not bewilderingly so) and superbly acted by

---

* *Aranyer Din-Ratri* (*Days and Nights in the Forest*).

the entire ensemble. Also certainly the most contemporary of my films in feeling.

The new film† starts shooting 1st February. This is the Calcutta story about a young man looking for a job. I've cast the entire film with newcomers—with two Poona boys in two key roles. I'm looking forward to the shooting.

Did I tell you that *Goupy* got an all time record for long run (8½ months) before it was taken off at the end of December.

† *Pratidwandi (Siddhartha and the City).* See following Postscript and plates.

POSTSCRIPT II—FROM THE AUTHOR

WITH the completion of *Aranyer Din-Ratri* (*Days and Nights in the Forest*), which Penelope Mortimer found to be the only film of the 1970 Berlin Film Festival she could remember, Ray embarked on a documentary interlude. He went to the semi-autonomous kingdom of Sikkim tucked away on the border of Tibet to capture its antique mode of life before the onset of modernity. One can say in doing this he momentarily went back into the living past.

Increasingly, during the second half of the 1960s criticism has been levelled at Satyajit Ray, particularly in India, that his films failed to reflect the immediately contemporary scene. The core of this criticism has been that Ray evaded grappling with the developing political situation. It is true that up to 1970 no Ray film touched directly upon politics. Objectively, Bengal has been in an increasing state of political flux since early in 1964. But only in 1969 did a clear-cut confrontation develop between the groups adhering to Left and Right, one that now affects the daily existance of everyone in Bengal and especially in the city of Calcutta.

Ray's latest film, *Pratidwandi* (*Siddhartha and The City*), plunges into the current climate of Calcutta and reflects the existing politicial situation. Based on a novel by Sunil Ganguly, author of *Aranyer Din-Ratri*, the exact period of the action is April 1970 when the shooting commenced with considerable use of Calcutta's streets and actual political demonstrations. The action of the film covers three or four days and reveals contemporary political attitudes as they affect family relationships, and the way in which opinions affect the matter of jobs. The predicament of today's Bengali youth is depicted through two brothers faced with social adjustments as a result of their father's death.

The elder, Siddhartha, whom Ray terms his hero, has to find a job within the difficult existing conditions. The younger, Tanu, has abandoned all hope in the existing system and has become an adherent of the Naxalites with faith in the ultimate outcome of a violent agarian guerrilla-tactic revolution. The intelligent and bright Siddhartha goes for his first job interview. A question is asked to probe his views: what has been the most memorable event of the last decade? He answers: War in Vietnam. Again he

313

is questioned: why does he not consider the conquest of Space and the Moon the most memorable of events? He replies that these conquests could be foreseen. Another question is put to him: "Are you a communist?" With this assumption the interview ends for the time being.

Siddhartha is left with time on his hands while his job application is considered. There develops the exploration of the family relations with the boy's mother, his younger sister who has obtained a job, and his brother. Beyond the family circle there is his relationship with a friend with whom he pals around, and a girl whom he accidentally meets and likes, and with her parents. As a background to the developing contact with the girl and her family problems, Ray introduces the largest demonstration ever to take place in Calcutta. He shot the real thing from the top of a high roof.

As in many of Ray's films, a subtle psychological change takes place in his central character during the course of the action. By the time the conclusive interview takes place, Siddhartha has reacted to bureaucratic indifference. He does not want the restricting job. He chooses a lesser job, that of a salesman of medical supplies, but one with more independence.

Satyajit Ray remarked years ago that sometime he would introduce his contact with political minded people into a film when he felt the time had come to do so. He had no intentions of being hurried.

London,
16th July, 1970

THE FILMS OF
SATYAJIT RAY

APPENDICES

by

SATYAJIT RAY

RENOIR IN CALCUTTA

I

"Mr. and Mrs. Renoir are occupying the Royal Suite on the second floor," informed the receptionist of the Great Eastern Hotel.

My decision to see Renoir at his hotel was a more or less desperate one. Although his arrival in Calcutta had been marked by a conspicuous lack of publicity, the stir it had created among local students of the cinema was considerable. For this was no chance visit, no casual passing through en route to important missions elsewhere. Renoir's mission was here, in Calcutta. He had come with the professed intention of making a film of Rumer Godden's novel *The River* against authentic backgrounds in Bengal. In all likelihood, therefore, his stay would be an extended one.

But fame invests a man with an aura of unapproachability, and I had all but despaired of a chance of meeting the great director when I stumbled upon Clyde DeVinna. A wizened, wisecracking American, DeVinna had acquired some reputation and a great deal of experience in the early nineteen-thirties by photographing *Trader Horn*. He was now considered something of an expert in outdoor photography, and had been engaged to supervise the preliminary shooting on *The River* (in monopack Technicolor). DeVinna had allayed my misgivings by cheerfully asserting that "John is a great guy, a great individualist, and *very* approachable. You can see him any day at his hotel in the evening."

As it turned out, Renoir was not only approachable, but so embarrassingly polite and modest that I felt if I wasn't too careful I would probably find myself discoursing upon the "Future of the Cinema" for his benefit. There were so many things I wanted to ask him. Why did he want to make *The River*? Did he enjoy making films in Hollywood? Was he thinking of going back to France? But when it came to asking them, I found that I was hopelessly mixed up, and came out with something inane like—How did he like India?

Renoir replied with great seriousness: "That I will tell you when I have known it better. At present I am only beginning to understand the city of Calcutta, which I find very interesting."

I didn't have to ask many more questions that evening, for Renoir had a great deal to say about the two or three trips he had already made around the city and on the Ganges. The river, with its old-fashioned boats, had charmed him, and he was fascinated by all the colourful things he had seen. "You know," he said, "India seems to have retained some of the charm and simplicity of primitive life. The way the boatmen pull the oars, and the farmers plough the fields, and the women draw water from the wells, they remind you of old Egyptian murals and bas-reliefs."

Renoir had met a family of refugees who had come all the way from Pakistan by boat. "And they had all sorts of fantastic adventures on the way," he said, "I'm sure their story would make a very good film." I said India was full of such stories which simply cried out for filming. "And no doubt they are going to be made," said Renoir with naive conviction. I said No, because the Indian director seems to find more inspiration in the slick artificiality of a Hollywood film than in the reality around him. "Ah, the American film . . ." Renoir shook his head sadly, "I know it's a bad influence."

II

Soon after this, attending a reception given in his honour by the Calcutta Film Society, Renoir submitted himself to a barrage of questions ranging from the most absurd to the most abstruse, all of which he answered with great ease and candour in his charming broken English. Asked about *The River*, Renoir said that he had chanced upon a review of the novel in *New Yorker*. The outline of the story, as *New Yorker* gave it, had seemed to him to contain the elements of an interesting film. A reading of the novel had confirmed the impression, and Renoir had set about preparing a treatment, shelving for the time being a project on a life of Goya which he had previously thought of making in Italy.

I had not read the novel, and had no idea what the story was about, except that it had something to do with a river in Bengal (presumably the Ganges). But after all the nightmarish versions and perversions of India perpetuated by Hollywood, I was looking forward with real eagerness to the prospect of a great director tackling the Indian scene. It was therefore an acute disappointment to hear Renoir declare that *The River* was being made expressly for an American audience, that it contained only one Indian character—a servant in a European household, and that we were not to expect much in the way of authentic India in it. Of course the background would be authentic, since all the shooting was to be done on location in Calcutta. I couldn't help feeling that it was overdoing it a bit, coming all the way from California merely to get the topography right . . .

"What goes wrong with the great continental directors when they go to Hollywood?" This was a question many of us had in mind but few had the temerity to ask. But when it did come Renoir's eagerness to answer it surprised and relieved us. "I'll tell you," he said. "I'll tell you what happens to them. It is the American mania for *organization* which frustrates them. You have heard of this mania of course, but you know nothing unless you have seen it in action. Suppose you are in the United States, and you want to go somewhere. So you go to a station to catch a train. And what do you find? You find the train arrives on time. *Exactly* on time. Now this is very strange. In France the trains don't run on time. You are not used to this punctuality, and it makes you feel uneasy. Then you go to work in a studio. You are on the floor, ready to begin work. And what do you find? You find you have to go by the schedules, and so many of them. Which means *you* are supposed to run on time too. And then they begin to check. They check the sound and double-check it, so that you get perfect sound, which is good. Then they check and double-check the lighting, so you get perfect lighting, which is also good. But then they check and double-check the director's inspiration—which is not so good!"

Renoir feels that the best intentions are apt to be thwarted in Hollywood owing to certain immutable factors. He mentioned the star system, the endless codes of censorship, and the general tendency to regard films as a mass-produced commodity, as being the three most obvious. Once in a rare while a director was lucky enough to find the right story, the right sort of players (not stars) to act in it, and the right sort of artistic freedom to make it, and the result was a worthwhile film. Only once, when he made *The Southerner*, was Renoir able to work in such ideal conditions in Hollywood.

Renoir also believes that the best films of a country are produced in times of stress; that an atmosphere of smug self-complacence is bad for the cinema. "Look what the war has done to Italian films," he said. "Look at *Brief Encounter*. I don't think a great film like that would have been possible without all those air raids London had to suffer. I think what Hollywood really needs is a good bombing . . ."

III

"Look at those flowers," said Renoir, pointing at a *palas* tree in full
bloom. It was the first of several occasions on which I was fortunate
enough to accompany him on his trips in search of locations.
"Those flowers," said Renoir, "are very beautiful. But you get
flowers in America too. Poinsettias, for instance. They grow wild
in California. But look at the clump of banana trees, and that
green pond at its foot. You don't get that in California. *That* is
Bengal."

One could see that while searching for locations, Renoir was also
searching for *la couleur locale*, for these quintessential elements
in the landscape which would be pictorially effective as well as
being truly evocative of the atmosphere of the country. As he put
it: "You don't have to show many things in a film, but you have to
be very careful to show only the right things."

For a man of his age and dimensions, Renoir's enthusiasm and
energy are phenomenal. He would trudge across miles of impossible
territory to find the right viewpoint for the right locale. At times
the absorption in his work was so complete that his wife would
have to administer some gentle admonishment like "You shouldn't
be out in the sun so long, Jean", or "Jean, you haven't forgotten
that appointment at six o'clock have you?"

During these trips Renoir spoke a great deal about himself. Of
his youth; of his father, and the other great figures of the impres-
sionist movement; of ceramics—his other great passion besides the
cinema; and of the cinema itself. It was during the first world war,
while convalescing in a hospital from a leg wound, that Renoir had
first toyed with the idea of a possible career in the films, although
the actual apprenticeship was to come later, after he had gone
through a spate of journalism. While he spoke in glowing terms of
the *avant-garde* movement, Renoir characterized the entire silent
period of the French commercial cinema as being largely stagnant
and ineffectual. With the coming of sound, however, there was a
sudden and magical transformation. As Renoir put it: "It was as
if someone had opened a secret door of communication between
the film-maker and his audience. It was a great feeling. Everything
we did the audience understood. The French cinema could not have
made those enormous strides towards maturity without this won-
derfully perceptive audience. They helped us all along the way, and
I for one feel grateful to them."

The rich period lasted till the occupation, after which—although
there was no loss in technical quality since the Germans were an-

xious to prove their munificence in regard to cultural activities—there was an inevitable falling off in content.

Of his early films, Renoir spoke of *La Chienne* as being one of his favourites. "It is a pity they had to remake it in Hollywood, and so badly," he said. (This second version, directed by Fritz Lang, was called *Scarlet Street.*) Among the great masterpieces of the late 'thirties, Renoir had a special affection for *La Règle du Jeu* because it was entirely his own creation. He even acted a role in it. The case of *Partie de Campagne* was peculiar. It appears that Renoir had wanted to experiment with the short story film. For ease of commercial exploitation, two such short films would have to be made, and Renoir had started on the Maupassant story, hoping to follow it up with a second one. But, unfortunately, the film had to be abandoned before it was quite finished. All through the occupation the negatives lay hidden away by a friend to prevent destruction at the hands of the Nazis. It was only after the liberation that prints were made and the film released with explanatory titles filling the gaps in the narrative.

Renoir himself had yet to see *Partie de Campagne.* For on the very day the Germans had marched into Paris, Renoir had marched out, taking with him his wife, and just such of his worldly belongings as could be got into one small suitcase.

IV

From Paris to Hollywood. The inevitable trammels of adjustment apart, Renoir had found life in California pleasant enough. The climate was good, and there were good friends. Chaplin—*le maître* —the mere mention of whose name would make him beam, was one of the best. Renoir was sorry for him. "He is a sad man now," he said. "Nobody understands him in America." I asked him if he was aware of his (Chaplin's) future plans. Renoir said: "Well, the last time I met him he was thinking of a musical burlesque in which the characters would represent contemporary political figures. But I don't think he'll make it, because he also seemed very anxious to displease nobody, and you can't make a film like that and displease nobody."

Of the five films he had made in Hollywood, Renoir never mentioned *The Diary of a Chambermaid* or *Swamp Water.* He had made *This Land is Mine* as a rejoinder to the notion then prevailing in America that the resistance movement in Europe was a myth, and that every person in an occupied country was a collaborationist. *The Southerner* he had enjoyed making mainly because it was a bit of authentic America, and the people in it were real. He considered it his best American film.

The Woman on the Beach was something of a misadventure. Originally what interested Renoir in the story was the character of the woman who "lived only for love". But after he had begun to make the film, he had discovered to his chagrin that the Codes prevented him from developing the character in the way it needed to be developed. As a result, in situations which called for a forthright emotional treatment, he had to fall back on subterfuge and extraneous technical claptrap (hence the near-surrealism of the setting and the distracting dissonances of Hanns Eisler's score).

To Renoir, there is nothing more important to a film than the emotional integrity of the human relationships it depicts. Technique is useful and necessary in so far as it contributes towards this integrity. Beyond that it is generally intrusive and exhibitionist. "In America," said Renoir, "they worry too much about technique, and neglect the human aspect."

I asked Renoir what he thought about the recent American trend towards documentary realism. "That is nothing new," he said. "I shot most of *La Bête Humaine* on location in Le Havre. I built very few sets for *The Southerner*. But I am not dogmatic about it. I think a set is a useful and necessary thing at times. And in any case, if the people don't behave in a realistic manner there is no point in having them perform against real backgrounds. I have also heard theories about using non-professional actors. This I don't understand at all. Can you think of a non-actor replacing Raimu or Gabin? I can't. Personally, I have a great respect for the acting profession." For all his vast experience, Renoir is surprisingly free from aesthetic dogmas. I think he summed up his attitude beautifully when he said: "Each time I make a new film, I want to feel like a child who is learning about the cinema for the first time."

v

The day before he left for Europe, I saw Renoir again at his hotel. He was taking with him a trunkful of mementoes, some of which had been given him by his admirers, and some he had picked up himself at bazaars and curio shops. In the four weeks of his stay in Calcutta he had travelled, and observed, and reflected. Bengal had grown on him. The enchantment and novelty of the landscape on the one hand, and the picture of filth and misery and poverty on the other. I had watched him go into ecstasies over a simple hut, and pass into gloomy despondency at the sight of a beggar. The visit to a coalmine had stirred him so deeply that he had talked of it for days on end. And he had said: "If you could only shake Hollywood out of your system and evolve your own style, you would be making great films here."

He was to return to Calcutta with his unit in November, which is the best time for shooting outdoors in India. Of course the script had to be rewritten. "This time, when I'm in London, I must sit down with Rumer Godden and discuss the story. I may want to make some changes in it; add some new characters, maybe. Maybe an Indian family to show the contrast between their way of life and the Indians." It would be a good idea . . .

As I came away from the hotel that evening, I felt convinced that there was any amount of creative vigour still left in Renoir. Perhaps *The River* would mark the beginning of a fresh and vital period after all the disappointments of Hollywood. As he had now become an American citizen, the chances of returning to Paris were somewhat remote. The important thing, however, was to get away from the synthetic environment of Hollywood, and India was as good a refuge as any. There is no doubt that here Renoir would get his freedom. There would be no schedules to distract him, and no checking and double-checking of inspiration. And of course, out here, the trains never will run on time.

Appendix II

TOKYO, KYOTO AND KUROSAWA

WE were on our way back to Tokyo from Kyoto. The time was around midday. Pink-cheeked girls in uniforms wheeled food-trolleys up and down the gangways of the compartment, selling packaged curry and rice. A loudspeaker offered the use of a tele-phone with connections to Osaka, Kyoto, Yokohama and Tokyo. Sitting by the large window and watching the landscape whizz past, one felt at the point of being airborne. And no wonder. This new electric train on the Hokkaido line had an average speed of 125 miles an hour—and I noticed no *ritardandi* for bridges and tunnels.

On the onward journey, we had been lucky to get a clear view of Fuji, its peak brushed pink by the low sun flattening perceptibly as it dipped towards the horizon. But this time, on the way back, Fuji was more characteristically shrouded in mist and chimney-smoke.

My all-too-brief Japanese visit was drawing to its end, and Fuji was one of a hundred impressions which formed a whirling collage in my mind. Tokyo itself—audaciously modern, aspiring, ebullient. I like big cities to engulf and bewilder me, and Tokyo does that with a persistence unapproached by other big cities. For a measure of the city's assault on the senses, one has only to take a walk down the Ginza of an evening, with one eye on the road for the traffic, and the other up on the animated neons which, for variety, inven-tion and rhythmic complexity, have no parallel.

Strange to reflect that the same Japanese mind produced the Zen gardens—surely the most subtle and self-effacing of artistic pursuits. One unresponsive to the feel and texture of rocks, foliage and water, or one who thinks of gardens in terms of the predictable symmetries of a Mughal Bagh will in all likelihood miss the gentle harmony of contrasts that permeates these gardens. The work of the artist—the order imposed on natural elements—is so muted as to be barely discernible. And yet that is what makes works of art of these gardens.

The temple of the Thousand Buddhas, in Kyoto, had the lifesize

328

idols ranged in galleries like crowds in a football stadium. The dull gold of the statues gleaming in the dim light of the cavernous hall, and the sheer weight of numbers, produced the right awe-inspiring effect. But one couldn't help feeling that the main preoccupation here was religious, not aesthetic. Art consisted, as in most Japanese temples, in the beauty of the woodwork, the titles, and the proportions of the architecture.

Deer roamed the famous park at Nara. As you walked up the driveway towards the temple, they came prancing up and nudged you with the soft tips of their lopped-off antlers, expecting biscuits which you could buy by the dozen from shops which lined the path. Inside the temple, the colossal Buddha sat obscured by incense-smoke between gigantic metal lotuses of an unbelievable art-nouveauish ugliness.

And yet how wonderful it was to roam the streets of old Kyoto and just look at the old houses. Doors, windows, rooftops, gates, cornices, were all works of art, and the balancing of beauty and function a consistent miracle.

The human element in Japan was dominated, in my mind, by schoolchildren. Wherever we went sightseeing, there they were, in great uniformed hordes, tumbling merrily out of sleek school buses, or gathered in earnest knots with necks craned to converge on Teacher scattering educative data.

A Lunch Appointment

On our way to Nara, a brief diversion had taken us through the woods where *Rasho Mon* was filmed. These were up in the mountains, and one could just as well have been on the Kalimpong Road. As I sat in the train, I thought of the woods, of the strange and powerful film shot there, and of my imminent encounter with the maker of that film: at the end of my journey lay a lunch appointment with Akira Kurosawa.

I only hoped it wouldn't be in a Japanese inn, as most other meals so far had been. The interiors of these inns—especially the old hallowed ones—afford great aesthetic delight. I never tired of running my eyes over the lines of the *tatame*, so spotlessly clean that the thought of cockroaches barely formed in the mind before it perished. But—and this was my only serious quarrel with Japan— I could accept neither the food they served, nor the fact that you had to genuflect in order to eat it. Moreover, I don't think the best food in the world can be truly relished unless transferred from plate to mouth with ease and in the right quantity. Chopsticks in the hands of a beginner are apt to thwart these basic functions.

As it turned out, the venue for the meeting was a Chinese restaurant in a quiet back street of Tokyo. "A favourite of Kurosawa's," said Mrs. Kawakita, my hostess and a close friend of the director. At least one could face the gastronomic hazards with more confidence here.

Kurosawa turned out to be that rarity—a tall Japanese. He also had a stoop, with an appropriate humility to go with it, kindly eyes which a ready smile thinned into mere slits, and a hushed and gentle tone of voice—all of which was in unexpected contrast to the ferocious image derived from his samurai films. But then, it is not unusual to find schizophrenics among people of the theatrical profession, and I knew Kurosawa had samurai blood in him. I had visions of his unbridled other self, pitching into that scene of combat with all the controlled fury of a samurai himself.

I started by talking of *Seven Samurai*, which turned out to be both his and my favourite amongst his films.

"It needs long and hard training to be a film samurai," he said. "There was so much about the samurai that was stylized—his ride, his run, the way he wielded the sword. A samurai would never be hunched over his saddle when charging. He would stand straight up with feet firmly on the stirrup and knees pressed tight against the flanks of the horse. His body would not be perpendicular, but leaning forward at an angle to prevent being thrown backwards by the force of the charge."

Kurosawa rose from his chair to demonstrate the stance of the charging samurai.

"And about the sword—it wouldn't cut at all if you only hacked with it. You would have to combine" (more demonstration here) "a *hacking* motion with a *slicing* motion. And when the samurai runs, his head shouldn't bob up and down with his footsteps. The effect should be like a swift floating. In other words, the head shouldn't trace a wavy curve, but a straight line."

A stickler for historical accuracy, Kurosawa, in his period films, makes his actors put on period costumes obtained from museums.

Grown Smaller

"But you know where the snag is," he said with a twinkle in his eyes, "The Japanese as a whole have grown smaller over the last five or six hundred years. It is difficult to find actors large enough for these costumes to fit."

I asked if he had any more samurai films in mind.

"None," he said. "And I doubt if I could ever make another one."

"Why not?"

"Because there's such a dearth of horses now. You see, most of the horses used in films came from farms. But now farmwork has been mechanized, and horses are bred only for racing."

The conversation now turned to Kurosawa's *Macbeth*, which had a most impressive array of horses in it. But I was more interested in the birds—the birds from Birnam wood which invade Macbeth's castle after the trees of the wood have been cut down. I said I thought the idea a brilliant one.

"Well, the trees obviously had birds nesting in them, and the birds obviously had to go somewhere, so I made them invade the castle. But", and here his eyes twinkled again, "we had trouble filming them. The idea was to have them wildly flapping about just above the heads of the actors. But they were not trained birds, and they just kept flopping down on the floor as we released them, and stayed there. Some even kept slipping, because we had polished the floor with wax. It took us a whole week to do that one scene properly."

It appeared that Laurence Olivier had liked Kurosawa's idea of showing Lady Macbeth as pregnant—because it gave a clear motivation to her actions—and had written to ask if he might borrow it for his production of the play. In course of the letter, Olivier had remarked, somewhat gratuitously, that he believed the child born of the Macbeths would be an ugly and deformed one. To Kurosawa this had seemed like a crude and inartistic comment, and he had consequently turned down Olivier's request.

I had heard that Kurosawa had been signed up by the American producer Joe Levine to direct a film in the U.S.A. The news had intrigued me, because this would be the first instance of an Asian director with only a rudimentary knowledge of English making an English-language film in the States.

Red Beard

Mrs. Kawakita had hinted earlier that Kurosawa had got into the bad books of the Japanese producers through his lordly unconcern with the financial aspects of a film. His last film, *Red Beard*, planned to be shot in six months took more than two years to complete. This had resulted in the termination of a twenty-year-old relationship with the actor Toshiro Mifune, who had been in every Kurosawa film except one since 1947. For *Red Beard*, Mifune had signed an exclusive contract for six months, and had grown a beard for the part. As the shooting dragged on, Mifune had to keep turning down offer after offer. While the film was in production, he did nothing to jeopardize its interests. But from the moment the shooting ended, he had been a stranger to Kurosawa, with no chance of *rapprochement* in sight.

The fact that *Red Beard* went way over budget was something Kurosawa couldn't care less about. All that mattered to him was perfection, which he believed he had achieved in the film. The critics applauded *Red Beard*. It also had a long run, but not long enough to bring back the cost. Kurosawa sensed trouble and cast about for backing from abroad.

"I had a story in mind," said Kurosawa. "I had saved up a clipping from an American newspaper which described how a goods train went tearing through Chicago at eighty miles an hour with three men on board but no one at the controls. For some unaccountable reason, the driver had jumped off and killed himself. The train as well as the passengers were ultimately saved, and the film will show how."

But there were snags. Kurosawa had stipulated that he would work with his own Japanese crew consisting of some twenty technicians. The producer Levine's drastic terms permitted only *one* English-speaking assistant.

The fact that Kurosawa had to concede could be indicative of either his great urge to film the story at any cost, or of the alarming situation of the serious film-maker in Japan. What is true of Kurosawa is also true of Ichikawa, Kobayashi and Shindo.

However, a truly gifted film-maker—as has often been proved in the history of the cinema—can rise above his circumstances: so that, Levine notwithstanding, one can look forward to *The Runaway Train*—if it ever gets made—with all the pleasurable anticipation of an authentic, Japanese Kurosawa. Let us hope that a charging train will prove just as inspiring as a charging samurai.

INDEX